D0941030

THE COMPLETE NEWSPAPER
Wallace & Gromit
COMIC STRIPS COLLECTION

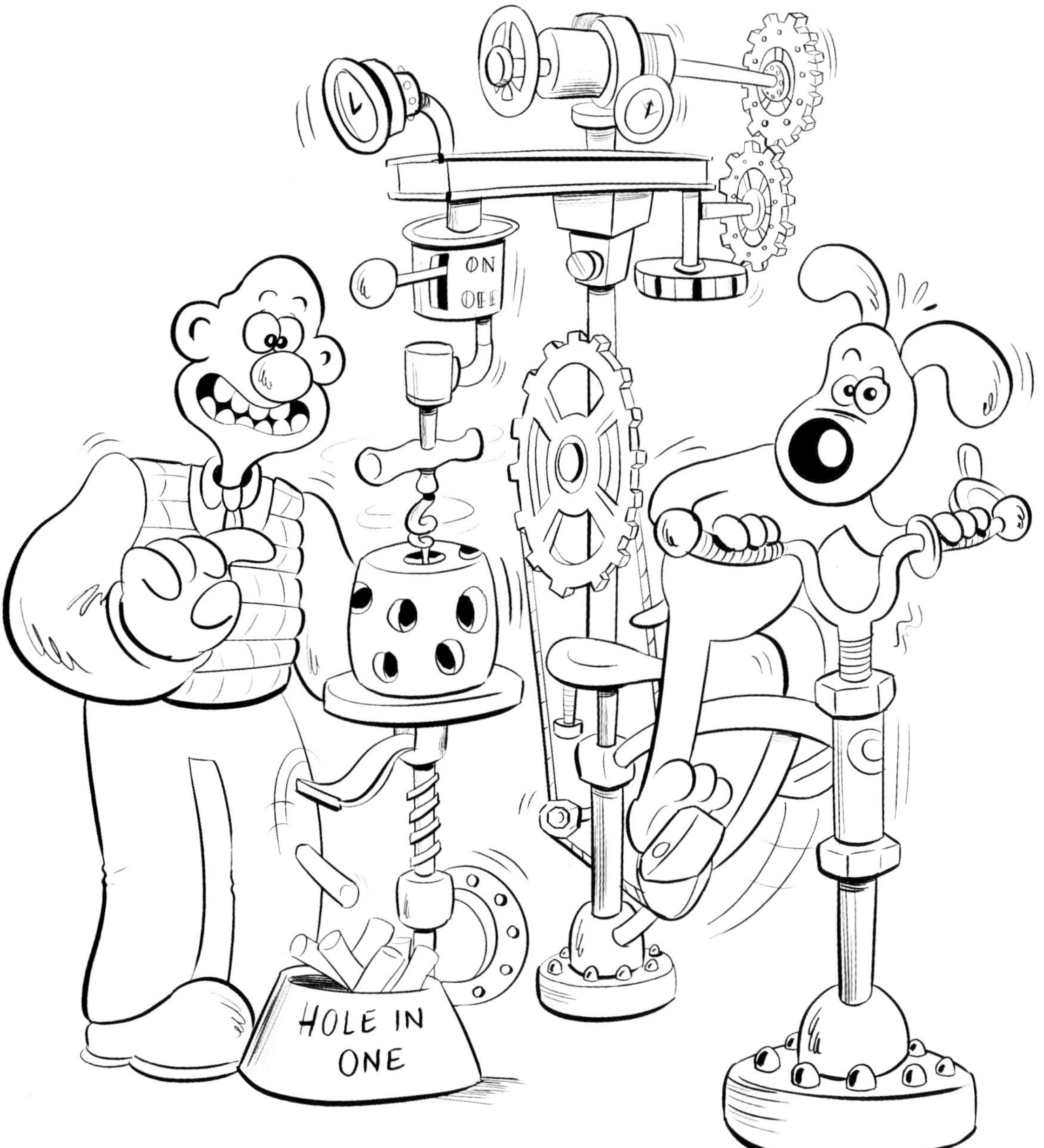
ON
OFF
HOLE IN ONE

Wallace & Gromit:
The Complete Newspaper Comic Strips Collection.
Volume 1: 2010 - 2011

ISBN: 978-1-78276-032-0
Published by Titan Comics, a division of Titan Publishing Group Ltd.,
144 Southwark St., London, SE1 0UP.

WALLACE & GROMIT, AARDMAN the logos, and all related characters and elements are
© and TM Aardman/Wallace & Gromit Limited 2013. All rights reserved.
Wallace & Gromit and the characters "Wallace" and "Gromit"
© and TM Aardman/Wallace & Gromit Ltd
All characters, events and institutions depicted herein are fictional.
Any similarity between any of the names, characters, persons, events and/or
institutions in this publication to actual names, characters, and persons,
whether living or dead and/or institutions are unintended and purely
coincidental.

A CIP catalogue record for this title is available from the British Library.

This edition first published: October 2013

Printed in China

10 9 8 7 6 5 4 3 2 1

We love to hear from our readers. Please email us at:
readercomments@titanemail.com, or write to us at the above
address. For all the latest news, information, competitions and exclusive
offers, sign up to our latest newsletter at:
www.titan-comics.com

THE COMPLETE NEWSPAPER
Wallace & Gromit
COMIC STRIPS COLLECTION

Volume 1: 2010 - 2011

HOLE IN
ONE

TITAN COMICS

Foreword by Nick Park

Strip cartoons have always been a big part of my life – when I was young, I used to go over to my Grandma's every Saturday and she'd have a comic for me. I'd read it from cover to cover, then read it in bed, and keep it so I could read it again and again over the years (until my mother threw them out!). I'd look forward to every strip – Lord Snooty, The Bash Street Kids – each one had its own special quality, a wacky but gentle sense of humour. I wasn't so keen on the football stories, and I found the war comics a bit boring. But I loved the funny strips and used to copy the drawings in my sketch pad.

There was something very exciting about the weekly comics – we didn't have computer games and 24 hour kids' channels in those days, just an hour of children's television every day – but in between, I used to enjoy reading the daily strips in the newspapers too. I loved Rupert Bear in the Daily Express, and Peanuts in The Observer. I suppose Snoopy may have been an unconscious influence on Gromit – they're both smart dogs.

And then at Christmas you'd get the Annuals – in fact, I've just bought an old Beezer annual from 1966 on Ebay, with 'Colonel Blink, the Short-Sighted Gink' on the cover – I don't think you could get away with that today! (Although he does remind me of the Farmer in Shaun The Sheep...) Then there were the collections of newspaper strips like Oor Wullie from the Sunday Post; it was great to get a book full of them. You could get lost in the cartoons – especially Rupert Bear and Tintin. And more recently, I've enjoyed the collections of Gary Larson's The Far Side strips as well.

So when Titan Books approached us about producing a daily Wallace & Gromit newspaper strip for The Sun, it seemed like a great idea. It was a chance to have them appear regularly, not just every few years in a new film. At first, we thought there could just be a daily gag, like Andy Capp or Peanuts. But there's an awful lot to fit in with Wallace & Gromit – the inventions, the puns, the constant references to cheese... We didn't seem to be able to do the characters justice in just three panels. So then we had the idea of telling continued stories over a week – each strip would work as a joke in its own right, but put them together and they would tell a bigger story.

The plan was always to collect them in book format so readers could enjoy seeing the complete stories all in one place. So I'm delighted to see our first collection published. And who knows – perhaps someone will be buying this very book on Ebay in 50 years time!

Nick Park

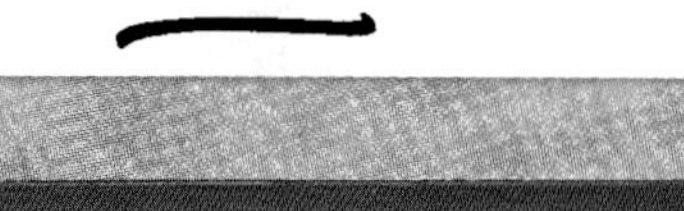

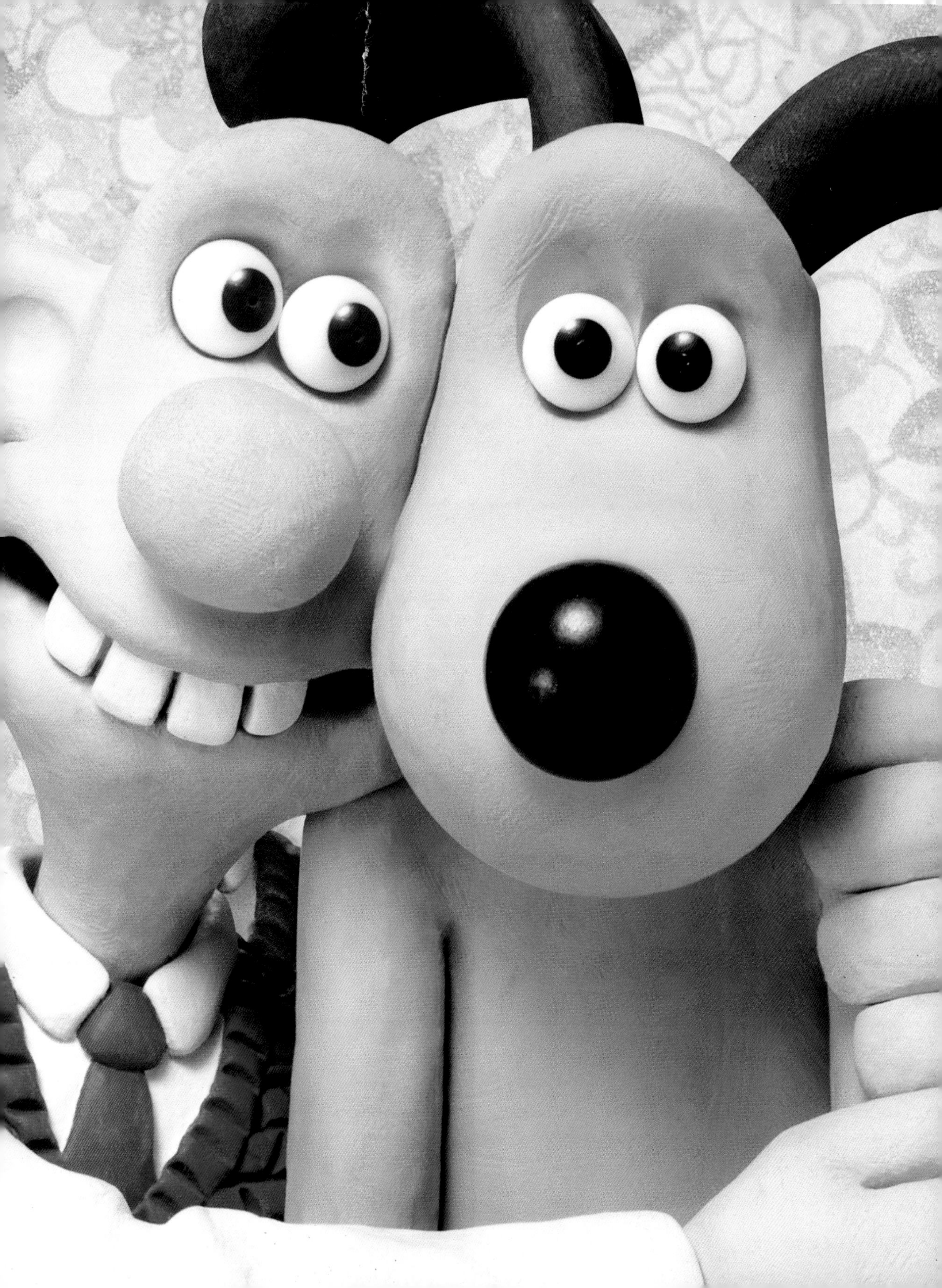

Wallace & Gromit - The Tooth Hurts

by Aardman & Titan Comics

ME *WISDOM TOOTH* IS DRIVING ME CRACKERS, *GROMIT!* BUT I JUST CAN'T *FACE* GOING TO THE *DENTIST.* GIVE IT A *SLAM*, LAD!

OOOAAAAAH!

SLAM!

OW. DON'T KNOW WHY THEY CALL THEM WISDOM TEETH, LAD -- THERE WAS NOTHING *CLEVER* ABOUT THAT!

© and TM Aardman/W&G Ltd 2010. All rights reserved.

1

Wallace & Gromit - The Tooth Hurts

by Aardman & Titan Comics

WE NEED A MORE *HI-TECH* SOLUTION TO MY *TOOTHACHE*, GROMIT LAD! A *MIRROR* HERE AND A LITTLE *MOUTHWASH* THERE... SOME *COTTON WOOL PADS* THERE...

A *MARVEL* OF MODERN MECHANICS! PEOPLE WILL GIVE THEIR *EYE TEETH* FOR OUR *CAVITRON*, GROMIT, LAD!

THERE... *FINISHED.* IT'LL BE THE FIRST ROBOT TO RUN ON *MOLAR*-POWER!

© and TM Aardman/W&G Ltd 2010. All rights reserved.

2

Wallace & Gromit - The Tooth Hurts

by Aardman & Titan Comics

BY 'ECK, GROMIT, THE TOOTH *HURTS!*

THE *CAVITRON* IS ALMOST READY... JUST ONE LAST SET OF PLIERS AND, *VOILA* --

OP-EN WIIIIIIIIIIIIDE!

-- THE NEW, *FRIENDLIER* FACE OF *ORAL CARE!*

© and TM Aardman/W&G Ltd 2010. All rights reserved.

3

Wallace & Gromit - The Tooth Hurts by Aardman & Titan Comics

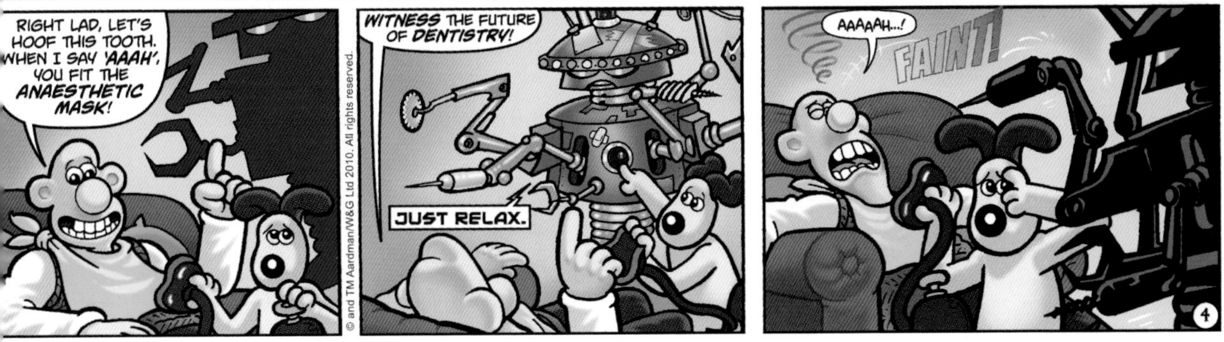

RIGHT LAD, LET'S HOOF THIS TOOTH. WHEN I SAY 'AAAH', YOU FIT THE ANAESTHETIC MASK!
WITNESS THE FUTURE OF DENTISTRY!
JUST RELAX.
AAAAAH...!
FAINT!
4

Wallace & Gromit - The Tooth Hurts by Aardman & Titan Comics

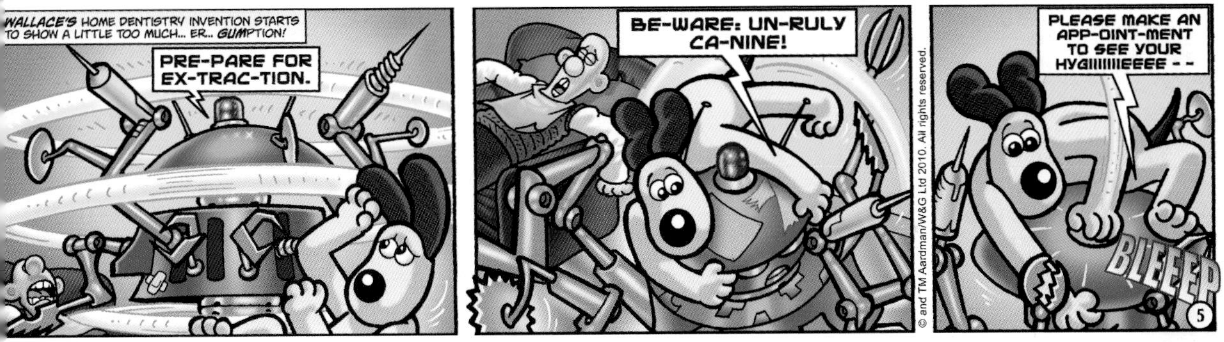

WALLACE'S HOME DENTISTRY INVENTION STARTS TO SHOW A LITTLE TOO MUCH... ER... GUMPTION!
PRE-PARE FOR EX-TRAC-TION.
BE-WARE: UN-RULY CA-NINE!
PLEASE MAKE AN APP-OINT-MENT TO SEE YOUR HYGIIIIIIEEEE - -
BLEEEP
5

Wallace & Gromit - The Tooth Hurts by Aardman & Titan Comics

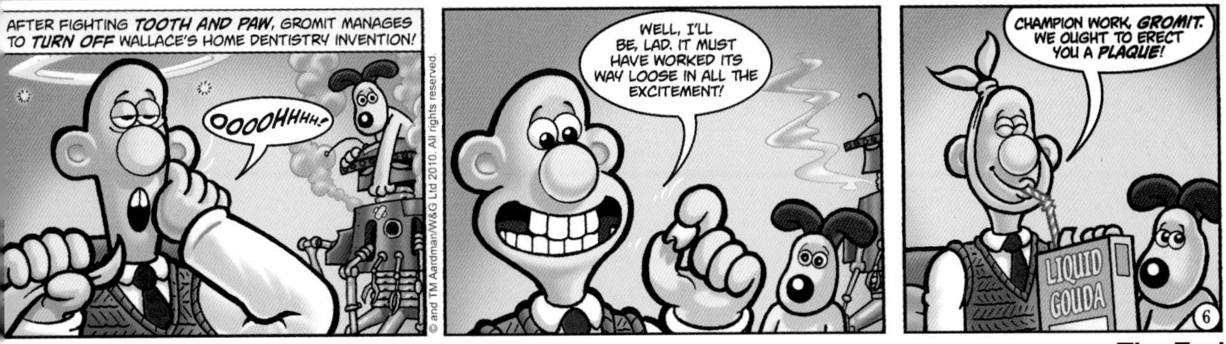

AFTER FIGHTING TOOTH AND PAW, GROMIT MANAGES TO TURN OFF WALLACE'S HOME DENTISTRY INVENTION!
OOOOHHHH!
WELL, I'LL BE, LAD. IT MUST HAVE WORKED ITS WAY LOOSE IN ALL THE EXCITEMENT!
CHAMPION WORK, GROMIT. WE OUGHT TO ERECT YOU A PLAQUE!
LIQUID GOUDA
6

The End

Wallace & Gromit - Helping Hands

by Aardman & Titan Comics

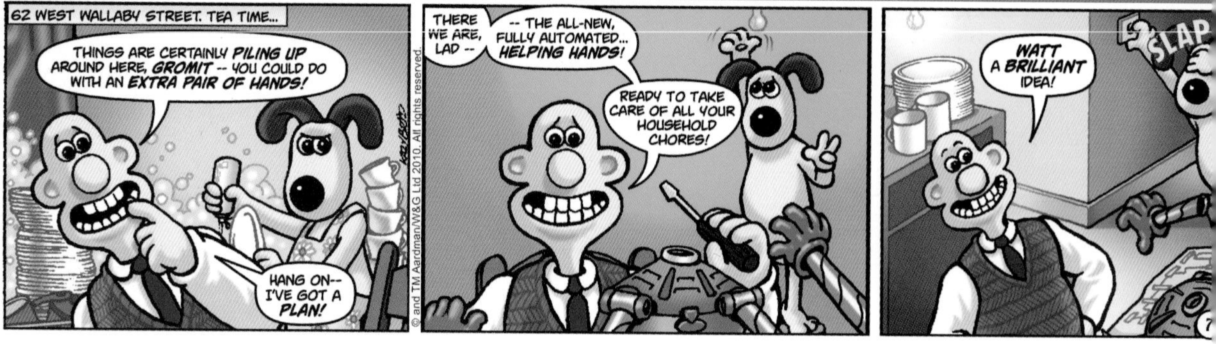

62 WEST WALLABY STREET. TEA TIME...
THINGS ARE CERTAINLY PILING UP AROUND HERE, GROMIT -- YOU COULD DO WITH AN EXTRA PAIR OF HANDS!
HANG ON-- I'VE GOT A PLAN!
© and TM Aardman/W&G Ltd 2010. All rights reserved.
THERE WE ARE, LAD --
-- THE ALL-NEW, FULLY AUTOMATED... HELPING HANDS!
READY TO TAKE CARE OF ALL YOUR HOUSEHOLD CHORES!
WATT A BRILLIANT IDEA!
SLAP
7

Wallace & Gromit - Helping Hands

by Aardman & Titan Comics

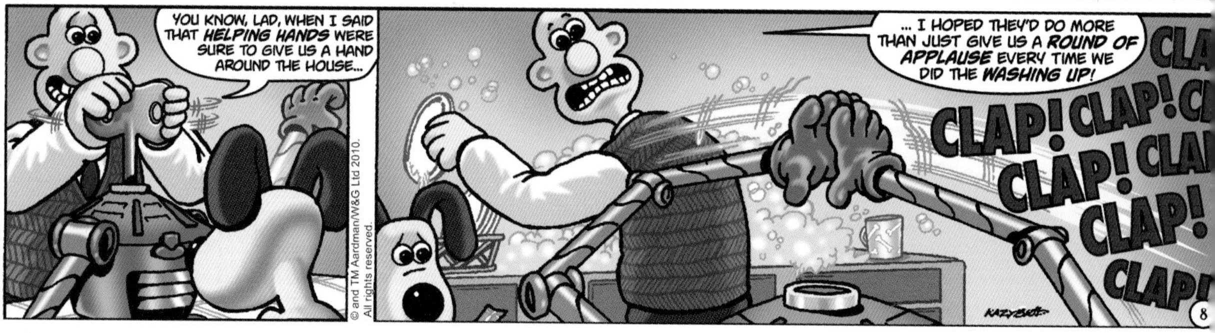

YOU KNOW, LAD, WHEN I SAID THAT HELPING HANDS WERE SURE TO GIVE US A HAND AROUND THE HOUSE...
© and TM Aardman/W&G Ltd 2010. All rights reserved.
... I HOPED THEY'D DO MORE THAN JUST GIVE US A ROUND OF APPLAUSE EVERY TIME WE DID THE WASHING UP!
CLAP! CLAP! CLAP! CLAP! CLAP!
8

Wallace & Gromit - Helping Hands

by Aardman & Titan Comics

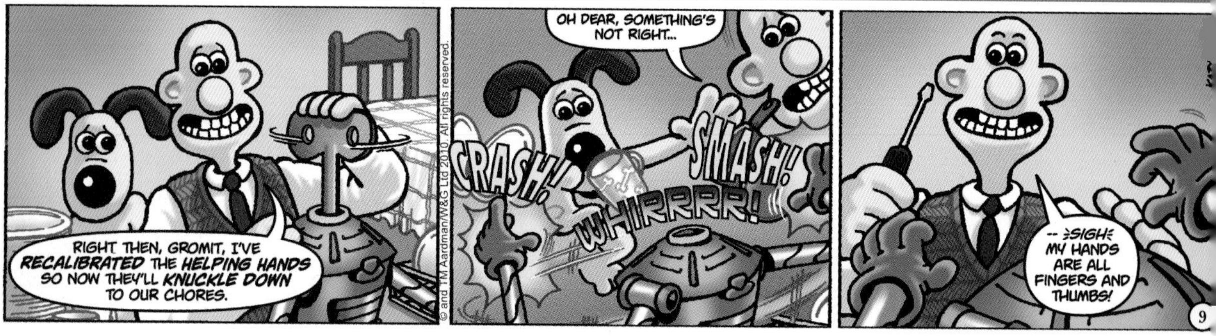

RIGHT THEN, GROMIT, I'VE RECALIBRATED THE HELPING HANDS SO NOW THEY'LL KNUCKLE DOWN TO OUR CHORES.
© and TM Aardman/W&G Ltd 2010. All rights reserved.
OH DEAR, SOMETHING'S NOT RIGHT...
CRASH!
SMASH!
WHIRRRR!
-- SIGH MY HANDS ARE ALL FINGERS AND THUMBS!
9

Wallace & Gromit - Helping Hands by Aardman & Titan Comics

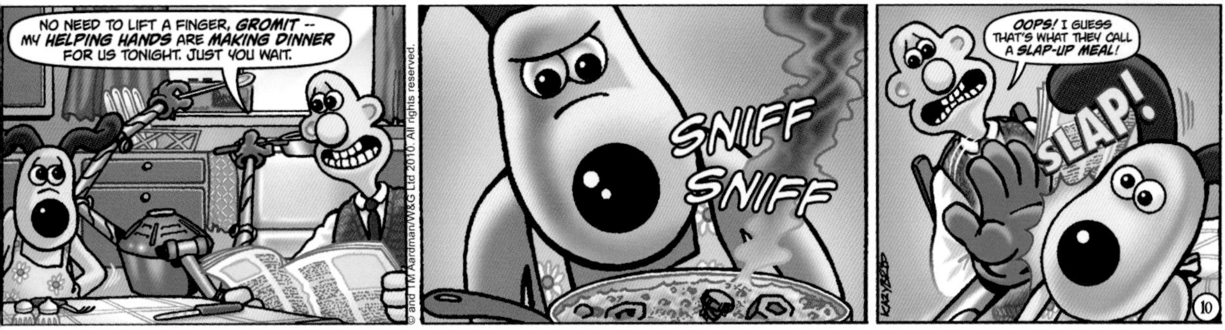

NO NEED TO LIFT A FINGER, GROMIT -- MY HELPING HANDS ARE MAKING DINNER FOR US TONIGHT. JUST YOU WAIT.
© and TM Aardman/W&G Ltd 2010. All rights reserved.
SNIFF SNIFF
OOPS! I GUESS THAT'S WHAT THEY CALL A SLAP-UP MEAL!
SLAP!
KAZYBRID
10

Wallace & Gromit - Helping Hands by Aardman & Titan Comics

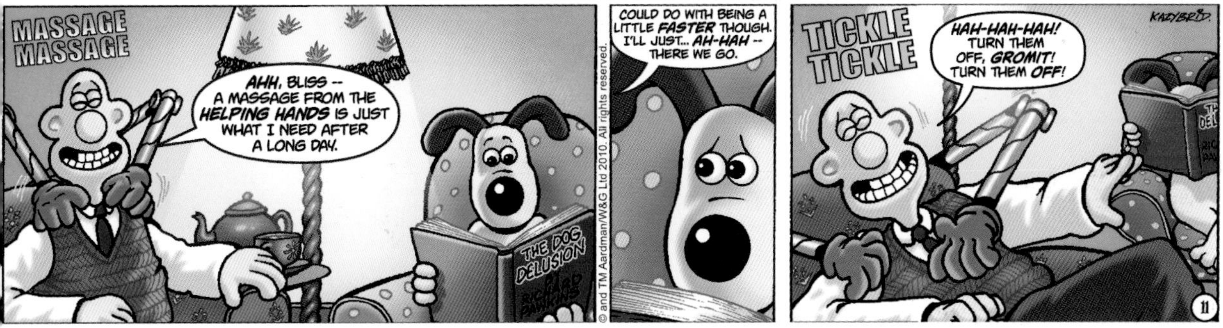

MASSAGE MASSAGE
AHH, BLISS -- A MASSAGE FROM THE HELPING HANDS IS JUST WHAT I NEED AFTER A LONG DAY.
THE DOG DELUSION
© and TM Aardman/W&G Ltd 2010. All rights reserved.
COULD DO WITH BEING A LITTLE FASTER THOUGH. I'LL JUST... AH-HAH -- THERE WE GO.
TICKLE TICKLE
HAH-HAH-HAH! TURN THEM OFF, GROMIT! TURN THEM OFF!
KAZYBRID
11

Wallace & Gromit - Helping Hands by Aardman & Titan Comics

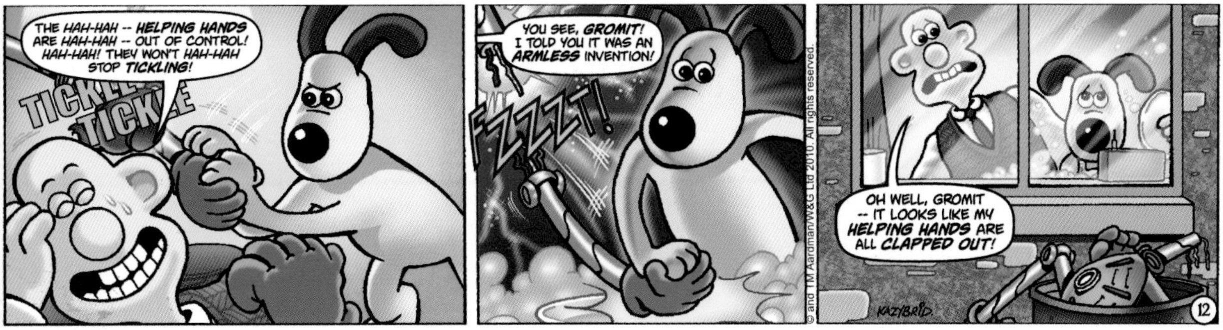

THE HAH-HAH -- HELPING HANDS ARE HAH-HAH -- OUT OF CONTROL! HAH-HAH! THEY WON'T HAH-HAH STOP TICKLING!
YOU SEE, GROMIT! I TOLD YOU IT WAS AN ARMLESS INVENTION!
FZZZT!
© and TM Aardman/W&G Ltd 2010. All rights reserved.
OH WELL, GROMIT -- IT LOOKS LIKE MY HELPING HANDS ARE ALL CLAPPED OUT!
KAZYBRID
12

The End

Wallace & Gromit - Hear Muffs

by Aardman & Titan Comics

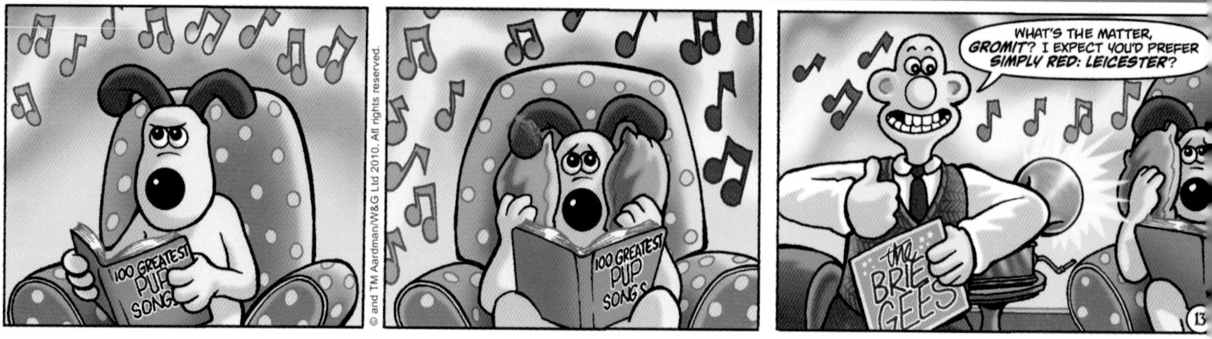
100 GREATEST PUP SONGS
100 GREATEST PUP SONGS
WHAT'S THE MATTER, GROMIT? I EXPECT YOU'D PREFER SIMPLY RED: LEICESTER?
THE BRIE GEES
13

Wallace & Gromit - Hear Muffs

by Aardman & Titan Comics

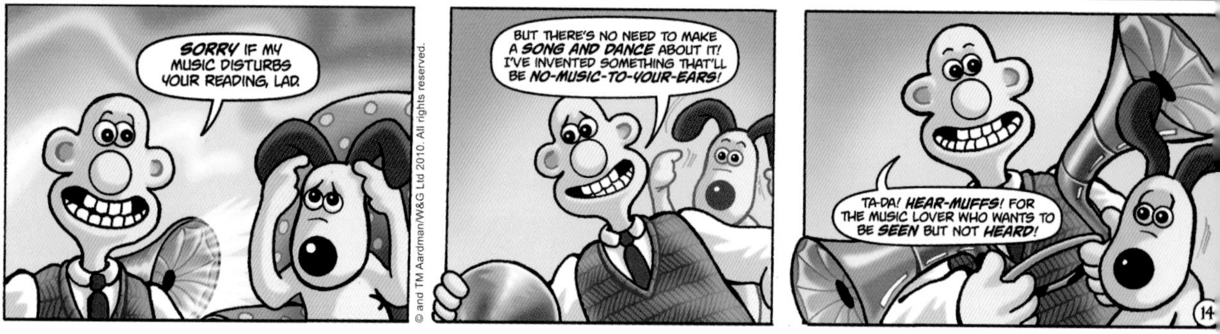
SORRY IF MY MUSIC DISTURBS YOUR READING, LAD.
BUT THERE'S NO NEED TO MAKE A SONG AND DANCE ABOUT IT! I'VE INVENTED SOMETHING THAT'LL BE NO-MUSIC-TO-YOUR-EARS!
TA-DA! HEAR-MUFFS! FOR THE MUSIC LOVER WHO WANTS TO BE SEEN BUT NOT HEARD!
14

Wallace & Gromit - Hear Muffs

by Aardman & Titan Comics

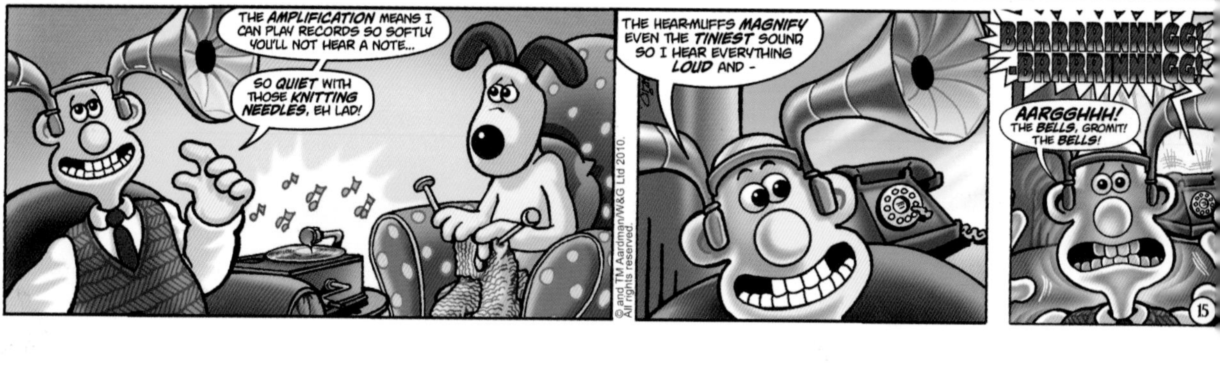
THE AMPLIFICATION MEANS I CAN PLAY RECORDS SO SOFTLY YOU'LL NOT HEAR A NOTE...
SO QUIET WITH THOSE KNITTING NEEDLES, EH LAD!
THE HEAR-MUFFS MAGNIFY EVEN THE TINIEST SOUND SO I HEAR EVERYTHING LOUD AND -
BRRRRRINNNGG! BRRRRINNNGG!
AARGGHHH! THE BELLS, GROMIT! THE BELLS!
15

by Aardman & Titan Comics

WALLACE'S NEW SUPER-HEARING DEVICE IS PROVING TO BE NOT SUCH A *SOUND* IDEA...

BRRRRRINNNGG! -BRRRRRINNNGG!

AARRGGHH!

DO SOMETHING, LAD! *UNPLUG ME!*

CLICK

I'LL HAVE TO FIND A WAY TO TURN THE VOLUME DOWN ON THESE BEFORE I DO MESELF ANY MORE *DECIBEL DAMAGE!*

© and TM Aardman/W&G Ltd 2010. All rights reserved.

16

by Aardman & Titan Comics

WALLACE'S NEW HEAR-MUFFS ARE TOO POWERFUL FOR THEIR OWN GOOD...

DING-DONG!

AARRGGHH!

GET THE DOOR GROMIT! AN' TELL THE *MILKMAN...*

...NO MILK TODAY! I CAN'T TAKE THE SOUND OF 'IM *RATTLING* HIS *EMPTIES!*

MORNING, GROMIT! ALL QUIET ON THE WEST WALLABY FRONT, I TRUST?

AARRGGH! NO IT'S BLINKIN' *NOT!*

© and TM Aardman/W&G Ltd 2010. All rights reserved.

17

by Aardman & Titan Comics

WALLACE IS DESPERATE TO PUMP DOWN THE VOLUME ON HIS NEW *HEAR-MUFFS...*

HERE'S YOUR WEEKLY CHEESE ORDER, MR WALLACE!

BLINKIN' NORA! PUT A *SOCK* IN IT WOULD YOU!

GOT TO TURN THE VOLUME *DOWN* 'TILL I CAN GET THIS BLASTED THING OFF ME HEAD!

CHEESEY CHOICE

AHHHH, THAT'S BETTER! NOW THAT'S WHAT I CALL *CHE-EASY LISTENING!*

CHEESEY CHOICE

© and TM Aardman/W&G Ltd 2010. All rights reserved.

18

The End

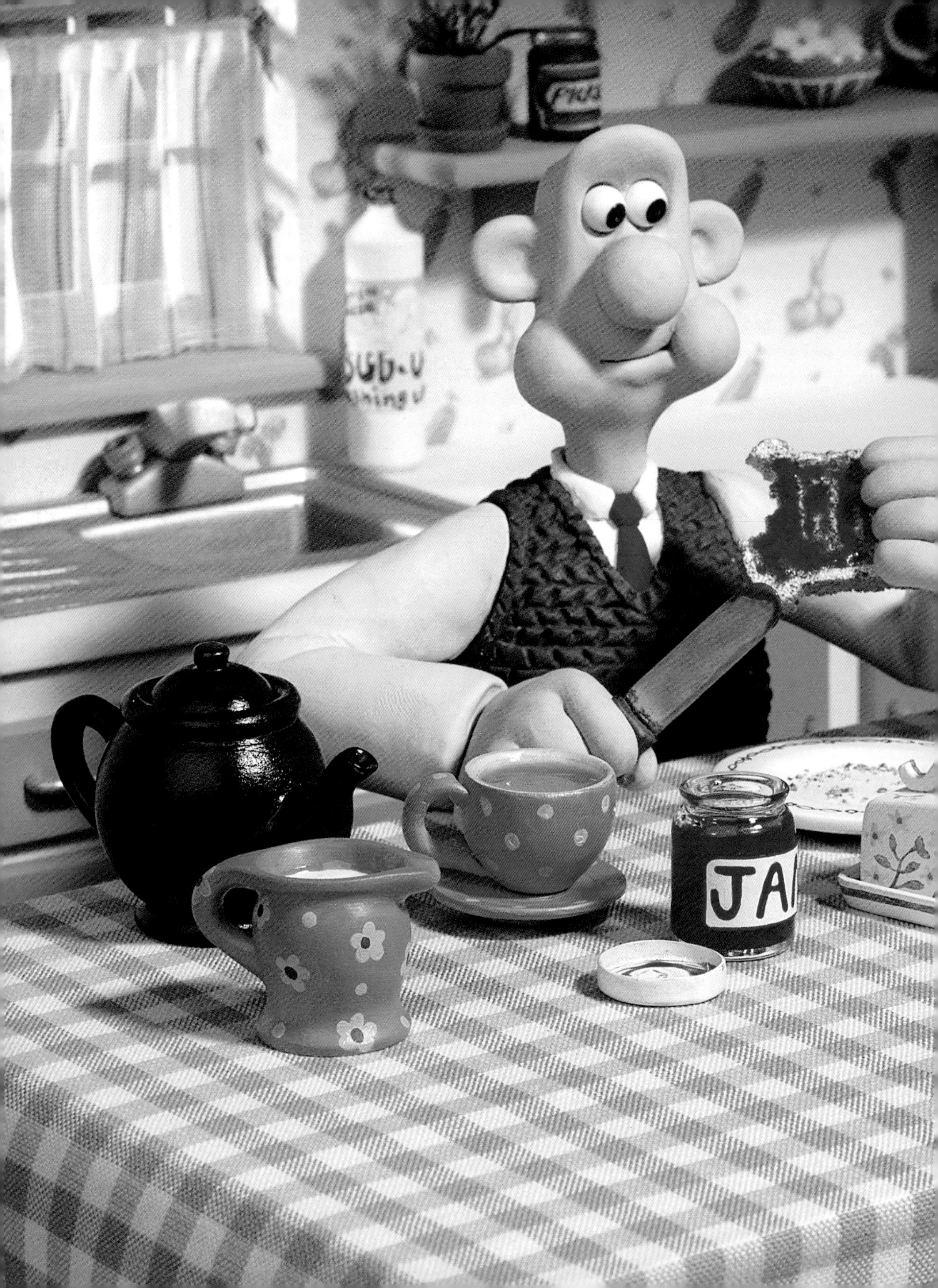
JA

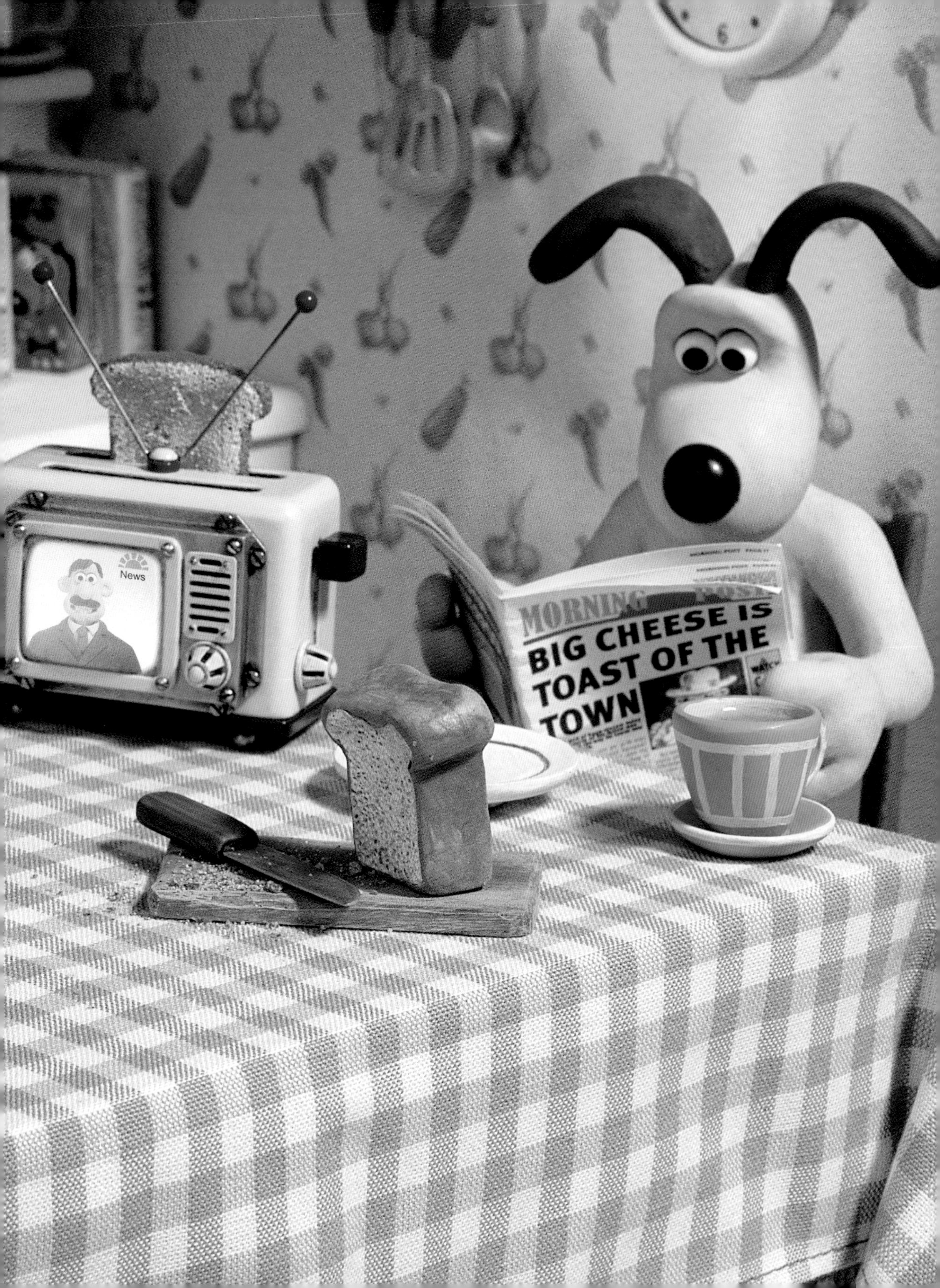
News
MORNING
BIG CHEESE IS
TOAST OF THE
TOWN

Wallace & Gromit - Knowing Bee, Knowing You

by Aardman & Titan Comics

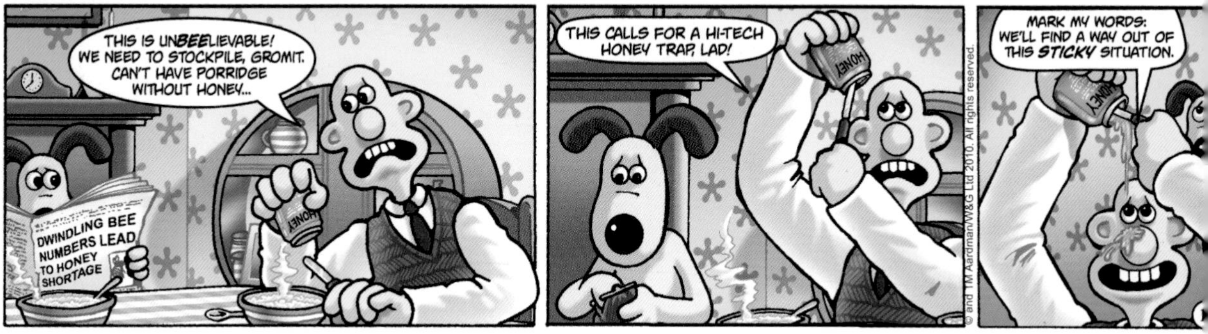

THIS IS UNBEELIEVABLE! WE NEED TO STOCKPILE, GROMIT. CAN'T HAVE PORRIDGE WITHOUT HONEY...
DWINDLING BEE NUMBERS LEAD TO HONEY SHORTAGE
HONEY
THIS CALLS FOR A HI-TECH HONEY TRAP, LAD!
HONEY
© and TM Aardman/W&G Ltd 2010. All rights reserved.
MARK MY WORDS: WE'LL FIND A WAY OUT OF THIS STICKY SITUATION.

Wallace & Gromit - Knowing Bee, Knowing You

by Aardman & Titan Comic

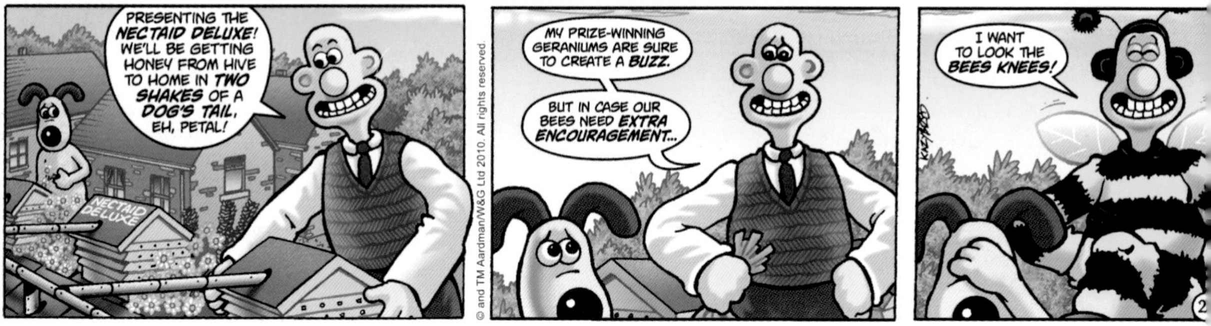

PRESENTING THE NECTAID DELUXE! WE'LL BE GETTING HONEY FROM HIVE TO HOME IN TWO SHAKES OF A DOG'S TAIL, EH, PETAL!
NECTAID DELUXE
© and TM Aardman/W&G Ltd 2010. All rights reserved.
MY PRIZE-WINNING GERANIUMS ARE SURE TO CREATE A BUZZ.
BUT IN CASE OUR BEES NEED EXTRA ENCOURAGEMENT...
I WANT TO LOOK THE BEES KNEES!

Wallace & Gromit - Knowing Bee, Knowing You

by Aardman & Titan Comic

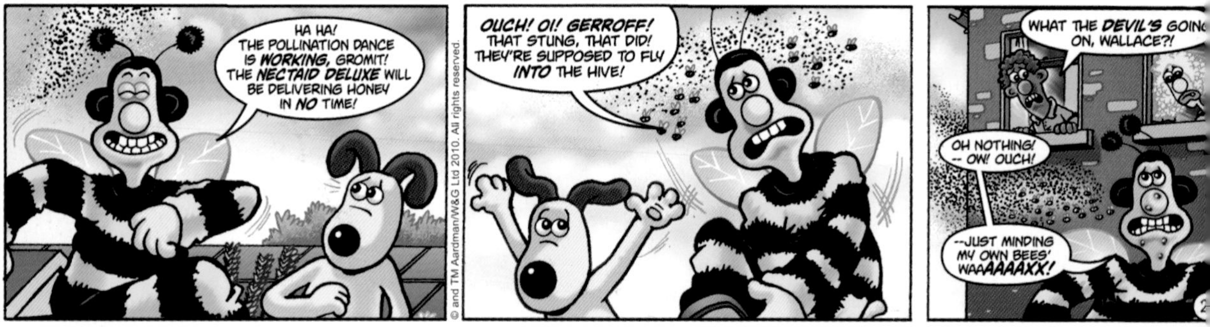

HA HA! THE POLLINATION DANCE IS WORKING, GROMIT! THE NECTAID DELUXE WILL BE DELIVERING HONEY IN NO TIME!
© and TM Aardman/W&G Ltd 2010. All rights reserved.
OUCH! OI! GERROFF! THAT STUNG, THAT DID! THEY'RE SUPPOSED TO FLY INTO THE HIVE!
WHAT THE DEVIL'S GOIN ON, WALLACE?!
OH NOTHING! -- OW! OUCH!
--JUST MINDING MY OWN BEES' WAAAAAAXX!

Wallace & Gromit - Knowing Bee, Knowing You by Aardman & Titan Comics

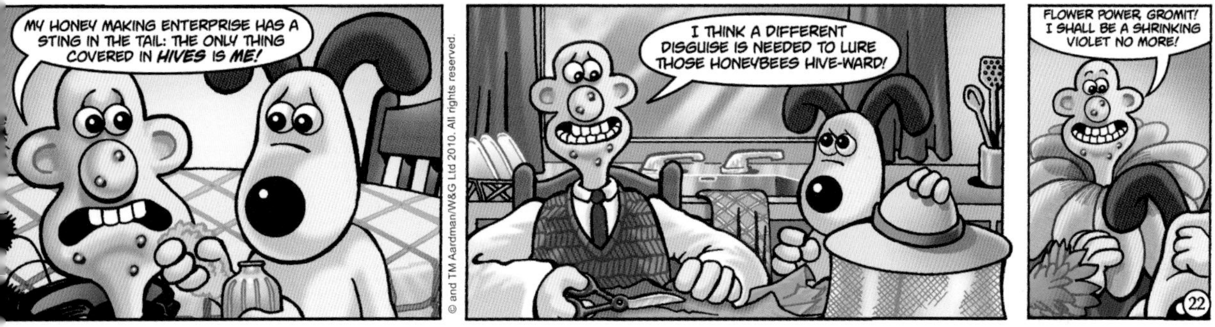

MY HONEY MAKING ENTERPRISE HAS A STING IN THE TAIL: THE ONLY THING COVERED IN HIVES IS ME!
© and TM Aardman/W&G Ltd 2010. All rights reserved.
I THINK A DIFFERENT DISGUISE IS NEEDED TO LURE THOSE HONEYBEES HIVE-WARD!
FLOWER POWER, GROMIT! I SHALL BE A SHRINKING VIOLET NO MORE!
22

Wallace & Gromit - Knowing Bee, Knowing You by Aardman & Titan Comics

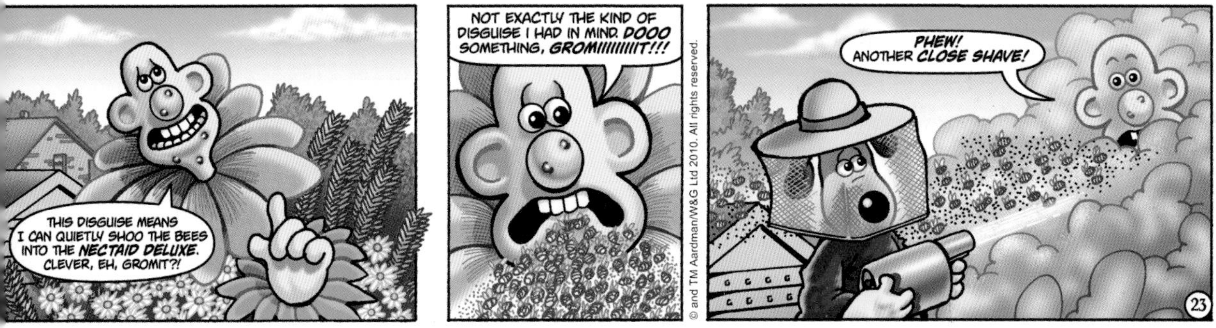

THIS DISGUISE MEANS I CAN QUIETLY SHOO THE BEES INTO THE NECTAID DELUXE. CLEVER, EH, GROMIT?!
NOT EXACTLY THE KIND OF DISGUISE I HAD IN MIND. DOOO SOMETHING, GROMIIIIIIIIIT!!!
© and TM Aardman/W&G Ltd 2010. All rights reserved.
PHEW! ANOTHER CLOSE SHAVE!
23

Wallace & Gromit - Knowing Bee, Knowing You by Aardman & Titan Comics

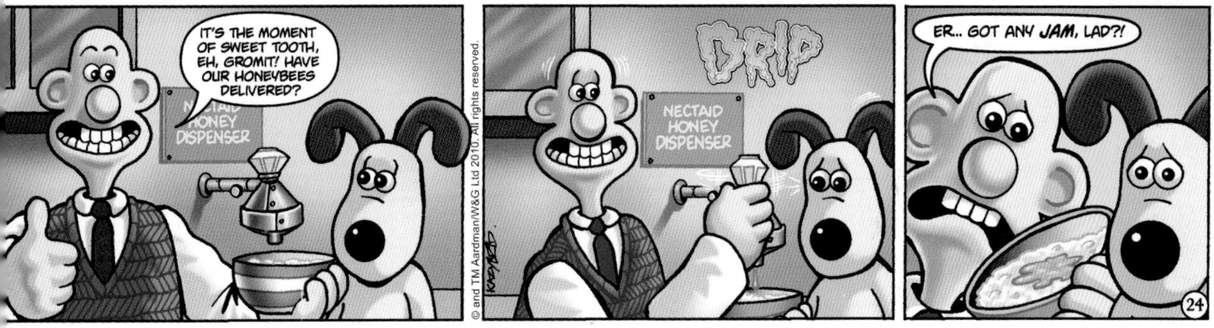

IT'S THE MOMENT OF SWEET TOOTH, EH, GROMIT! HAVE OUR HONEYBEES DELIVERED?
NECTAID HONEY DISPENSER
© and TM Aardman/W&G Ltd 2010. All rights reserved.
DRIP
NECTAID HONEY DISPENSER
ER... GOT ANY JAM, LAD?!
24

The End

Wallace & Gromit - Jurassic Lark
by Aardman & Titan Comic

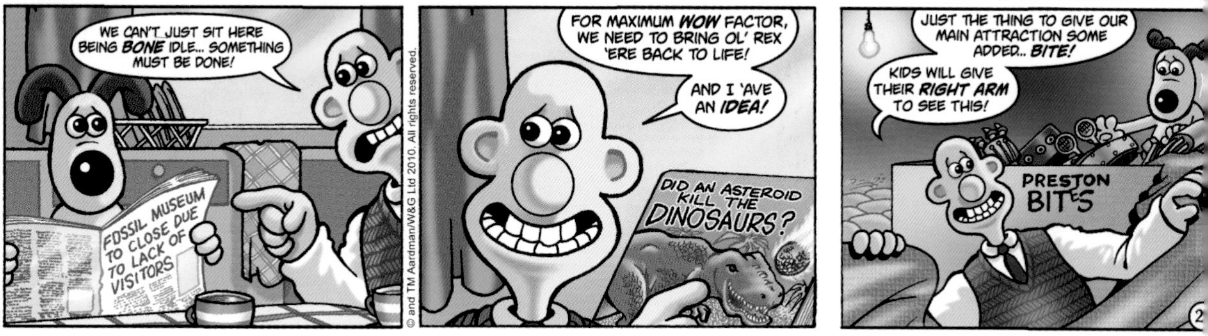
WE CAN'T JUST SIT HERE BEING BONE IDLE... SOMETHING MUST BE DONE!
FOSSIL MUSEUM TO CLOSE DUE TO LACK OF VISITORS
© and TM Aardman/W&G Ltd 2010. All rights reserved.
FOR MAXIMUM WOW FACTOR, WE NEED TO BRING OL' REX 'ERE BACK TO LIFE!
AND I 'AVE AN IDEA!
DID AN ASTEROID KILL THE DINOSAURS?
JUST THE THING TO GIVE OUR MAIN ATTRACTION SOME ADDED.. BITE!
KIDS WILL GIVE THEIR RIGHT ARM TO SEE THIS!
PRESTON BITS

Wallace & Gromit - Jurassic Lark
by Aardman & Titan Comics

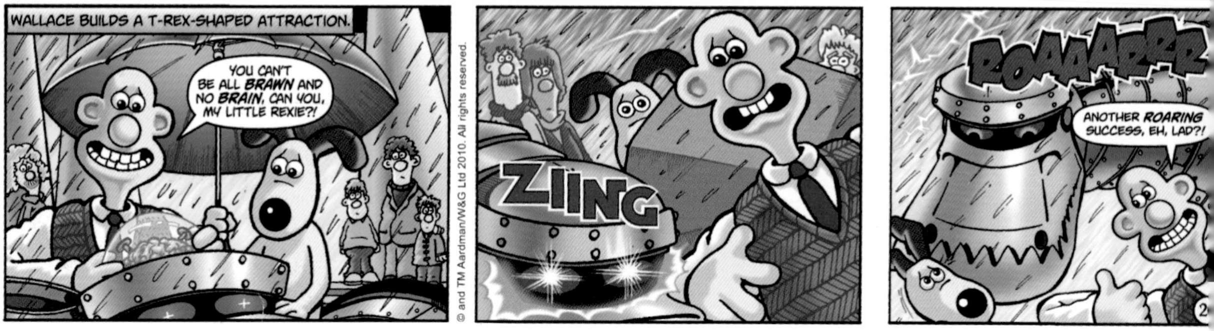
WALLACE BUILDS A T-REX-SHAPED ATTRACTION.
YOU CAN'T BE ALL BRAWN AND NO BRAIN, CAN YOU, MY LITTLE REXIE?!
© and TM Aardman/W&G Ltd 2010. All rights reserved.
ZIING
ROAAARRR
ANOTHER ROARING SUCCESS, EH, LAD?!

Wallace & Gromit - Jurassic Lark
by Aardman & Titan Comics

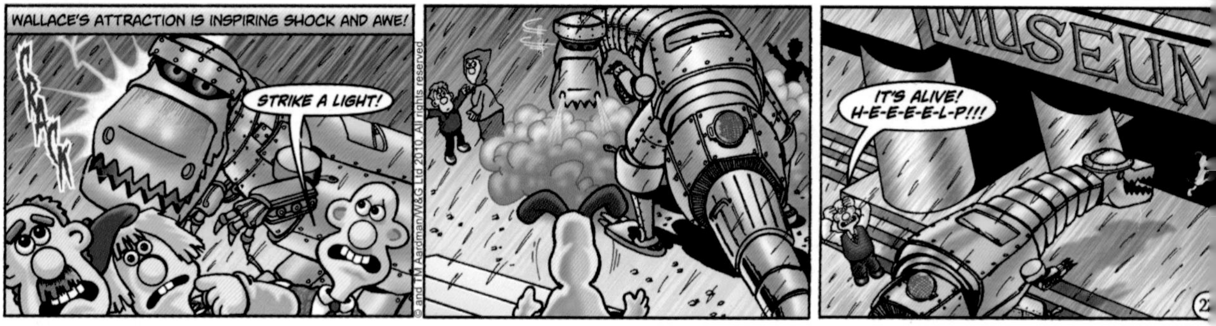
WALLACE'S ATTRACTION IS INSPIRING SHOCK AND AWE!
CRACK
STRIKE A LIGHT!
© and TM Aardman/W&G Ltd 2010. All rights reserved.
MUSEUM
IT'S ALIVE! H-E-E-E-E-L-P!!!

Wallace & Gromit - Jurassic Lark
by Aardman & Titan Comics

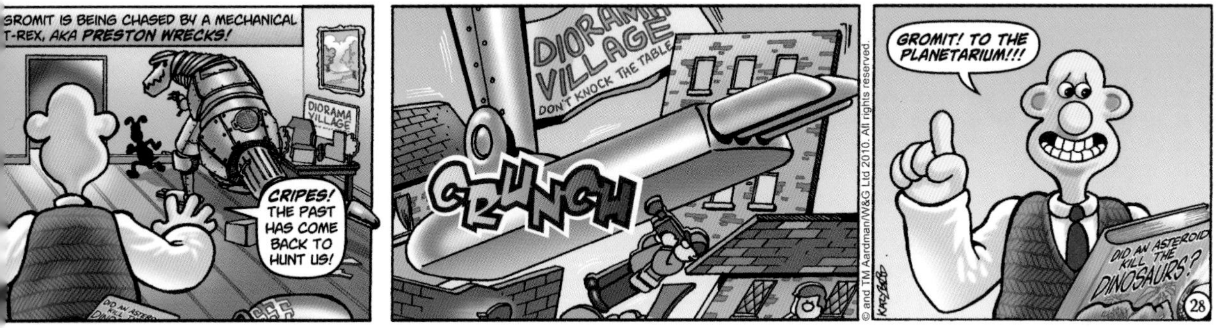
GROMIT IS BEING CHASED BY A MECHANICAL T-REX, AKA PRESTON WRECKS!
DIORAMA VILLAGE
CRIPES! THE PAST HAS COME BACK TO HUNT US!
DIORAMA VILLAGE
DON'T KNOCK THE TABLE
CRUNCH
GROMIT! TO THE PLANETARIUM!!!
DID AN ASTEROID KILL THE DINOSAURS?
28

Wallace & Gromit - Jurassic Lark
by Aardman & Titan Comics

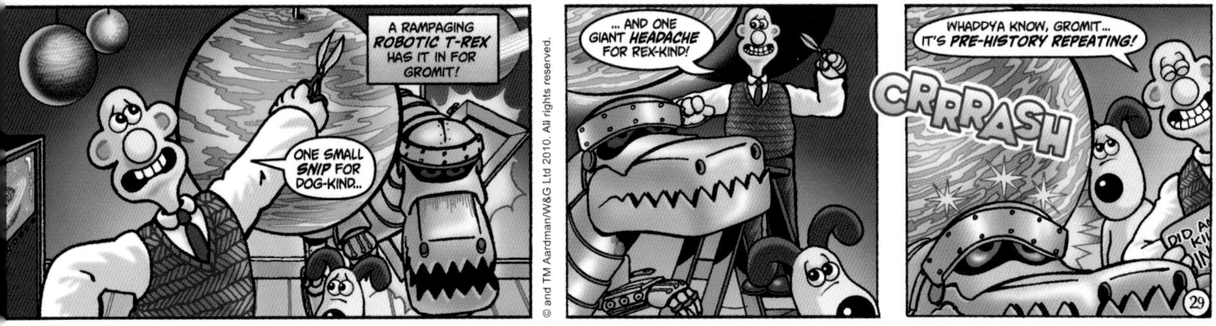
A RAMPAGING ROBOTIC T-REX HAS IT IN FOR GROMIT!
ONE SMALL SNIP FOR DOG-KIND..
... AND ONE GIANT HEADACHE FOR REX-KIND!
WHADDYA KNOW, GROMIT... IT'S PRE-HISTORY REPEATING!
CRRRASH
29

Wallace & Gromit - Jurassic Lark
by Aardman & Titan Comics

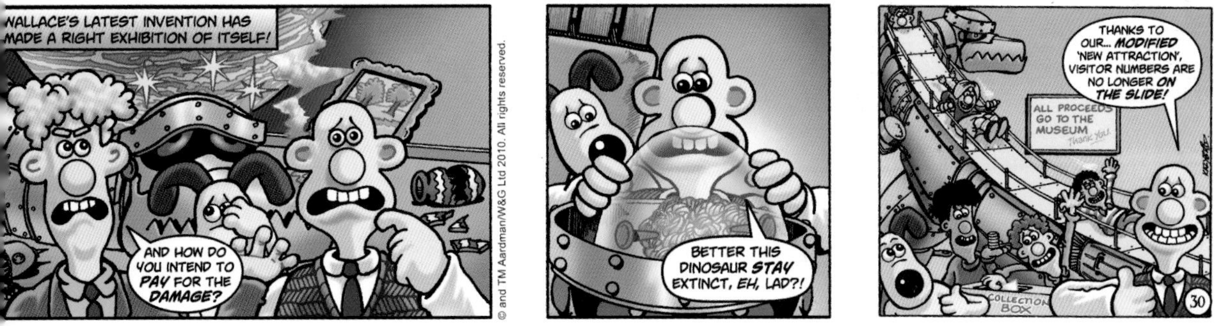
WALLACE'S LATEST INVENTION HAS MADE A RIGHT EXHIBITION OF ITSELF!
AND HOW DO YOU INTEND TO PAY FOR THE DAMAGE?
BETTER THIS DINOSAUR STAY EXTINCT, EH, LAD?!
THANKS TO OUR... MODIFIED 'NEW ATTRACTION', VISITOR NUMBERS ARE NO LONGER ON THE SLIDE!
ALL PROCEEDS GO TO THE MUSEUM
Thank You
COLLECTION BOX
30

The End

Wallace & Gromit - Roboplod
by Aardman & Titan Comics

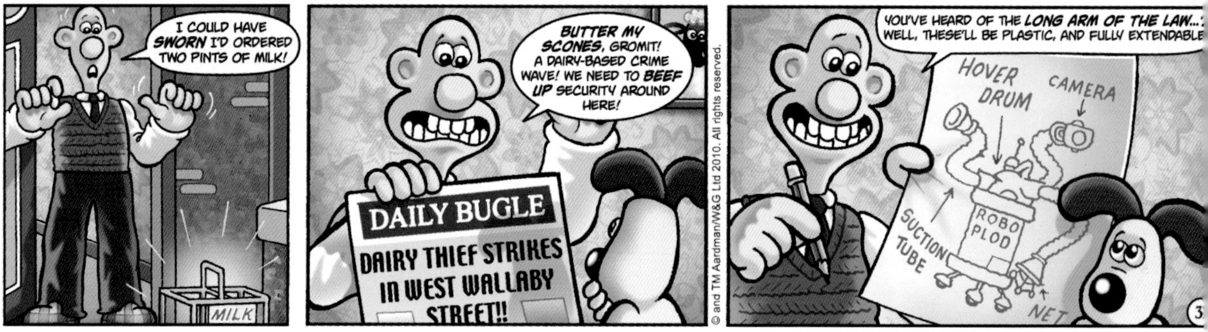

I COULD HAVE SWORN I'D ORDERED TWO PINTS OF MILK!
MILK
BUTTER MY SCONES, GROMIT! A DAIRY-BASED CRIME WAVE! WE NEED TO BEEF UP SECURITY AROUND HERE!
DAILY BUGLE
DAIRY THIEF STRIKES IN WEST WALLABY STREET!!
YOU'VE HEARD OF THE LONG ARM OF THE LAW...? WELL, THESE'LL BE PLASTIC, AND FULLY EXTENDABLE
HOVER DRUM
CAMERA
SUCTION TUBE
ROBO PLOD
NET

Wallace & Gromit - Roboplod
by Aardman & Titan Comics

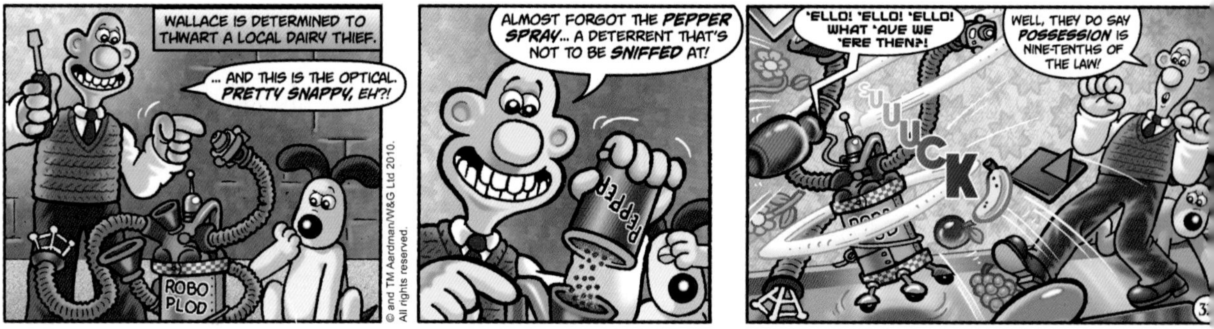

WALLACE IS DETERMINED TO THWART A LOCAL DAIRY THIEF.
... AND THIS IS THE OPTICAL. PRETTY SNAPPY, EH?!
ROBO PLOD
ALMOST FORGOT THE PEPPER SPRAY... A DETERRENT THAT'S NOT TO BE SNIFFED AT!
PEPPER
'ELLO! 'ELLO! 'ELLO! WHAT 'AVE WE 'ERE THEN?!
SUUUCK
WELL, THEY DO SAY POSSESSION IS NINE-TENTHS OF THE LAW!

Wallace & Gromit - Roboplod
by Aardman & Titan Comics

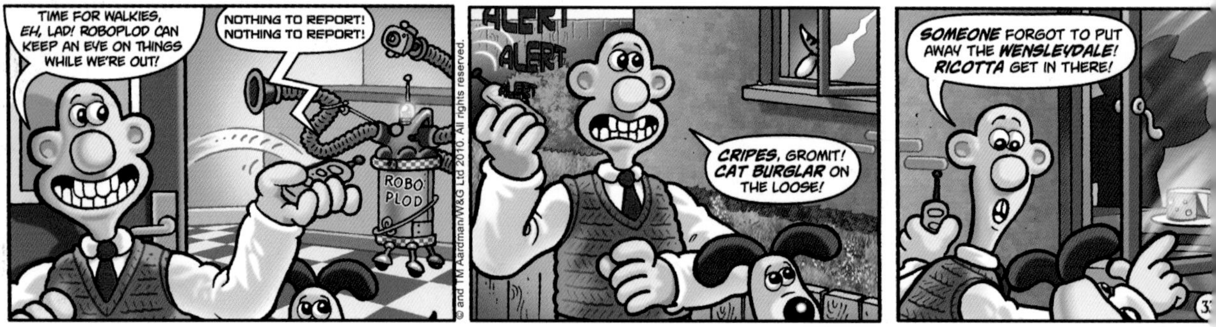

TIME FOR WALKIES, EH, LAD! ROBOPLOD CAN KEEP AN EYE ON THINGS WHILE WE'RE OUT!
NOTHING TO REPORT! NOTHING TO REPORT!
ROBO PLOD
ALERT
ALERT
CRIPES, GROMIT! CAT BURGLAR ON THE LOOSE!
SOMEONE FORGOT TO PUT AWAY THE WENSLEYDALE! RICOTTA GET IN THERE!

Wallace & Gromit - Roboplod **by Aardman & Titan Comics**

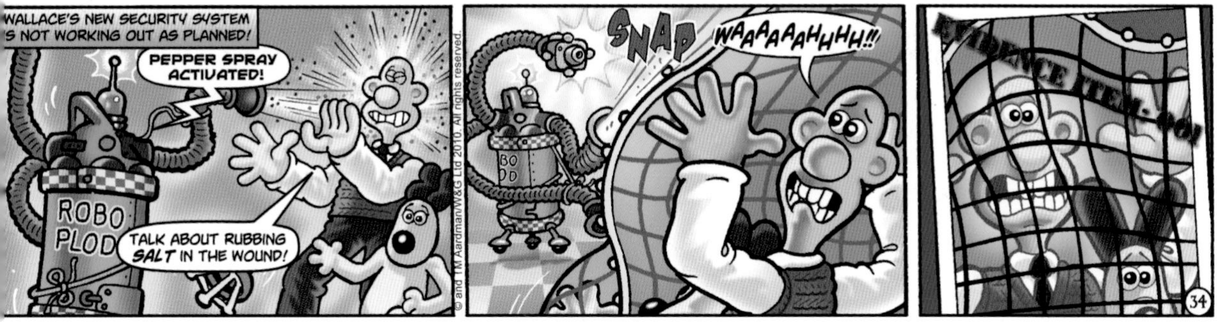

WALLACE'S NEW SECURITY SYSTEM IS NOT WORKING OUT AS PLANNED!
PEPPER SPRAY ACTIVATED!
TALK ABOUT RUBBING SALT IN THE WOUND!
ROBO PLOD
© and TM Aardman/W&G Ltd 2010. All rights reserved.
SNAP
WAAAAAAHHHH!!
EVIDENCE ITEM - 001
34

Wallace & Gromit - Roboplod **by Aardman & Titan Comics**

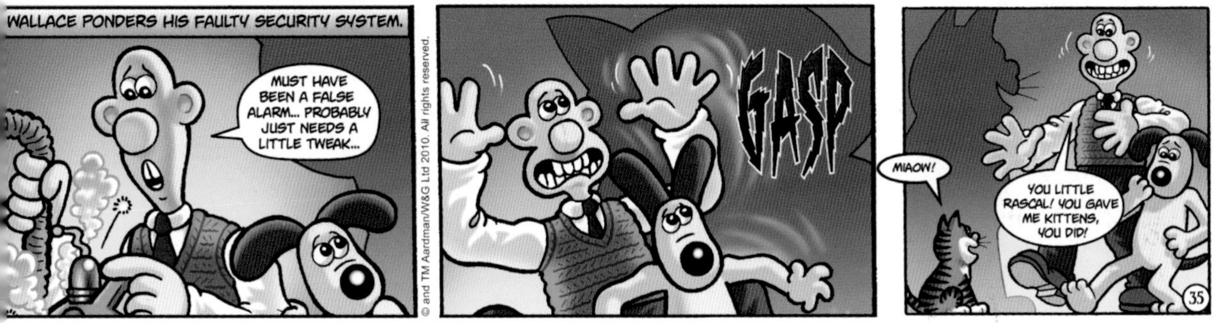

WALLACE PONDERS HIS FAULTY SECURITY SYSTEM.
MUST HAVE BEEN A FALSE ALARM... PROBABLY JUST NEEDS A LITTLE TWEAK...
© and TM Aardman/W&G Ltd 2010. All rights reserved.
GASP
MIAOW!
YOU LITTLE RASCAL! YOU GAVE ME KITTENS, YOU DID!
35

Wallace & Gromit - Roboplod **by Aardman & Titan Comics**

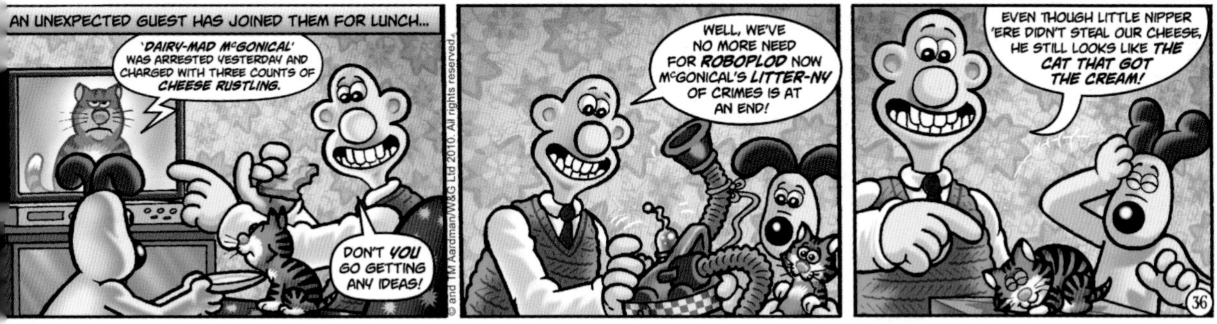

AN UNEXPECTED GUEST HAS JOINED THEM FOR LUNCH...
'DAIRY-MAD McGONICAL' WAS ARRESTED YESTERDAY AND CHARGED WITH THREE COUNTS OF CHEESE RUSTLING.
DON'T YOU GO GETTING ANY IDEAS!
© and TM Aardman/W&G Ltd 2010. All rights reserved.
WELL, WE'VE NO MORE NEED FOR ROBOPLOD NOW McGONICAL'S LITTER-NY OF CRIMES IS AT AN END!
EVEN THOUGH LITTLE NIPPER 'ERE DIDN'T STEAL OUR CHEESE, HE STILL LOOKS LIKE THE CAT THAT GOT THE CREAM!
36

The End

Wallace & Gromit - Pet Detectives

by Aardman & Titan Comics

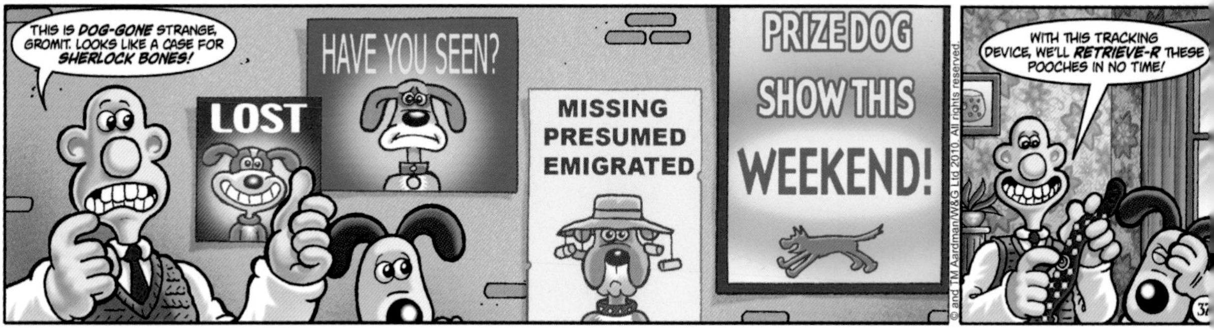

THIS IS DOG-GONE STRANGE, GROMIT. LOOKS LIKE A CASE FOR SHERLOCK BONES!
HAVE YOU SEEN?
LOST
MISSING PRESUMED EMIGRATED
PRIZE DOG SHOW THIS WEEKEND!
WITH THIS TRACKING DEVICE, WE'LL RETRIEVE-R THESE POOCHES IN NO TIME!
© and TM Aardman/W&G Ltd 2010. All rights reserved.

Wallace & Gromit - Pet Detectives

by Aardman & Titan Comics

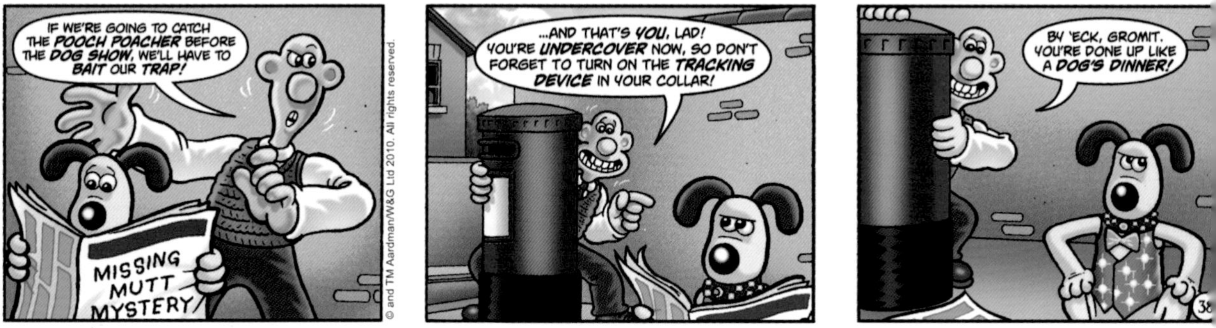

IF WE'RE GOING TO CATCH THE POOCH POACHER BEFORE THE DOG SHOW, WE'LL HAVE TO BAIT OUR TRAP!
MISSING MUTT MYSTERY
© and TM Aardman/W&G Ltd 2010. All rights reserved.
...AND THAT'S YOU, LAD! YOU'RE UNDERCOVER NOW, SO DON'T FORGET TO TURN ON THE TRACKING DEVICE IN YOUR COLLAR!
BY 'ECK, GROMIT. YOU'RE DONE UP LIKE A DOG'S DINNER!

Wallace & Gromit - Pet Detectives

by Aardman & Titan Comics

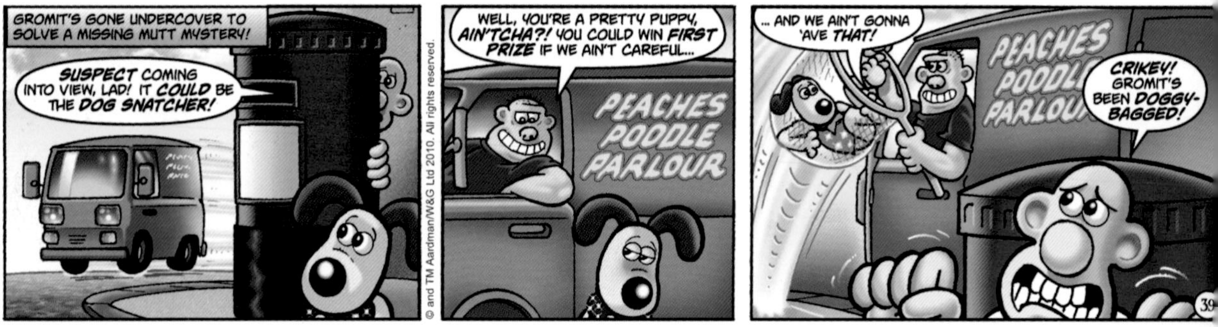

GROMIT'S GONE UNDERCOVER TO SOLVE A MISSING MUTT MYSTERY!
SUSPECT COMING INTO VIEW, LAD! IT COULD BE THE DOG SNATCHER!
© and TM Aardman/W&G Ltd 2010. All rights reserved.
WELL, YOU'RE A PRETTY PUPPY, AIN'TCHA?! YOU COULD WIN FIRST PRIZE IF WE AIN'T CAREFUL...
PEACHES POODLE PARLOUR
... AND WE AIN'T GONNA 'AVE THAT!
CRIKEY! GROMIT'S BEEN DOGGY-BAGGED!

Vallace & Gromit - Pet Detectives — by Aardman & Titan Comics

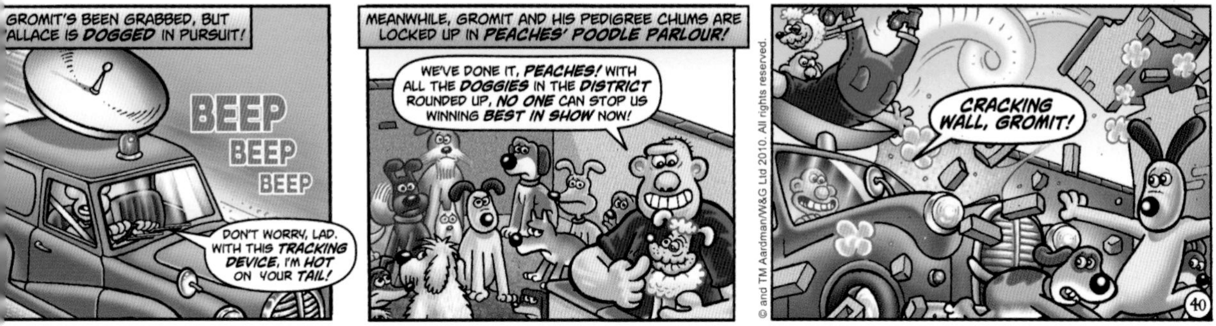

GROMIT'S BEEN GRABBED, BUT 'ALLACE IS DOGGED IN PURSUIT!
BEEP BEEP BEEP
DON'T WORRY, LAD. WITH THIS TRACKING DEVICE, I'M HOT ON YOUR TAIL!
MEANWHILE, GROMIT AND HIS PEDIGREE CHUMS ARE LOCKED UP IN PEACHES' POODLE PARLOUR!
WE'VE DONE IT, PEACHES! WITH ALL THE DOGGIES IN THE DISTRICT ROUNDED UP, NO ONE CAN STOP US WINNING BEST IN SHOW NOW!
© and TM Aardman/W&G Ltd 2010. All rights reserved.
CRACKING WALL, GROMIT!
40

Vallace & Gromit - Pet Detectives — by Aardman & Titan Comics

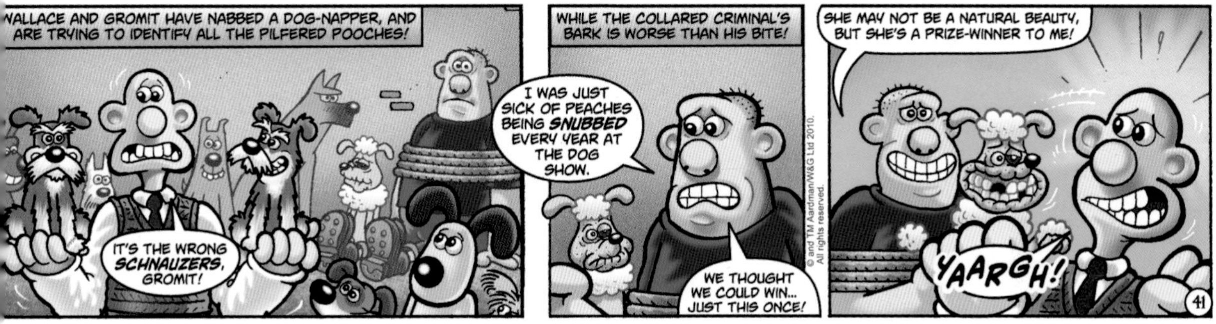

VALLACE AND GROMIT HAVE NABBED A DOG-NAPPER, AND ARE TRYING TO IDENTIFY ALL THE PILFERED POOCHES!
IT'S THE WRONG SCHNAUZERS, GROMIT!
WHILE THE COLLARED CRIMINAL'S BARK IS WORSE THAN HIS BITE!
I WAS JUST SICK OF PEACHES BEING SNUBBED EVERY YEAR AT THE DOG SHOW.
WE THOUGHT WE COULD WIN... JUST THIS ONCE!
© and TM Aardman/W&G Ltd 2010. All rights reserved.
SHE MAY NOT BE A NATURAL BEAUTY, BUT SHE'S A PRIZE-WINNER TO ME!
YAARGH!
41

Vallace & Gromit - Pet Detectives — by Aardman & Titan Comics

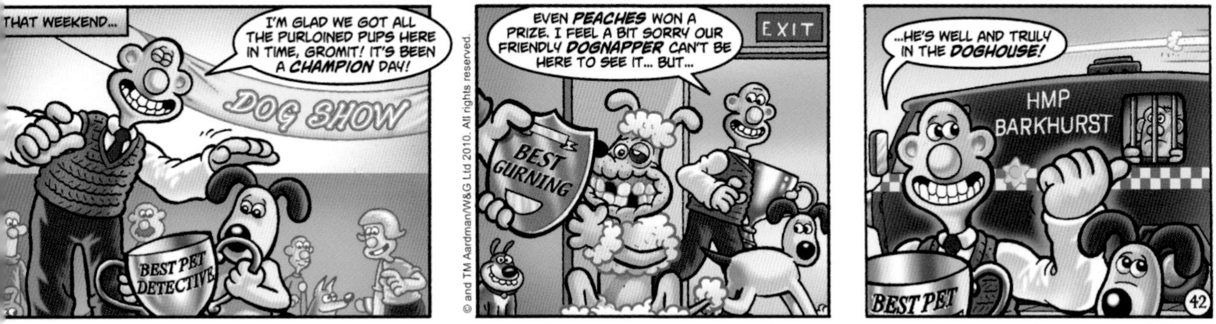

THAT WEEKEND...
I'M GLAD WE GOT ALL THE PURLOINED PUPS HERE IN TIME, GROMIT! IT'S BEEN A CHAMPION DAY!
DOG SHOW
BEST PET DETECTIVE
© and TM Aardman/W&G Ltd 2010. All rights reserved.
EVEN PEACHES WON A PRIZE. I FEEL A BIT SORRY OUR FRIENDLY DOGNAPPER CAN'T BE HERE TO SEE IT... BUT...
EXIT
BEST GURNING
...HE'S WELL AND TRULY IN THE DOGHOUSE!
HMP BARKHURST
BEST PET
42

The End

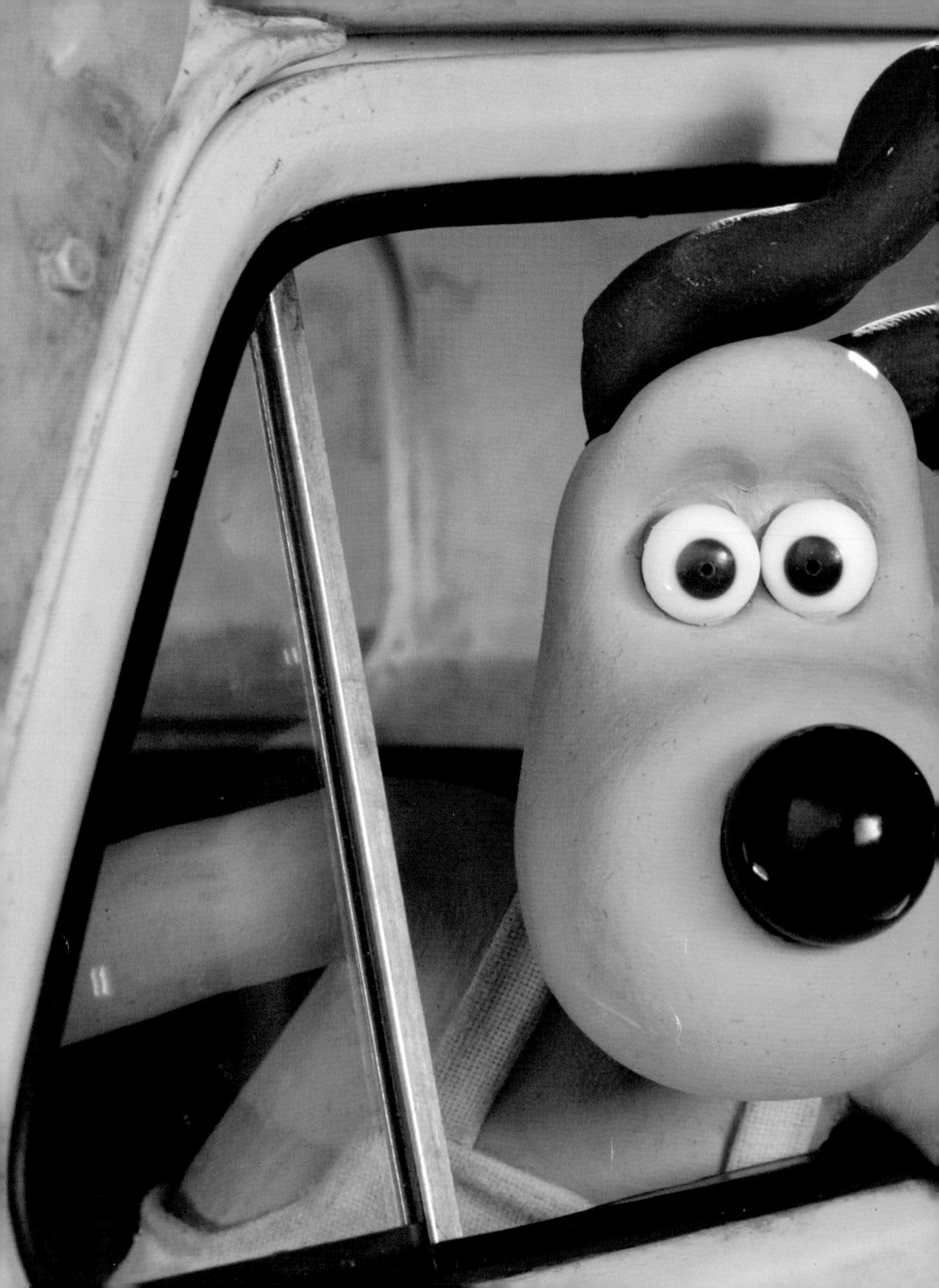

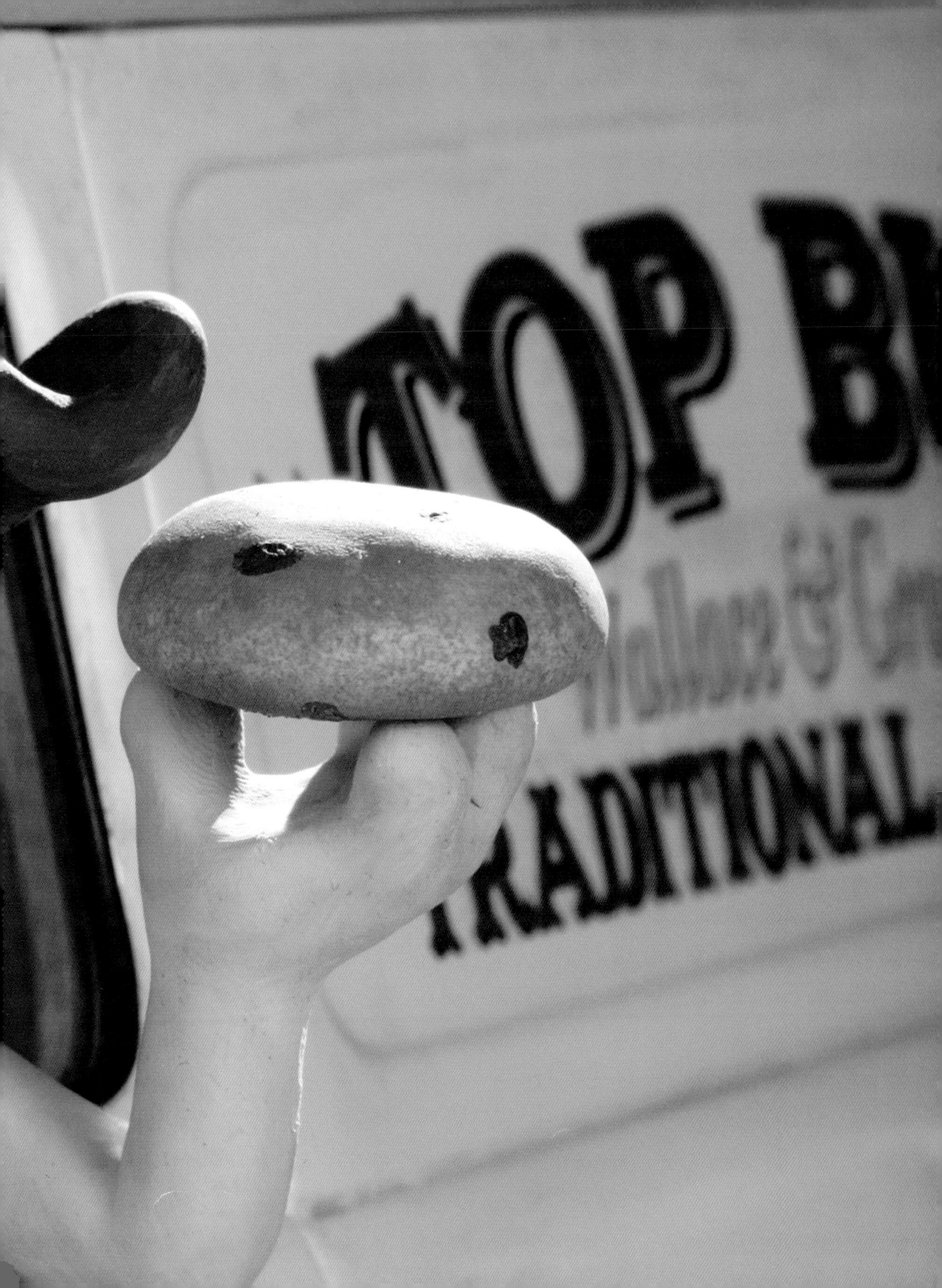
TOP
TRADITIONAL

Wallace & Gromit - The Restaurant

by Aardman & Titan Comics

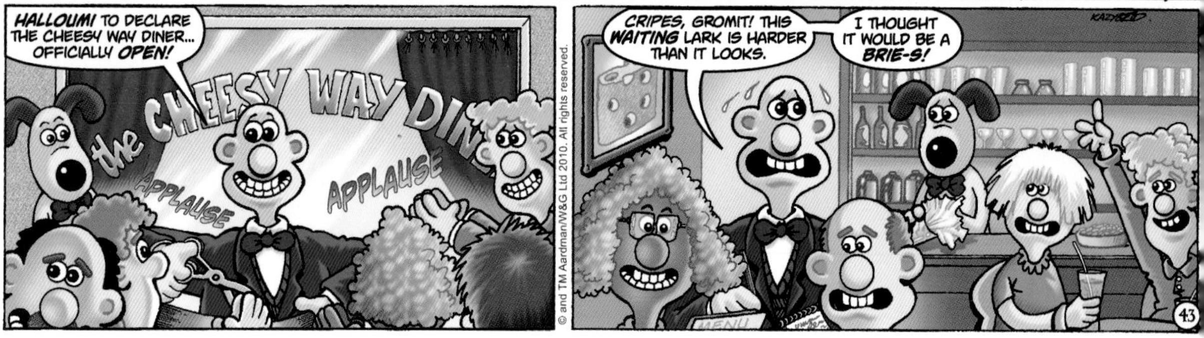

HALLOUMI TO DECLARE THE CHEESY WAY DINER... OFFICIALLY OPEN!
the CHEESY WAY DINER
APPLAUSE
APPLAUSE
© and TM Aardman/W&G Ltd 2010. All rights reserved.
CRIPES, GROMIT! THIS WAITING LARK IS HARDER THAN IT LOOKS.
I THOUGHT IT WOULD BE A BRIE-S!
43

Wallace & Gromit - The Restaurant

by Aardman & Titan Comics

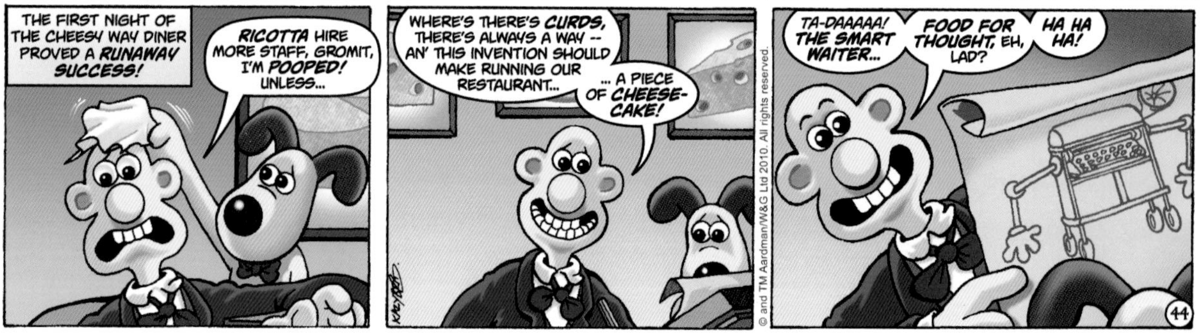

THE FIRST NIGHT OF THE CHEESY WAY DINER PROVED A RUNAWAY SUCCESS!
RICOTTA HIRE MORE STAFF, GROMIT, I'M POOPED! UNLESS...
WHERE'S THERE'S CURDS, THERE'S ALWAYS A WAY -- AN' THIS INVENTION SHOULD MAKE RUNNING OUR RESTAURANT...
... A PIECE OF CHEESE-CAKE!
© and TM Aardman/W&G Ltd 2010. All rights reserved.
TA-DAAAAA! THE SMART WAITER...
FOOD FOR THOUGHT, EH, LAD?
HA HA HA!
44

Wallace & Gromit - The Restaurant

by Aardman & Titan Comics

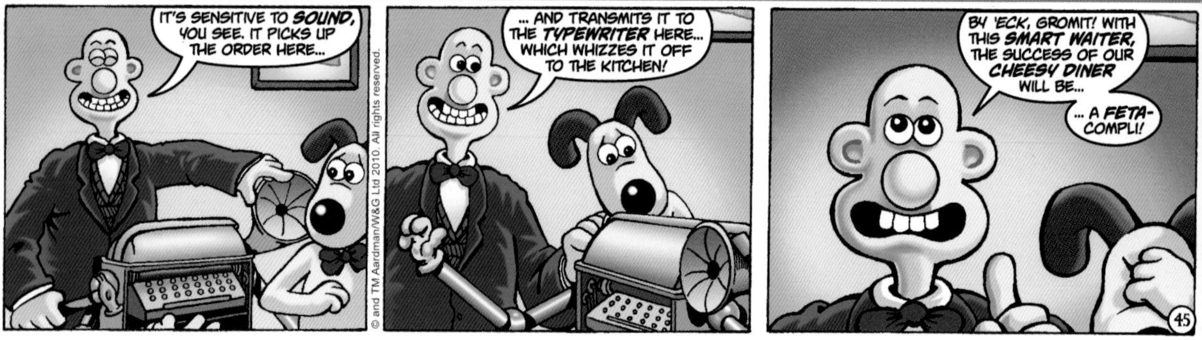

IT'S SENSITIVE TO SOUND, YOU SEE. IT PICKS UP THE ORDER HERE...
© and TM Aardman/W&G Ltd 2010. All rights reserved.
... AND TRANSMITS IT TO THE TYPEWRITER HERE... WHICH WHIZZES IT OFF TO THE KITCHEN!
BY 'ECK, GROMIT! WITH THIS SMART WAITER, THE SUCCESS OF OUR CHEESY DINER WILL BE...
... A FETA-COMPLI!
45

Wallace & Gromit - The Restaurant by Aardman & Titan Comics

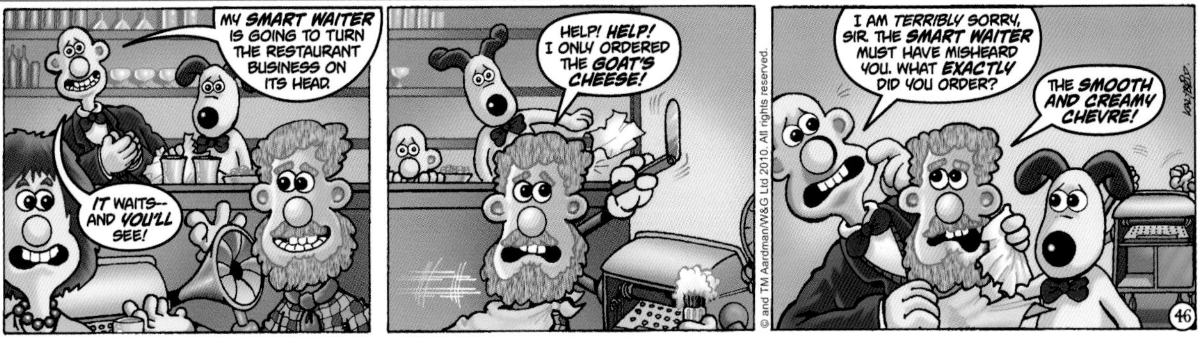

MY SMART WAITER IS GOING TO TURN THE RESTAURANT BUSINESS ON ITS HEAD.
IT WAITS-- AND YOU'LL SEE!
HELP! HELP! I ONLY ORDERED THE GOAT'S CHEESE!
I AM TERRIBLY SORRY, SIR. THE SMART WAITER MUST HAVE MISHEARD YOU. WHAT EXACTLY DID YOU ORDER?
THE SMOOTH AND CREAMY CHEVRE!
46

Wallace & Gromit - The Restaurant by Aardman & Titan Comics

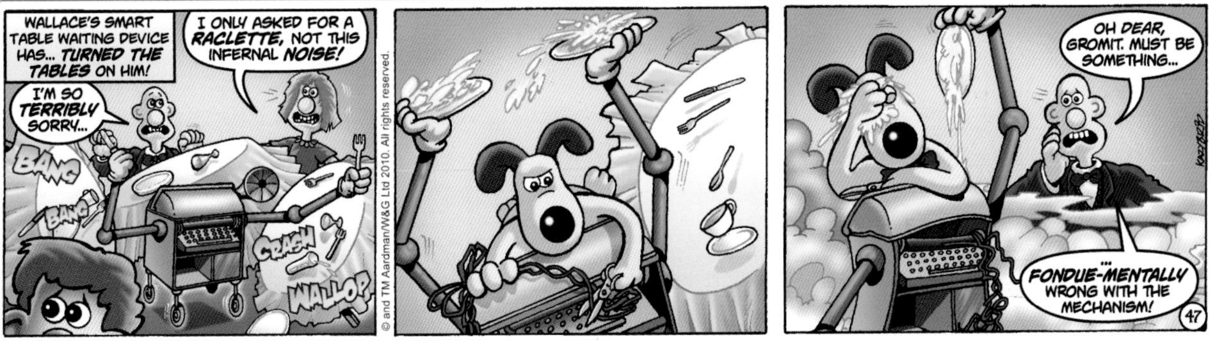

WALLACE'S SMART TABLE WAITING DEVICE HAS... TURNED THE TABLES ON HIM!
I ONLY ASKED FOR A RACLETTE, NOT THIS INFERNAL NOISE!
I'M SO TERRIBLY SORRY...
BANG
BANG
CRASH
WALLOP
OH DEAR, GROMIT. MUST BE SOMETHING...
...FONDUE-MENTALLY WRONG WITH THE MECHANISM!
47

Wallace & Gromit - The Restaurant by Aardman & Titan Comics

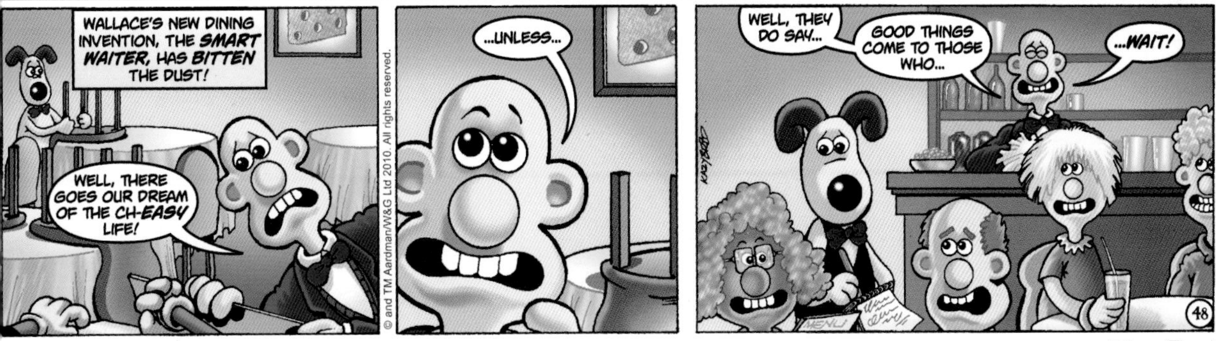

WALLACE'S NEW DINING INVENTION, THE SMART WAITER, HAS BITTEN THE DUST!
WELL, THERE GOES OUR DREAM OF THE CH-EASY LIFE!
...UNLESS...
WELL, THEY DO SAY...
GOOD THINGS COME TO THOSE WHO...
...WAIT!
MENU
48

The End

Wallace & Gromit - The House Next Door
by Aardman & Titan Comics

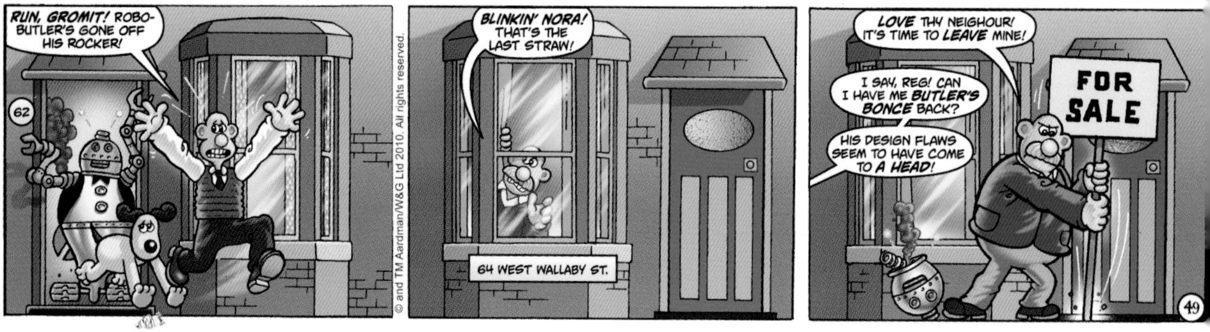
RUN, GROMIT! ROBO-BUTLER'S GONE OFF HIS ROCKER!
62
© and TM Aardman/W&G Ltd 2010. All rights reserved.
BLINKIN' NORA! THAT'S THE LAST STRAW!
64 WEST WALLABY ST.
LOVE THY NEIGHOUR! IT'S TIME TO LEAVE MINE!
I SAY, REG! CAN I HAVE ME BUTLER'S BONCE BACK?
HIS DESIGN FLAWS SEEM TO HAVE COME TO A HEAD!
FOR SALE
49

Wallace & Gromit - The House Next Door
by Aardman & Titan Comics

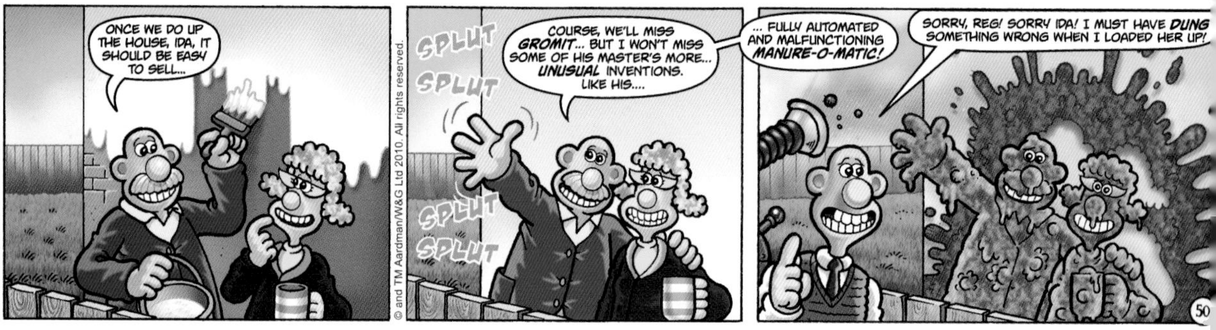
ONCE WE DO UP THE HOUSE, IDA, IT SHOULD BE EASY TO SELL...
© and TM Aardman/W&G Ltd 2010. All rights reserved.
SPLUT
SPLUT
COURSE, WE'LL MISS GROMIT... BUT I WON'T MISS SOME OF HIS MASTER'S MORE... UNUSUAL INVENTIONS. LIKE HIS....
SPLUT
SPLUT
... FULLY AUTOMATED AND MALFUNCTIONING MANURE-O-MATIC!
SORRY, REG! SORRY IDA! I MUST HAVE DUNG SOMETHING WRONG WHEN I LOADED HER UP!
50

Wallace & Gromit - The House Next Door
by Aardman & Titan Comics

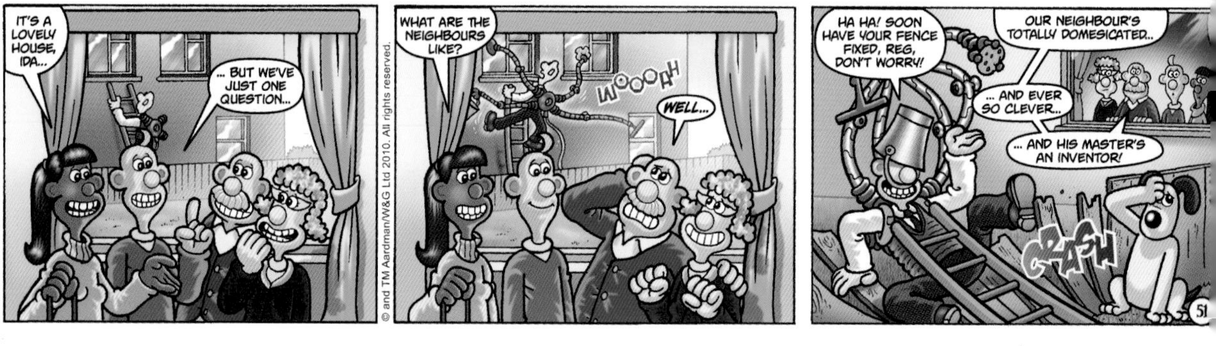
IT'S A LOVELY HOUSE, IDA...
... BUT WE'VE JUST ONE QUESTION...
© and TM Aardman/W&G Ltd 2010. All rights reserved.
WHAT ARE THE NEIGHBOURS LIKE?
WOOOAH
WELL...
HA HA! SOON HAVE YOUR FENCE FIXED, REG, DON'T WORRY!
OUR NEIGHBOUR'S TOTALLY DOMESICATED...
... AND EVER SO CLEVER...
... AND HIS MASTER'S AN INVENTOR!
CRASH
51

Wallace & Gromit - The House Next Door by Aardman & Titan Comics

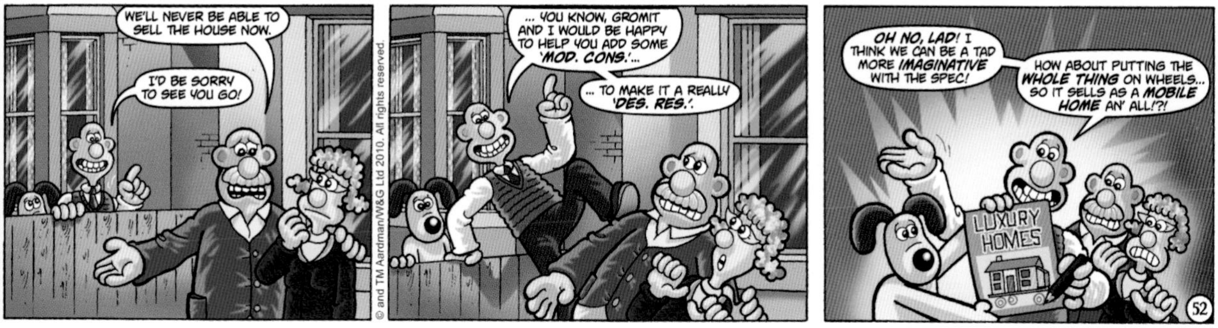
WE'LL NEVER BE ABLE TO SELL THE HOUSE NOW.
I'D BE SORRY TO SEE YOU GO!
... YOU KNOW, GROMIT AND I WOULD BE HAPPY TO HELP YOU ADD SOME 'MOD. CONS.'...
... TO MAKE IT A REALLY 'DES. RES.'.
OH NO, LAD! I THINK WE CAN BE A TAD MORE IMAGINATIVE WITH THE SPEC!
HOW ABOUT PUTTING THE WHOLE THING ON WHEELS... SO IT SELLS AS A MOBILE HOME AN' ALL!?!
LUXURY HOMES
52

Wallace & Gromit - The House Next Door by Aardman & Titan Comics

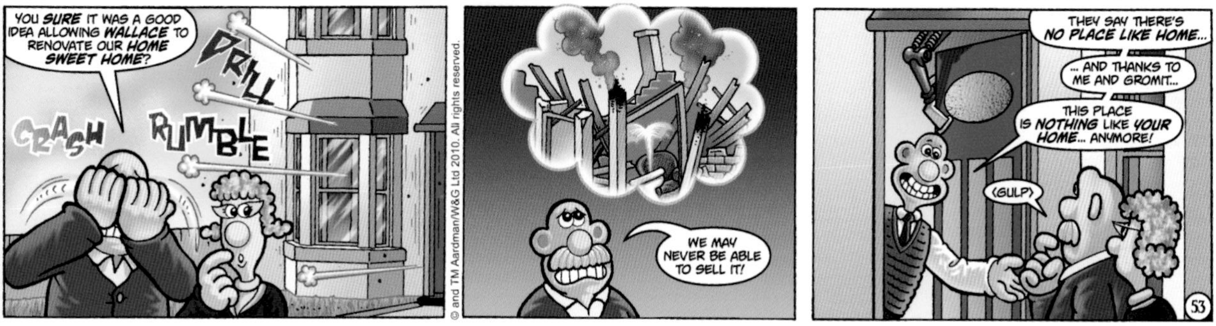
YOU SURE IT WAS A GOOD IDEA ALLOWING WALLACE TO RENOVATE OUR HOME SWEET HOME?
DRILL
CRASH
RUMBLE
WE MAY NEVER BE ABLE TO SELL IT!
THEY SAY THERE'S NO PLACE LIKE HOME...
... AND THANKS TO ME AND GROMIT...
THIS PLACE IS NOTHING LIKE YOUR HOME... ANYMORE!
{GULP}
53

Wallace & Gromit - The House Next Door by Aardman & Titan Comics

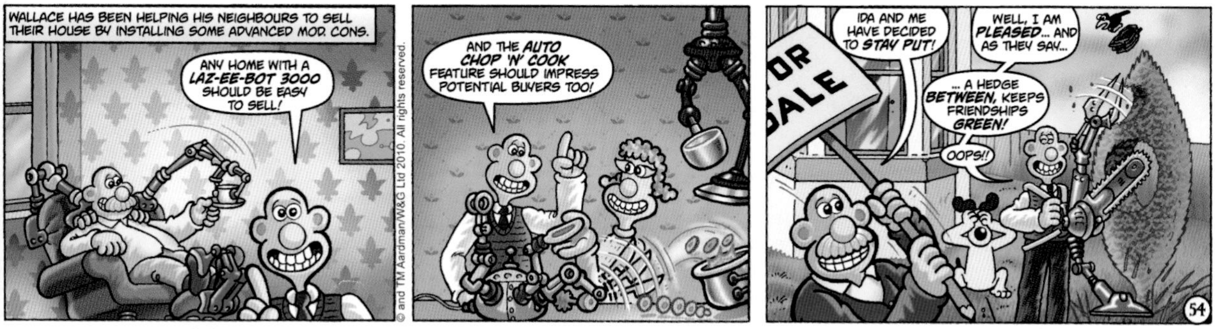
WALLACE HAS BEEN HELPING HIS NEIGHBOURS TO SELL THEIR HOUSE BY INSTALLING SOME ADVANCED MOD. CONS.
ANY HOME WITH A LAZ-EE-BOT 3000 SHOULD BE EASY TO SELL!
AND THE AUTO CHOP 'N' COOK FEATURE SHOULD IMPRESS POTENTIAL BUYERS TOO!
IDA AND ME HAVE DECIDED TO STAY PUT!
WELL, I AM PLEASED... AND AS THEY SAY...
... A HEDGE BETWEEN, KEEPS FRIENDSHIPS GREEN!
OOPS!!
OR SALE
54

The End

Wallace & Gromit - The Spaghetti Incident

by Aardman & Titan Comics

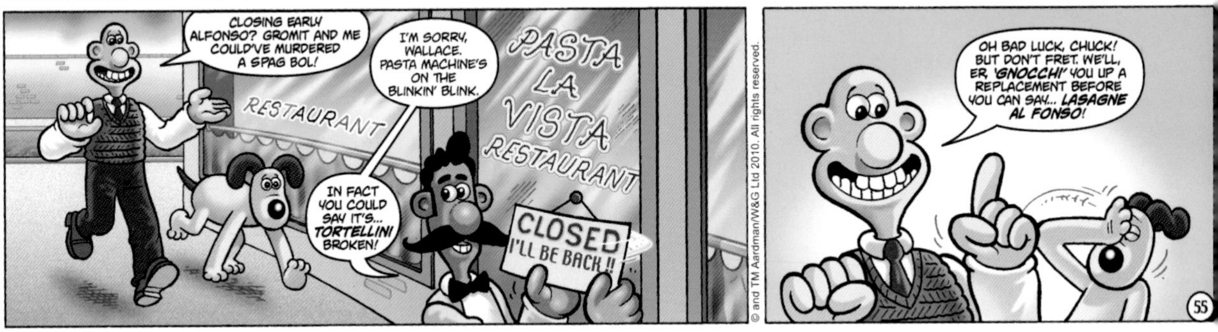
CLOSING EARLY ALFONSO? GROMIT AND ME COULD'VE MURDERED A SPAG BOL!
I'M SORRY, WALLACE. PASTA MACHINE'S ON THE BLINKIN' BLINK.
PASTA LA VISTA RESTAURANT
RESTAURANT
IN FACT YOU COULD SAY IT'S... TORTELLINI BROKEN!
CLOSED I'LL BE BACK!!
OH BAD LUCK, CHUCK! BUT DON'T FRET. WE'LL, ER, 'GNOCCHI' YOU UP A REPLACEMENT BEFORE YOU CAN SAY... LASAGNE AL FONSO!
55

Wallace & Gromit - The Spaghetti Incident

by Aardman & Titan Comics

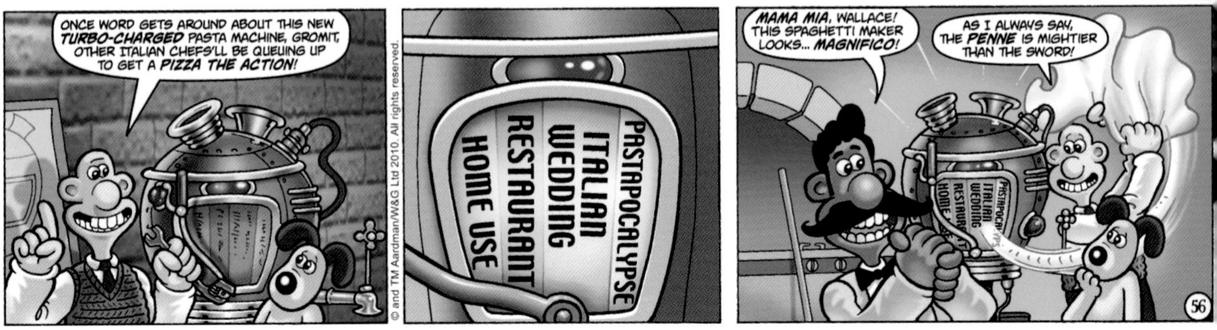
ONCE WORD GETS AROUND ABOUT THIS NEW TURBO-CHARGED PASTA MACHINE, GROMIT, OTHER ITALIAN CHEFS'LL BE QUEUING UP TO GET A PIZZA THE ACTION!
PASTAPOCALYPSE
ITALIAN
WEDDING
RESTAURANT
HOME USE
MAMA MIA, WALLACE! THIS SPAGHETTI MAKER LOOKS... MAGNIFICO!
AS I ALWAYS SAY, THE PENNE IS MIGHTIER THAN THE SWORD!
56

Wallace & Gromit - The Spaghetti Incident

by Aardman & Titan Comics

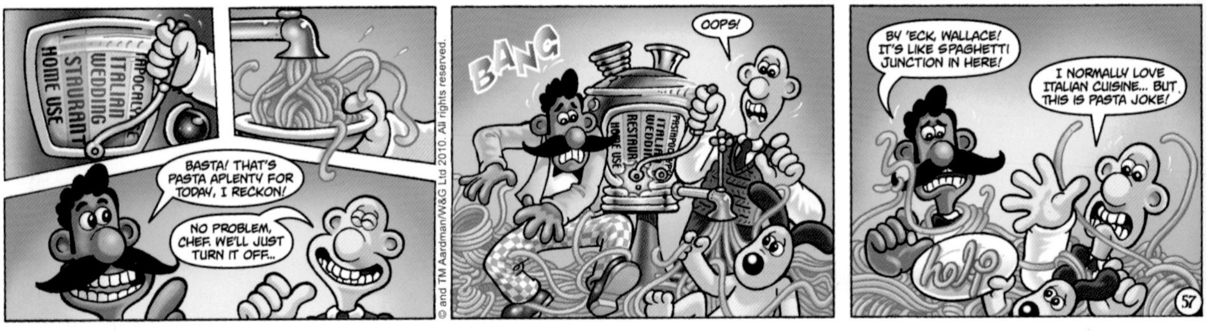
BASTA! THAT'S PASTA APLENTY FOR TODAY, I RECKON!
NO PROBLEM, CHEF. WE'LL JUST TURN IT OFF...
BANG
OOPS!
BY 'ECK, WALLACE! IT'S LIKE SPAGHETTI JUNCTION IN HERE!
I NORMALLY LOVE ITALIAN CUISINE... BUT THIS IS PASTA JOKE!
help
57

Wallace & Gromit - The Spaghetti Incident by Aardman & Titan Comics

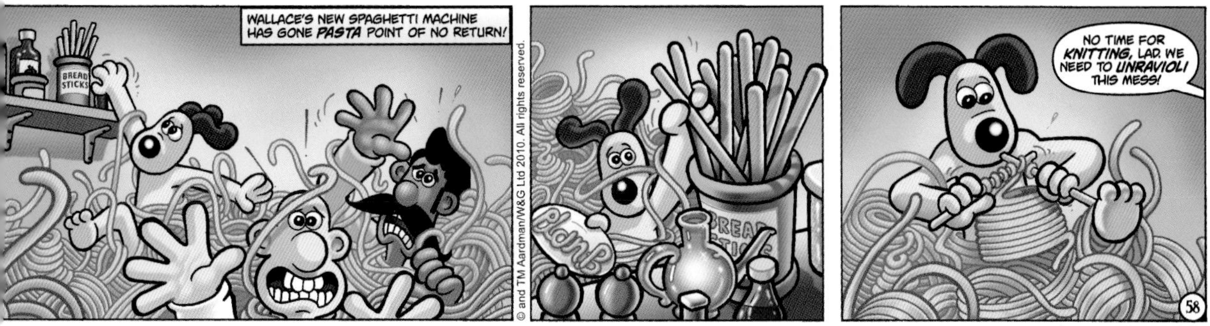

WALLACE'S NEW SPAGHETTI MACHINE HAS GONE PASTA POINT OF NO RETURN!
BREAD STICKS
NO TIME FOR KNITTING, LAD. WE NEED TO UNRAVIOLI THIS MESS!
58

Wallace & Gromit - The Spaghetti Incident by Aardman & Titan Comics

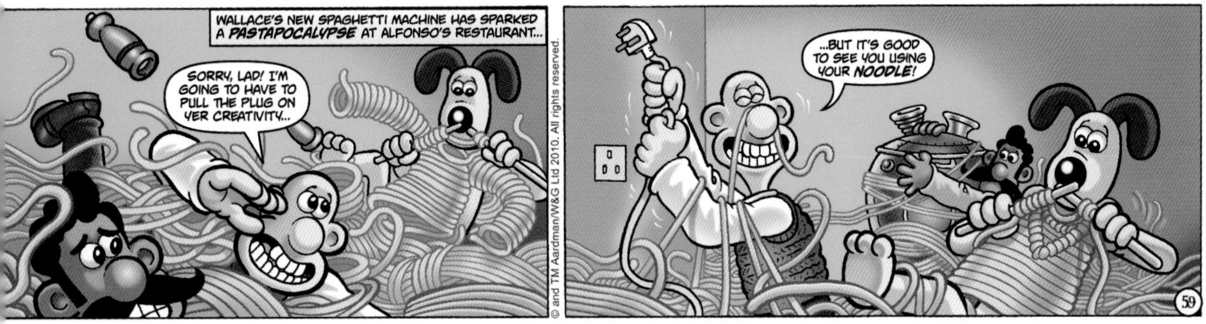

WALLACE'S NEW SPAGHETTI MACHINE HAS SPARKED A PASTAPOCALYPSE AT ALFONSO'S RESTAURANT...
SORRY, LAD! I'M GOING TO HAVE TO PULL THE PLUG ON YER CREATIVITY...
...BUT IT'S GOOD TO SEE YOU USING YOUR NOODLE!
59

Wallace & Gromit - The Spaghetti Incident by Aardman & Titan Comics

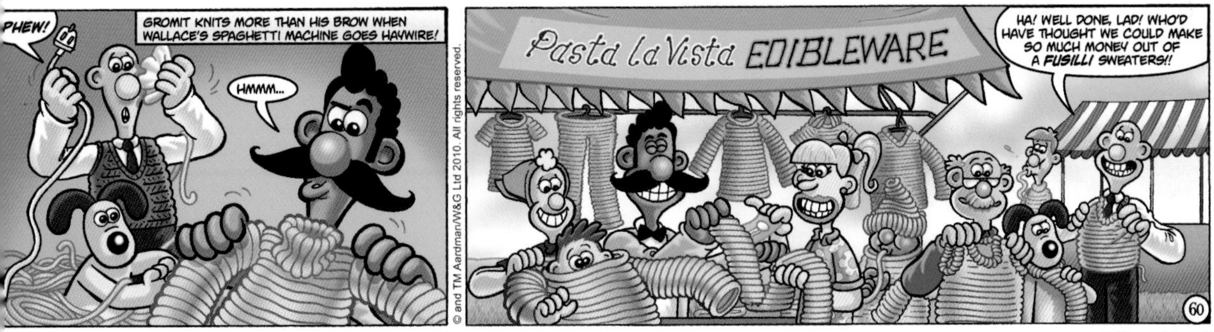

PHEW!
GROMIT KNITS MORE THAN HIS BROW WHEN WALLACE'S SPAGHETTI MACHINE GOES HAYWIRE!
HMMM...
Pasta la Vista EDIBLEWARE
HA! WELL DONE, LAD! WHO'D HAVE THOUGHT WE COULD MAKE SO MUCH MONEY OUT OF A FUSILLI SWEATERS!!
60

The End

Wallace & Gromit - Raiders of the Lost Bark by Aardman & Titan Comics

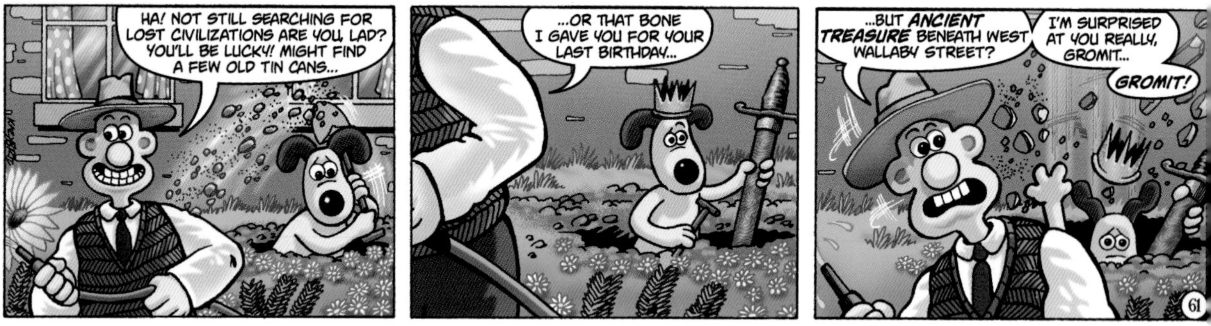
HA! NOT STILL SEARCHING FOR LOST CIVILIZATIONS ARE YOU, LAD? YOU'LL BE LUCKY! MIGHT FIND A FEW OLD TIN CANS...
...OR THAT BONE I GAVE YOU FOR YOUR LAST BIRTHDAY...
...BUT ANCIENT TREASURE BENEATH WEST WALLABY STREET?
I'M SURPRISED AT YOU REALLY, GROMIT...
GROMIT!
61

Wallace & Gromit - Raiders of the Lost Bark by Aardman & Titan Comics

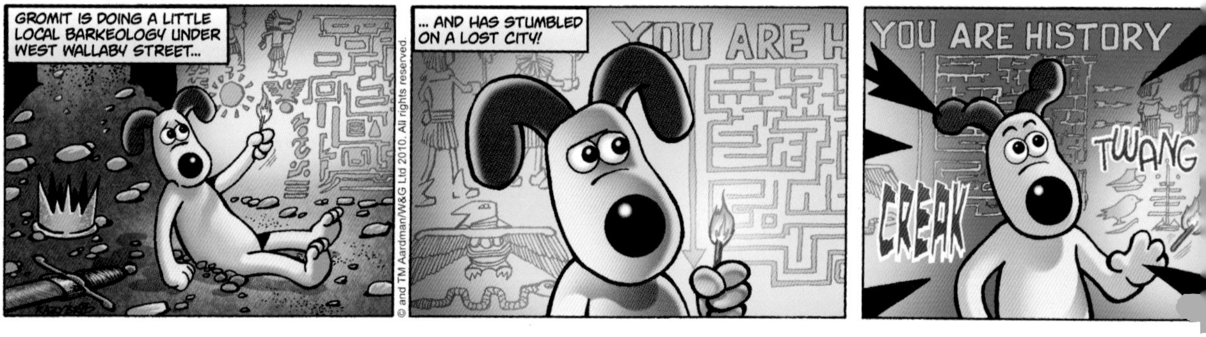
GROMIT IS DOING A LITTLE LOCAL BARKEOLOGY UNDER WEST WALLABY STREET...
... AND HAS STUMBLED ON A LOST CITY!
YOU ARE H
YOU ARE HISTORY
TWANG
CREAK

Wallace & Gromit - Raiders of the Lost Bark by Aardman & Titan Comics

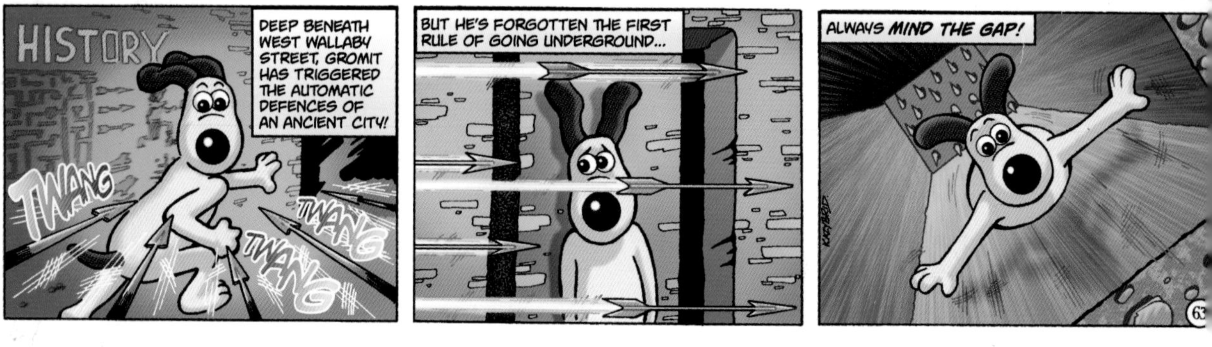
HISTORY
DEEP BENEATH WEST WALLABY STREET, GROMIT HAS TRIGGERED THE AUTOMATIC DEFENCES OF AN ANCIENT CITY!
TWANG
TWANG
TWANG
BUT HE'S FORGOTTEN THE FIRST RULE OF GOING UNDERGROUND...
ALWAYS MIND THE GAP!
63

Wallace & Gromit - Raiders of the Lost Bark by Aardman & Titan Comics

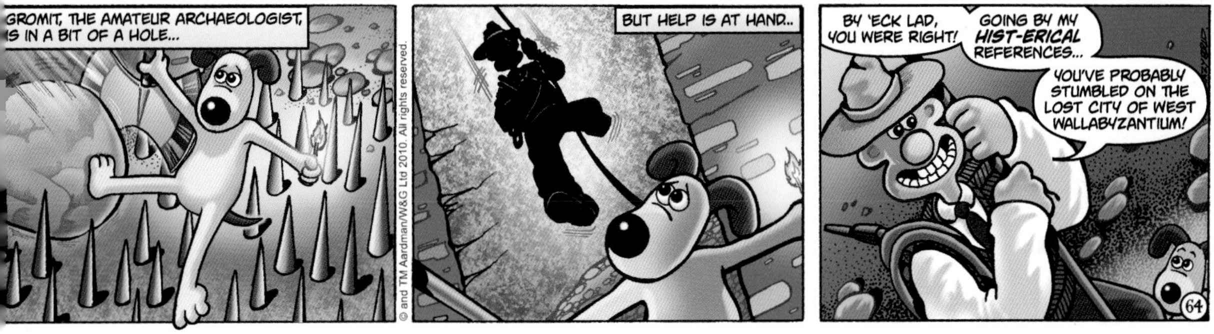
GROMIT, THE AMATEUR ARCHAEOLOGIST, IS IN A BIT OF A HOLE...
BUT HELP IS AT HAND...
BY 'ECK LAD, YOU WERE RIGHT!
GOING BY MY HIST-ERICAL REFERENCES...
YOU'VE PROBABLY STUMBLED ON THE LOST CITY OF WEST WALLABYZANTIUM!
64

Wallace & Gromit - Raiders of the Lost Bark by Aardman & Titan Comics

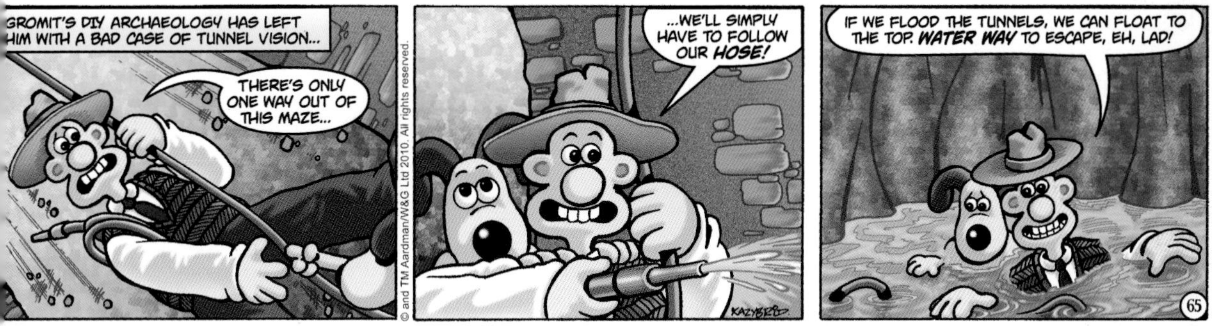
GROMIT'S DIY ARCHAEOLOGY HAS LEFT HIM WITH A BAD CASE OF TUNNEL VISION...
THERE'S ONLY ONE WAY OUT OF THIS MAZE...
...WE'LL SIMPLY HAVE TO FOLLOW OUR HOSE!
IF WE FLOOD THE TUNNELS, WE CAN FLOAT TO THE TOP. WATER WAY TO ESCAPE, EH, LAD!
65

Wallace & Gromit - Raiders of the Lost Bark by Aardman & Titan Comics

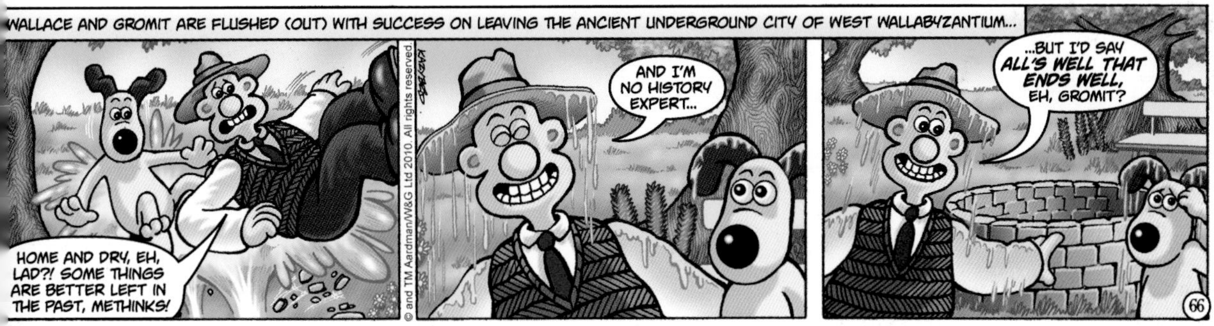
WALLACE AND GROMIT ARE FLUSHED (OUT) WITH SUCCESS ON LEAVING THE ANCIENT UNDERGROUND CITY OF WEST WALLABYZANTIUM...
HOME AND DRY, EH, LAD?! SOME THINGS ARE BETTER LEFT IN THE PAST, METHINKS!
AND I'M NO HISTORY EXPERT...
...BUT I'D SAY ALL'S WELL THAT ENDS WELL, EH, GROMIT?
66

The End

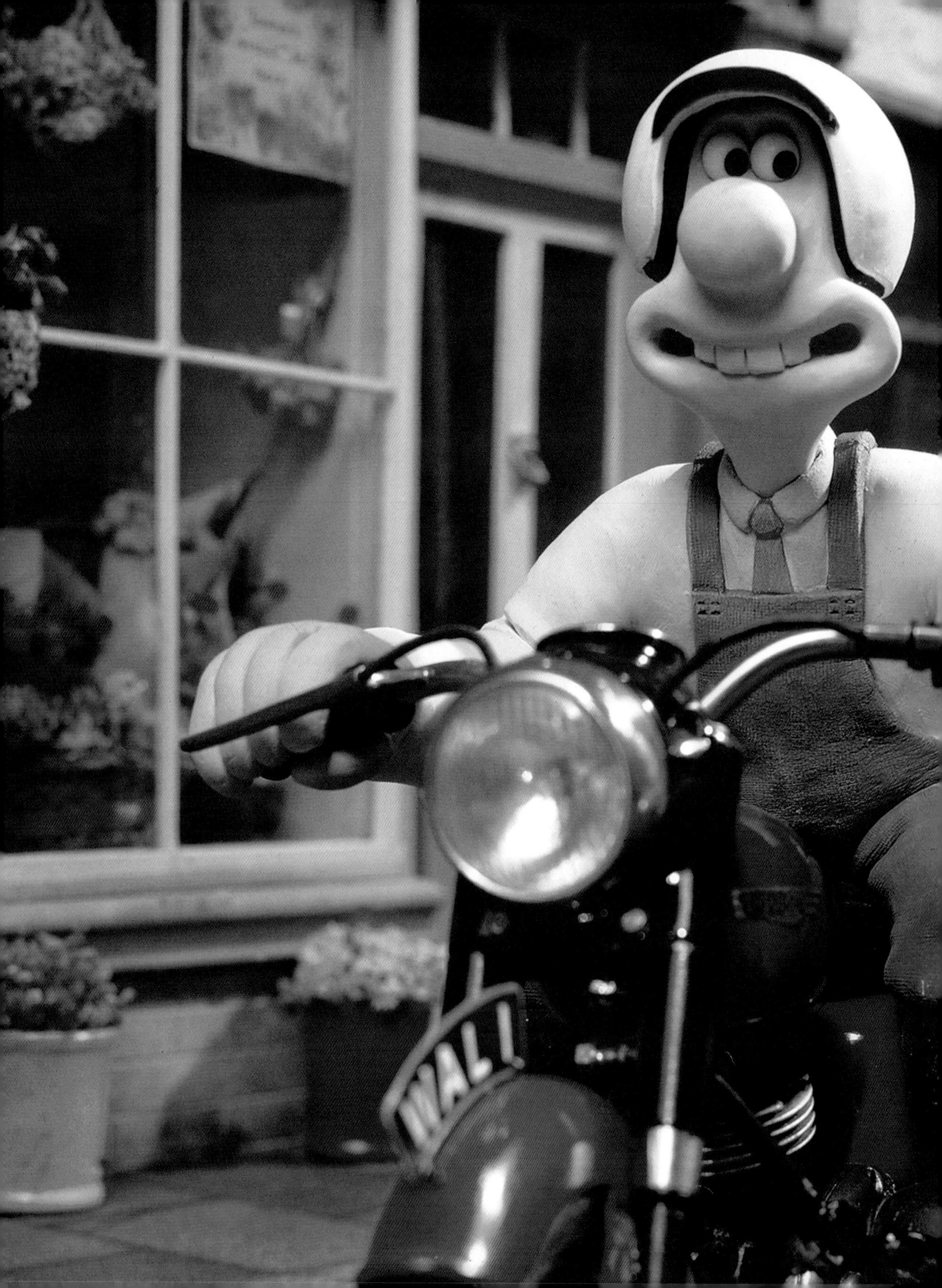
WAL 1

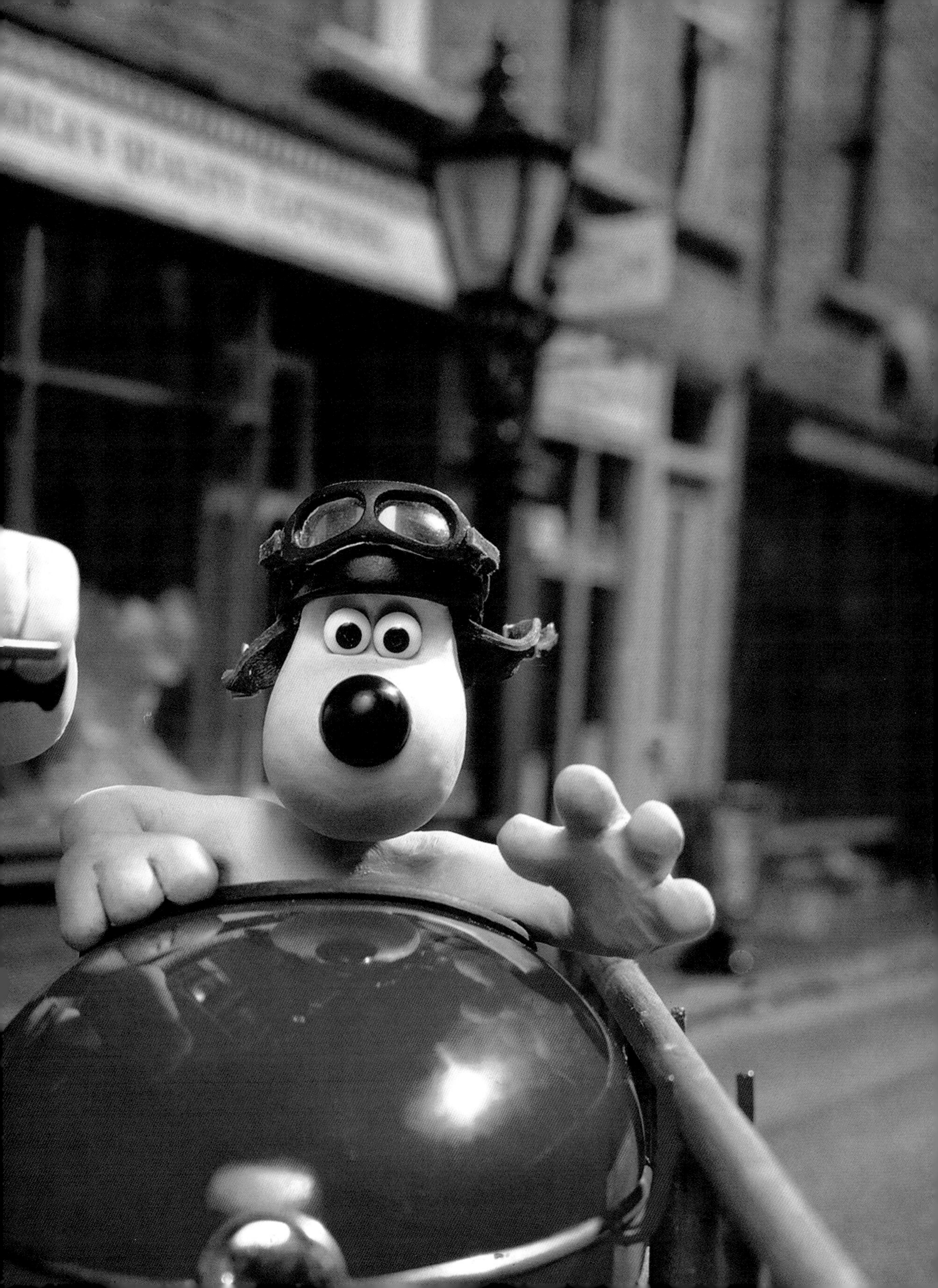

Wallace & Gromit - Gromit Time

by Aardman & Titan Comic

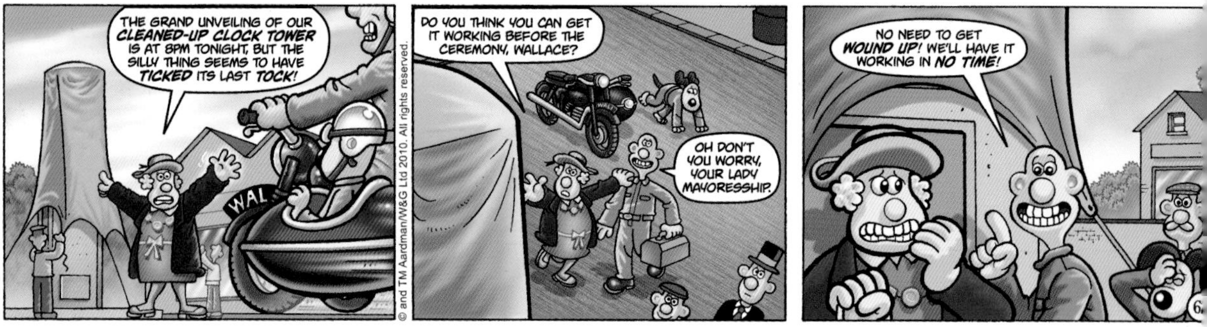

THE GRAND UNVEILING OF OUR CLEANED-UP CLOCK TOWER IS AT 8PM TONIGHT, BUT THE SILLY THING SEEMS TO HAVE TICKED ITS LAST TOCK!
WAL
© and TM Aardman/W&G Ltd 2010. All rights reserved.
DO YOU THINK YOU CAN GET IT WORKING BEFORE THE CEREMONY, WALLACE?
OH DON'T YOU WORRY, YOUR LADY MAYORESSHIP.
NO NEED TO GET WOUND UP! WE'LL HAVE IT WORKING IN NO TIME!

Wallace & Gromit - Gromit Time

by Aardman & Titan Comic

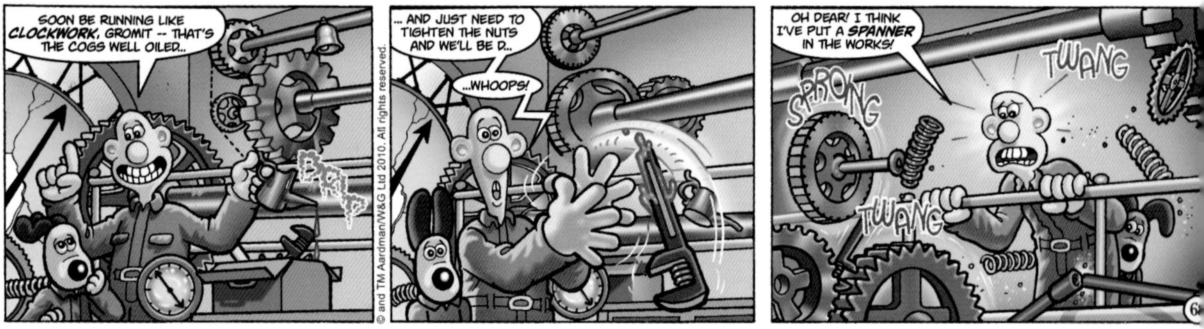

SOON BE RUNNING LIKE CLOCKWORK, GROMIT -- THAT'S THE COGS WELL OILED...
© and TM Aardman/W&G Ltd 2010. All rights reserved.
... AND JUST NEED TO TIGHTEN THE NUTS AND WE'LL BE D...
...WHOOPS!
OH DEAR! I THINK I'VE PUT A SPANNER IN THE WORKS!
SPROING
TWANG
TWANG

Wallace & Gromit - Gromit Time

by Aardman & Titan Comic

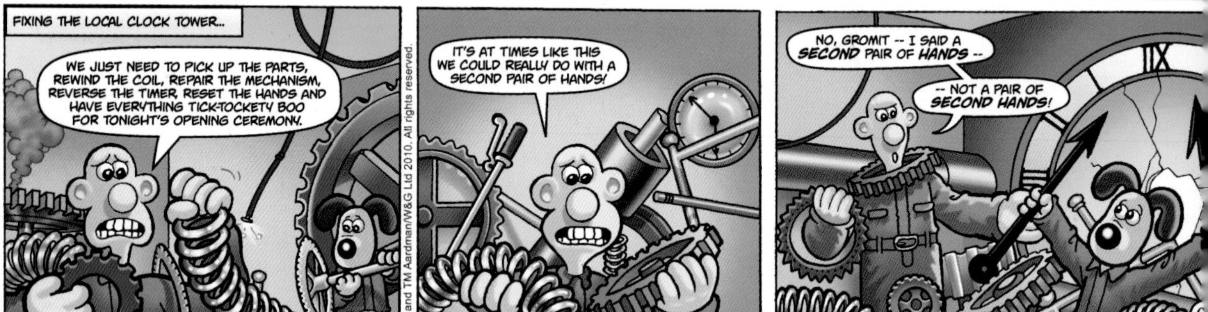

FIXING THE LOCAL CLOCK TOWER...
WE JUST NEED TO PICK UP THE PARTS, REWIND THE COIL, REPAIR THE MECHANISM, REVERSE THE TIMER, RESET THE HANDS AND HAVE EVERYTHING TICK-TOCKETY BOO FOR TONIGHT'S OPENING CEREMONY.
© and TM Aardman/W&G Ltd 2010. All rights reserved.
IT'S AT TIMES LIKE THIS WE COULD REALLY DO WITH A SECOND PAIR OF HANDS!
NO, GROMIT -- I SAID A SECOND PAIR OF HANDS --
-- NOT A PAIR OF SECOND HANDS!

Wallace & Gromit - Gromit Time by Aardman & Titan Comics

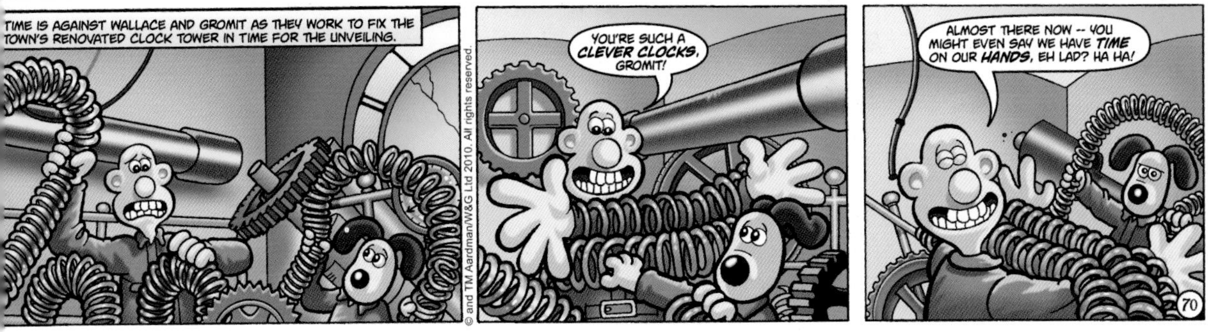

TIME IS AGAINST WALLACE AND GROMIT AS THEY WORK TO FIX THE TOWN'S RENOVATED CLOCK TOWER IN TIME FOR THE UNVEILING.
YOU'RE SUCH A CLEVER CLOCKS, GROMIT!
ALMOST THERE NOW -- YOU MIGHT EVEN SAY WE HAVE TIME ON OUR HANDS, EH LAD? HA HA!
70

Wallace & Gromit - Gromit Time by Aardman & Titan Comics

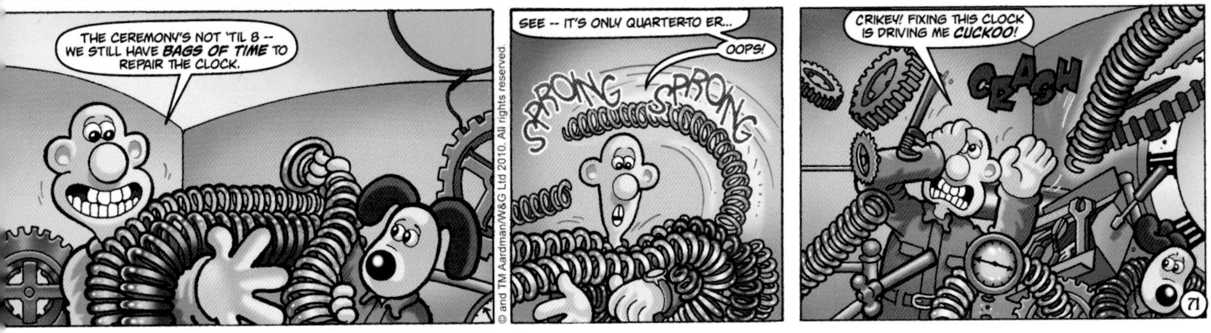

THE CEREMONY'S NOT 'TIL 8 -- WE STILL HAVE BAGS OF TIME TO REPAIR THE CLOCK.
SEE -- IT'S ONLY QUARTER-TO ER...
OOPS!
SPROING
SPROING
CRIKEY! FIXING THIS CLOCK IS DRIVING ME CUCKOO!
CRASH
71

Wallace & Gromit - Gromit Time by Aardman & Titan Comics

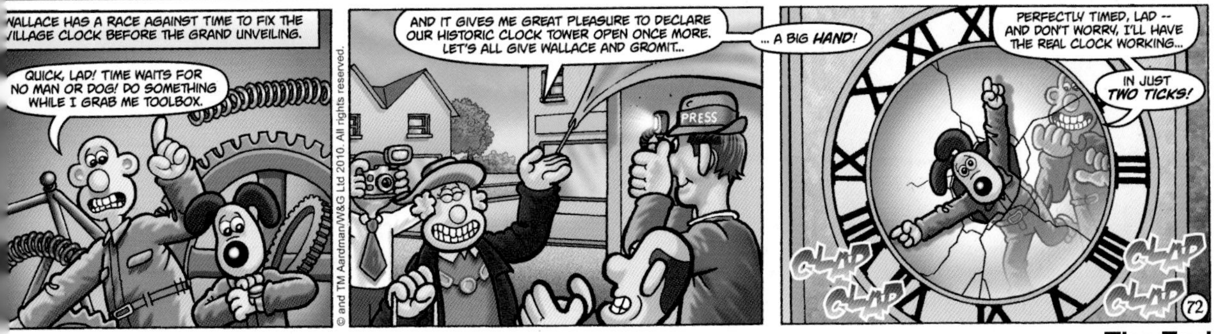

WALLACE HAS A RACE AGAINST TIME TO FIX THE VILLAGE CLOCK BEFORE THE GRAND UNVEILING.
QUICK, LAD! TIME WAITS FOR NO MAN OR DOG! DO SOMETHING WHILE I GRAB ME TOOLBOX.
AND IT GIVES ME GREAT PLEASURE TO DECLARE OUR HISTORIC CLOCK TOWER OPEN ONCE MORE. LET'S ALL GIVE WALLACE AND GROMIT...
... A BIG HAND!
PRESS
PERFECTLY TIMED, LAD -- AND DON'T WORRY, I'LL HAVE THE REAL CLOCK WORKING...
IN JUST TWO TICKS!
CLAP
CLAP
CLAP
CLAP
72

The End

Wallace & Gromit - Life's a Beach

by Aardman & Titan Comic

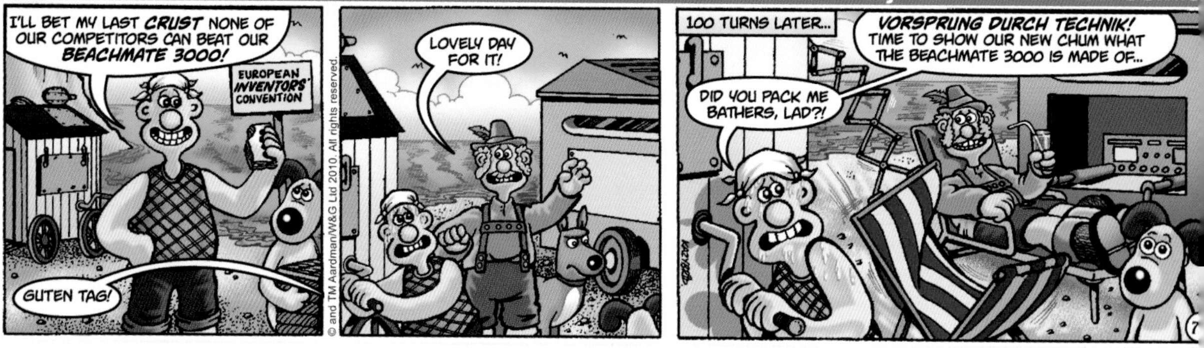
I'LL BET MY LAST CRUST NONE OF OUR COMPETITORS CAN BEAT OUR BEACHMATE 3000!
EUROPEAN INVENTORS' CONVENTION
GUTEN TAG!
© and TM Aardman/W&G Ltd 2010. All rights reserved.
LOVELY DAY FOR IT!
100 TURNS LATER...
VORSPRUNG DURCH TECHNIK! TIME TO SHOW OUR NEW CHUM WHAT THE BEACHMATE 3000 IS MADE OF...
DID YOU PACK ME BATHERS, LAD?!

Wallace & Gromit - Life's a Beach

by Aardman & Titan Comic

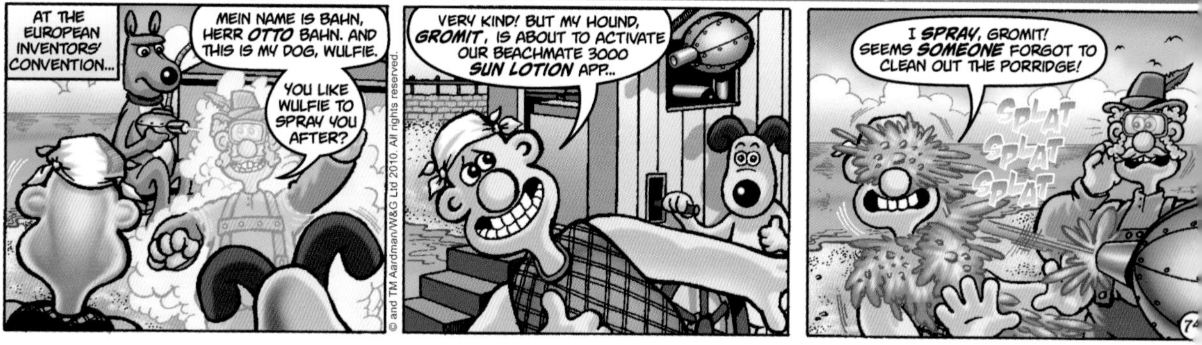
AT THE EUROPEAN INVENTORS' CONVENTION...
MEIN NAME IS BAHN, HERR OTTO BAHN. AND THIS IS MY DOG, WULFIE.
YOU LIKE WULFIE TO SPRAY YOU AFTER?
© and TM Aardman/W&G Ltd 2010. All rights reserved.
VERY KIND! BUT MY HOUND, GROMIT, IS ABOUT TO ACTIVATE OUR BEACHMATE 3000 SUN LOTION APP...
I SPRAY, GROMIT! SEEMS SOMEONE FORGOT TO CLEAN OUT THE PORRIDGE!
SPLAT
SPLAT
SPLAT

Wallace & Gromit - Life's a Beach

by Aardman & Titan Comic

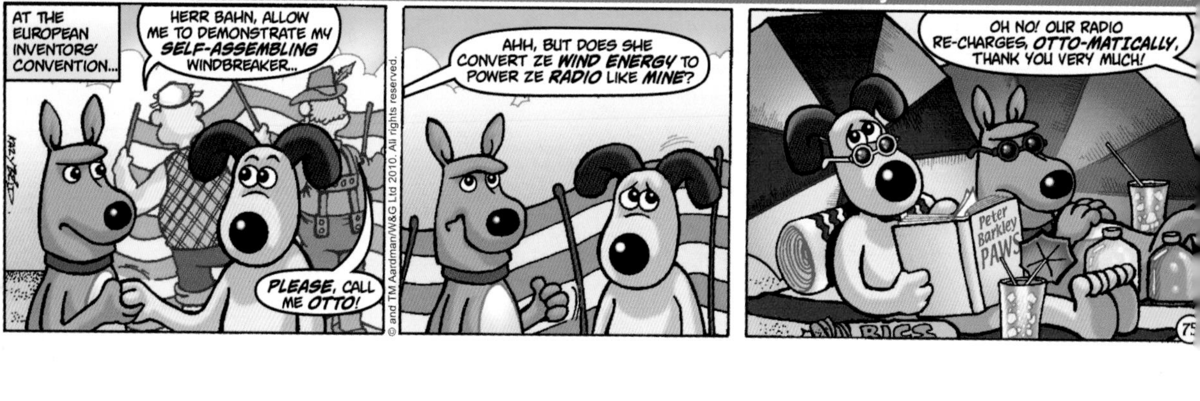
AT THE EUROPEAN INVENTORS' CONVENTION...
HERR BAHN, ALLOW ME TO DEMONSTRATE MY SELF-ASSEMBLING WINDBREAKER...
PLEASE, CALL ME OTTO!
© and TM Aardman/W&G Ltd 2010. All rights reserved.
AHH, BUT DOES SHE CONVERT ZE WIND ENERGY TO POWER ZE RADIO LIKE MINE?
OH NO! OUR RADIO RE-CHARGES, OTTO-MATICALLY, THANK YOU VERY MUCH!
Peter Barkley PAWS

Wallace & Gromit - Life's a Beach by Aardman & Titan Comics

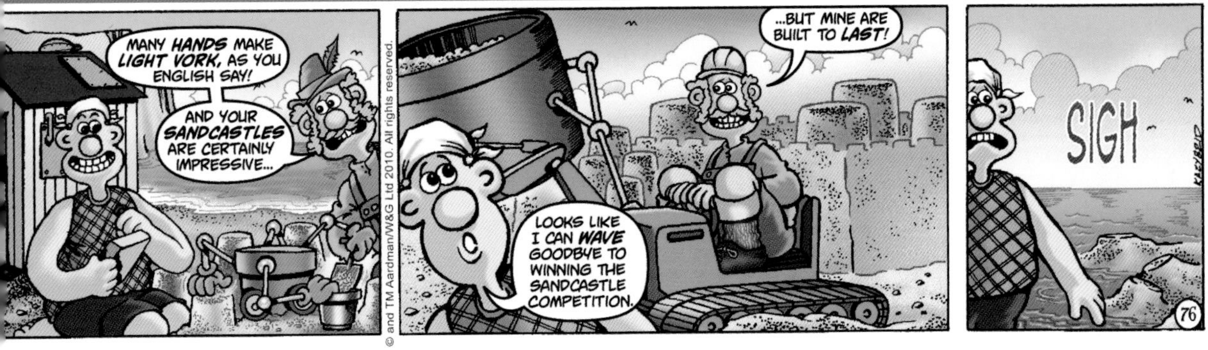

MANY HANDS MAKE LIGHT VORK, AS YOU ENGLISH SAY!
AND YOUR SANDCASTLES ARE CERTAINLY IMPRESSIVE...
© and TM Aardman/W&G Ltd 2010. All rights reserved.
...BUT MINE ARE BUILT TO LAST!
LOOKS LIKE I CAN WAVE GOODBYE TO WINNING THE SANDCASTLE COMPETITION.
SIGH
76

Wallace & Gromit - Life's a Beach by Aardman & Titan Comics

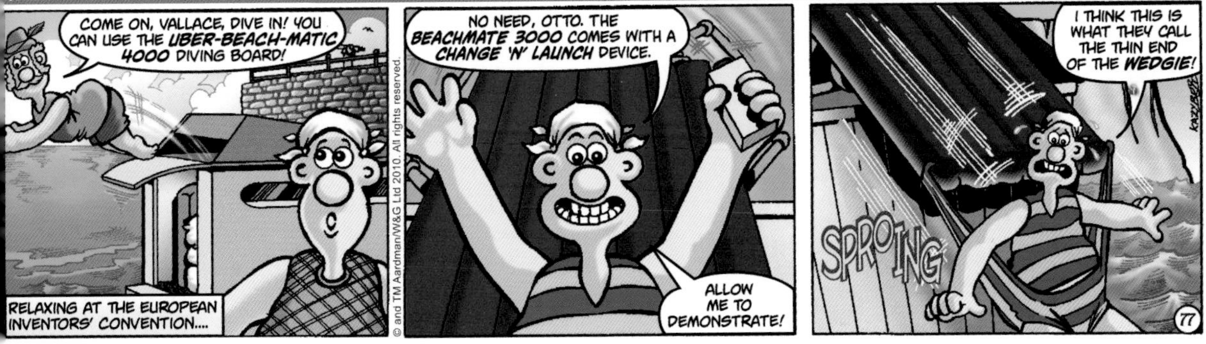

COME ON, VALLACE, DIVE IN! YOU CAN USE THE UBER-BEACH-MATIC 4000 DIVING BOARD!
RELAXING AT THE EUROPEAN INVENTORS' CONVENTION....
© and TM Aardman/W&G Ltd 2010. All rights reserved.
NO NEED, OTTO. THE BEACHMATE 3000 COMES WITH A CHANGE 'N' LAUNCH DEVICE.
ALLOW ME TO DEMONSTRATE!
I THINK THIS IS WHAT THEY CALL THE THIN END OF THE WEDGIE!
SPROING
77

Wallace & Gromit - Life's a Beach by Aardman & Titan Comics

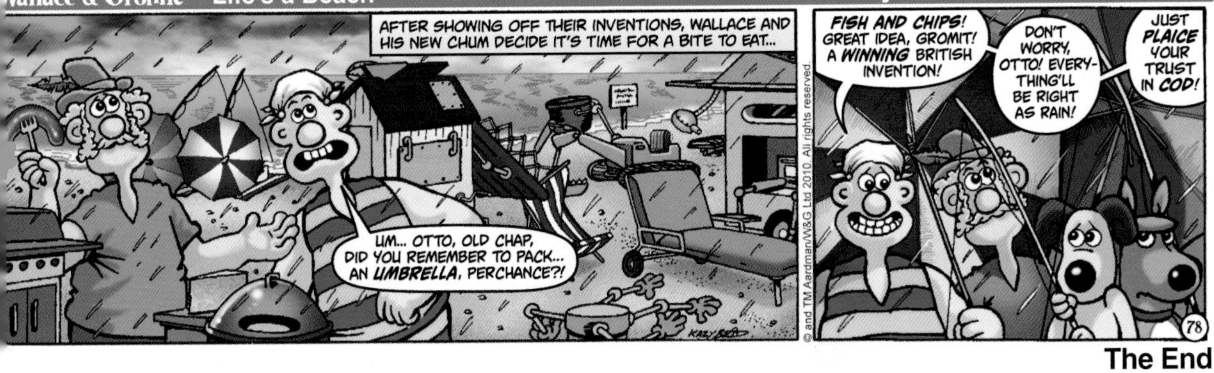

AFTER SHOWING OFF THEIR INVENTIONS, WALLACE AND HIS NEW CHUM DECIDE IT'S TIME FOR A BITE TO EAT...
UM... OTTO, OLD CHAP, DID YOU REMEMBER TO PACK... AN UMBRELLA, PERCHANCE?!
© and TM Aardman/W&G Ltd 2010. All rights reserved.
FISH AND CHIPS! GREAT IDEA, GROMIT! A WINNING BRITISH INVENTION!
DON'T WORRY, OTTO! EVERY-THING'LL BE RIGHT AS RAIN!
JUST PLAICE YOUR TRUST IN COD!
78

The End

Wallace & Gromit - Wallace's Sharp Idea

by Aardman & Titan Comic

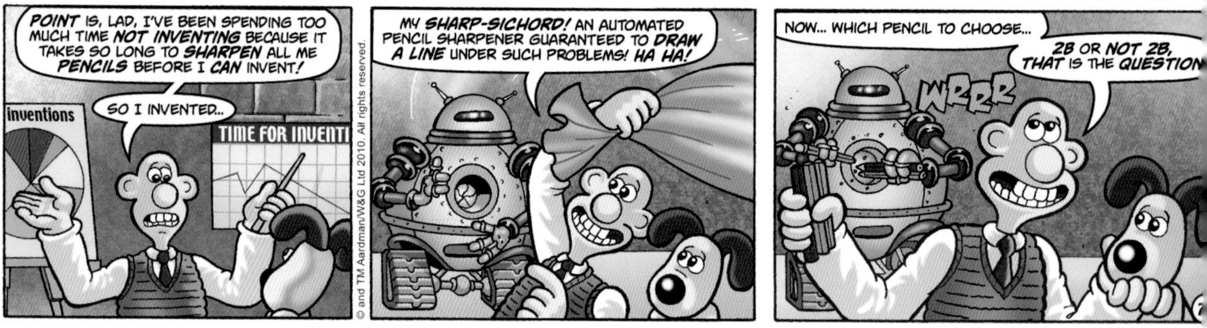

POINT IS, LAD, I'VE BEEN SPENDING TOO MUCH TIME NOT INVENTING BECAUSE IT TAKES SO LONG TO SHARPEN ALL ME PENCILS BEFORE I CAN INVENT!
SO I INVENTED...
inventions
TIME FOR INVENTI
© and TM Aardman/W&G Ltd 2010. All rights reserved.
MY SHARP-SICHORD! AN AUTOMATED PENCIL SHARPENER GUARANTEED TO DRAW A LINE UNDER SUCH PROBLEMS! HA HA!
NOW... WHICH PENCIL TO CHOOSE...
WRRR
2B OR NOT 2B, THAT IS THE QUESTION

Wallace & Gromit - Wallace's Sharp Idea

by Aardman & Titan Comic

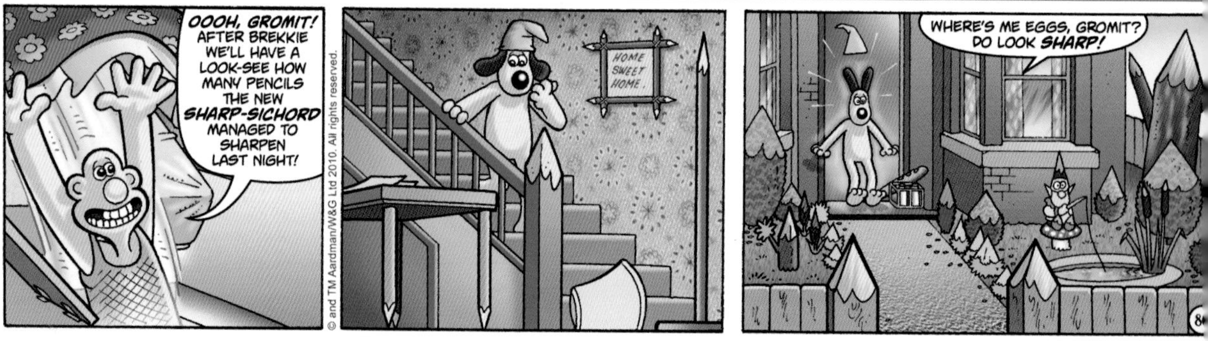

OOOH, GROMIT! AFTER BREKKIE WE'LL HAVE A LOOK-SEE HOW MANY PENCILS THE NEW SHARP-SICHORD MANAGED TO SHARPEN LAST NIGHT!
© and TM Aardman/W&G Ltd 2010. All rights reserved.
HOME SWEET HOME
WHERE'S ME EGGS, GROMIT? DO LOOK SHARP!

Wallace & Gromit - Wallace's Sharp Idea

by Aardman & Titan Comic

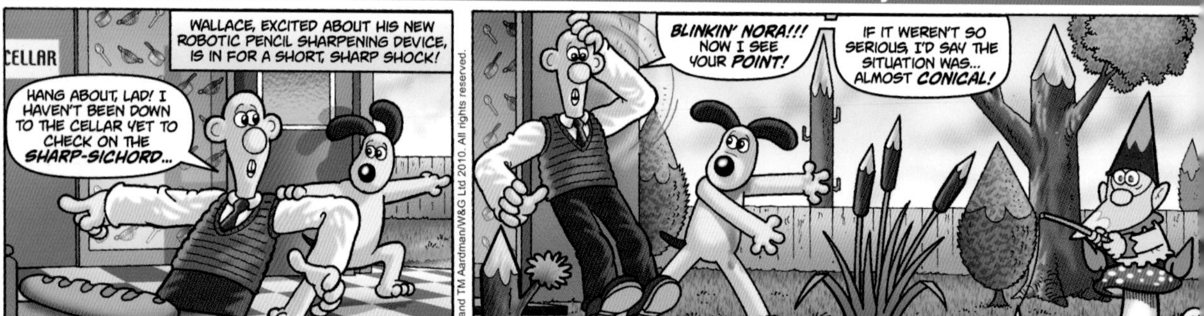

WALLACE, EXCITED ABOUT HIS NEW ROBOTIC PENCIL SHARPENING DEVICE, IS IN FOR A SHORT, SHARP SHOCK!
CELLAR
HANG ABOUT, LAD! I HAVEN'T BEEN DOWN TO THE CELLAR YET TO CHECK ON THE SHARP-SICHORD...
© and TM Aardman/W&G Ltd 2010. All rights reserved.
BLINKIN' NORA!!! NOW I SEE YOUR POINT!
IF IT WEREN'T SO SERIOUS, I'D SAY THE SITUATION WAS... ALMOST CONICAL!

Wallace & Gromit - Wallace's Sharp Idea by Aardman & Titan Comics

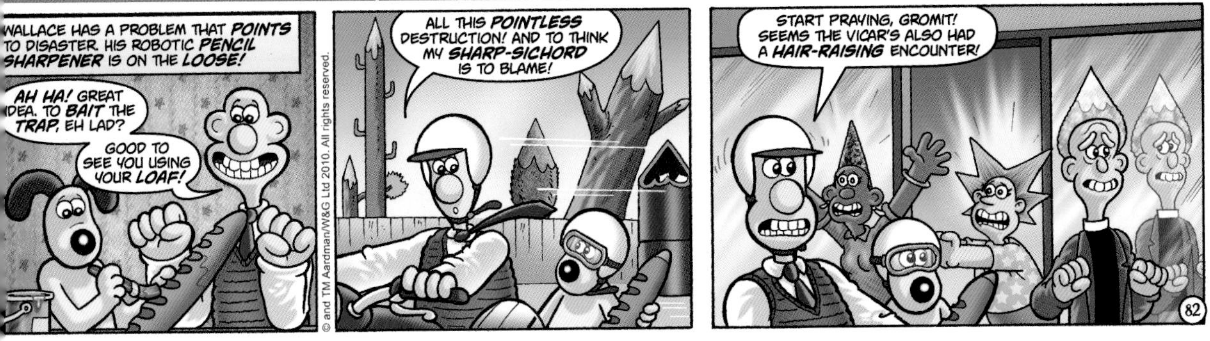
WALLACE HAS A PROBLEM THAT POINTS TO DISASTER. HIS ROBOTIC PENCIL SHARPENER IS ON THE LOOSE!
AH HA! GREAT IDEA. TO BAIT THE TRAP, EH LAD?
GOOD TO SEE YOU USING YOUR LOAF!
© and TM Aardman/W&G Ltd 2010. All rights reserved.
ALL THIS POINTLESS DESTRUCTION! AND TO THINK MY SHARP-SICHORD IS TO BLAME!
START PRAYING, GROMIT! SEEMS THE VICAR'S ALSO HAD A HAIR-RAISING ENCOUNTER!
82

Wallace & Gromit - Wallace's Sharp Idea by Aardman & Titan Comics

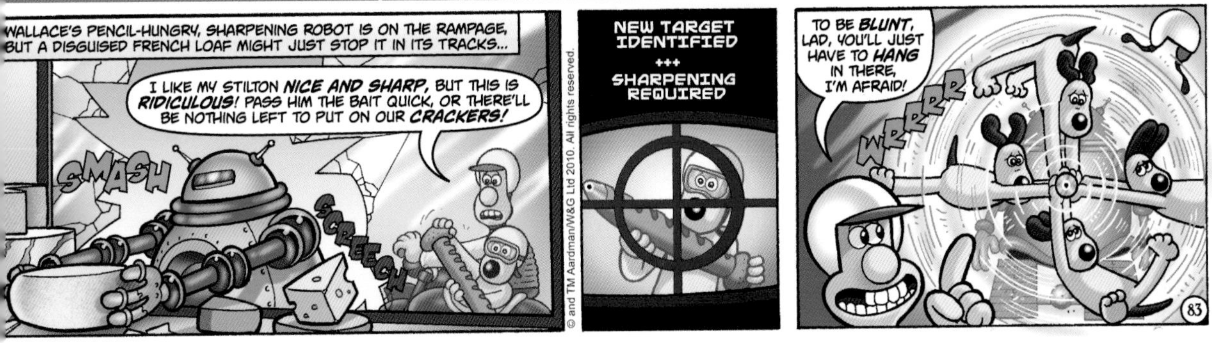
WALLACE'S PENCIL-HUNGRY, SHARPENING ROBOT IS ON THE RAMPAGE, BUT A DISGUISED FRENCH LOAF MIGHT JUST STOP IT IN ITS TRACKS...
I LIKE MY STILTON NICE AND SHARP, BUT THIS IS RIDICULOUS! PASS HIM THE BAIT QUICK, OR THERE'LL BE NOTHING LEFT TO PUT ON OUR CRACKERS!
SMASH
SCREEECH
© and TM Aardman/W&G Ltd 2010. All rights reserved.
NEW TARGET IDENTIFIED
+++
SHARPENING REQUIRED
TO BE BLUNT, LAD, YOU'LL JUST HAVE TO HANG IN THERE, I'M AFRAID!
WRRRRR
83

Wallace & Gromit - Wallace's Sharp Idea by Aardman & Titan Comics

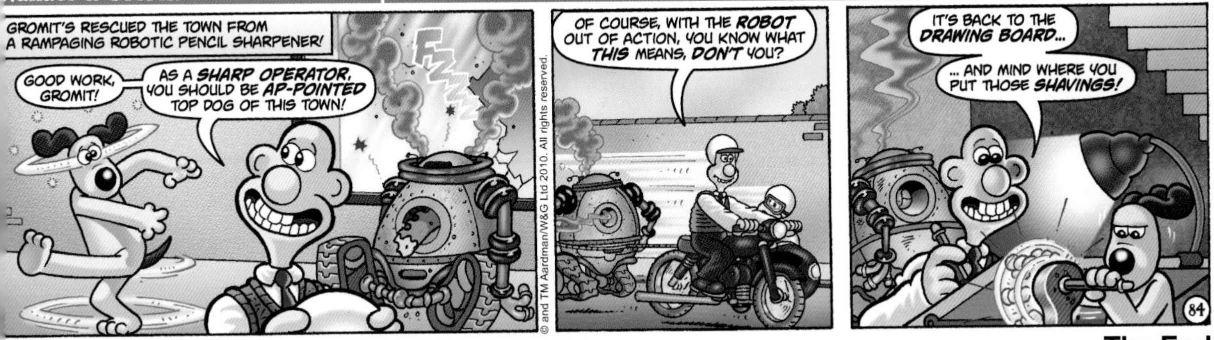
GROMIT'S RESCUED THE TOWN FROM A RAMPAGING ROBOTIC PENCIL SHARPENER!
GOOD WORK, GROMIT!
AS A SHARP OPERATOR, YOU SHOULD BE AP-POINTED TOP DOG OF THIS TOWN!
FZZZ
© and TM Aardman/W&G Ltd 2010. All rights reserved.
OF COURSE, WITH THE ROBOT OUT OF ACTION, YOU KNOW WHAT THIS MEANS, DON'T YOU?
IT'S BACK TO THE DRAWING BOARD...
... AND MIND WHERE YOU PUT THOSE SHAVINGS!
84

The End

Wallace & Gromit - A Safe Pair of Hands

by Aardman & Titan Comic

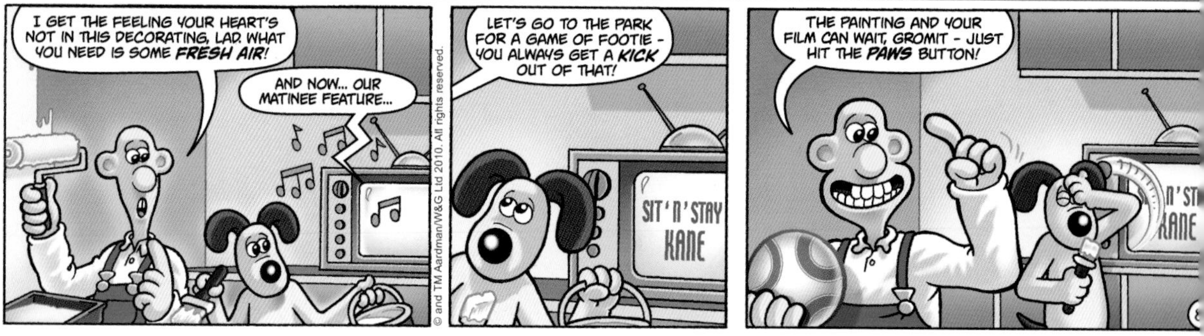

I GET THE FEELING YOUR HEART'S NOT IN THIS DECORATING, LAD. WHAT YOU NEED IS SOME **FRESH AIR**!
AND NOW... OUR MATINEE FEATURE...
LET'S GO TO THE PARK FOR A GAME OF FOOTIE - YOU ALWAYS GET A **KICK** OUT OF THAT!
SIT 'N' STAY KANE
THE PAINTING AND YOUR FILM CAN WAIT, GROMIT - JUST HIT THE **PAWS** BUTTON!

Wallace & Gromit - A Safe Pair of Hands

by Aardman & Titan Comic

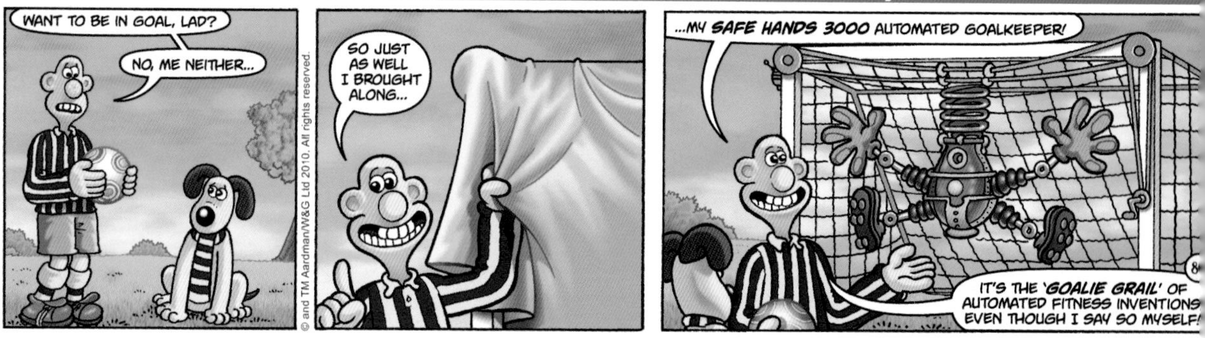

WANT TO BE IN GOAL, LAD?
NO, ME NEITHER...
SO JUST AS WELL I BROUGHT ALONG...
...MY **SAFE HANDS 3000** AUTOMATED GOALKEEPER!
IT'S THE '**GOALIE GRAIL**' OF AUTOMATED FITNESS INVENTIONS EVEN THOUGH I SAY SO MYSELF!

Wallace & Gromit - A Safe Pair of Hands

by Aardman & Titan Comic

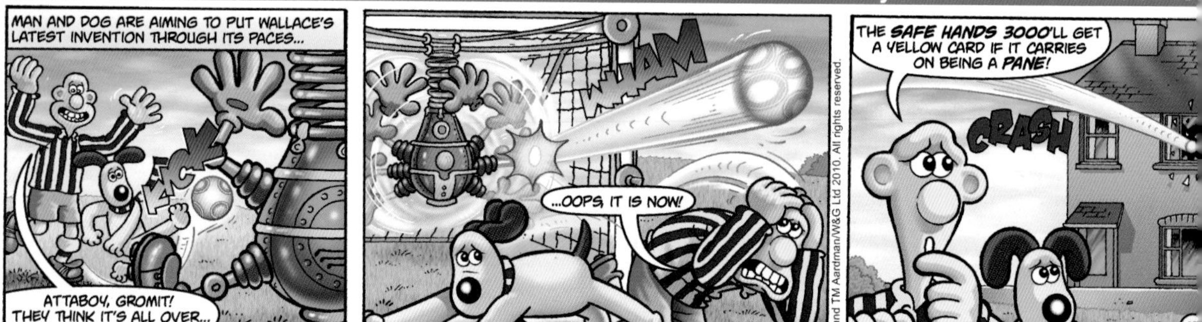

MAN AND DOG ARE AIMING TO PUT WALLACE'S LATEST INVENTION THROUGH ITS PACES...
KICK
ATTABOY, GROMIT! THEY THINK IT'S ALL OVER...
WHAM
...OOPS, IT IS NOW!
THE **SAFE HANDS 3000**'LL GET A YELLOW CARD IF IT CARRIES ON BEING A **PANE**!
CRASH

Wallace & Gromit - A Safe Pair of Hands by Aardman & Titan Comics

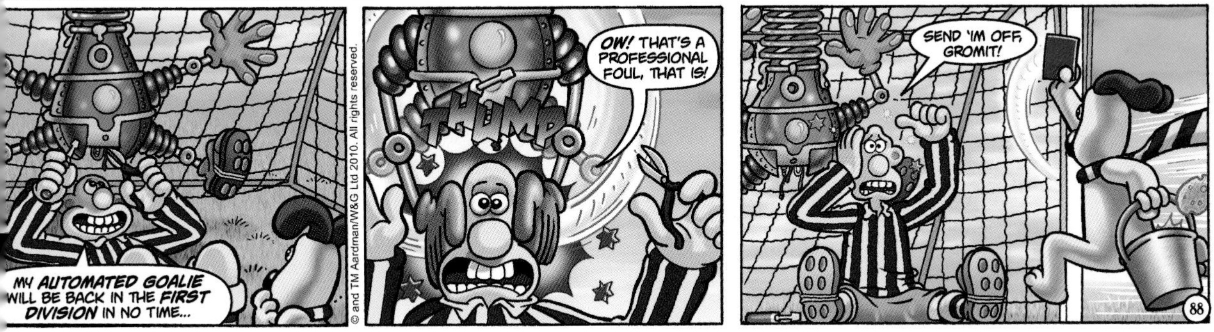
MY AUTOMATED GOALIE WILL BE BACK IN THE FIRST DIVISION IN NO TIME...
THUMP
OW! THAT'S A PROFESSIONAL FOUL, THAT IS!
SEND 'IM OFF, GROMIT!
88

Wallace & Gromit - A Safe Pair of Hands by Aardman & Titan Comics

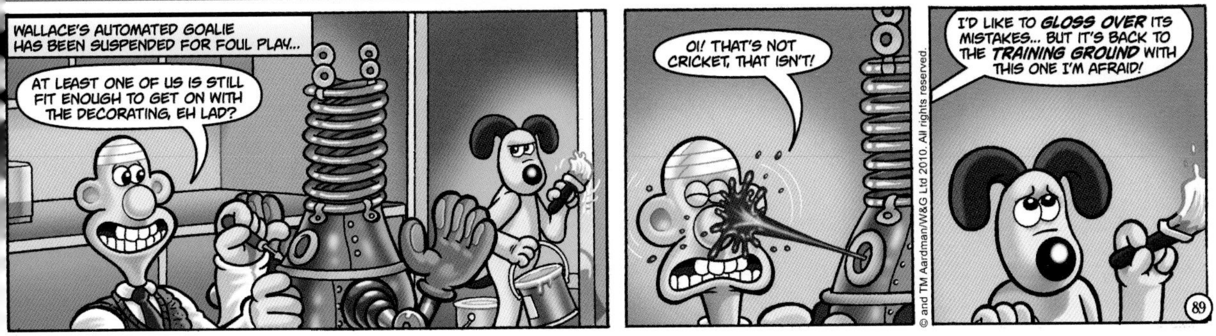
WALLACE'S AUTOMATED GOALIE HAS BEEN SUSPENDED FOR FOUL PLAY...
AT LEAST ONE OF US IS STILL FIT ENOUGH TO GET ON WITH THE DECORATING, EH LAD?
OI! THAT'S NOT CRICKET, THAT ISN'T!
I'D LIKE TO GLOSS OVER ITS MISTAKES... BUT IT'S BACK TO THE TRAINING GROUND WITH THIS ONE I'M AFRAID!
89

Wallace & Gromit - A Safe Pair of Hands by Aardman & Titan Comics

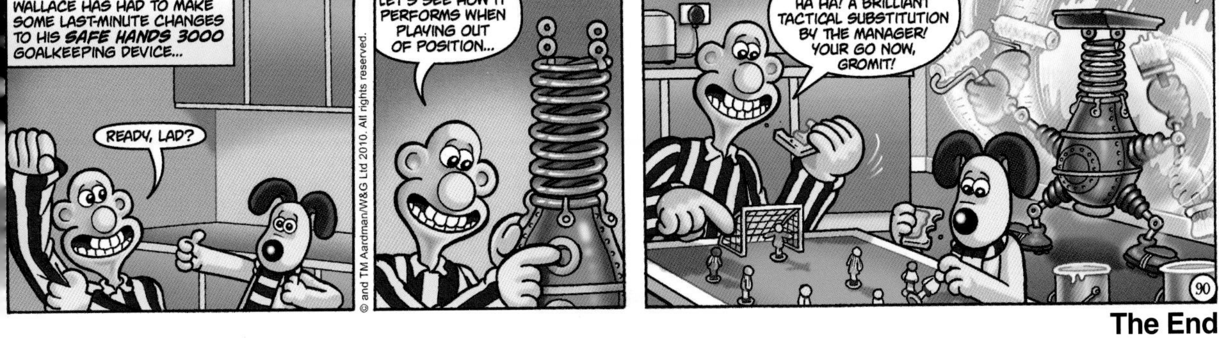
WALLACE HAS HAD TO MAKE SOME LAST-MINUTE CHANGES TO HIS SAFE HANDS 3000 GOALKEEPING DEVICE...
READY, LAD?
LET'S SEE HOW IT PERFORMS WHEN PLAYING OUT OF POSITION...
HA HA! A BRILLIANT TACTICAL SUBSTITUTION BY THE MANAGER! YOUR GO NOW, GROMIT!
90

The End

Wallace & Gromit - The Edam Busters

by Aardman & Titan Comics

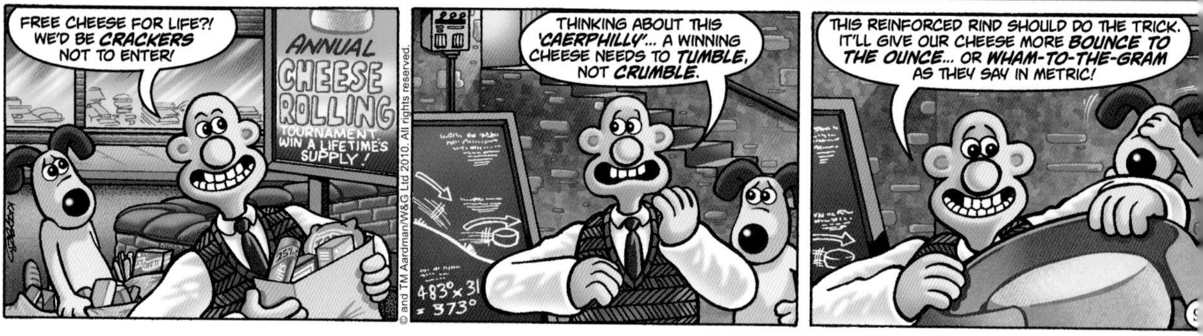
FREE CHEESE FOR LIFE?! WE'D BE *CRACKERS* NOT TO ENTER!
ANNUAL CHEESE ROLLING TOURNAMENT. WIN A LIFETIME'S SUPPLY!
© and TM Aardman/W&G Ltd 2010. All rights reserved.
THINKING ABOUT THIS *'CAERPHILLY'*... A WINNING CHEESE NEEDS TO *TUMBLE*, NOT *CRUMBLE*.
483° x 31 = 373°
THIS REINFORCED RIND SHOULD DO THE TRICK. IT'LL GIVE OUR CHEESE MORE *BOUNCE TO THE OUNCE*... OR *WHAM-TO-THE-GRAM* AS THEY SAY IN METRIC!

Wallace & Gromit - The Edam Busters

by Aardman & Titan Comics

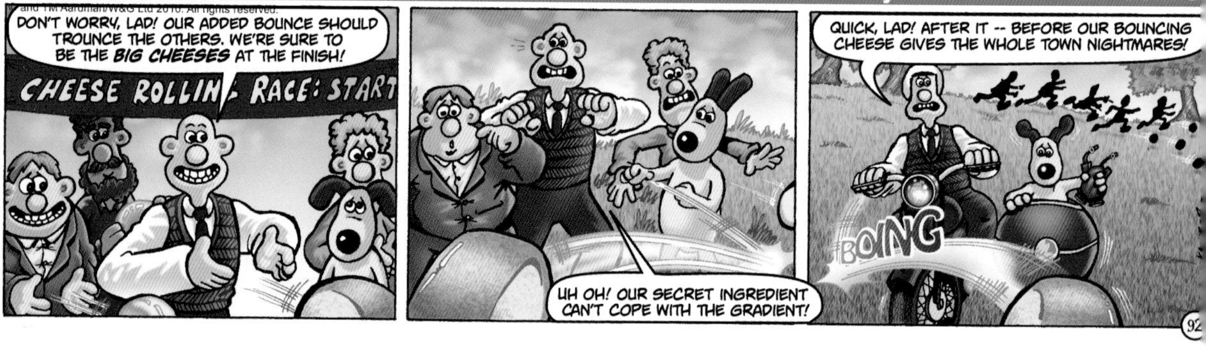
DON'T WORRY, LAD! OUR ADDED BOUNCE SHOULD TROUNCE THE OTHERS. WE'RE SURE TO BE THE *BIG CHEESES* AT THE FINISH!
CHEESE ROLLIN RACE: START
UH OH! OUR SECRET INGREDIENT CAN'T COPE WITH THE GRADIENT!
QUICK, LAD! AFTER IT -- BEFORE OUR BOUNCING CHEESE GIVES THE WHOLE TOWN NIGHTMARES!
BOING

Wallace & Gromit - The Edam Busters

by Aardman & Titan Comics

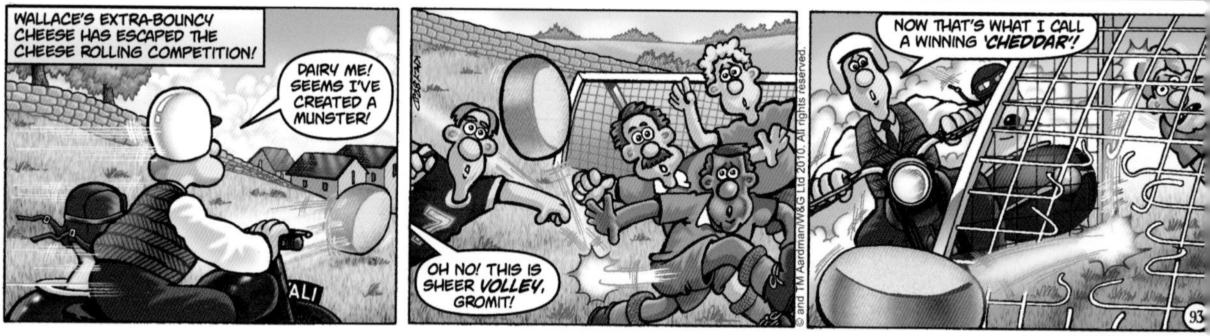
WALLACE'S EXTRA-BOUNCY CHEESE HAS ESCAPED THE CHEESE ROLLING COMPETITION!
DAIRY ME! SEEMS I'VE CREATED A MUNSTER!
OH NO! THIS IS SHEER *VOLLEY*, GROMIT!
© and TM Aardman/W&G Ltd 2010. All rights reserved.
NOW THAT'S WHAT I CALL A WINNING *'CHEDDAR'!*

Wallace & Gromit - The Edam Busters by Aardman & Titan Comics

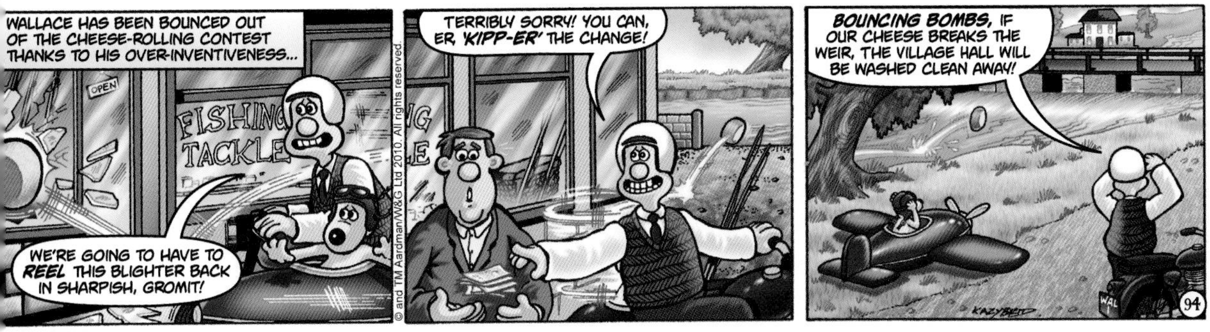
WALLACE HAS BEEN BOUNCED OUT OF THE CHEESE-ROLLING CONTEST THANKS TO HIS OVER-INVENTIVENESS...
OPEN
FISHING TACKLE
WE'RE GOING TO HAVE TO REEL THIS BLIGHTER BACK IN SHARPISH, GROMIT!
© and TM Aardman/W&G Ltd 2010. All rights reserved.
TERRIBLY SORRY! YOU CAN, ER, 'KIPP-ER' THE CHANGE!
BOUNCING BOMBS, IF OUR CHEESE BREAKS THE WEIR, THE VILLAGE HALL WILL BE WASHED CLEAN AWAY!
94

Wallace & Gromit - The Edam Busters by Aardman & Titan Comics

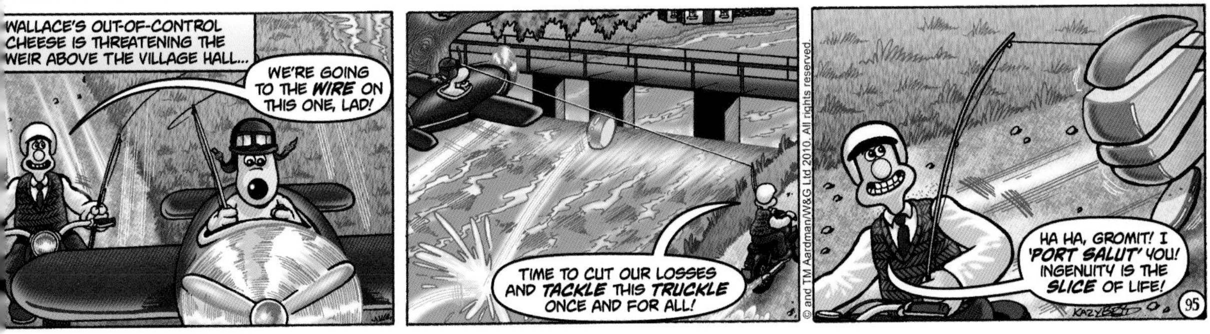
WALLACE'S OUT-OF-CONTROL CHEESE IS THREATENING THE WEIR ABOVE THE VILLAGE HALL...
WE'RE GOING TO THE WIRE ON THIS ONE, LAD!
TIME TO CUT OUR LOSSES AND TACKLE THIS TRUCKLE ONCE AND FOR ALL!
© and TM Aardman/W&G Ltd 2010. All rights reserved.
HA HA, GROMIT! I 'PORT SALUT' YOU! INGENUITY IS THE SLICE OF LIFE!
95

Wallace & Gromit - The Edam Busters by Aardman & Titan Comics

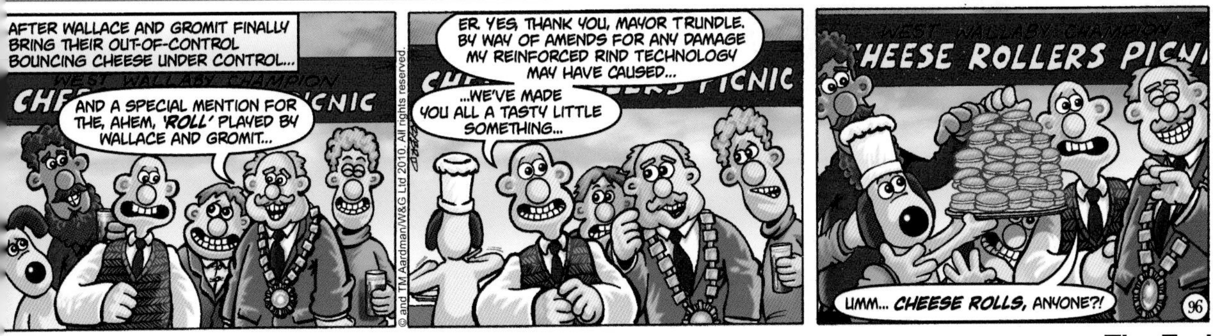
AFTER WALLACE AND GROMIT FINALLY BRING THEIR OUT-OF-CONTROL BOUNCING CHEESE UNDER CONTROL...
AND A SPECIAL MENTION FOR THE, AHEM, 'ROLL' PLAYED BY WALLACE AND GROMIT...
© and TM Aardman/W&G Ltd 2010. All rights reserved.
ER, YES, THANK YOU, MAYOR TRUNDLE. BY WAY OF AMENDS FOR ANY DAMAGE MY REINFORCED RIND TECHNOLOGY MAY HAVE CAUSED...
...WE'VE MADE YOU ALL A TASTY LITTLE SOMETHING...
WEST WALLABY CHAMPION CHEESE ROLLERS PICNI
UMM... CHEESE ROLLS, ANYONE?!
96

The End

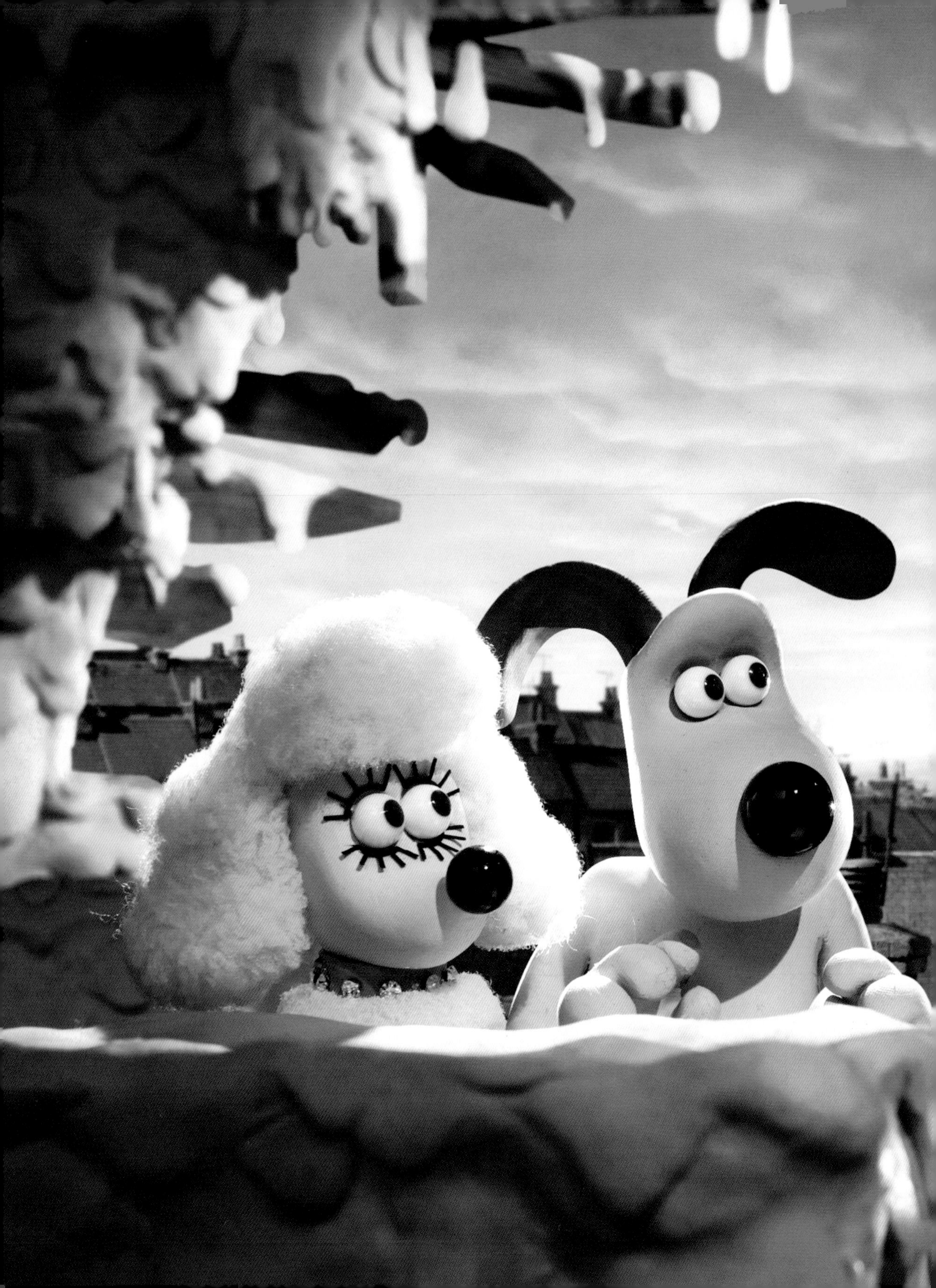

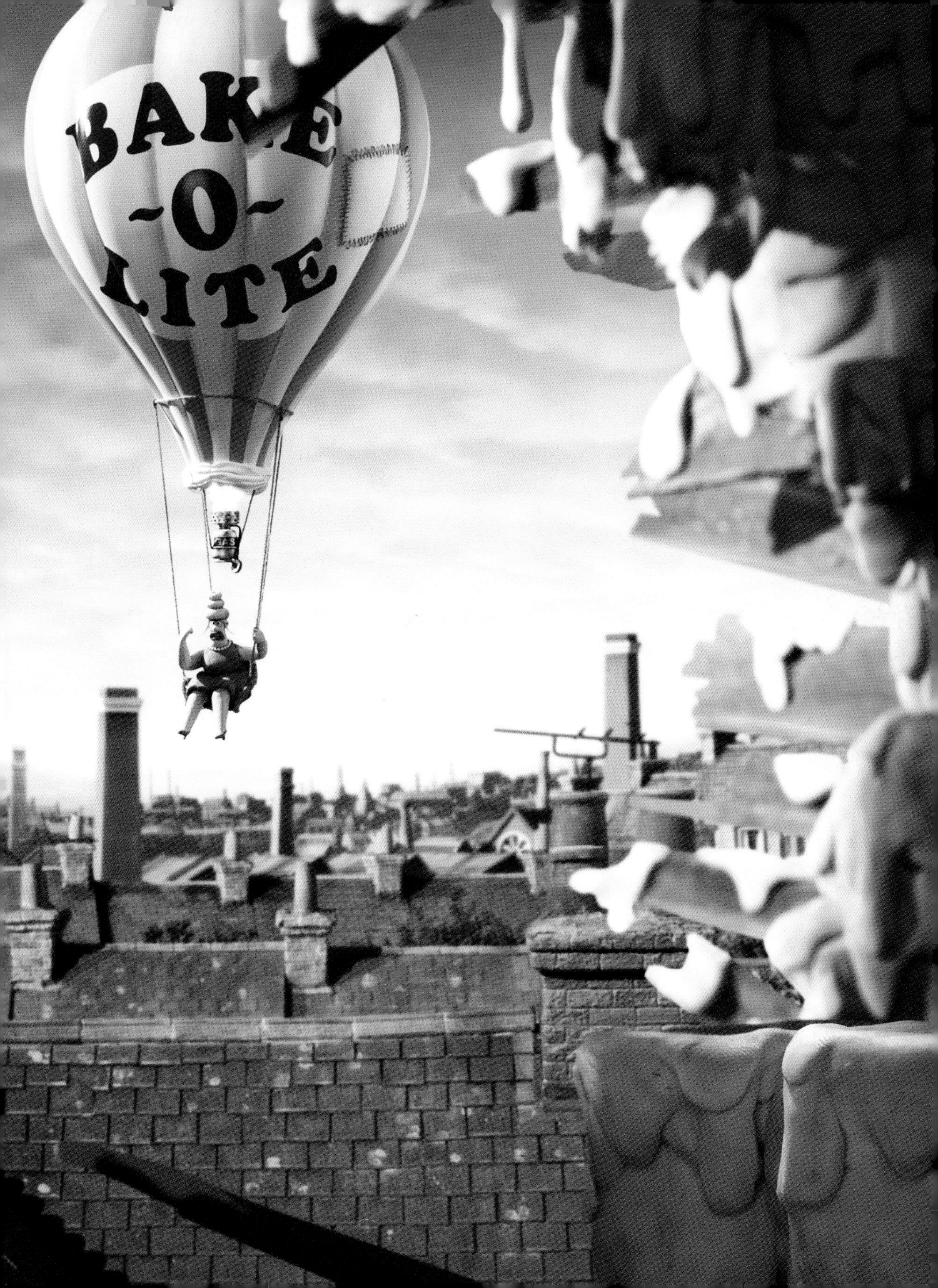
BAKE
-O-
LITE

Wallace & Gromit - Funnies #1
by Aardman & Titan Comics

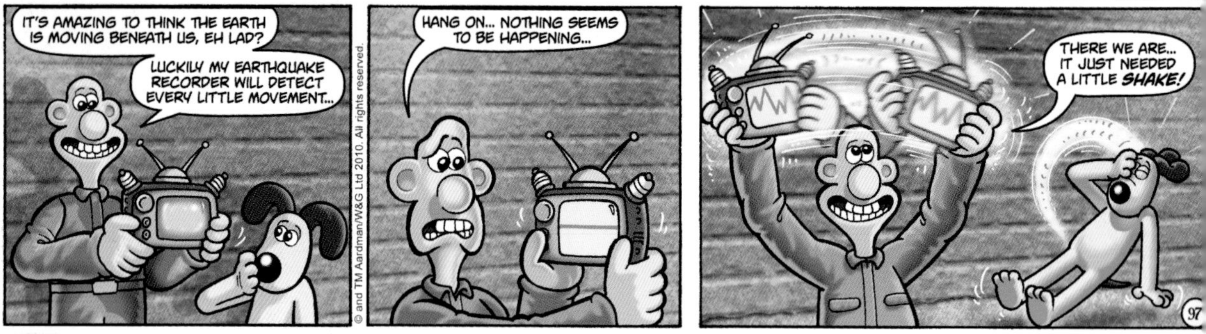
IT'S AMAZING TO THINK THE EARTH IS MOVING BENEATH US, EH LAD?
LUCKILY MY EARTHQUAKE RECORDER WILL DETECT EVERY LITTLE MOVEMENT...
HANG ON... NOTHING SEEMS TO BE HAPPENING...
THERE WE ARE... IT JUST NEEDED A LITTLE **SHAKE!**

Wallace & Gromit - Funnies #1
by Aardman & Titan Comics

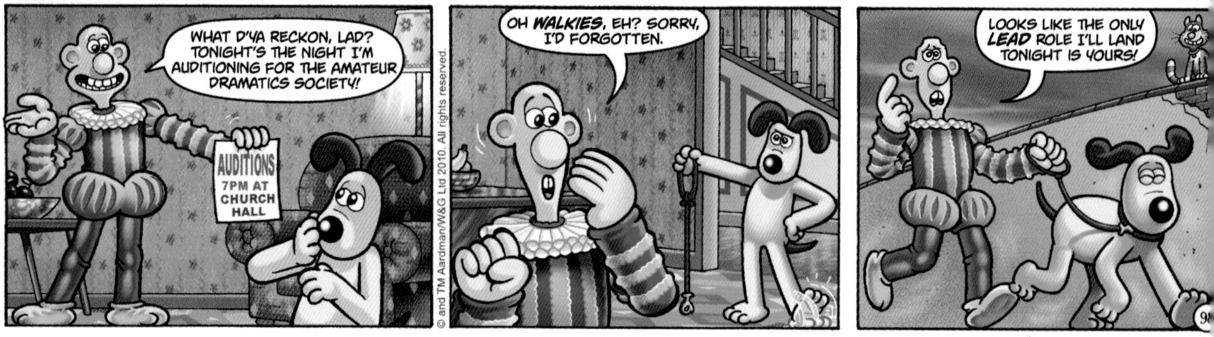
WHAT D'YA RECKON, LAD? TONIGHT'S THE NIGHT I'M AUDITIONING FOR THE AMATEUR DRAMATICS SOCIETY!
AUDITIONS 7PM AT CHURCH HALL
OH **WALKIES**, EH? SORRY, I'D FORGOTTEN.
LOOKS LIKE THE ONLY **LEAD** ROLE I'LL LAND TONIGHT IS YOURS!

Wallace & Gromit - Funnies #1
by Aardman & Titan Comics

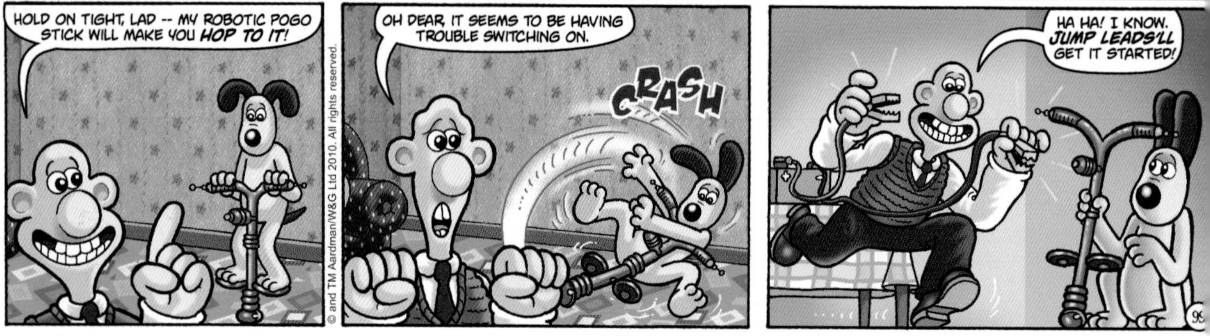
HOLD ON TIGHT, LAD -- MY ROBOTIC POGO STICK WILL MAKE YOU **HOP TO IT!**
OH DEAR, IT SEEMS TO BE HAVING TROUBLE SWITCHING ON.
CRASH
HA HA! I KNOW. **JUMP LEADS'LL** GET IT STARTED!

/allace & Gromit - Funnies #1 by Aardman & Titan Comics

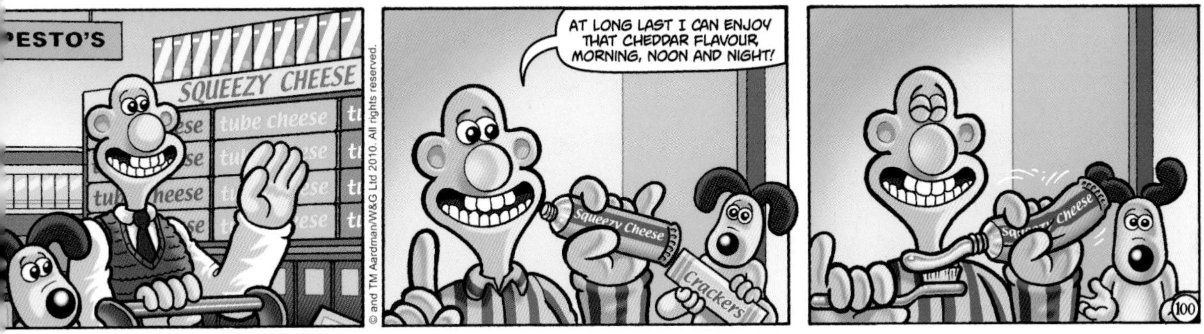

PESTO'S
SQUEEZY CHEESE
tube cheese
© and TM Aardman/W&G Ltd 2010. All rights reserved.
AT LONG LAST I CAN ENJOY THAT CHEDDAR FLAVOUR, MORNING, NOON AND NIGHT!
Squeezy Cheese
Crackers
100

/allace & Gromit - Funnies #1 by Aardman & Titan Comics

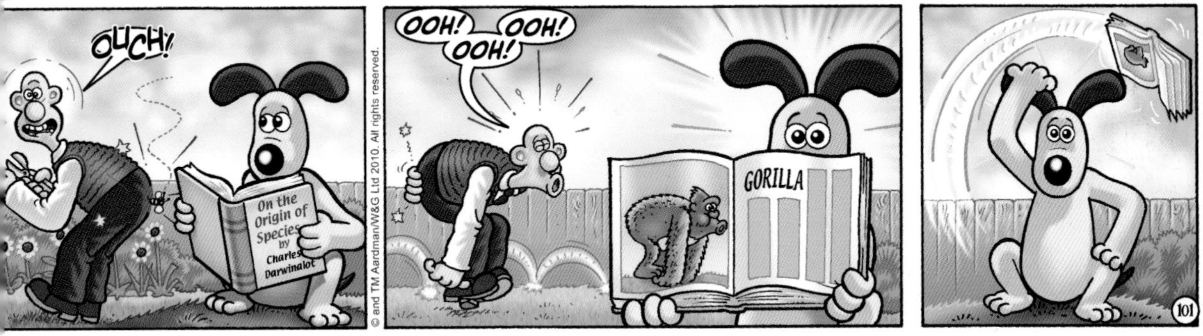

OUCH!
On the Origin of Species by Charles Darwinalot
© and TM Aardman/W&G Ltd 2010. All rights reserved.
OOH! OOH! OOH!
GORILLA
101

/allace & Gromit - Funnies #1 by Aardman & Titan Comics

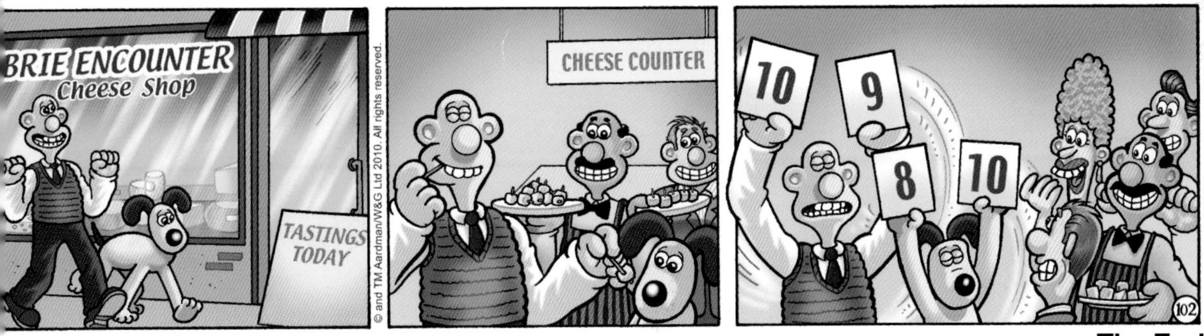

BRIE ENCOUNTER
Cheese Shop
TASTINGS TODAY
© and TM Aardman/W&G Ltd 2010. All rights reserved.
CHEESE COUNTER
10
9
8
10
102

The End

Wallace & Gromit - Jolley-Goode Jewels by Aardman & Titan Comic

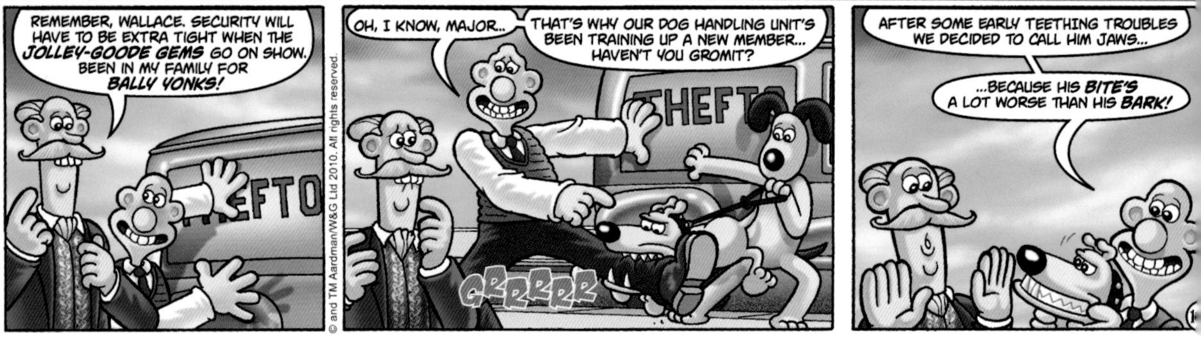
REMEMBER, WALLACE. SECURITY WILL HAVE TO BE EXTRA TIGHT WHEN THE JOLLEY-GOODE GEMS GO ON SHOW. BEEN IN MY FAMILY FOR BALLY YONKS!
THEFTO
© and TM Aardman/W&G Ltd 2010. All rights reserved.
OH, I KNOW, MAJOR...
THAT'S WHY OUR DOG HANDLING UNIT'S BEEN TRAINING UP A NEW MEMBER... HAVEN'T YOU GROMIT?
THEFTO
GRRRRR
AFTER SOME EARLY TEETHING TROUBLES WE DECIDED TO CALL HIM JAWS...
...BECAUSE HIS BITE'S A LOT WORSE THAN HIS BARK!

Wallace & Gromit - Jolley-Goode Jewels by Aardman & Titan Comic

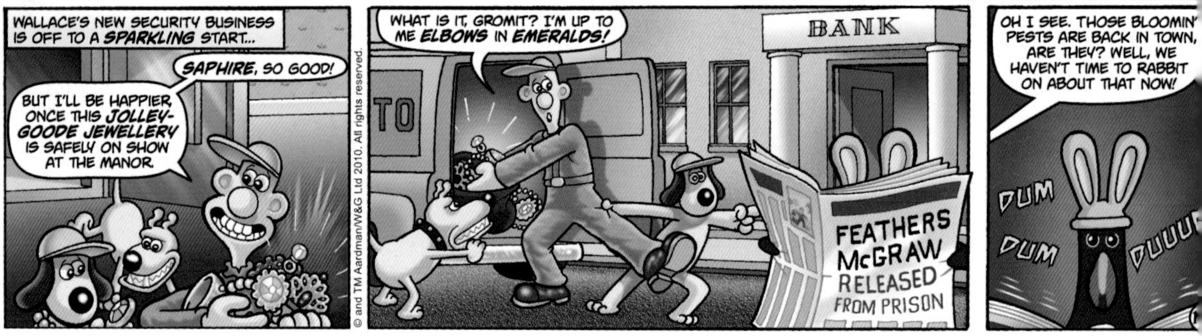
WALLACE'S NEW SECURITY BUSINESS IS OFF TO A SPARKLING START...
SAPHIRE, SO GOOD!
BUT I'LL BE HAPPIER ONCE THIS JOLLEY-GOODE JEWELLERY IS SAFELY ON SHOW AT THE MANOR.
© and TM Aardman/W&G Ltd 2010. All rights reserved.
WHAT IS IT, GROMIT? I'M UP TO ME ELBOWS IN EMERALDS!
BANK
TO
FEATHERS McGRAW RELEASED FROM PRISON
OH I SEE. THOSE BLOOMIN' PESTS ARE BACK IN TOWN, ARE THEY? WELL, WE HAVEN'T TIME TO RABBIT ON ABOUT THAT NOW!
DUM
DUM
DUUU

Wallace & Gromit - Jolley-Goode Jewels by Aardman & Titan Comic

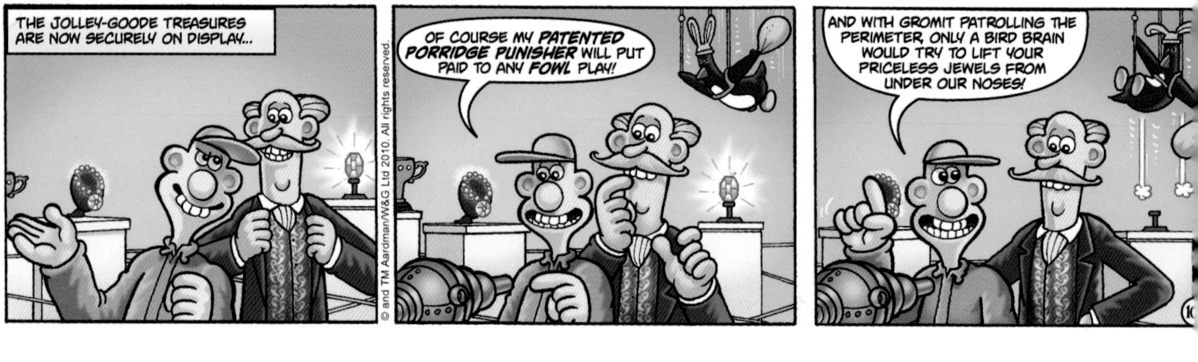
THE JOLLEY-GOODE TREASURES ARE NOW SECURELY ON DISPLAY...
© and TM Aardman/W&G Ltd 2010. All rights reserved.
OF COURSE MY PATENTED PORRIDGE PUNISHER WILL PUT PAID TO ANY FOWL PLAY!
AND WITH GROMIT PATROLLING THE PERIMETER, ONLY A BIRD BRAIN WOULD TRY TO LIFT YOUR PRICELESS JEWELS FROM UNDER OUR NOSES!

allace & Gromit - Jolley-Goode Jewels by Aardman & Titan Comics

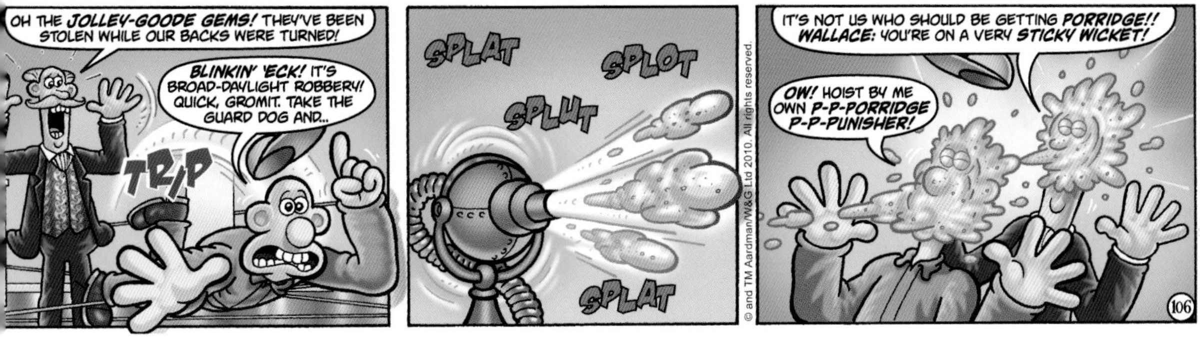

OH THE JOLLEY-GOODE GEMS! THEY'VE BEEN STOLEN WHILE OUR BACKS WERE TURNED!
BLINKIN' 'ECK! IT'S BROAD-DAYLIGHT ROBBERY! QUICK, GROMIT. TAKE THE GUARD DOG AND...
TRIP
SPLAT
SPLOT
SPLUT
SPLAT
IT'S NOT US WHO SHOULD BE GETTING PORRIDGE!! WALLACE: YOU'RE ON A VERY STICKY WICKET!
OW! HOIST BY ME OWN P-P-PORRIDGE P-P-PUNISHER!
106

allace & Gromit - Jolley-Goode Jewels by Aardman & Titan Comics

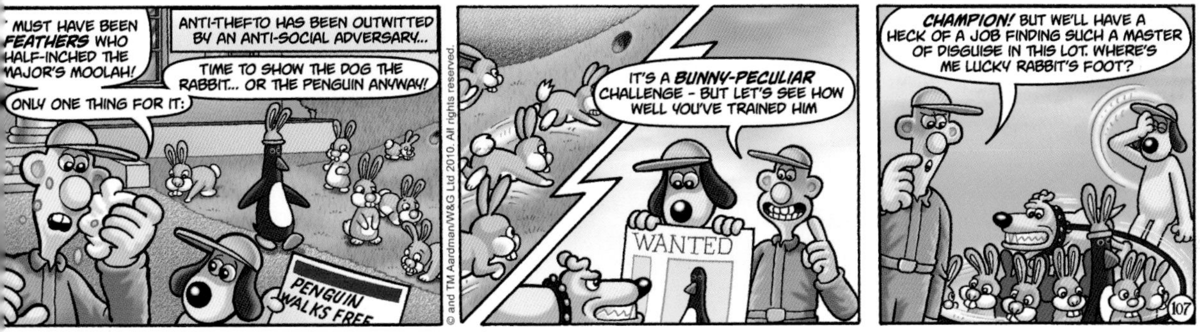

' MUST HAVE BEEN FEATHERS WHO HALF-INCHED THE MAJOR'S MOOLAH!
ANTI-THEFTO HAS BEEN OUTWITTED BY AN ANTI-SOCIAL ADVERSARY...
TIME TO SHOW THE DOG THE RABBIT... OR THE PENGUIN ANYWAY!
ONLY ONE THING FOR IT:
PENGUIN WALKS FREE
IT'S A BUNNY-PECULIAR CHALLENGE - BUT LET'S SEE HOW WELL YOU'VE TRAINED HIM
WANTED
CHAMPION! BUT WE'LL HAVE A HECK OF A JOB FINDING SUCH A MASTER OF DISGUISE IN THIS LOT. WHERE'S ME LUCKY RABBIT'S FOOT?
107

allace & Gromit - Jolley-Goode Jewels by Aardman & Titan Comics

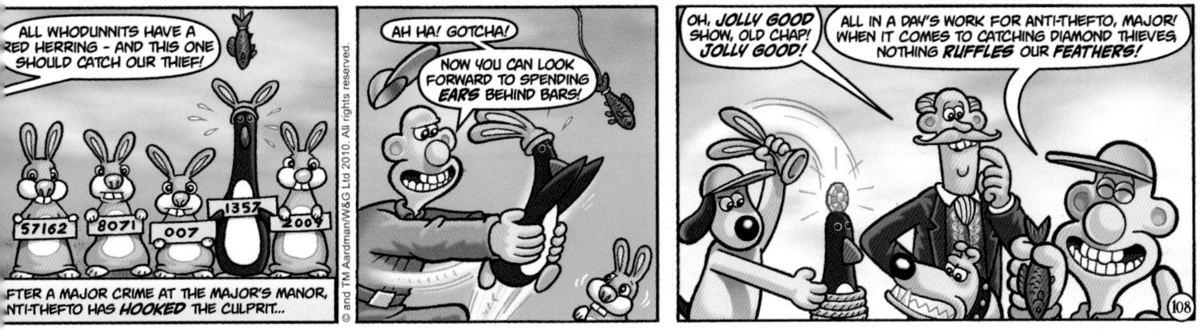

ALL WHODUNNITS HAVE A RED HERRING - AND THIS ONE SHOULD CATCH OUR THIEF!
57162
8071
007
1357
2009
FTER A MAJOR CRIME AT THE MAJOR'S MANOR, NTI-THEFTO HAS HOOKED THE CULPRIT...
AH HA! GOTCHA!
NOW YOU CAN LOOK FORWARD TO SPENDING EARS BEHIND BARS!
OH, JOLLY GOOD SHOW, OLD CHAP! JOLLY GOOD!
ALL IN A DAY'S WORK FOR ANTI-THEFTO, MAJOR! WHEN IT COMES TO CATCHING DIAMOND THIEVES, NOTHING RUFFLES OUR FEATHERS!
108

The End

Wallace & Gromit - Watch the Birdy

by Aardman & Titan Comi

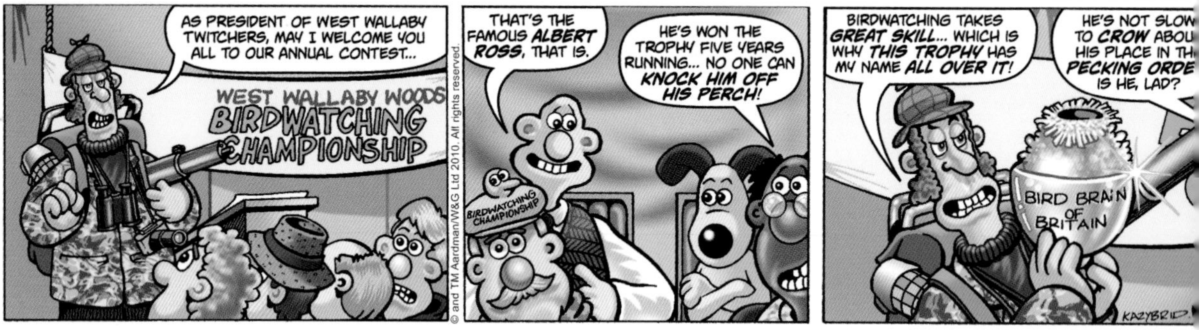

AS PRESIDENT OF WEST WALLABY TWITCHERS, MAY I WELCOME YOU ALL TO OUR ANNUAL CONTEST...
WEST WALLABY WOODS BIRDWATCHING CHAMPIONSHIP
THAT'S THE FAMOUS ALBERT ROSS, THAT IS.
HE'S WON THE TROPHY FIVE YEARS RUNNING... NO ONE CAN KNOCK HIM OFF HIS PERCH!
BIRDWATCHING CHAMPIONSHIP
BIRDWATCHING TAKES GREAT SKILL... WHICH IS WHY THIS TROPHY HAS MY NAME ALL OVER IT!
HE'S NOT SLOW TO CROW ABOU HIS PLACE IN TH PECKING ORDE IS HE, LAD?
BIRD BRAIN OF BRITAIN

Wallace & Gromit - Watch the Birdy

by Aardman & Titan Comic

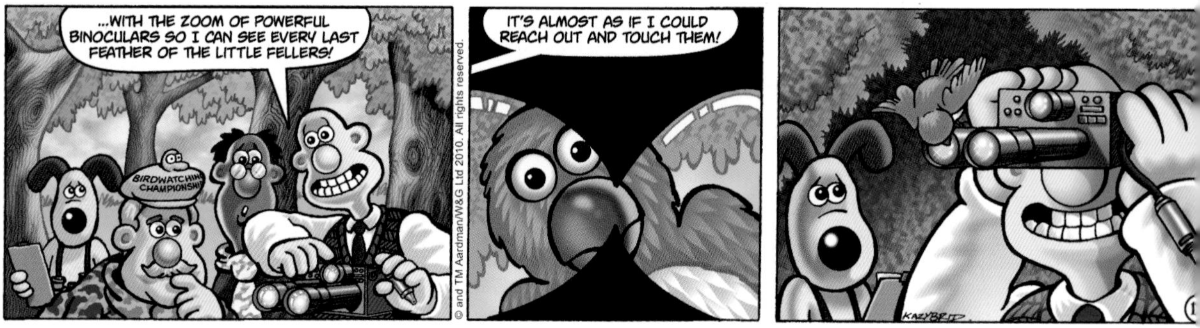

...WITH THE ZOOM OF POWERFUL BINOCULARS SO I CAN SEE EVERY LAST FEATHER OF THE LITTLE FELLERS!
BIRDWATCHING CHAMPIONSHI
IT'S ALMOST AS IF I COULD REACH OUT AND TOUCH THEM!

Wallace & Gromit - Watch the Birdy

by Aardman & Titan Comic

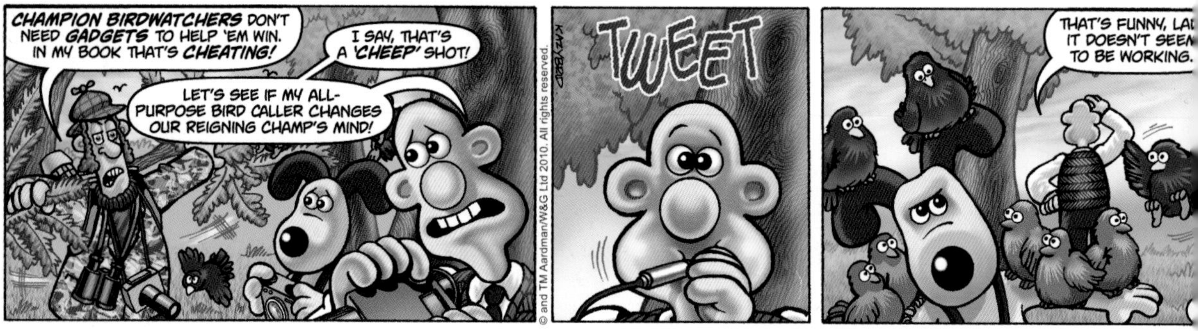

CHAMPION BIRDWATCHERS DON'T NEED GADGETS TO HELP 'EM WIN. IN MY BOOK THAT'S CHEATING!
I SAY, THAT'S A 'CHEEP' SHOT!
LET'S SEE IF MY ALL-PURPOSE BIRD CALLER CHANGES OUR REIGNING CHAMP'S MIND!
TWEET
THAT'S FUNNY, LA IT DOESN'T SEEM TO BE WORKING.

Vallace & Gromit - Watch the Birdy by Aardman & Titan Comics

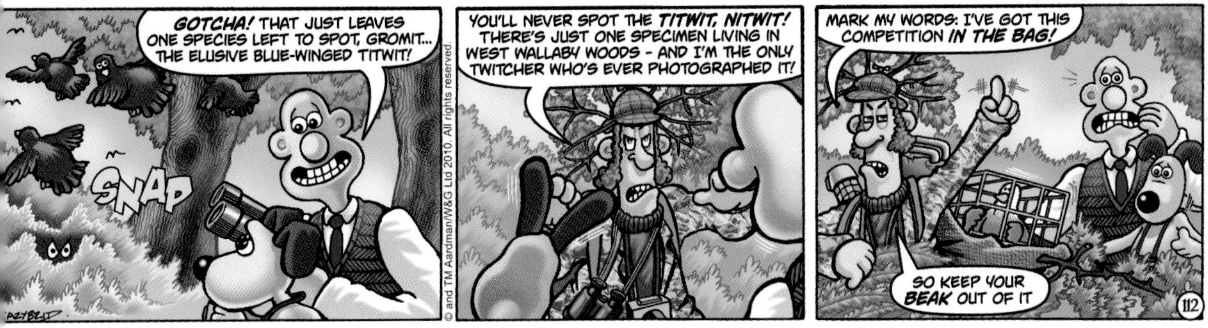
GOTCHA! THAT JUST LEAVES ONE SPECIES LEFT TO SPOT, GROMIT... THE ELUSIVE BLUE-WINGED TITWIT!
SNAP
YOU'LL NEVER SPOT THE TITWIT, NITWIT! THERE'S JUST ONE SPECIMEN LIVING IN WEST WALLABY WOODS - AND I'M THE ONLY TWITCHER WHO'S EVER PHOTOGRAPHED IT!
MARK MY WORDS: I'VE GOT THIS COMPETITION IN THE BAG!
SO KEEP YOUR BEAK OUT OF IT
112
© and TM Aardman/W&G Ltd 2010. All rights reserved.

Vallace & Gromit - Watch the Birdy by Aardman & Titan Comics

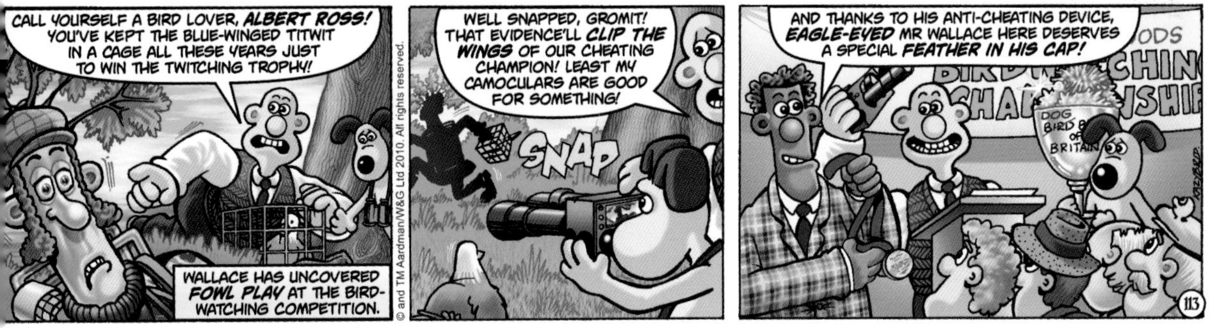
CALL YOURSELF A BIRD LOVER, ALBERT ROSS! YOU'VE KEPT THE BLUE-WINGED TITWIT IN A CAGE ALL THESE YEARS JUST TO WIN THE TWITCHING TROPHY!
WALLACE HAS UNCOVERED FOWL PLAY AT THE BIRD-WATCHING COMPETITION.
WELL SNAPPED, GROMIT! THAT EVIDENCE'LL CLIP THE WINGS OF OUR CHEATING CHAMPION! LEAST MY CAMOCULARS ARE GOOD FOR SOMETHING!
SNAP
AND THANKS TO HIS ANTI-CHEATING DEVICE, EAGLE-EYED MR WALLACE HERE DESERVES A SPECIAL FEATHER IN HIS CAP!
DOG BIRD BRAIN OF BRITAIN
113
© and TM Aardman/W&G Ltd 2010. All rights reserved.

Vallace & Gromit - Watch the Birdy by Aardman & Titan Comics

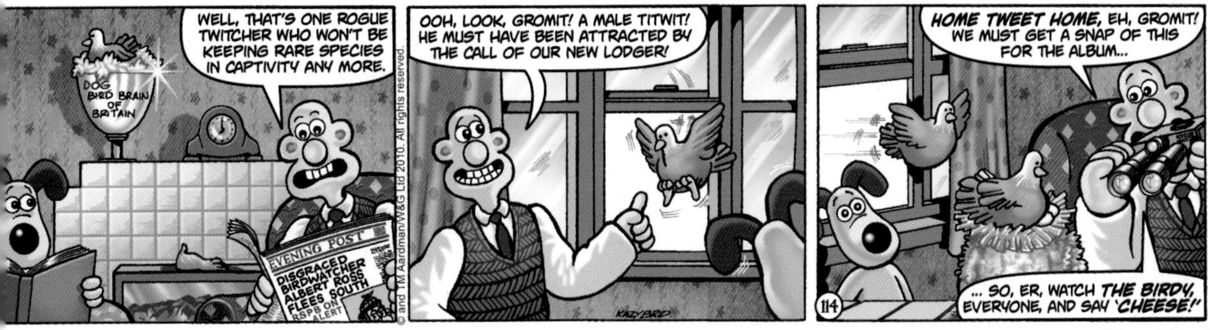
WELL, THAT'S ONE ROGUE TWITCHER WHO WON'T BE KEEPING RARE SPECIES IN CAPTIVITY ANY MORE.
DOG BIRD BRAIN OF BRITAIN
EVENING POST
DISGRACED BIRDWATCHER ALBERT ROSS FLEES SOUTH
OOH, LOOK, GROMIT! A MALE TITWIT! HE MUST HAVE BEEN ATTRACTED BY THE CALL OF OUR NEW LODGER!
HOME TWEET HOME, EH, GROMIT! WE MUST GET A SNAP OF THIS FOR THE ALBUM...
... SO, ER, WATCH THE BIRDY, EVERYONE, AND SAY 'CHEESE!'
114
© and TM Aardman/W&G Ltd 2010. All rights reserved.

The End

Wallace & Gromit - A Snip Above

by Aardman & Titan Comics

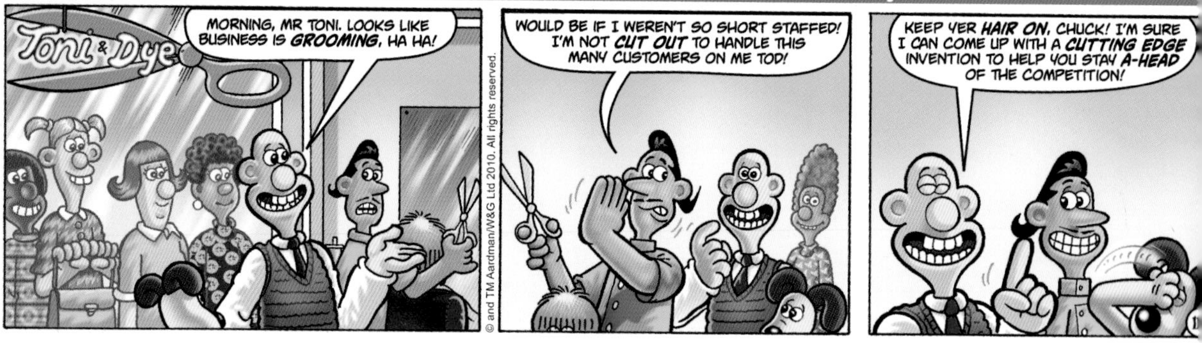
Toni & Dye
MORNING, MR TONI. LOOKS LIKE BUSINESS IS GROOMING, HA HA!
WOULD BE IF I WEREN'T SO SHORT STAFFED! I'M NOT CUT OUT TO HANDLE THIS MANY CUSTOMERS ON ME TOD!
KEEP YER HAIR ON, CHUCK! I'M SURE I CAN COME UP WITH A CUTTING EDGE INVENTION TO HELP YOU STAY A-HEAD OF THE COMPETITION!

Wallace & Gromit - A Snip Above

by Aardman & Titan Comics

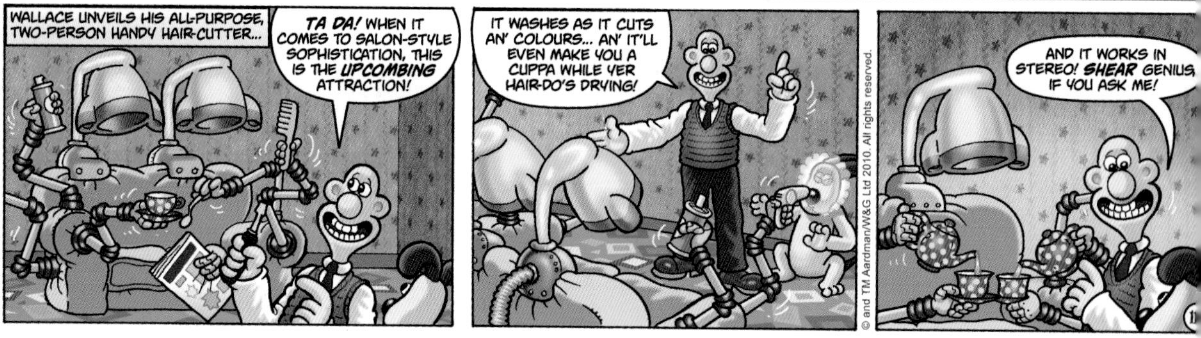
WALLACE UNVEILS HIS ALL-PURPOSE, TWO-PERSON HANDY HAIR-CUTTER...
TA DA! WHEN IT COMES TO SALON-STYLE SOPHISTICATION, THIS IS THE UPCOMBING ATTRACTION!
IT WASHES AS IT CUTS AN' COLOURS... AN' IT'LL EVEN MAKE YOU A CUPPA WHILE YER HAIR-DO'S DRYING!
AND IT WORKS IN STEREO! SHEAR GENIUS, IF YOU ASK ME!

Wallace & Gromit - A Snip Above

by Aardman & Titan Comics

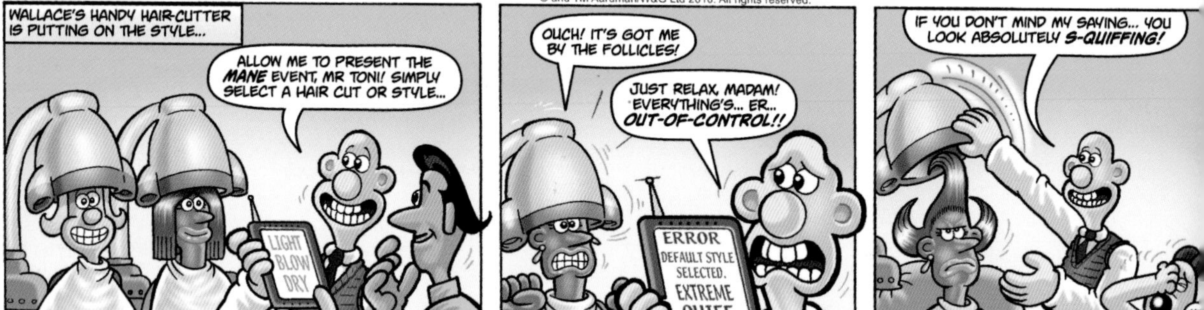
WALLACE'S HANDY HAIR-CUTTER IS PUTTING ON THE STYLE...
ALLOW ME TO PRESENT THE MANE EVENT, MR TONI! SIMPLY SELECT A HAIR CUT OR STYLE...
LIGHT BLOW DRY
OUCH! IT'S GOT ME BY THE FOLLICLES!
JUST RELAX, MADAM! EVERYTHING'S... ER... OUT-OF-CONTROL!!
ERROR DEFAULT STYLE SELECTED. EXTREME QUIFF
IF YOU DON'T MIND MY SAYING... YOU LOOK ABSOLUTELY S-QUIFFING!

Vallace & Gromit - A Snip Above by Aardman & Titan Comics

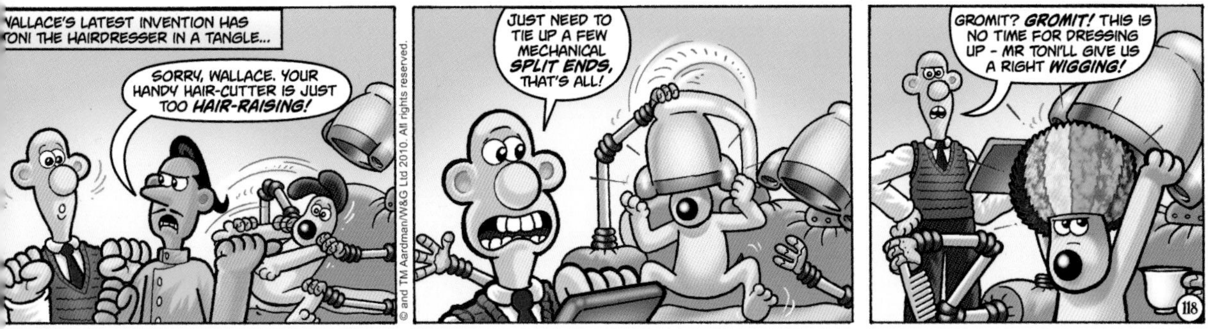
VALLACE'S LATEST INVENTION HAS
ONI THE HAIRDRESSER IN A TANGLE...
SORRY, WALLACE. YOUR HANDY HAIR-CUTTER IS JUST TOO HAIR-RAISING!
JUST NEED TO TIE UP A FEW MECHANICAL SPLIT ENDS, THAT'S ALL!
GROMIT? GROMIT! THIS IS NO TIME FOR DRESSING UP - MR TONI'LL GIVE US A RIGHT WIGGING!
118

Vallace & Gromit - A Snip Above by Aardman & Titan Comics

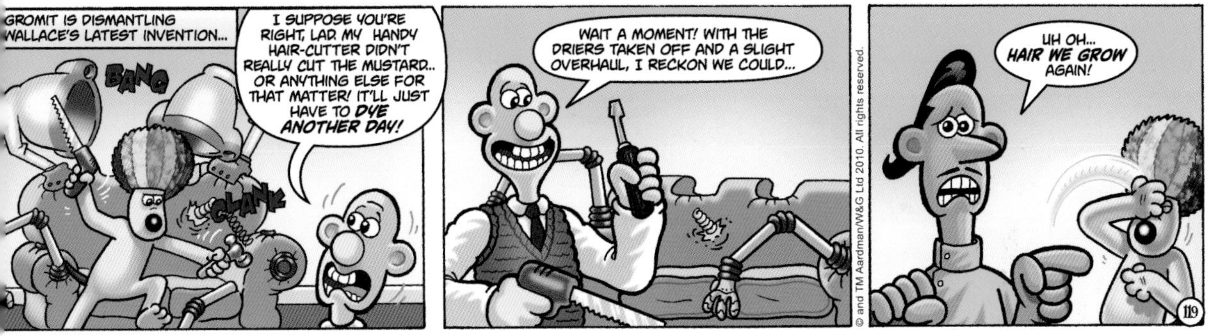
GROMIT IS DISMANTLING
VALLACE'S LATEST INVENTION...
BANG
CLANK
I SUPPOSE YOU'RE RIGHT, LAD. MY HANDY HAIR-CUTTER DIDN'T REALLY CUT THE MUSTARD.. OR ANYTHING ELSE FOR THAT MATTER! IT'LL JUST HAVE TO DYE ANOTHER DAY!
WAIT A MOMENT! WITH THE DRIERS TAKEN OFF AND A SLIGHT OVERHAUL, I RECKON WE COULD...
UH OH... HAIR WE GROW AGAIN!
119

Vallace & Gromit - A Snip Above by Aardman & Titan Comics

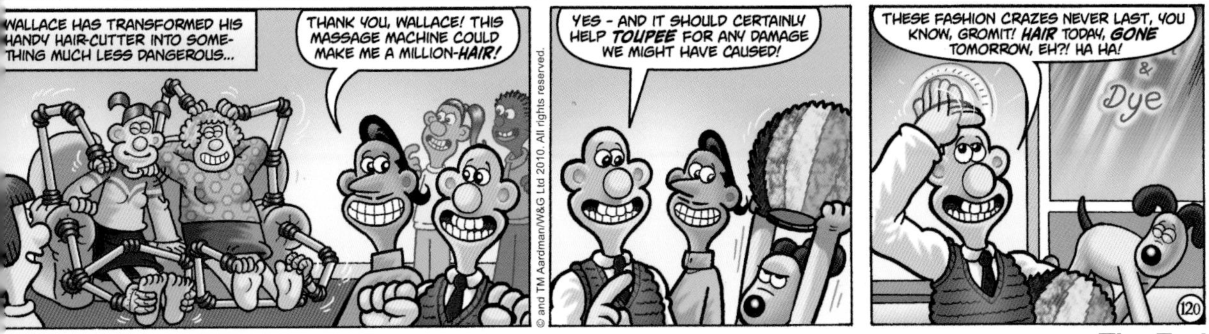
VALLACE HAS TRANSFORMED HIS
HANDY HAIR-CUTTER INTO SOME-
THING MUCH LESS DANGEROUS...
THANK YOU, WALLACE! THIS MASSAGE MACHINE COULD MAKE ME A MILLION-HAIR!
YES - AND IT SHOULD CERTAINLY HELP TOUPEE FOR ANY DAMAGE WE MIGHT HAVE CAUSED!
THESE FASHION CRAZES NEVER LAST, YOU KNOW, GROMIT! HAIR TODAY, GONE TOMORROW, EH?! HA HA!
& Dye
120

The End

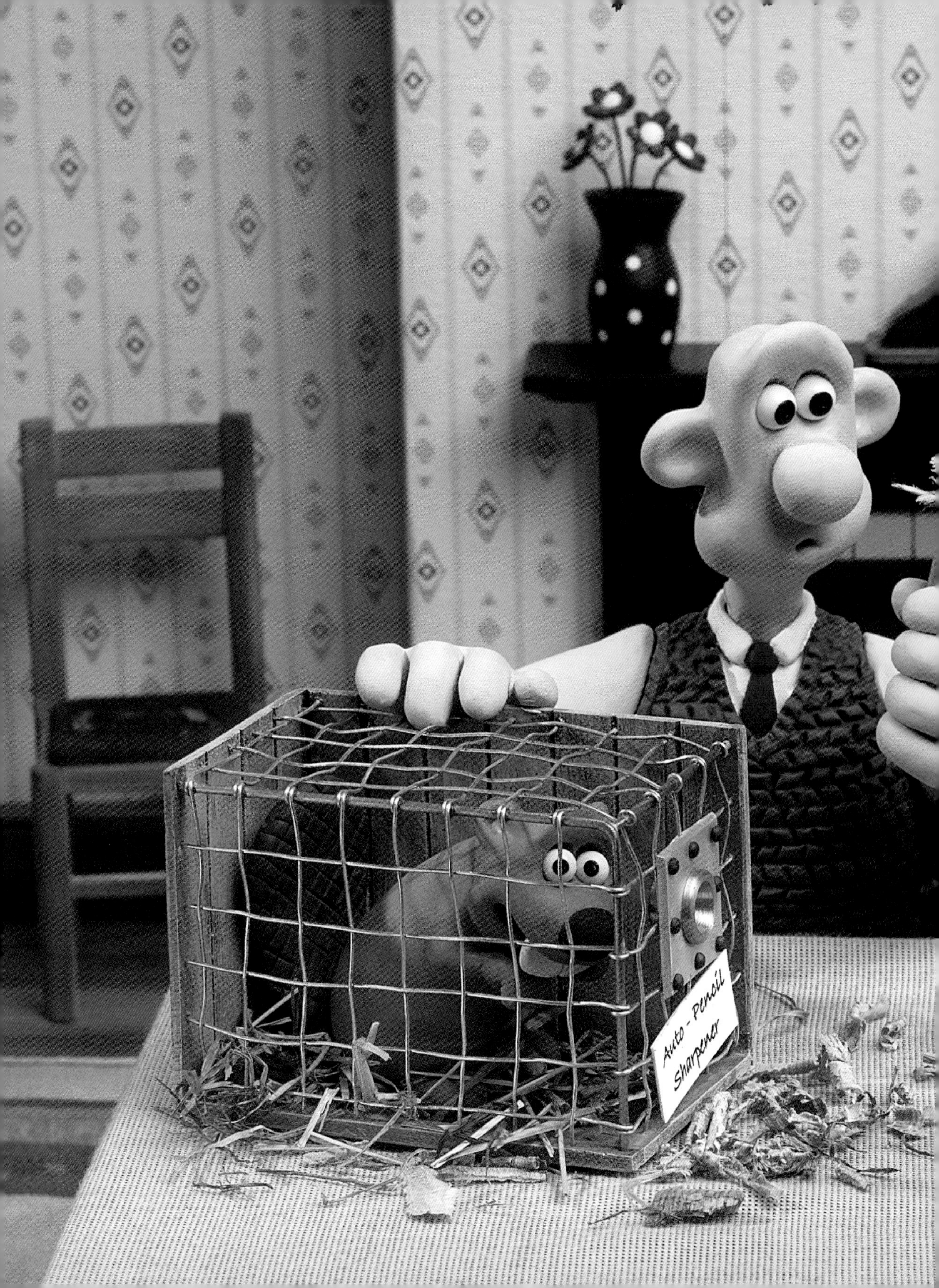
Auto - Pencil
Sharpener

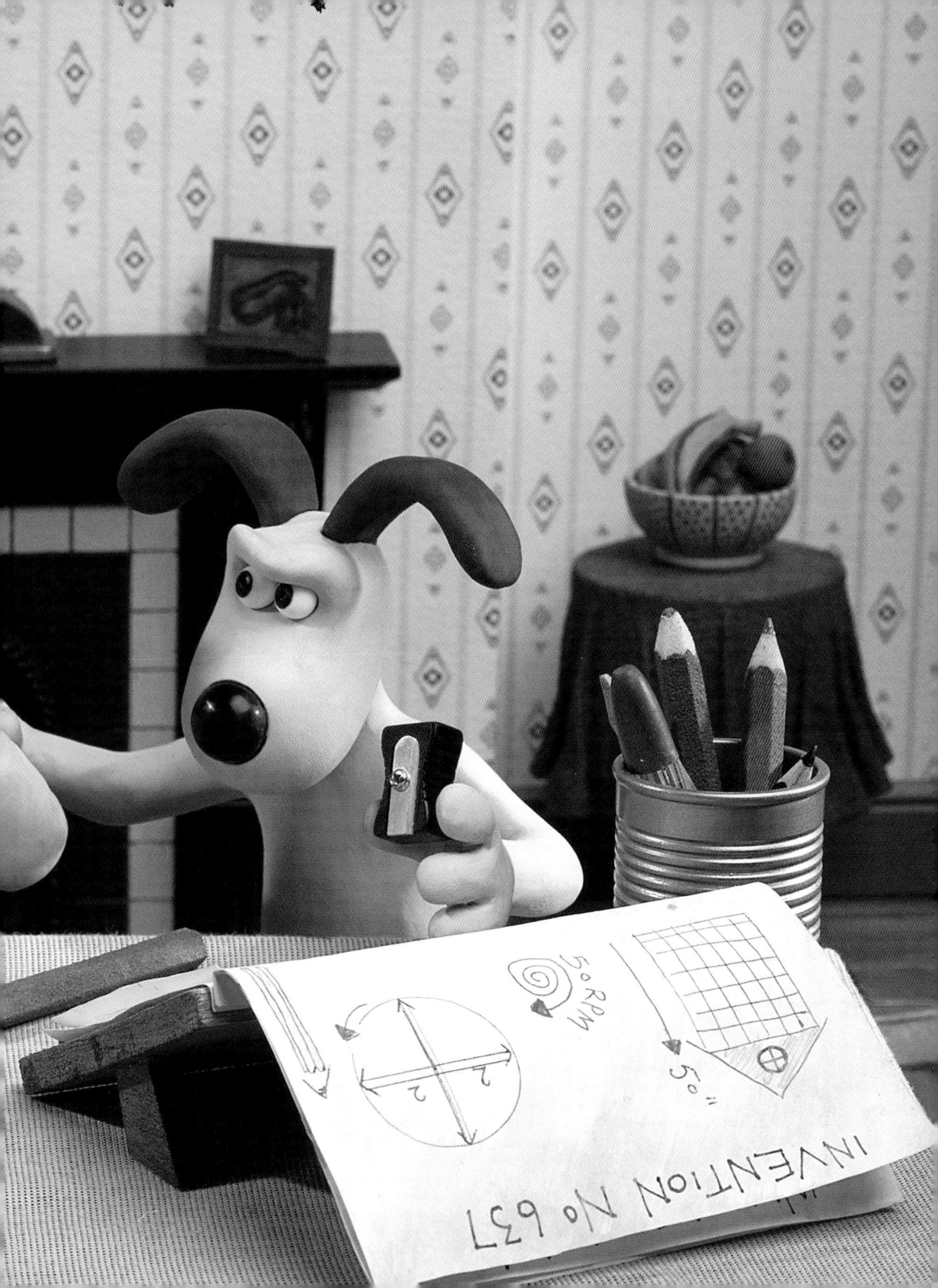
INVENTION No 637
50 RPM

Wallace & Gromit - It Had to be Zoo

by Aardman & Titan Comics

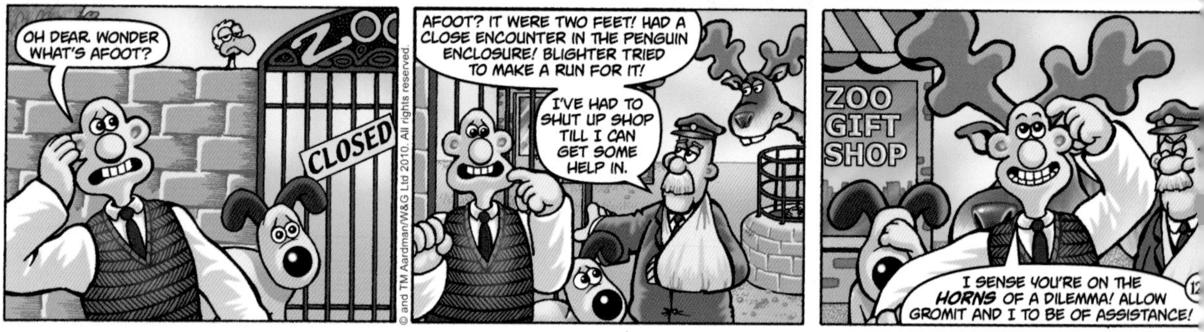

OH DEAR. WONDER WHAT'S AFOOT?
ZOO
CLOSED
© and TM Aardman/W&G Ltd 2010. All rights reserved.
AFOOT? IT WERE TWO FEET! HAD A CLOSE ENCOUNTER IN THE PENGUIN ENCLOSURE! BLIGHTER TRIED TO MAKE A RUN FOR IT!
I'VE HAD TO SHUT UP SHOP TILL I CAN GET SOME HELP IN.
ZOO GIFT SHOP
I SENSE YOU'RE ON THE HORNS OF A DILEMMA! ALLOW GROMIT AND I TO BE OF ASSISTANCE!

Wallace & Gromit - It Had to be Zoo

by Aardman & Titan Comics

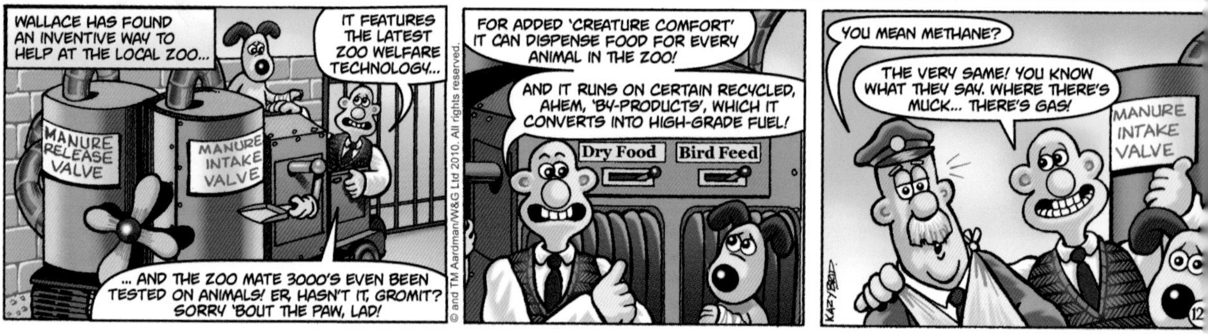

WALLACE HAS FOUND AN INVENTIVE WAY TO HELP AT THE LOCAL ZOO...
IT FEATURES THE LATEST ZOO WELFARE TECHNOLOGY...
MANURE RELEASE VALVE
MANURE INTAKE VALVE
... AND THE ZOO MATE 3000'S EVEN BEEN TESTED ON ANIMALS! ER, HASN'T IT, GROMIT? SORRY 'BOUT THE PAW, LAD!
© and TM Aardman/W&G Ltd 2010. All rights reserved.
FOR ADDED 'CREATURE COMFORT' IT CAN DISPENSE FOOD FOR EVERY ANIMAL IN THE ZOO!
AND IT RUNS ON CERTAIN RECYCLED, AHEM, 'BY-PRODUCTS', WHICH IT CONVERTS INTO HIGH-GRADE FUEL!
Dry Food
Bird Feed
YOU MEAN METHANE?
THE VERY SAME! YOU KNOW WHAT THEY SAY. WHERE THERE'S MUCK... THERE'S GAS!
MANURE INTAKE VALVE

Wallace & Gromit - It Had to be Zoo

by Aardman & Titan Comics

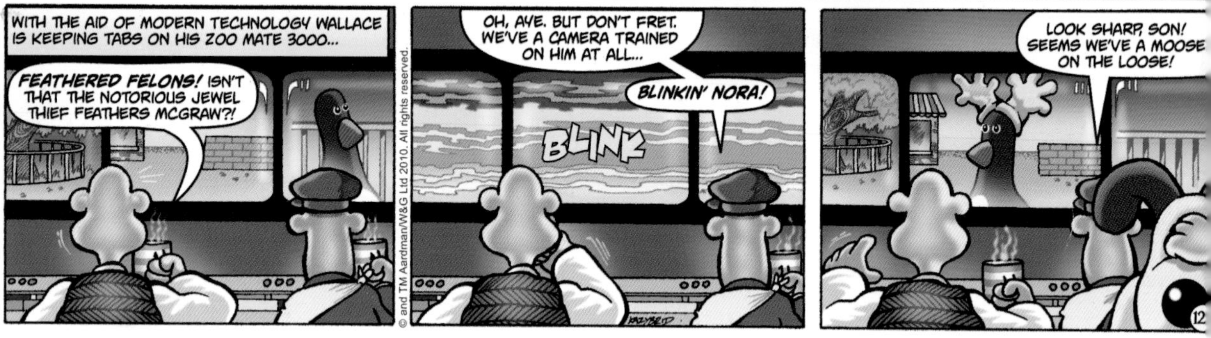

WITH THE AID OF MODERN TECHNOLOGY WALLACE IS KEEPING TABS ON HIS ZOO MATE 3000...
FEATHERED FELONS! ISN'T THAT THE NOTORIOUS JEWEL THIEF FEATHERS MCGRAW?!
© and TM Aardman/W&G Ltd 2010. All rights reserved.
OH, AYE. BUT DON'T FRET. WE'VE A CAMERA TRAINED ON HIM AT ALL...
BLINKIN' NORA!
BLINK
LOOK SHARP, SON! SEEMS WE'VE A MOOSE ON THE LOOSE!

Vallace & Gromit - It Had to be Zoo by Aardman & Titan Comics

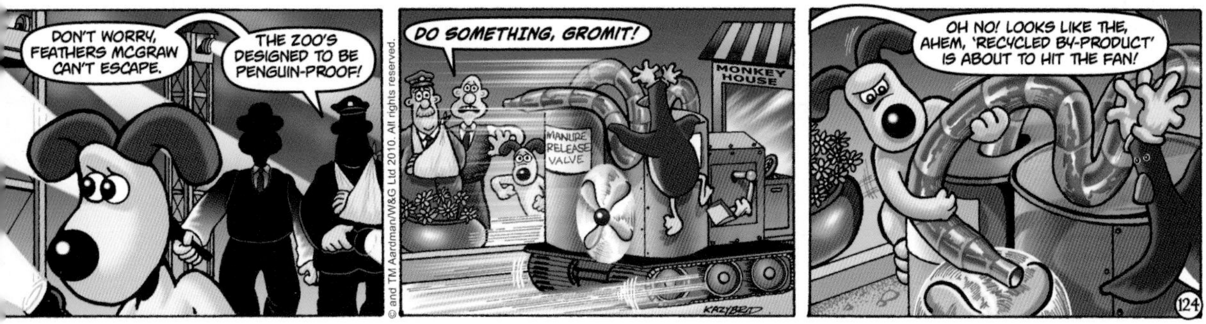

DON'T WORRY, FEATHERS MCGRAW CAN'T ESCAPE.
THE ZOO'S DESIGNED TO BE PENGUIN-PROOF!
DO SOMETHING, GROMIT!
MONKEY HOUSE
MANURE RELEASE VALVE
© and TM Aardman/W&G Ltd 2010. All rights reserved.
OH NO! LOOKS LIKE THE, AHEM, 'RECYCLED BY-PRODUCT' IS ABOUT TO HIT THE FAN!
124

Vallace & Gromit - It Had to be Zoo by Aardman & Titan Comics

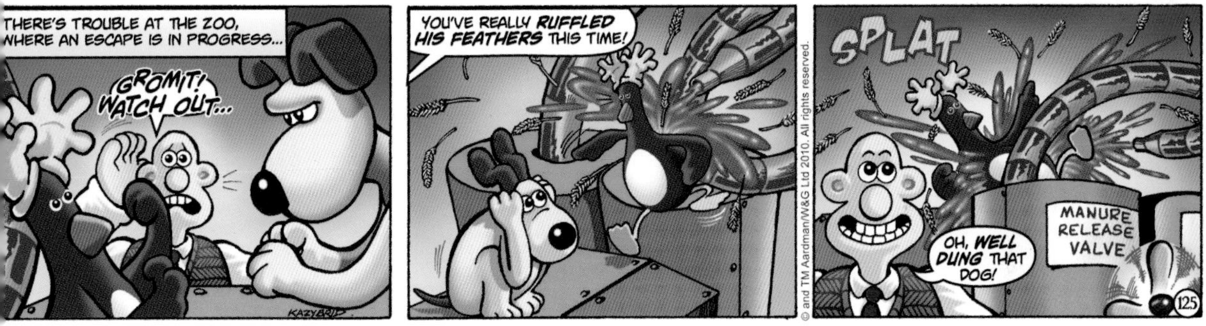

THERE'S TROUBLE AT THE ZOO, WHERE AN ESCAPE IS IN PROGRESS...
GROMIT! WATCH OUT...
YOU'VE REALLY RUFFLED HIS FEATHERS THIS TIME!
© and TM Aardman/W&G Ltd 2010. All rights reserved.
SPLAT
MANURE RELEASE VALVE
OH, WELL DUNG THAT DOG!
125

Vallace & Gromit - It Had to be Zoo by Aardman & Titan Comics

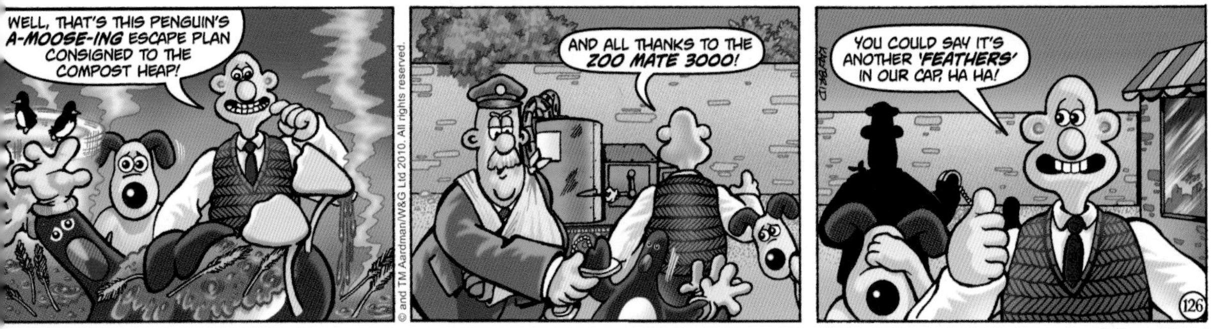

WELL, THAT'S THIS PENGUIN'S A-MOOSE-ING ESCAPE PLAN CONSIGNED TO THE COMPOST HEAP!
© and TM Aardman/W&G Ltd 2010. All rights reserved.
AND ALL THANKS TO THE ZOO MATE 3000!
YOU COULD SAY IT'S ANOTHER 'FEATHERS' IN OUR CAP, HA HA!
126

The End

Wallace & Gromit - Driving Miss Crazy
by Aardman & Titan Comic

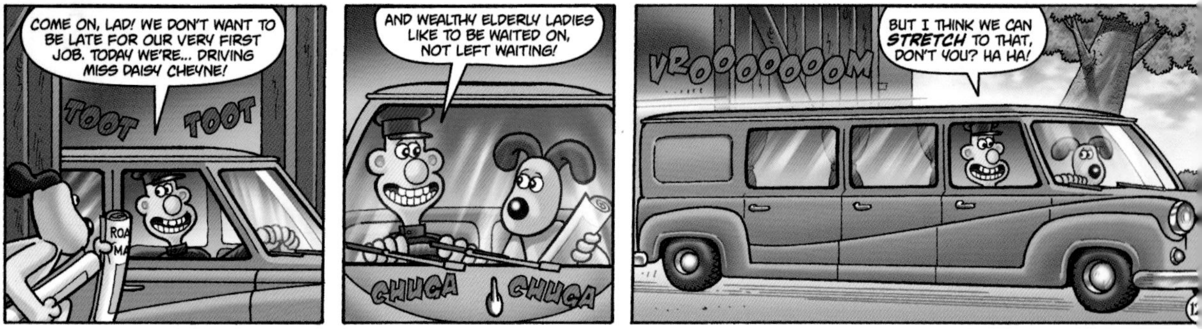
COME ON, LAD! WE DON'T WANT TO BE LATE FOR OUR VERY FIRST JOB. TODAY WE'RE... DRIVING MISS DAISY CHEYNE!
TOOT TOOT
AND WEALTHY ELDERLY LADIES LIKE TO BE WAITED ON, NOT LEFT WAITING!
CHUGA CHUGA
VROOOOOOOOM
BUT I THINK WE CAN STRETCH TO THAT, DON'T YOU? HA HA!

Wallace & Gromit - Driving Miss Crazy
by Aardman & Titan Comic

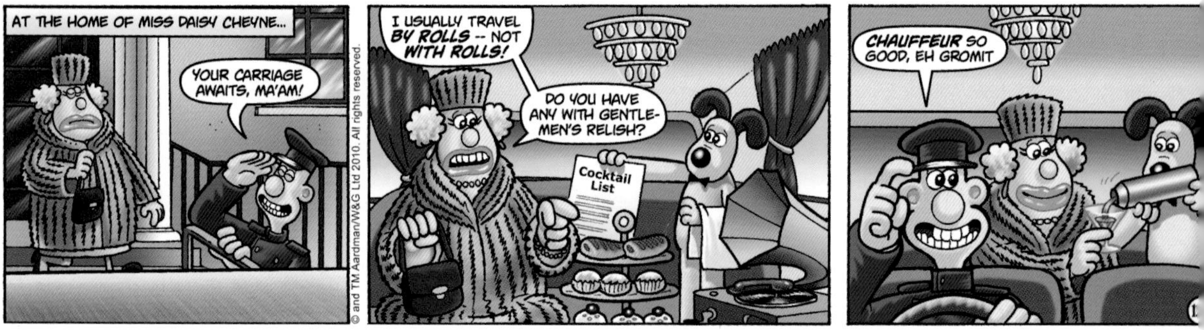
AT THE HOME OF MISS DAISY CHEYNE...
YOUR CARRIAGE AWAITS, MA'AM!
I USUALLY TRAVEL BY ROLLS -- NOT WITH ROLLS!
DO YOU HAVE ANY WITH GENTLE-MEN'S RELISH?
Cocktail List
CHAUFFEUR SO GOOD, EH GROMIT

Wallace & Gromit - Driving Miss Crazy
by Aardman & Titan Comic

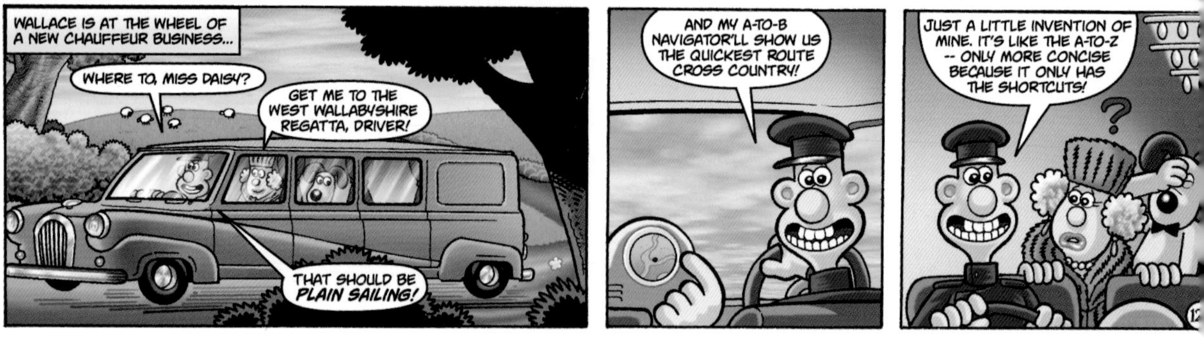
WALLACE IS AT THE WHEEL OF A NEW CHAUFFEUR BUSINESS...
WHERE TO, MISS DAISY?
GET ME TO THE WEST WALLABYSHIRE REGATTA, DRIVER!
THAT SHOULD BE PLAIN SAILING!
AND MY A-TO-B NAVIGATOR'LL SHOW US THE QUICKEST ROUTE CROSS COUNTRY!
JUST A LITTLE INVENTION OF MINE. IT'S LIKE THE A-TO-Z -- ONLY MORE CONCISE BECAUSE IT ONLY HAS THE SHORTCUTS!
?

Wallace & Gromit - Driving Miss Crazy by Aardman & Titan Comics

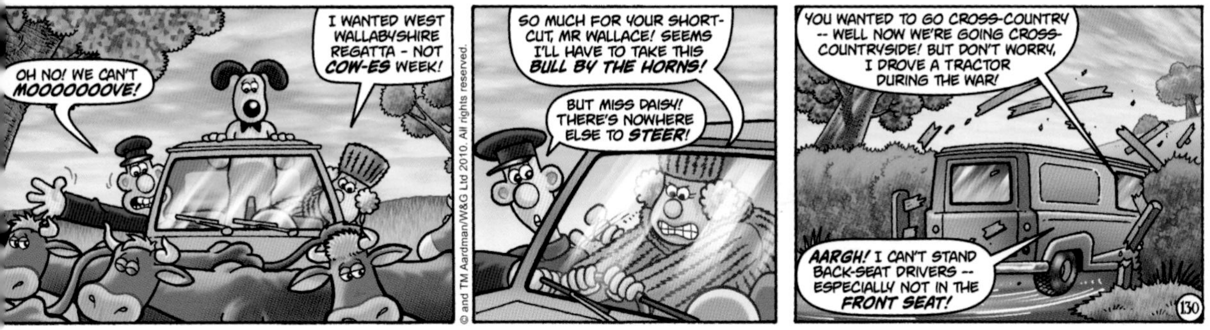
OH NO! WE CAN'T MOOOOOOOVE!
I WANTED WEST WALLABYSHIRE REGATTA - NOT COW-ES WEEK!
© and TM Aardman/W&G Ltd 2010. All rights reserved.
SO MUCH FOR YOUR SHORT-CUT, MR WALLACE! SEEMS I'LL HAVE TO TAKE THIS BULL BY THE HORNS!
BUT MISS DAISY! THERE'S NOWHERE ELSE TO STEER!
YOU WANTED TO GO CROSS-COUNTRY -- WELL NOW WE'RE GOING CROSS-COUNTRYSIDE! BUT DON'T WORRY, I DROVE A TRACTOR DURING THE WAR!
AARGH! I CAN'T STAND BACK-SEAT DRIVERS -- ESPECIALLY NOT IN THE FRONT SEAT!
130

Wallace & Gromit - Driving Miss Crazy by Aardman & Titan Comics

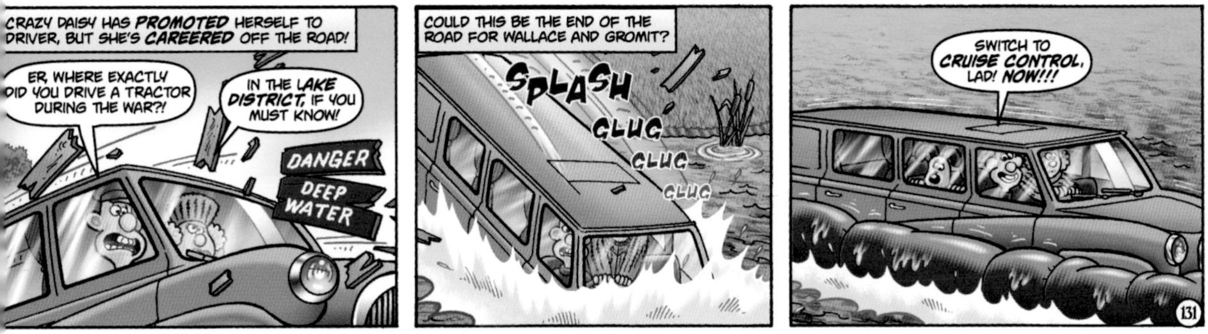
CRAZY DAISY HAS PROMOTED HERSELF TO DRIVER, BUT SHE'S CAREERED OFF THE ROAD!
ER, WHERE EXACTLY DID YOU DRIVE A TRACTOR DURING THE WAR?!
IN THE LAKE DISTRICT, IF YOU MUST KNOW!
DANGER
DEEP WATER
COULD THIS BE THE END OF THE ROAD FOR WALLACE AND GROMIT?
SPLASH
GLUG
GLUG
GLUG
SWITCH TO CRUISE CONTROL, LAD! NOW!!!
131

Wallace & Gromit - Driving Miss Crazy by Aardman & Titan Comics

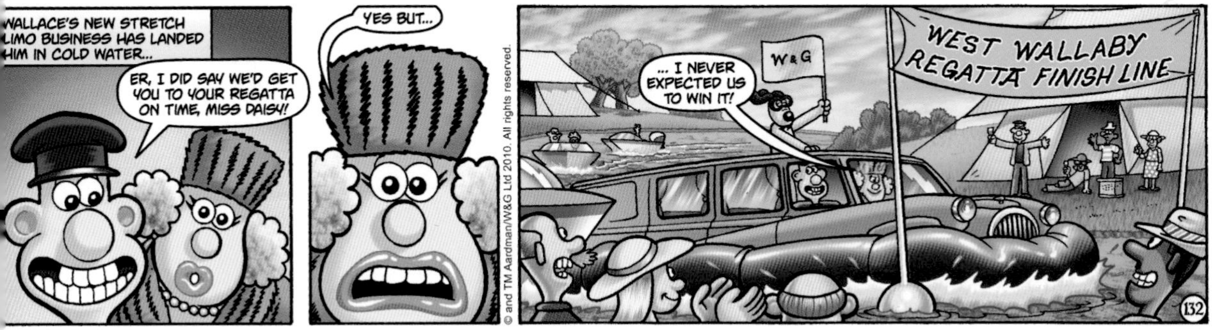
WALLACE'S NEW STRETCH LIMO BUSINESS HAS LANDED HIM IN COLD WATER...
ER, I DID SAY WE'D GET YOU TO YOUR REGATTA ON TIME, MISS DAISY!
YES BUT...
© and TM Aardman/W&G Ltd 2010. All rights reserved.
... I NEVER EXPECTED US TO WIN IT!
W&G
WEST WALLABY REGATTA FINISH LINE
132

The End

Wallace & Gromit - Gone Camping

by Aardman & Titan Comics

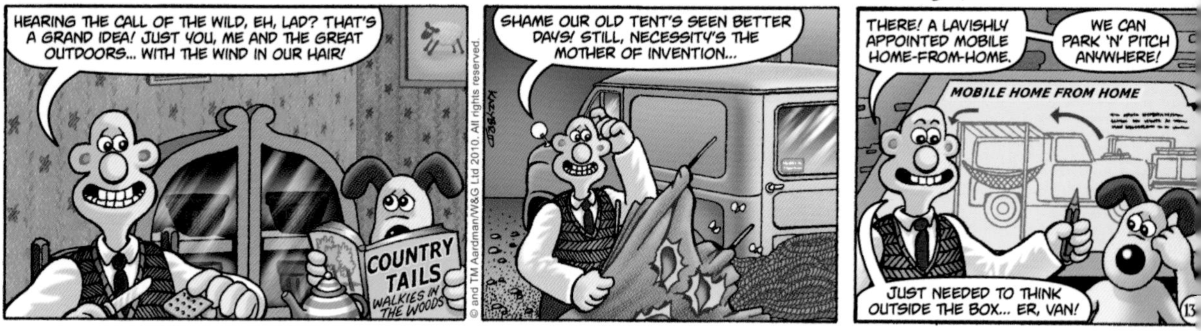
HEARING THE CALL OF THE WILD, EH, LAD? THAT'S A GRAND IDEA! JUST YOU, ME AND THE GREAT OUTDOORS... WITH THE WIND IN OUR HAIR!
COUNTRY TAILS
WALKIES IN THE WOODS
© and TM Aardman/W&G Ltd 2010. All rights reserved.
SHAME OUR OLD TENT'S SEEN BETTER DAYS! STILL, NECESSITY'S THE MOTHER OF INVENTION...
THERE! A LAVISHLY APPOINTED MOBILE HOME-FROM-HOME.
WE CAN PARK 'N' PITCH ANYWHERE!
MOBILE HOME FROM HOME
JUST NEEDED TO THINK OUTSIDE THE BOX... ER, VAN!

Wallace & Gromit - Gone Camping

by Aardman & Titan Comics

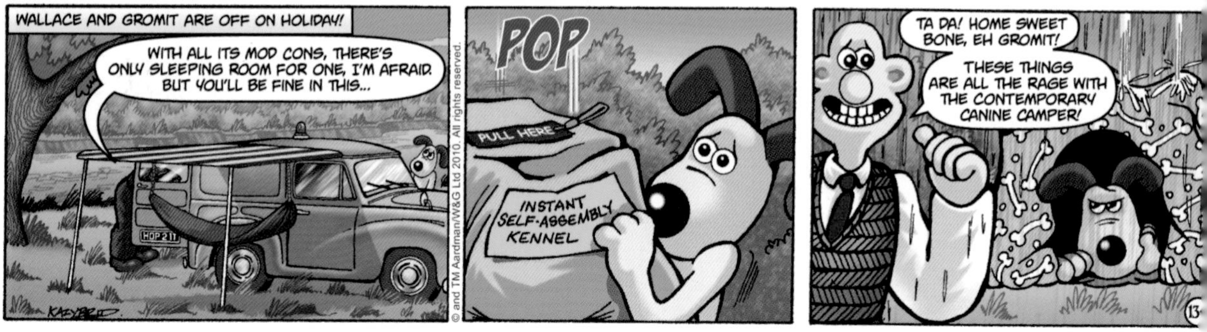
WALLACE AND GROMIT ARE OFF ON HOLIDAY!
WITH ALL ITS MOD CONS, THERE'S ONLY SLEEPING ROOM FOR ONE, I'M AFRAID. BUT YOU'LL BE FINE IN THIS...
HOP 211
© and TM Aardman/W&G Ltd 2010. All rights reserved.
POP
PULL HERE
INSTANT SELF-ASSEMBLY KENNEL
TA DA! HOME SWEET BONE, EH GROMIT!
THESE THINGS ARE ALL THE RAGE WITH THE CONTEMPORARY CANINE CAMPER!

Wallace & Gromit - Gone Camping

by Aardman & Titan Comics

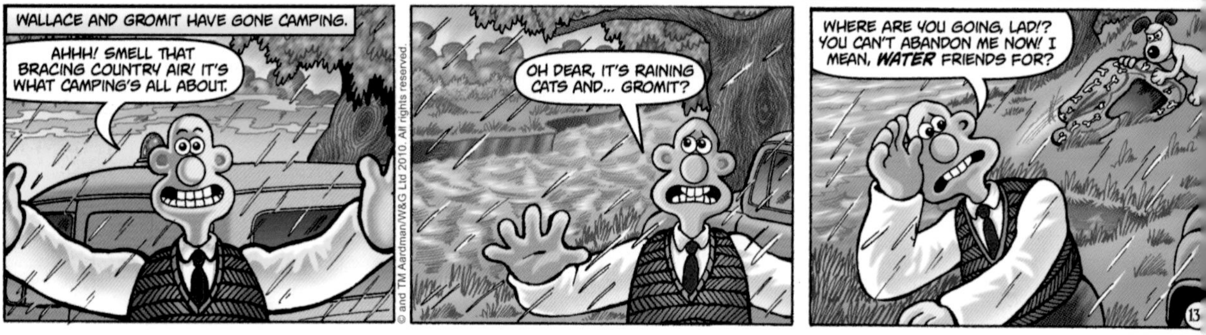
WALLACE AND GROMIT HAVE GONE CAMPING.
AHHH! SMELL THAT BRACING COUNTRY AIR! IT'S WHAT CAMPING'S ALL ABOUT.
© and TM Aardman/W&G Ltd 2010. All rights reserved.
OH DEAR, IT'S RAINING CATS AND... GROMIT?
WHERE ARE YOU GOING, LAD!? YOU CAN'T ABANDON ME NOW! I MEAN, WATER FRIENDS FOR?

Wallace & Gromit - Gone Camping by Aardman & Titan Comics

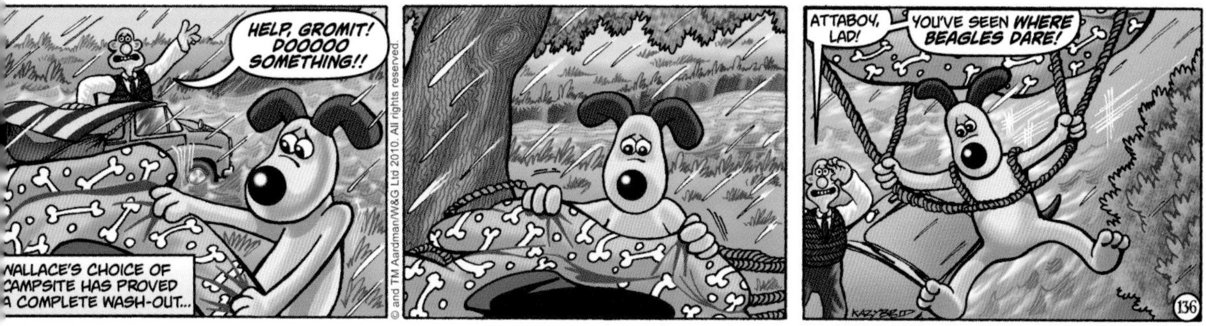
HELP, GROMIT! DOOOOO SOMETHING!!
WALLACE'S CHOICE OF CAMPSITE HAS PROVED A COMPLETE WASH-OUT...
ATTABOY, LAD!
YOU'VE SEEN WHERE BEAGLES DARE!
136

Wallace & Gromit - Gone Camping by Aardman & Titan Comics

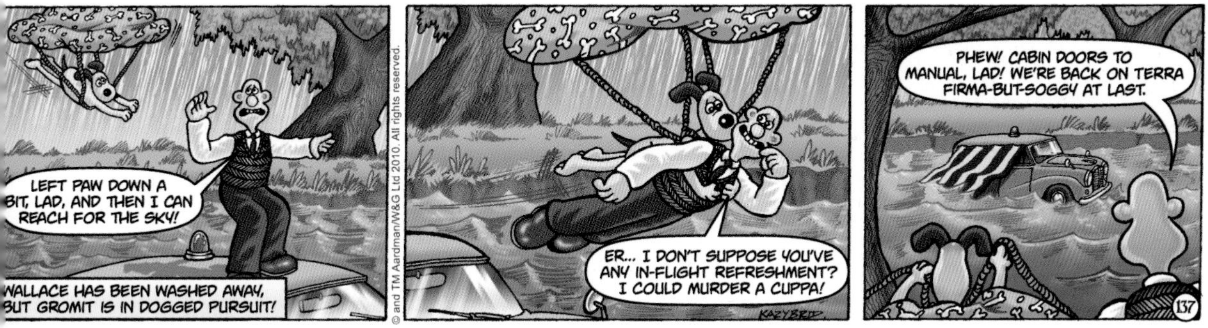
LEFT PAW DOWN A BIT, LAD, AND THEN I CAN REACH FOR THE SKY!
WALLACE HAS BEEN WASHED AWAY, BUT GROMIT IS IN DOGGED PURSUIT!
ER... I DON'T SUPPOSE YOU'VE ANY IN-FLIGHT REFRESHMENT? I COULD MURDER A CUPPA!
PHEW! CABIN DOORS TO MANUAL, LAD! WE'RE BACK ON TERRA FIRMA-BUT-SOGGY AT LAST.
137

© and TM Aardman/W&G Ltd 2010. All rights reserved.

Wallace & Gromit - Gone Camping by Aardman & Titan Comics

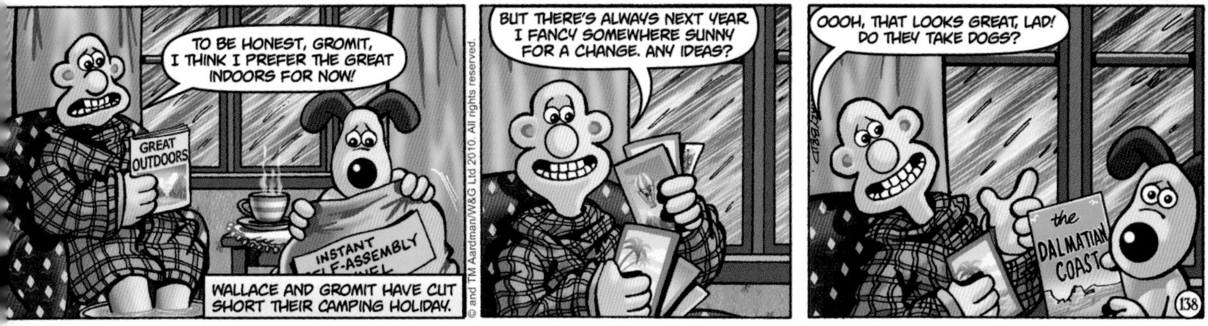
TO BE HONEST, GROMIT, I THINK I PREFER THE GREAT INDOORS FOR NOW!
GREAT OUTDOORS
INSTANT SELF-ASSEMBLY
WALLACE AND GROMIT HAVE CUT SHORT THEIR CAMPING HOLIDAY.
BUT THERE'S ALWAYS NEXT YEAR. I FANCY SOMEWHERE SUNNY FOR A CHANGE. ANY IDEAS?
OOOH, THAT LOOKS GREAT, LAD! DO THEY TAKE DOGS?
the DALMATIAN COAST
138

© and TM Aardman/W&G Ltd 2010. All rights reserved.

The End

Wallace & Gromit - Ghostblusters

by Aardman & Titan Comic

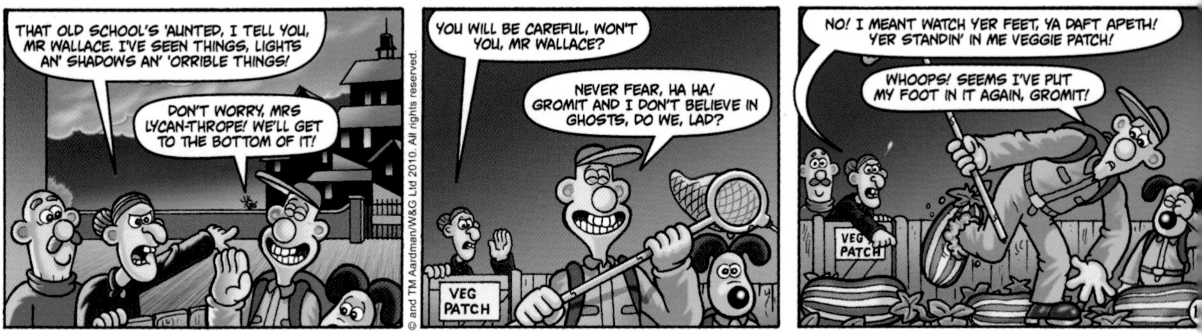

THAT OLD SCHOOL'S 'AUNTED, I TELL YOU, MR WALLACE. I'VE SEEN THINGS, LIGHTS AN' SHADOWS AN' 'ORRIBLE THINGS!
DON'T WORRY, MRS LYCAN-THROPE! WE'LL GET TO THE BOTTOM OF IT!
YOU WILL BE CAREFUL, WON'T YOU, MR WALLACE?
NEVER FEAR, HA HA! GROMIT AND I DON'T BELIEVE IN GHOSTS, DO WE, LAD?
VEG PATCH
NO! I MEANT WATCH YER FEET, YA DAFT APETH! YER STANDIN' IN ME VEGGIE PATCH!
WHOOPS! SEEMS I'VE PUT MY FOOT IN IT AGAIN, GROMIT!
VEG PATCH

Wallace & Gromit - Ghostblusters

by Aardman & Titan Comic

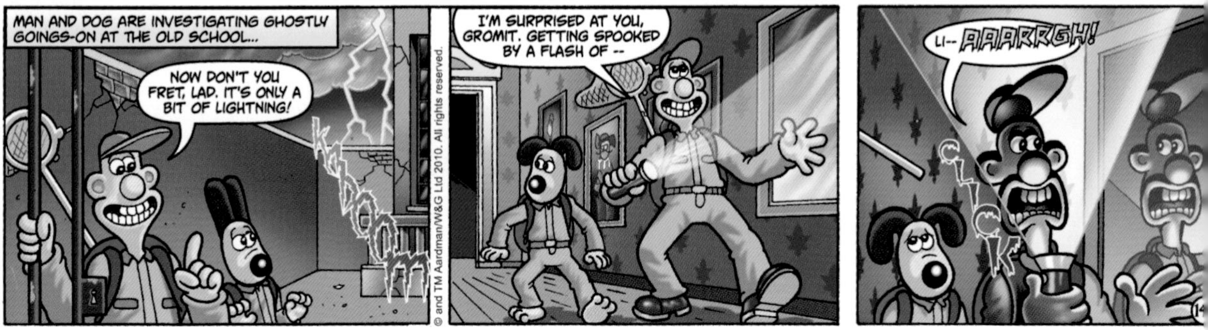

MAN AND DOG ARE INVESTIGATING GHOSTLY GOINGS-ON AT THE OLD SCHOOL...
NOW DON'T YOU FRET, LAD. IT'S ONLY A BIT OF LIGHTNING!
KABOOM
I'M SURPRISED AT YOU, GROMIT. GETTING SPOOKED BY A FLASH OF --
LI-- AAARRGH!
CLICK

Wallace & Gromit - Ghostblusters

by Aardman & Titan Comic

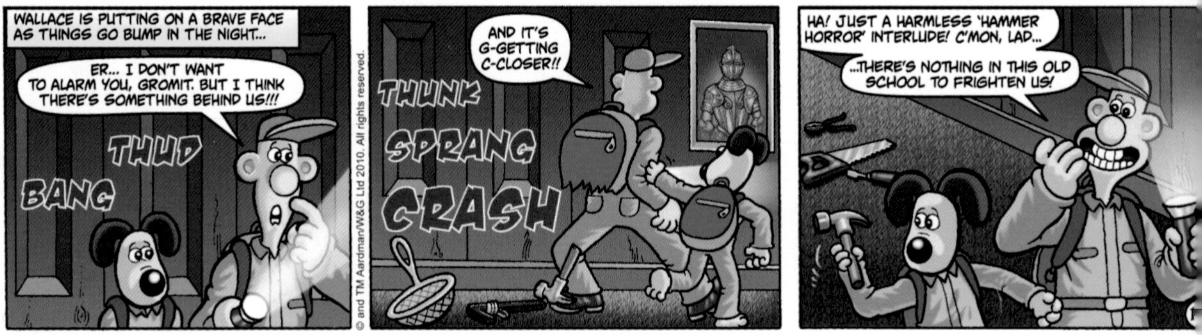

WALLACE IS PUTTING ON A BRAVE FACE AS THINGS GO BUMP IN THE NIGHT...
ER... I DON'T WANT TO ALARM YOU, GROMIT. BUT I THINK THERE'S SOMETHING BEHIND US!!!
THUD
BANG
AND IT'S G-GETTING C-CLOSER!!
THUNK
SPRANG
CRASH
HA! JUST A HARMLESS 'HAMMER HORROR' INTERLUDE! C'MON, LAD...
...THERE'S NOTHING IN THIS OLD SCHOOL TO FRIGHTEN US!

Wallace & Gromit - Ghostblusters **by Aardman & Titan Comics**

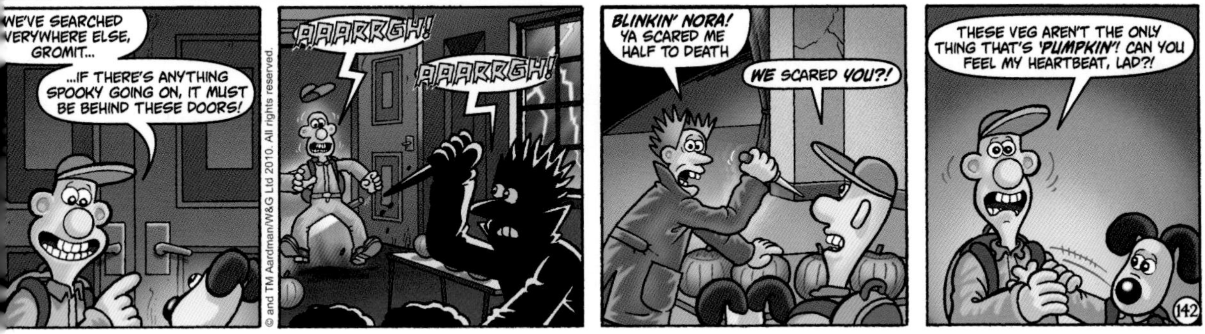

WE'VE SEARCHED VERYWHERE ELSE, GROMIT...
...IF THERE'S ANYTHING SPOOKY GOING ON, IT MUST BE BEHIND THESE DOORS!
AAARRGH!
AAARRGH!
© and TM Aardman/W&G Ltd 2010. All rights reserved.
BLINKIN' NORA! YA SCARED ME HALF TO DEATH
WE SCARED YOU?!
THESE VEG AREN'T THE ONLY THING THAT'S 'PUMPKIN'! CAN YOU FEEL MY HEARTBEAT, LAD?!
142

Wallace & Gromit - Ghostblusters **by Aardman & Titan Comics**

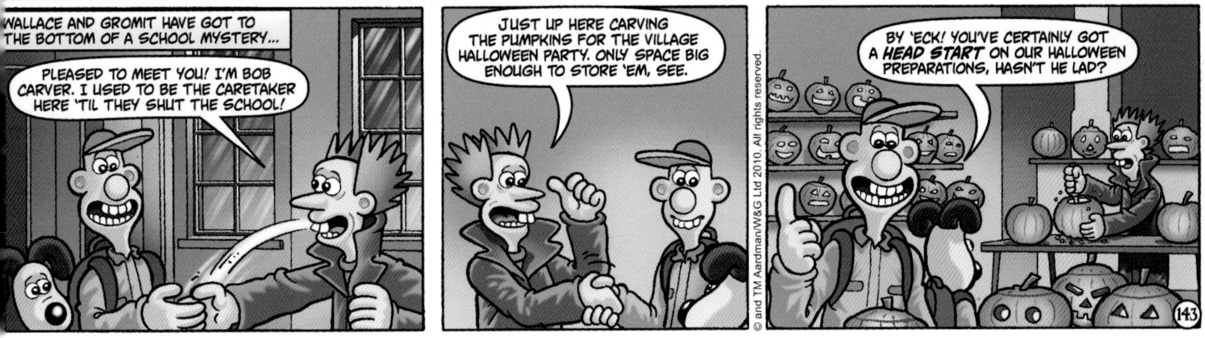

WALLACE AND GROMIT HAVE GOT TO THE BOTTOM OF A SCHOOL MYSTERY...
PLEASED TO MEET YOU! I'M BOB CARVER. I USED TO BE THE CARETAKER HERE 'TIL THEY SHUT THE SCHOOL!
JUST UP HERE CARVING THE PUMPKINS FOR THE VILLAGE HALLOWEEN PARTY. ONLY SPACE BIG ENOUGH TO STORE 'EM, SEE.
© and TM Aardman/W&G Ltd 2010. All rights reserved.
BY 'ECK! YOU'VE CERTAINLY GOT A HEAD START ON OUR HALLOWEEN PREPARATIONS, HASN'T HE LAD?
143

Wallace & Gromit - Ghostblusters **by Aardman & Titan Comics**

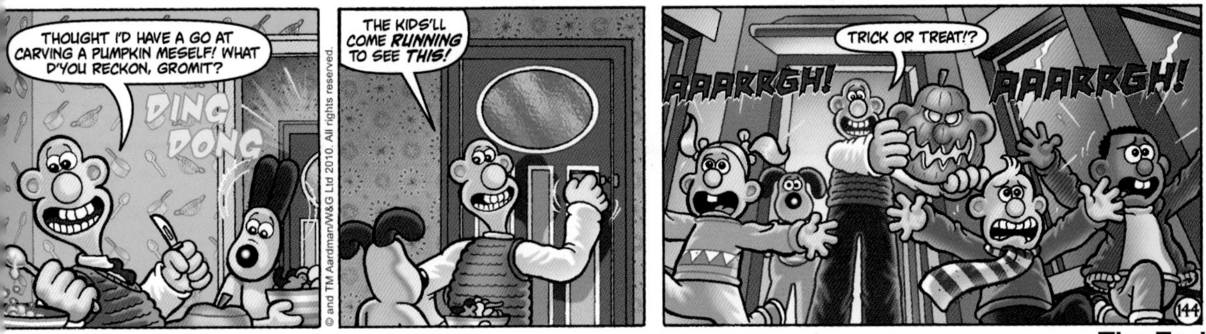

THOUGHT I'D HAVE A GO AT CARVING A PUMPKIN MESELF! WHAT D'YOU RECKON, GROMIT?
DING DONG
© and TM Aardman/W&G Ltd 2010. All rights reserved.
THE KIDS'LL COME RUNNING TO SEE THIS!
TRICK OR TREAT!?
AAARRGH!
AAARRGH!
144

The End

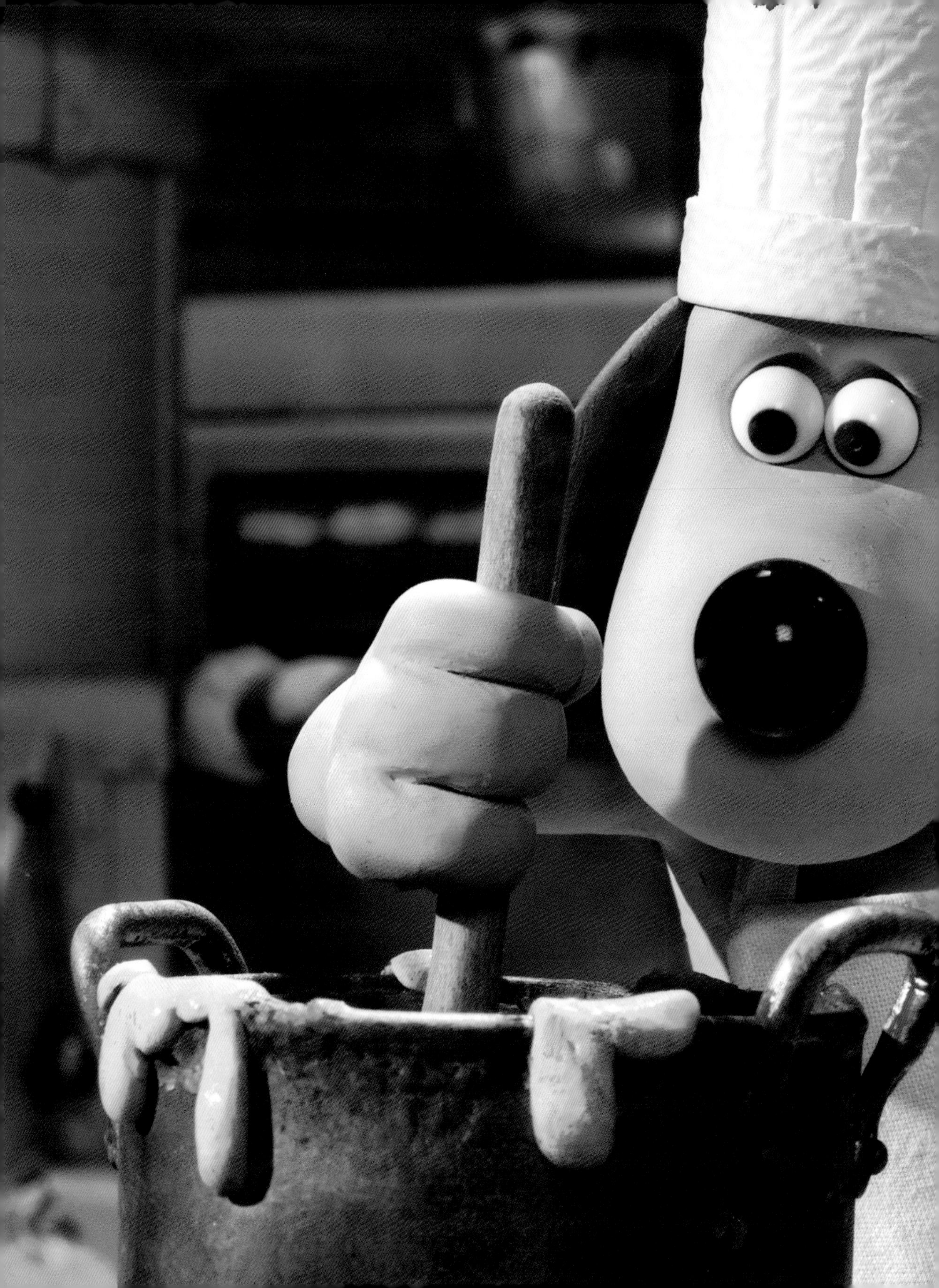

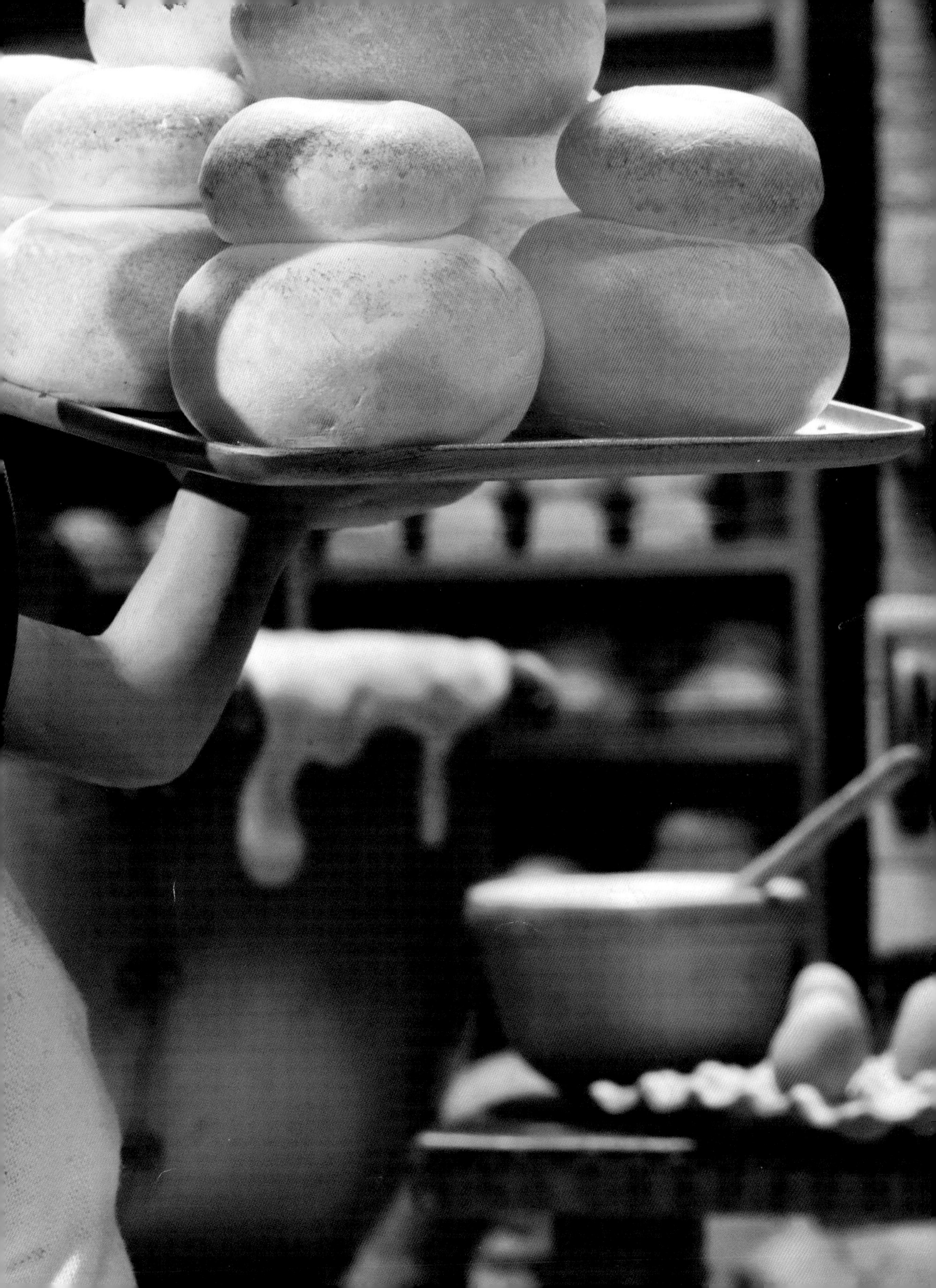

Wallace & Gromit - A Fridge Too Far

by Aardman & Titan Comic

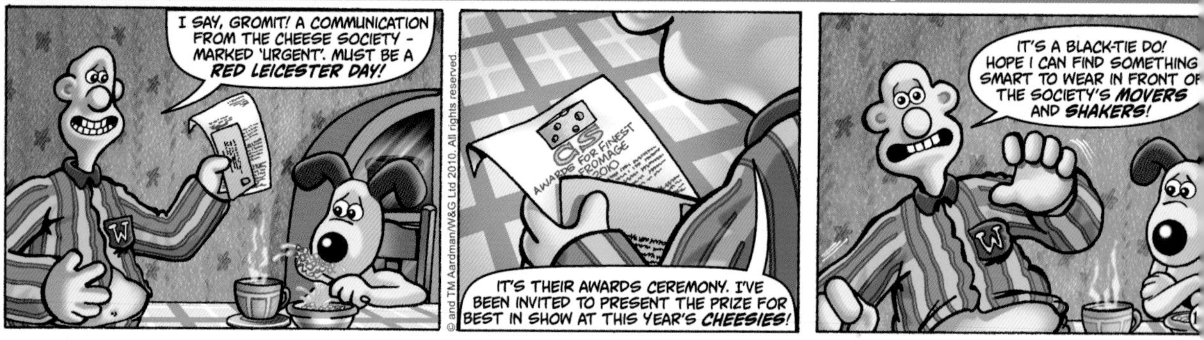
I SAY, GROMIT! A COMMUNICATION FROM THE CHEESE SOCIETY - MARKED 'URGENT'. MUST BE A RED LEICESTER DAY!
© and TM Aardman/W&G Ltd 2010. All rights reserved.
CS AWARDS FOR FINEST FROMAGE 2010
IT'S THEIR AWARDS CEREMONY. I'VE BEEN INVITED TO PRESENT THE PRIZE FOR BEST IN SHOW AT THIS YEAR'S CHEESIES!
IT'S A BLACK-TIE DO! HOPE I CAN FIND SOMETHING SMART TO WEAR IN FRONT OF THE SOCIETY'S MOVERS AND SHAKERS!

Wallace & Gromit - A Fridge Too Far

by Aardman & Titan Comic

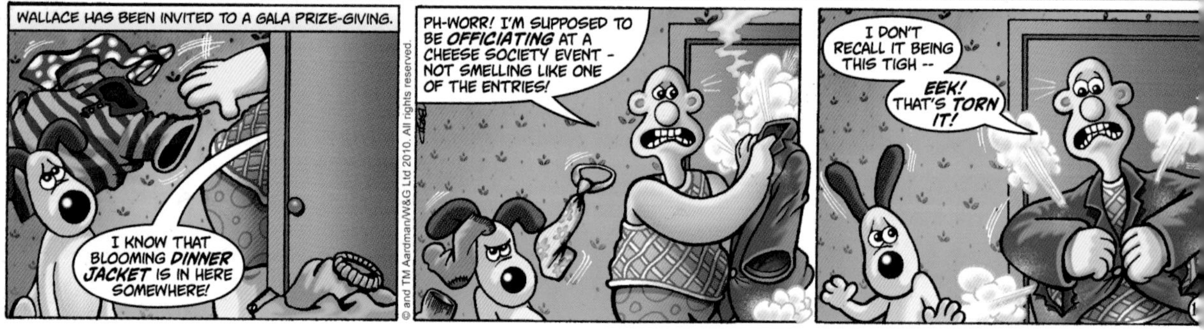
WALLACE HAS BEEN INVITED TO A GALA PRIZE-GIVING.
I KNOW THAT BLOOMING DINNER JACKET IS IN HERE SOMEWHERE!
© and TM Aardman/W&G Ltd 2010. All rights reserved.
PH-WORR! I'M SUPPOSED TO BE OFFICIATING AT A CHEESE SOCIETY EVENT - NOT SMELLING LIKE ONE OF THE ENTRIES!
I DON'T RECALL IT BEING THIS TIGH --
EEK! THAT'S TORN IT!

Wallace & Gromit - A Fridge Too Far

by Aardman & Titan Comic

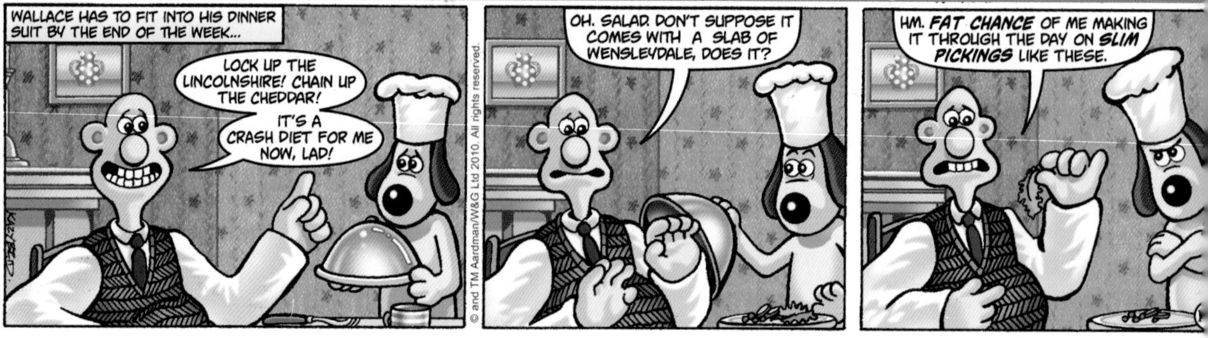
WALLACE HAS TO FIT INTO HIS DINNER SUIT BY THE END OF THE WEEK...
LOCK UP THE LINCOLNSHIRE! CHAIN UP THE CHEDDAR!
IT'S A CRASH DIET FOR ME NOW, LAD!
© and TM Aardman/W&G Ltd 2010. All rights reserved.
OH. SALAD. DON'T SUPPOSE IT COMES WITH A SLAB OF WENSLEYDALE, DOES IT?
HM. FAT CHANCE OF ME MAKING IT THROUGH THE DAY ON SLIM PICKINGS LIKE THESE.

Wallace & Gromit - A Fridge Too Far by Aardman & Titan Comics

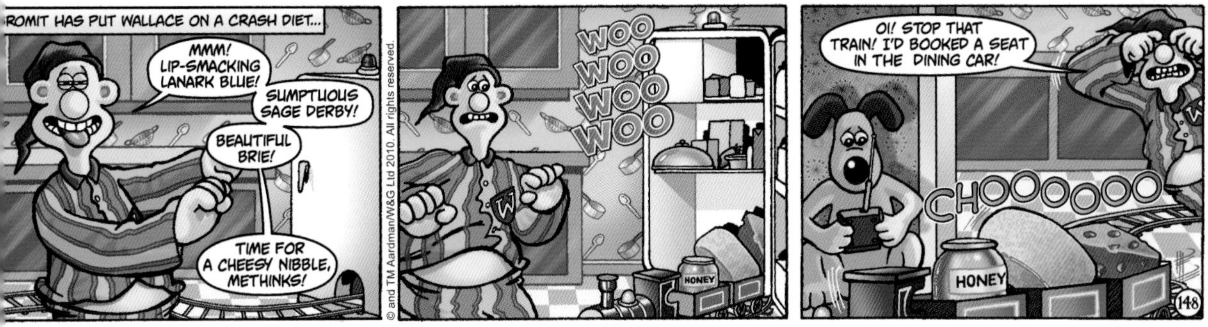

ROMIT HAS PUT WALLACE ON A CRASH DIET...
MMM! LIP-SMACKING LANARK BLUE!
SUMPTUOUS SAGE DERBY!
BEAUTIFUL BRIE!
TIME FOR A CHEESY NIBBLE, METHINKS!
© and TM Aardman/W&G Ltd 2010. All rights reserved.
WOO WOO WOO WOO
HONEY
OI! STOP THAT TRAIN! I'D BOOKED A SEAT IN THE DINING CAR!
CHOOOOOOO
HONEY
148

Wallace & Gromit - A Fridge Too Far by Aardman & Titan Comics

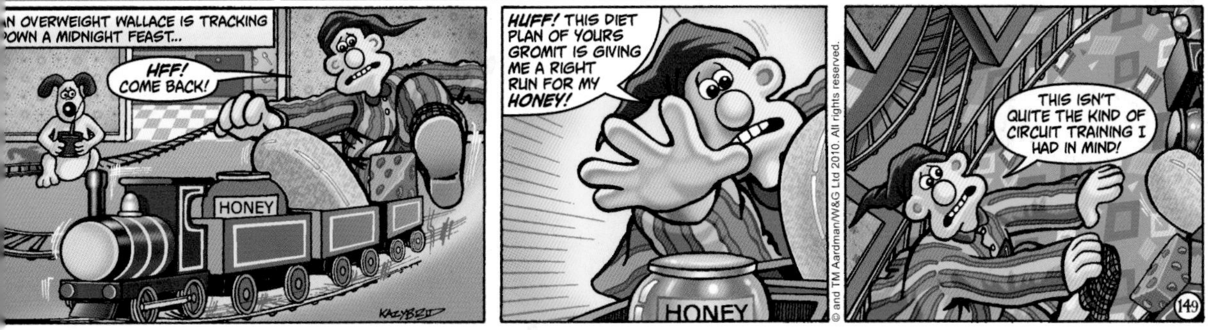

N OVERWEIGHT WALLACE IS TRACKING OWN A MIDNIGHT FEAST...
HFF! COME BACK!
HONEY
HUFF! THIS DIET PLAN OF YOURS GROMIT IS GIVING ME A RIGHT RUN FOR MY HONEY!
HONEY
© and TM Aardman/W&G Ltd 2010. All rights reserved.
THIS ISN'T QUITE THE KIND OF CIRCUIT TRAINING I HAD IN MIND!
149

Wallace & Gromit - A Fridge Too Far by Aardman & Titan Comics

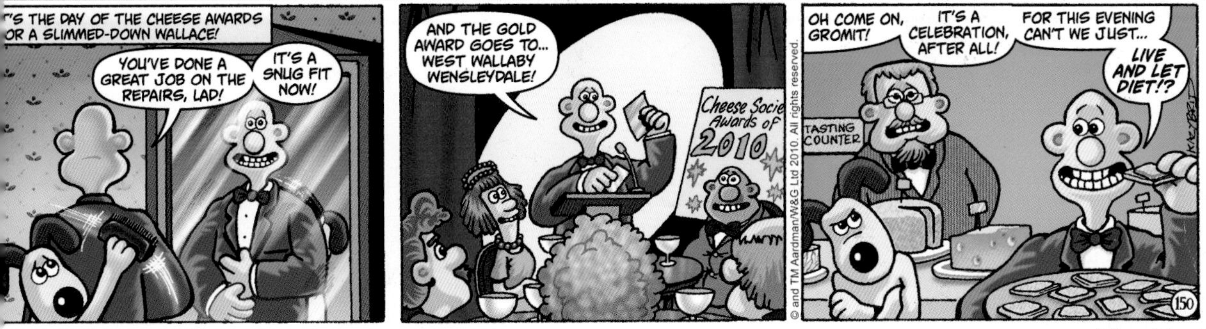

'S THE DAY OF THE CHEESE AWARDS OR A SLIMMED-DOWN WALLACE!
YOU'VE DONE A GREAT JOB ON THE REPAIRS, LAD!
IT'S A SNUG FIT NOW!
AND THE GOLD AWARD GOES TO... WEST WALLABY WENSLEYDALE!
Cheese Socie Awards of 2010
© and TM Aardman/W&G Ltd 2010. All rights reserved.
OH COME ON, GROMIT!
IT'S A CELEBRATION, AFTER ALL!
FOR THIS EVENING CAN'T WE JUST...
LIVE AND LET DIET!?
TASTING COUNTER
150

The End

Wallace & Gromit - Funnies #2

by Aardman & Titan Comic

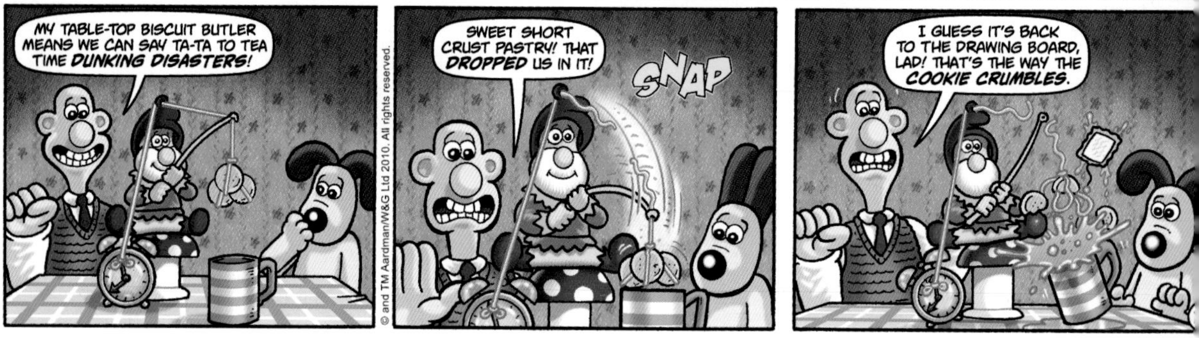

MY TABLE-TOP BISCUIT BUTLER MEANS WE CAN SAY TA-TA TO TEA TIME DUNKING DISASTERS!
SWEET SHORT CRUST PASTRY! THAT DROPPED US IN IT!
SNAP
I GUESS IT'S BACK TO THE DRAWING BOARD, LAD! THAT'S THE WAY THE COOKIE CRUMBLES.

Wallace & Gromit - Funnies #2

by Aardman & Titan Comic

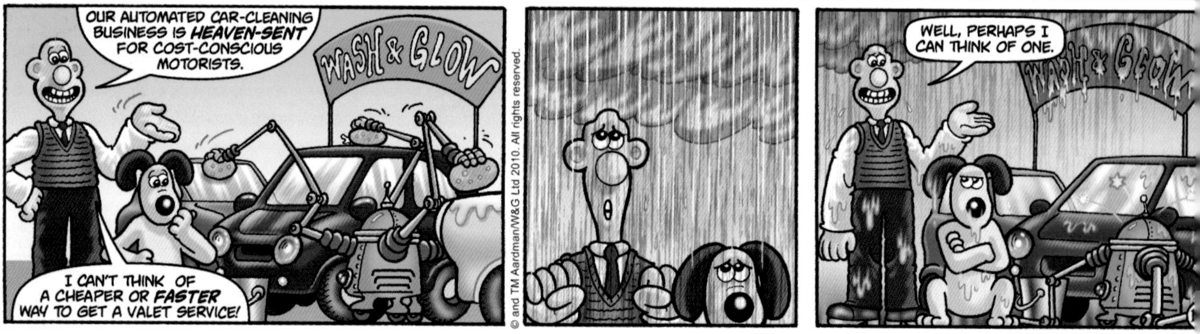

OUR AUTOMATED CAR-CLEANING BUSINESS IS HEAVEN-SENT FOR COST-CONSCIOUS MOTORISTS.
WASH & GLOW
I CAN'T THINK OF A CHEAPER OR FASTER WAY TO GET A VALET SERVICE!
WELL, PERHAPS I CAN THINK OF ONE.

Wallace & Gromit - Funnies #2

by Aardman & Titan Comic

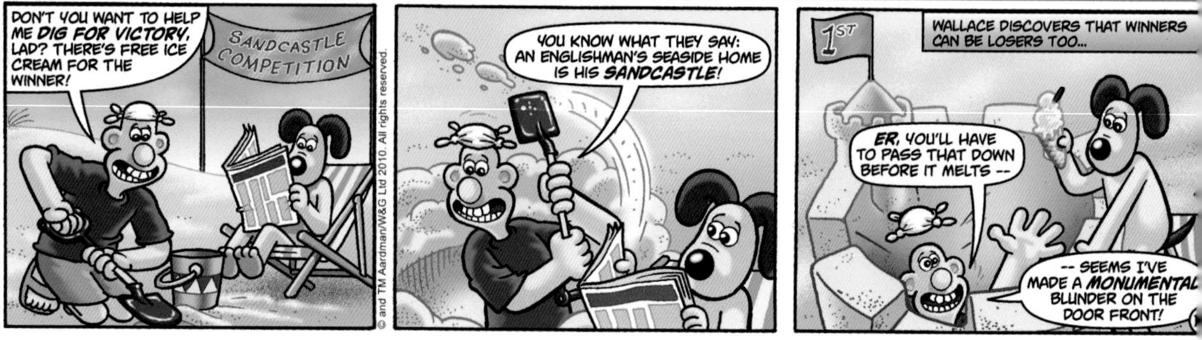

DON'T YOU WANT TO HELP ME DIG FOR VICTORY, LAD? THERE'S FREE ICE CREAM FOR THE WINNER!
SANDCASTLE COMPETITION
YOU KNOW WHAT THEY SAY: AN ENGLISHMAN'S SEASIDE HOME IS HIS SANDCASTLE!
WALLACE DISCOVERS THAT WINNERS CAN BE LOSERS TOO...
1ST
ER, YOU'LL HAVE TO PASS THAT DOWN BEFORE IT MELTS --
-- SEEMS I'VE MADE A MONUMENTAL BLUNDER ON THE DOOR FRONT!

Wallace & Gromit - Funnies #2 by Aardman & Titan Comics

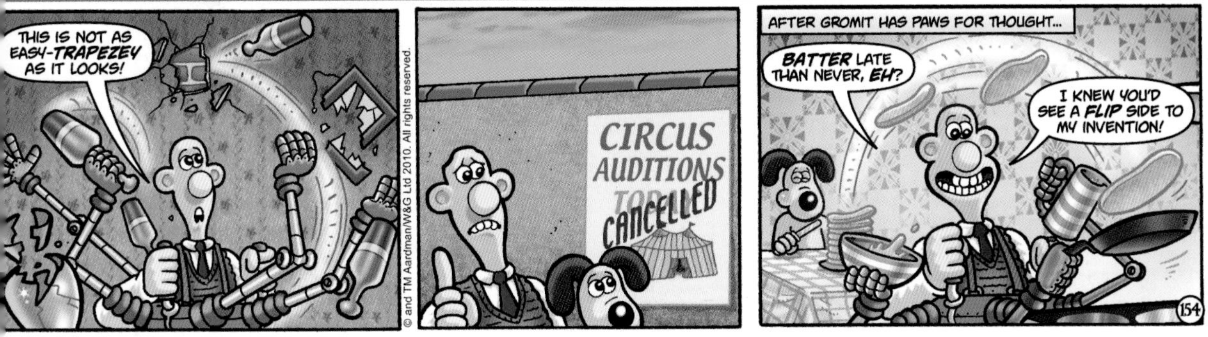

THIS IS NOT AS EASY-*TRAPEZEY* AS IT LOOKS!
© and TM Aardman/W&G Ltd 2010. All rights reserved.
CIRCUS AUDITIONS
CANCELLED
AFTER GROMIT HAS PAWS FOR THOUGHT...
BATTER LATE THAN NEVER, *EH*?
I KNEW YOU'D SEE A *FLIP* SIDE TO MY INVENTION!
154

Wallace & Gromit - Funnies #2 by Aardman & Titan Comics

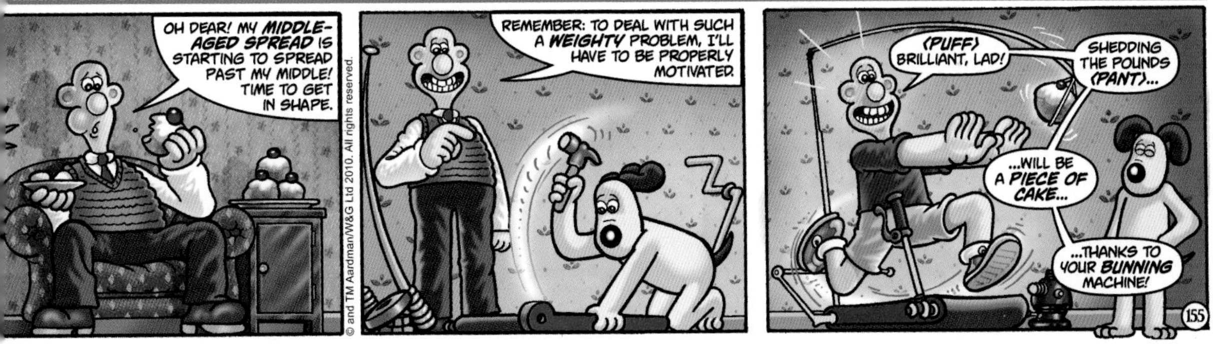

OH DEAR! MY *MIDDLE-AGED SPREAD* IS STARTING TO SPREAD PAST MY MIDDLE! TIME TO GET IN SHAPE.
© and TM Aardman/W&G Ltd 2010. All rights reserved.
REMEMBER: TO DEAL WITH SUCH A *WEIGHTY* PROBLEM, I'LL HAVE TO BE PROPERLY MOTIVATED.
(PUFF) BRILLIANT, LAD!
SHEDDING THE POUNDS *(PANT)*...
...WILL BE A *PIECE OF CAKE*...
...THANKS TO YOUR *BUNNING* MACHINE!
155

Wallace & Gromit - Funnies #2 by Aardman & Titan Comics

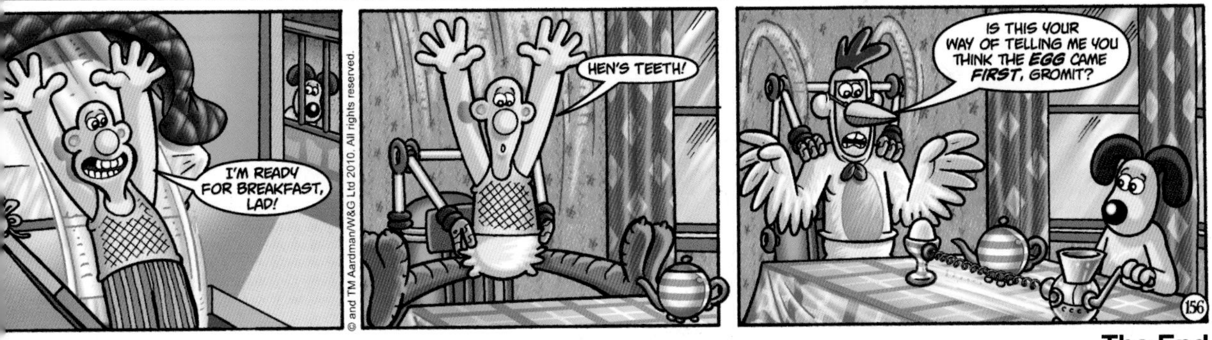

I'M READY FOR BREAKFAST, LAD!
© and TM Aardman/W&G Ltd 2010. All rights reserved.
HEN'S TEETH!
IS THIS YOUR WAY OF TELLING ME YOU THINK THE *EGG* CAME *FIRST*, GROMIT?
156

The End

Wallace & Gromit - Bonkers About Conkers by Aardman & Titan Comic

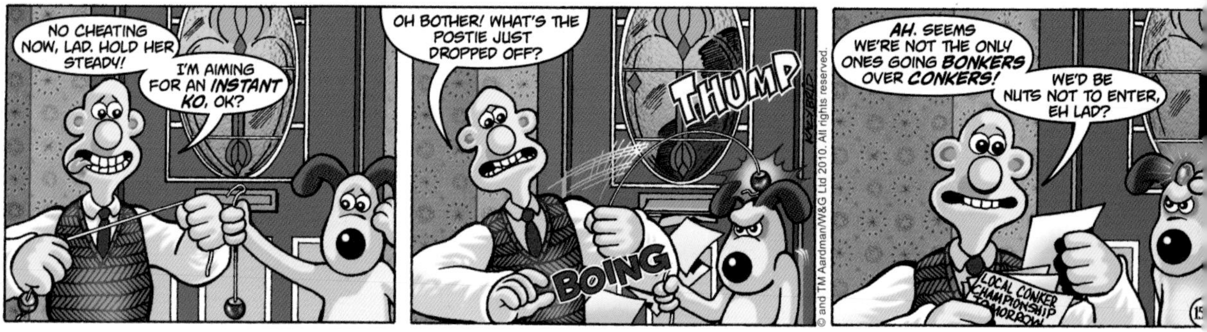
NO CHEATING NOW, LAD. HOLD HER STEADY!
I'M AIMING FOR AN INSTANT KO, OK?
OH BOTHER! WHAT'S THE POSTIE JUST DROPPED OFF?
THUMP
BOING
© and TM Aardman/W&G Ltd 2010. All rights reserved.
AH. SEEMS WE'RE NOT THE ONLY ONES GOING BONKERS OVER CONKERS!
WE'D BE NUTS NOT TO ENTER, EH LAD?
LOCAL CONKER CHAMPIONSHIP TOMORROW

Wallace & Gromit - Bonkers About Conkers by Aardman & Titan Comic

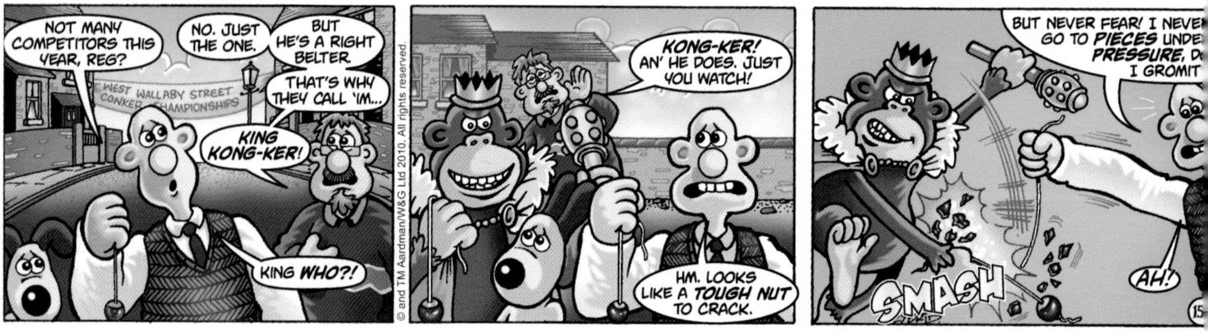
NOT MANY COMPETITORS THIS YEAR, REG?
NO. JUST THE ONE.
BUT HE'S A RIGHT BELTER.
THAT'S WHY THEY CALL 'IM...
KING KONG-KER!
KING WHO?!
WEST WALLABY STREET CONKER CHAMPIONSHIPS
© and TM Aardman/W&G Ltd 2010. All rights reserved.
KONG-KER! AN' HE DOES. JUST YOU WATCH!
HM. LOOKS LIKE A TOUGH NUT TO CRACK.
BUT NEVER FEAR! I NEVE GO TO PIECES UNDE PRESSURE, D I GROMIT
SMASH
AH!

Wallace & Gromit - Bonkers About Conkers by Aardman & Titan Comic

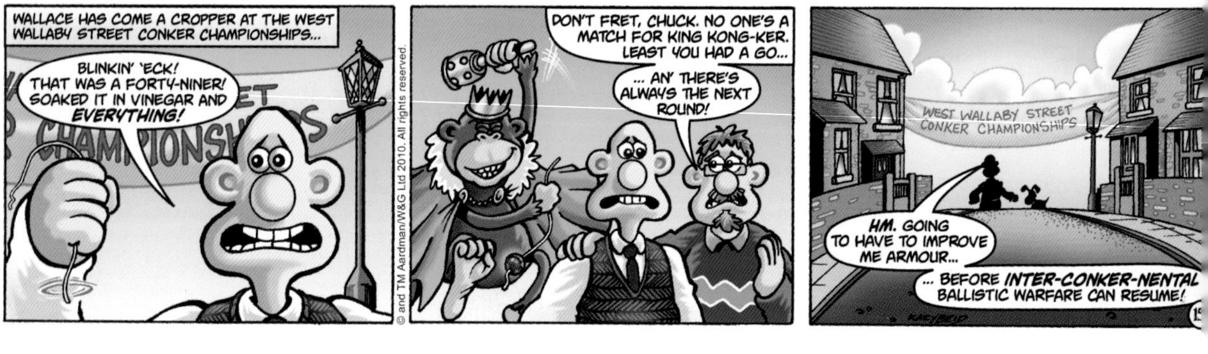
WALLACE HAS COME A CROPPER AT THE WEST WALLABY STREET CONKER CHAMPIONSHIPS...
BLINKIN' 'ECK! THAT WAS A FORTY-NINER! SOAKED IT IN VINEGAR AND EVERYTHING!
© and TM Aardman/W&G Ltd 2010. All rights reserved.
DON'T FRET, CHUCK. NO ONE'S A MATCH FOR KING KONG-KER. LEAST YOU HAD A GO...
... AN' THERE'S ALWAYS THE NEXT ROUND!
WEST WALLABY STREET CONKER CHAMPIONSHIPS
HM. GOING TO HAVE TO IMPROVE ME ARMOUR...
... BEFORE INTER-CONKER-NENTAL BALLISTIC WARFARE CAN RESUME!

Wallace & Gromit - Bonkers About Conkers — by Aardman & Titan Comics

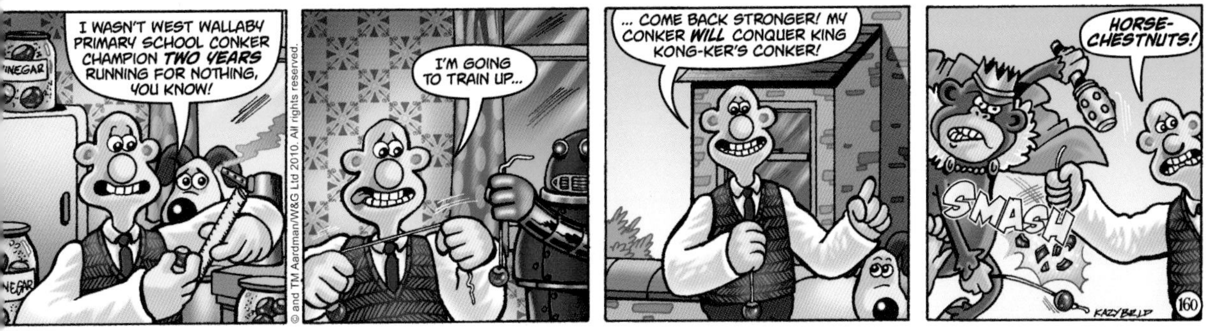
I WASN'T WEST WALLABY PRIMARY SCHOOL CONKER CHAMPION TWO YEARS RUNNING FOR NOTHING, YOU KNOW!
VINEGAR
I'M GOING TO TRAIN UP...
... COME BACK STRONGER! MY CONKER WILL CONQUER KING KONG-KER'S CONKER!
HORSE-CHESTNUTS!
SMASH
160
© and TM Aardman/W&G Ltd 2010. All rights reserved.

Wallace & Gromit - Bonkers About Conkers — by Aardman & Titan Comics

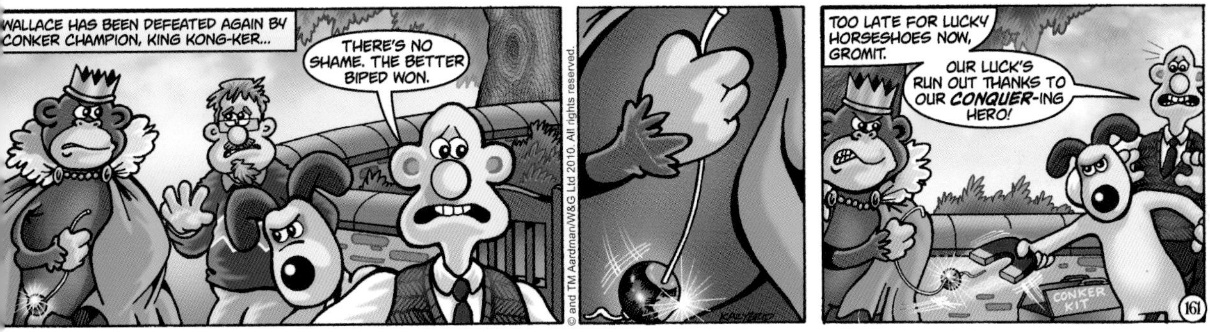
WALLACE HAS BEEN DEFEATED AGAIN BY CONKER CHAMPION, KING KONG-KER...
THERE'S NO SHAME. THE BETTER BIPED WON.
TOO LATE FOR LUCKY HORSESHOES NOW, GROMIT.
OUR LUCK'S RUN OUT THANKS TO OUR CONQUER-ING HERO!
CONKER KIT
161
© and TM Aardman/W&G Ltd 2010. All rights reserved.

Wallace & Gromit - Bonkers About Conkers — by Aardman & Titan Comics

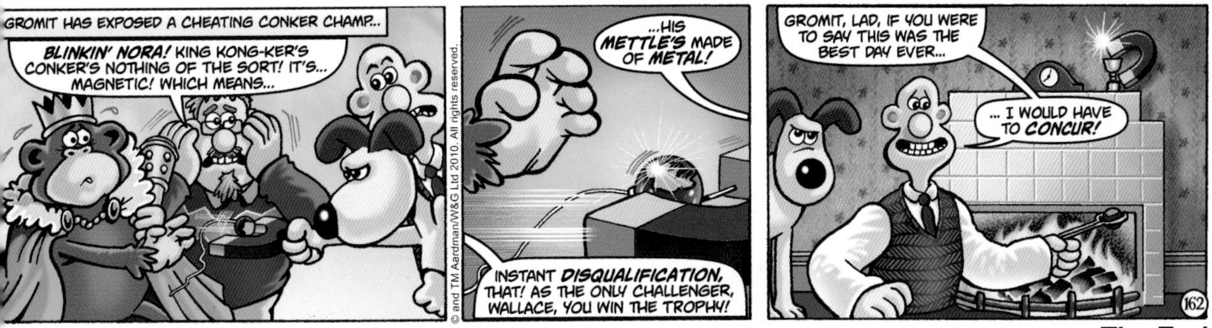
GROMIT HAS EXPOSED A CHEATING CONKER CHAMP..
BLINKIN' NORA! KING KONG-KER'S CONKER'S NOTHING OF THE SORT! IT'S... MAGNETIC! WHICH MEANS...
...HIS METTLE'S MADE OF METAL!
INSTANT DISQUALIFICATION, THAT! AS THE ONLY CHALLENGER, WALLACE, YOU WIN THE TROPHY!
GROMIT, LAD, IF YOU WERE TO SAY THIS WAS THE BEST DAY EVER...
... I WOULD HAVE TO CONCUR!
162
© and TM Aardman/W&G Ltd 2010. All rights reserved.

The End

Wallace & Gromit - A Family Affair

by Aardman & Titan Comic

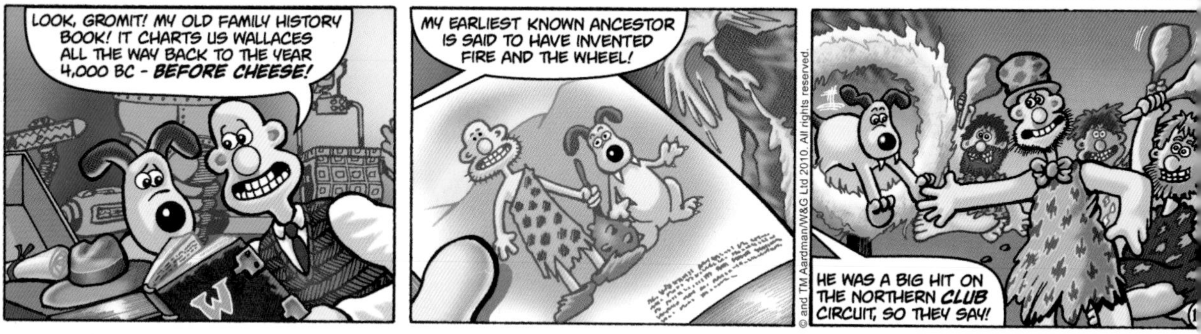
LOOK, GROMIT! MY OLD FAMILY HISTORY BOOK! IT CHARTS US WALLACES ALL THE WAY BACK TO THE YEAR 4,000 BC - BEFORE CHEESE!
MY EARLIEST KNOWN ANCESTOR IS SAID TO HAVE INVENTED FIRE AND THE WHEEL!
© and TM Aardman/W&G Ltd 2010. All rights reserved.
HE WAS A BIG HIT ON THE NORTHERN CLUB CIRCUIT, SO THEY SAY!

Wallace & Gromit - A Family Affair

by Aardman & Titan Comic

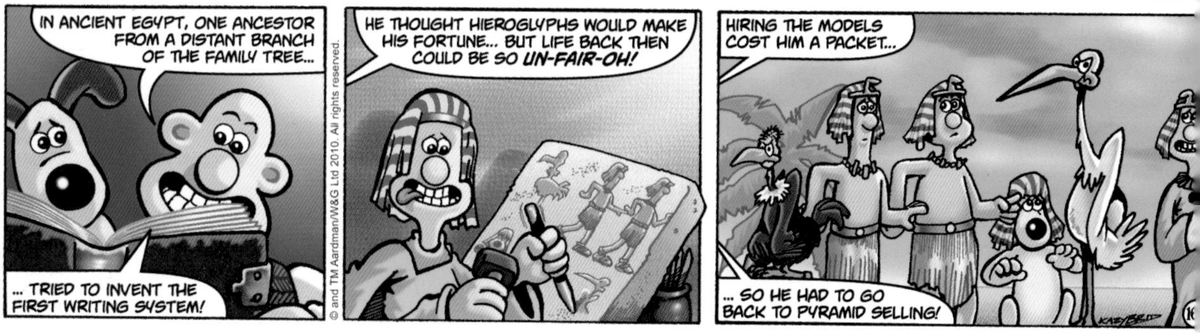
IN ANCIENT EGYPT, ONE ANCESTOR FROM A DISTANT BRANCH OF THE FAMILY TREE...
... TRIED TO INVENT THE FIRST WRITING SYSTEM!
© and TM Aardman/W&G Ltd 2010. All rights reserved.
HE THOUGHT HIEROGLYPHS WOULD MAKE HIS FORTUNE... BUT LIFE BACK THEN COULD BE SO UN-FAIR-OH!
HIRING THE MODELS COST HIM A PACKET...
... SO HE HAD TO GO BACK TO PYRAMID SELLING!

Wallace & Gromit - A Family Affair

by Aardman & Titan Comic

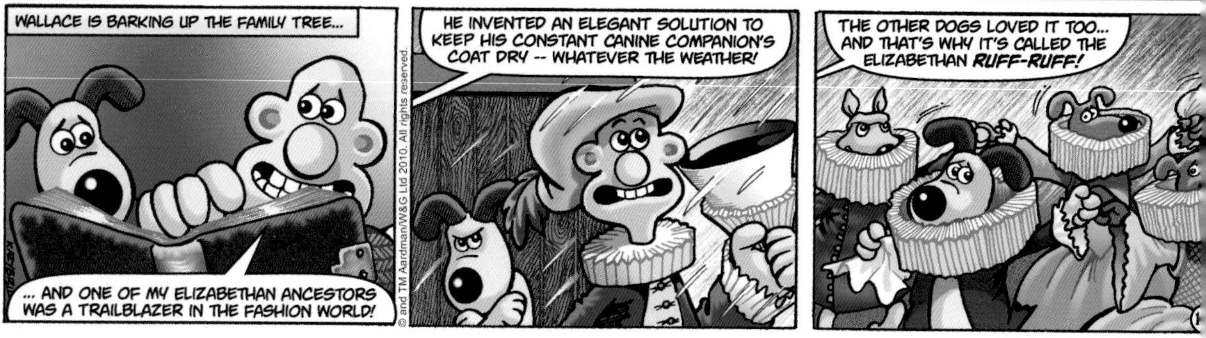
WALLACE IS BARKING UP THE FAMILY TREE...
... AND ONE OF MY ELIZABETHAN ANCESTORS WAS A TRAILBLAZER IN THE FASHION WORLD!
© and TM Aardman/W&G Ltd 2010. All rights reserved.
HE INVENTED AN ELEGANT SOLUTION TO KEEP HIS CONSTANT CANINE COMPANION'S COAT DRY -- WHATEVER THE WEATHER!
THE OTHER DOGS LOVED IT TOO... AND THAT'S WHY IT'S CALLED THE ELIZABETHAN RUFF-RUFF!

Wallace & Gromit - A Family Affair by Aardman & Titan Comics

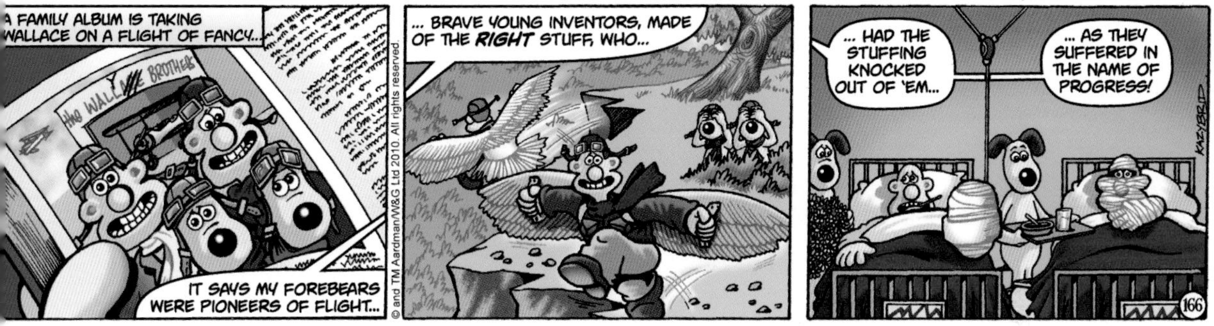
A FAMILY ALBUM IS TAKING WALLACE ON A FLIGHT OF FANCY...
IT SAYS MY FOREBEARS WERE PIONEERS OF FLIGHT...
© and TM Aardman/W&G Ltd 2010. All rights reserved.
... BRAVE YOUNG INVENTORS, MADE OF THE *RIGHT* STUFF, WHO...
... HAD THE STUFFING KNOCKED OUT OF 'EM...
... AS THEY SUFFERED IN THE NAME OF PROGRESS!
166

Wallace & Gromit - A Family Affair by Aardman & Titan Comics

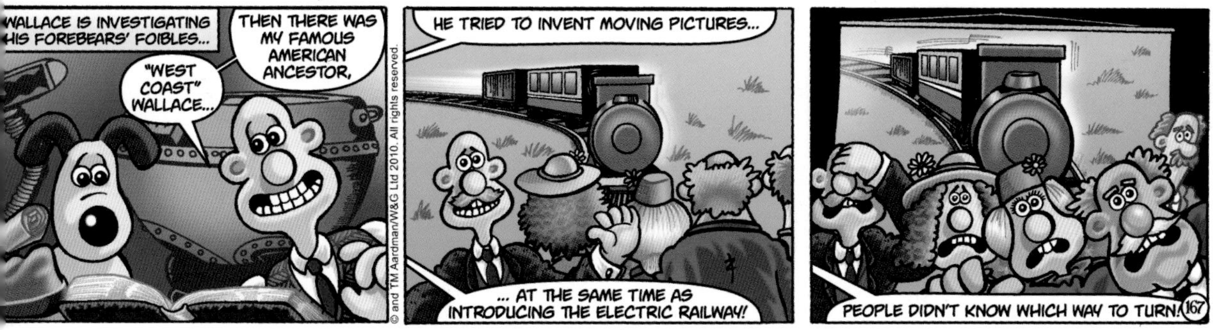
WALLACE IS INVESTIGATING HIS FOREBEARS' FOIBLES...
THEN THERE WAS MY FAMOUS AMERICAN ANCESTOR,
"WEST COAST" WALLACE...
© and TM Aardman/W&G Ltd 2010. All rights reserved.
HE TRIED TO INVENT MOVING PICTURES...
... AT THE SAME TIME AS INTRODUCING THE ELECTRIC RAILWAY!
PEOPLE DIDN'T KNOW WHICH WAY TO TURN!
167

Wallace & Gromit - A Family Affair by Aardman & Titan Comics

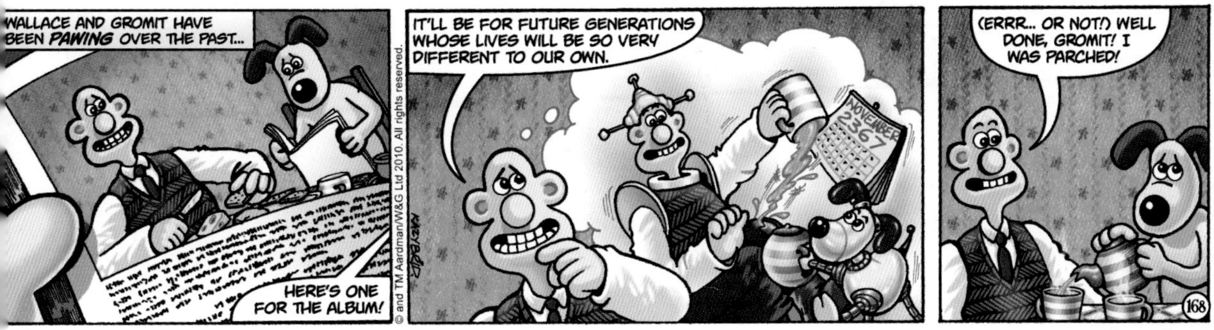
WALLACE AND GROMIT HAVE BEEN *PAWING* OVER THE PAST...
HERE'S ONE FOR THE ALBUM!
© and TM Aardman/W&G Ltd 2010. All rights reserved.
IT'LL BE FOR FUTURE GENERATIONS WHOSE LIVES WILL BE SO VERY DIFFERENT TO OUR OWN.
NOVEMBER 2367
(ERRR... OR NOT!) WELL DONE, GROMIT! I WAS PARCHED!
168

The End

Wallace & Gromit - Strictly Wallace

by Aardman & Titan Comics

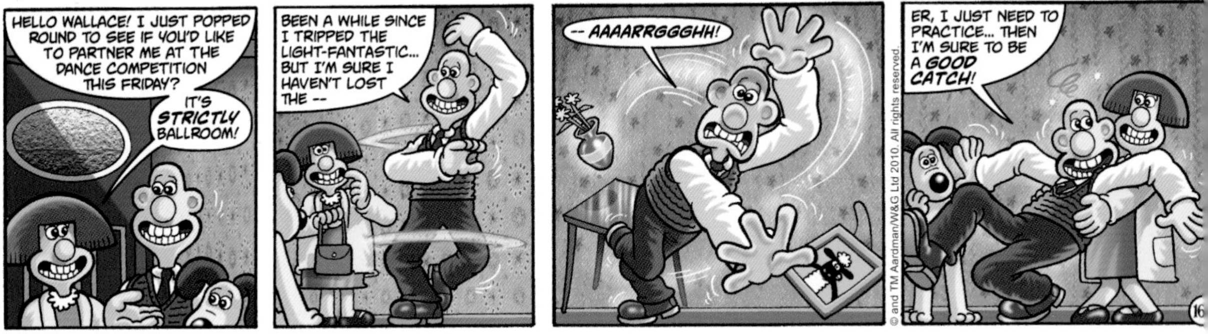
HELLO WALLACE! I JUST POPPED ROUND TO SEE IF YOU'D LIKE TO PARTNER ME AT THE DANCE COMPETITION THIS FRIDAY?
IT'S STRICTLY BALLROOM!
BEEN A WHILE SINCE I TRIPPED THE LIGHT-FANTASTIC... BUT I'M SURE I HAVEN'T LOST THE --
-- AAAARRGGGHH!
© and TM Aardman/W&G Ltd 2010. All rights reserved.
ER, I JUST NEED TO PRACTICE... THEN I'M SURE TO BE A GOOD CATCH!
16

Wallace & Gromit - Strictly Wallace

by Aardman & Titan Comics

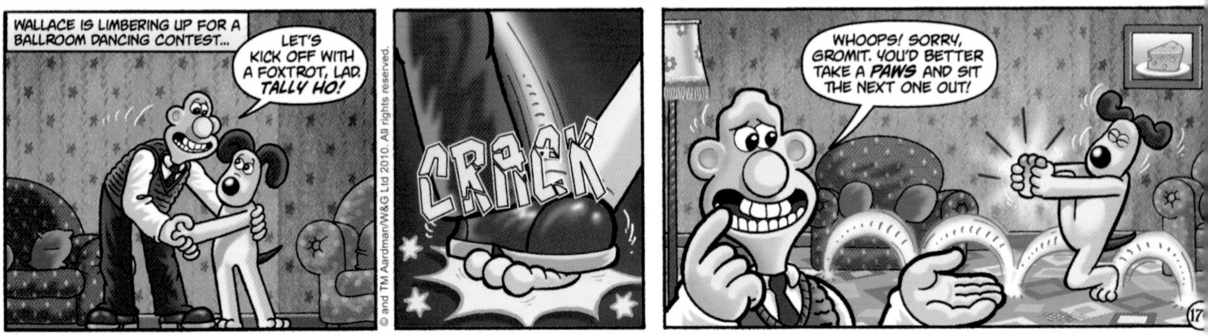
WALLACE IS LIMBERING UP FOR A BALLROOM DANCING CONTEST...
LET'S KICK OFF WITH A FOXTROT, LAD. TALLY HO!
© and TM Aardman/W&G Ltd 2010. All rights reserved.
CRACK
WHOOPS! SORRY, GROMIT. YOU'D BETTER TAKE A PAWS AND SIT THE NEXT ONE OUT!
17

Wallace & Gromit - Strictly Wallace

by Aardman & Titan Comics

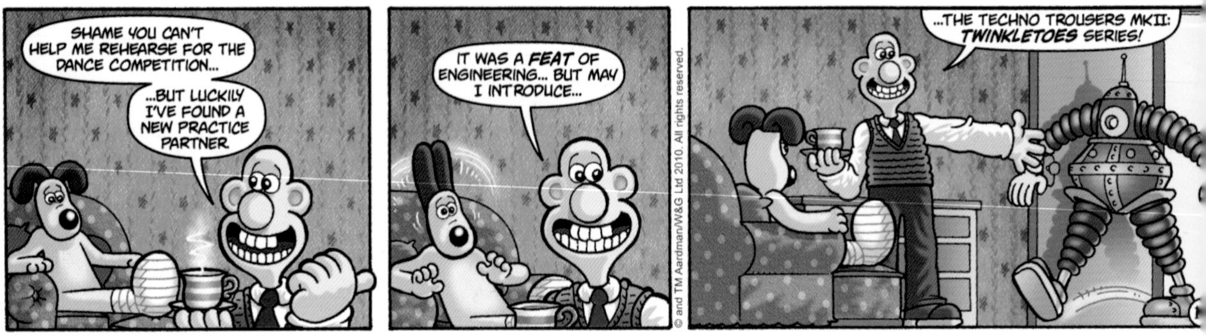
SHAME YOU CAN'T HELP ME REHEARSE FOR THE DANCE COMPETITION...
...BUT LUCKILY I'VE FOUND A NEW PRACTICE PARTNER.
IT WAS A FEAT OF ENGINEERING... BUT MAY I INTRODUCE...
© and TM Aardman/W&G Ltd 2010. All rights reserved.
...THE TECHNO TROUSERS MKII: TWINKLETOES SERIES!

Wallace & Gromit - Strictly Wallace by Aardman & Titan Comics

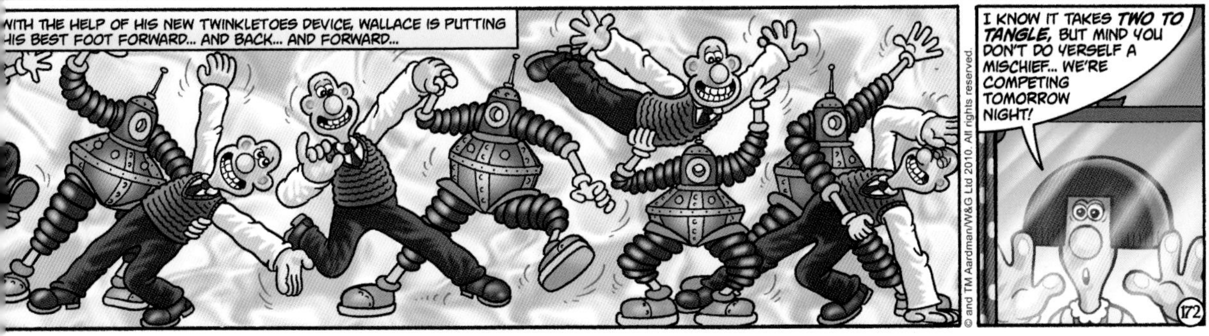
WITH THE HELP OF HIS NEW TWINKLETOES DEVICE, WALLACE IS PUTTING HIS BEST FOOT FORWARD... AND BACK... AND FORWARD...
I KNOW IT TAKES **TWO TO TANGLE,** BUT MIND YOU DON'T DO YERSELF A MISCHIEF... WE'RE COMPETING TOMORROW NIGHT!
172

Wallace & Gromit - Strictly Wallace by Aardman & Titan Comics

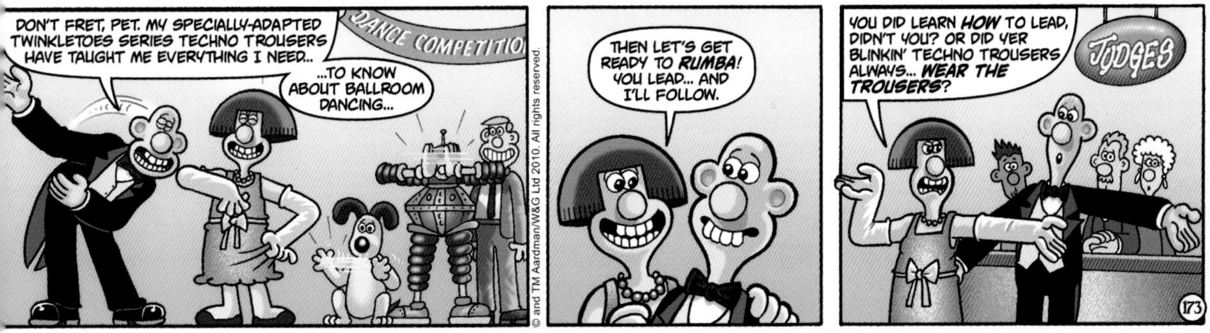
DON'T FRET, PET. MY SPECIALLY-ADAPTED TWINKLETOES SERIES TECHNO TROUSERS HAVE TAUGHT ME EVERYTHING I NEED...
...TO KNOW ABOUT BALLROOM DANCING...
DANCE COMPETITIO
THEN LET'S GET READY TO **RUMBA!** YOU LEAD... AND I'LL FOLLOW.
YOU DID LEARN **HOW** TO LEAD, DIDN'T YOU? OR DID YER BLINKIN' TECHNO TROUSERS ALWAYS... **WEAR THE TROUSERS**?
JUDGES
173

Wallace & Gromit - Strictly Wallace by Aardman & Titan Comics

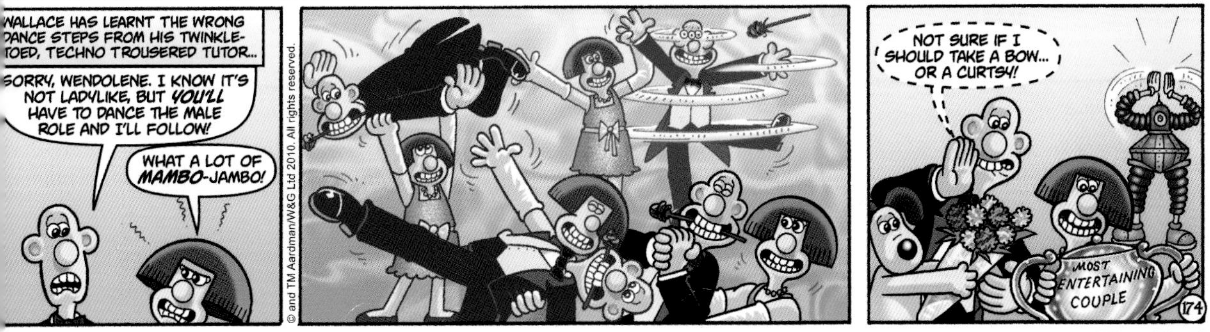
WALLACE HAS LEARNT THE WRONG DANCE STEPS FROM HIS TWINKLE-TOED, TECHNO TROUSERED TUTOR...
SORRY, WENDOLENE. I KNOW IT'S NOT LADYLIKE, BUT **YOU'LL** HAVE TO DANCE THE MALE ROLE AND I'LL FOLLOW!
WHAT A LOT OF **MAMBO**-JAMBO!
NOT SURE IF I SHOULD TAKE A BOW... OR A CURTSY!
MOST ENTERTAINING COUPLE
174

The End

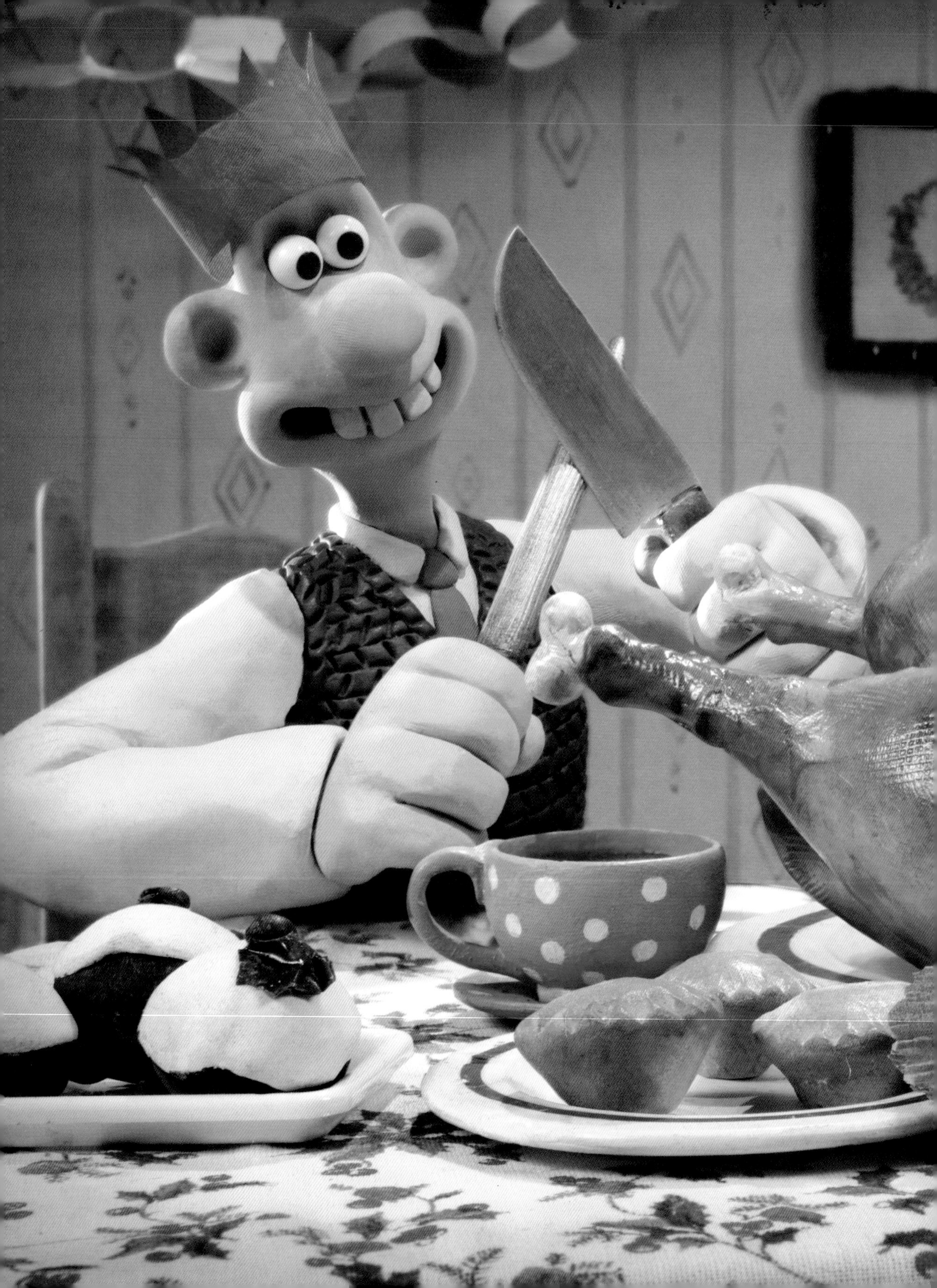

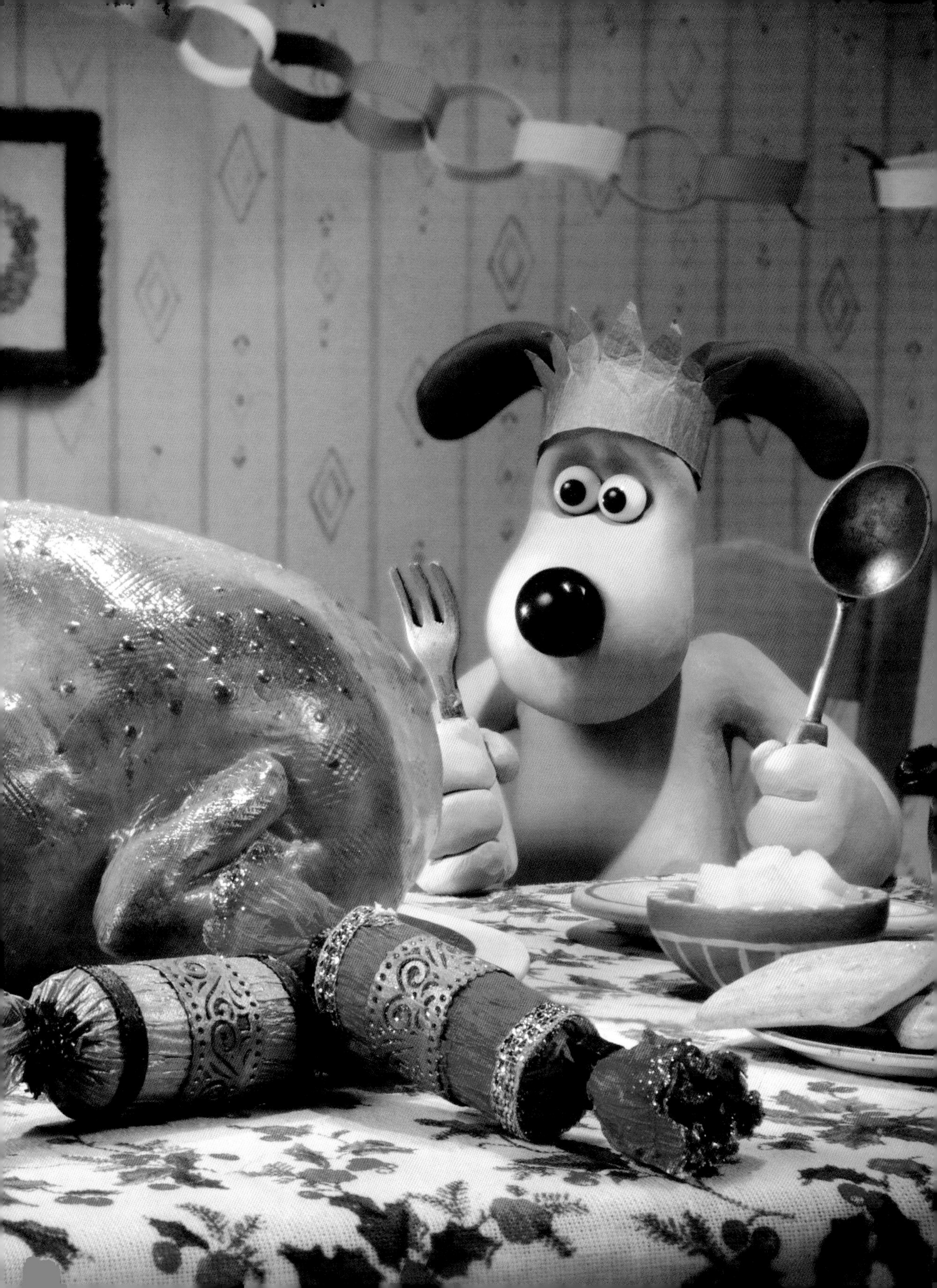

Wallace & Gromit - Cake-While-You-Wait by Aardman & Titan Comic

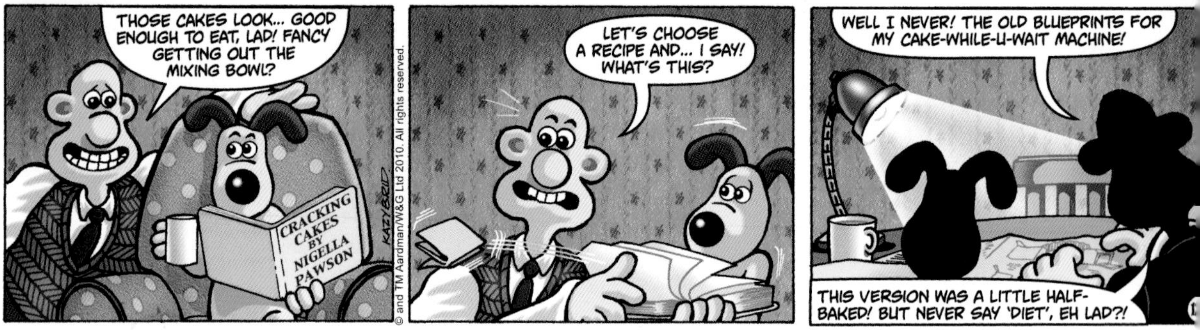
THOSE CAKES LOOK... GOOD ENOUGH TO EAT, LAD! FANCY GETTING OUT THE MIXING BOWL?
CRACKING CAKES BY NIGELLA PAWSON
© and TM Aardman/W&G Ltd 2010. All rights reserved.
LET'S CHOOSE A RECIPE AND... I SAY! WHAT'S THIS?
WELL I NEVER! THE OLD BLUEPRINTS FOR MY CAKE-WHILE-U-WAIT MACHINE!
THIS VERSION WAS A LITTLE HALF-BAKED! BUT NEVER SAY 'DIET', EH LAD?!

Wallace & Gromit - Cake-While-You-Wait by Aardman & Titan Comic

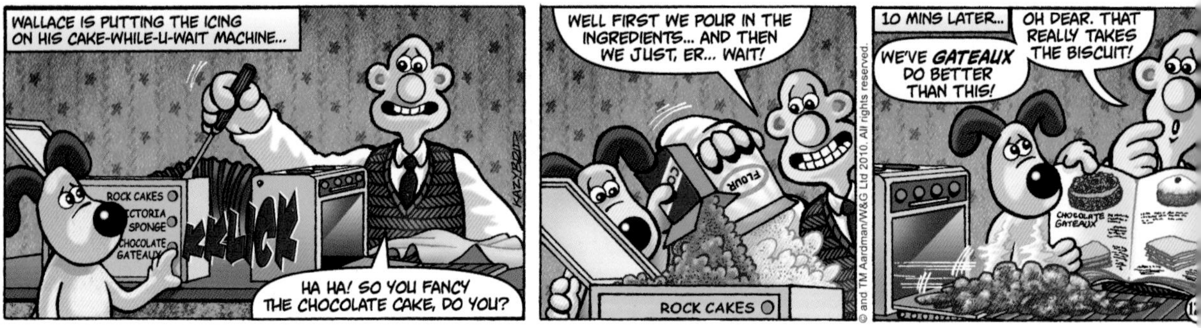
WALLACE IS PUTTING THE ICING ON HIS CAKE-WHILE-U-WAIT MACHINE...
ROCK CAKES
VICTORIA SPONGE
CHOCOLATE GATEAUX
HA HA! SO YOU FANCY THE CHOCOLATE CAKE, DO YOU?
WELL FIRST WE POUR IN THE INGREDIENTS... AND THEN WE JUST, ER... WAIT!
FLOUR
ROCK CAKES
© and TM Aardman/W&G Ltd 2010. All rights reserved.
10 MINS LATER...
WE'VE GATEAUX DO BETTER THAN THIS!
OH DEAR. THAT REALLY TAKES THE BISCUIT!
CHOCOLATE GATEAUX

Wallace & Gromit - Cake-While-You-Wait by Aardman & Titan Comic

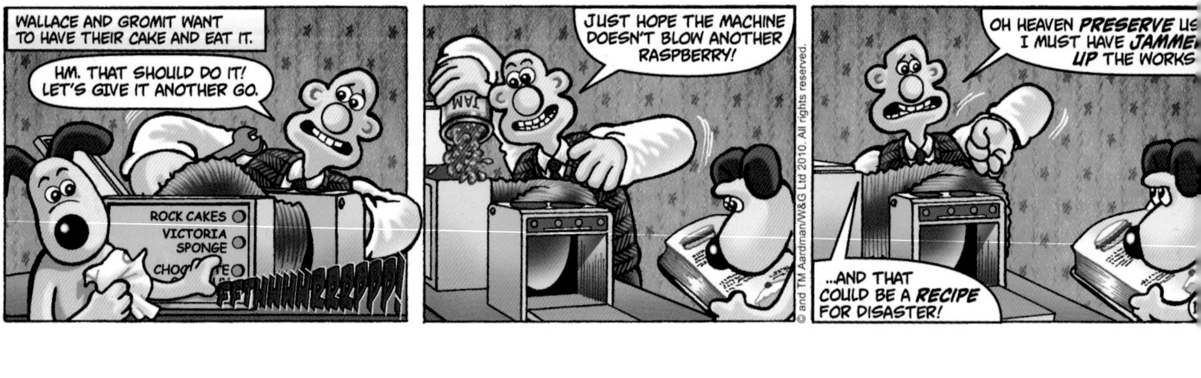
WALLACE AND GROMIT WANT TO HAVE THEIR CAKE AND EAT IT.
HM. THAT SHOULD DO IT! LET'S GIVE IT ANOTHER GO.
ROCK CAKES
VICTORIA SPONGE
JUST HOPE THE MACHINE DOESN'T BLOW ANOTHER RASPBERRY!
JAM
© and TM Aardman/W&G Ltd 2010. All rights reserved.
OH HEAVEN PRESERVE US I MUST HAVE JAMMED UP THE WORKS
...AND THAT COULD BE A RECIPE FOR DISASTER!

allace & Gromit - Cake-While-You-Wait **by Aardman & Titan Comics**

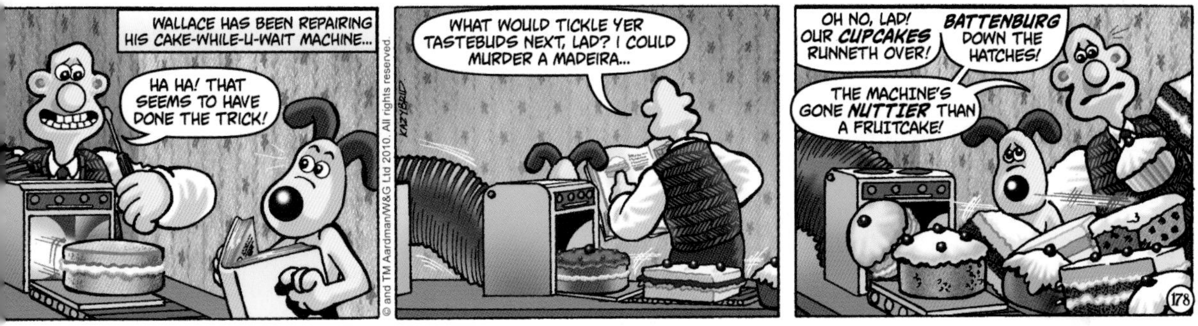

WALLACE HAS BEEN REPAIRING HIS CAKE-WHILE-U-WAIT MACHINE...
HA HA! THAT SEEMS TO HAVE DONE THE TRICK!
WHAT WOULD TICKLE YER TASTEBUDS NEXT, LAD? I COULD MURDER A MADEIRA...
OH NO, LAD! OUR ***CUPCAKES*** RUNNETH OVER!
BATTENBURG DOWN THE HATCHES!
THE MACHINE'S GONE ***NUTTIER*** THAN A FRUITCAKE!
178
© and TM Aardman/W&G Ltd 2010. All rights reserved.

allace & Gromit - Cake-While-You-Wait **by Aardman & Titan Comics**

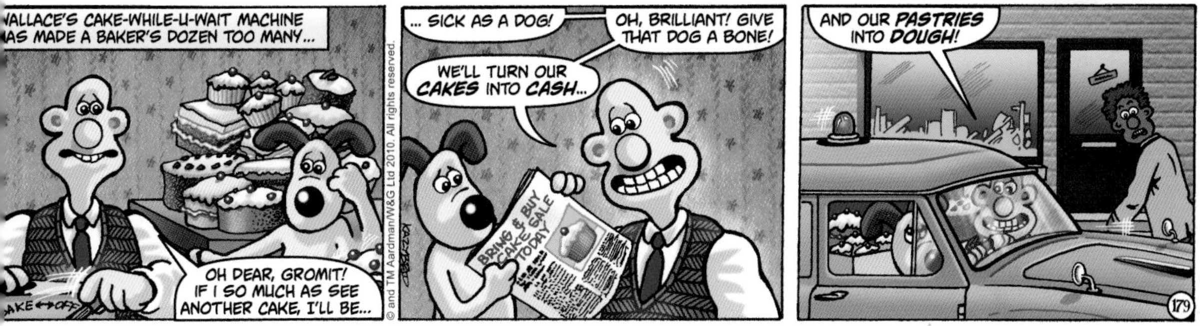

ALLACE'S CAKE-WHILE-U-WAIT MACHINE AS MADE A BAKER'S DOZEN TOO MANY...
OH DEAR, GROMIT! IF I SO MUCH AS SEE ANOTHER CAKE, I'LL BE...
... SICK AS A DOG!
OH, BRILLIANT! GIVE THAT DOG A BONE!
WE'LL TURN OUR ***CAKES*** INTO ***CASH***...
BRING & BUY CAKE SALE TODAY
AND OUR ***PASTRIES*** INTO ***DOUGH***!
179
© and TM Aardman/W&G Ltd 2010. All rights reserved.

allace & Gromit - Cake-While-You-Wait **by Aardman & Titan Comics**

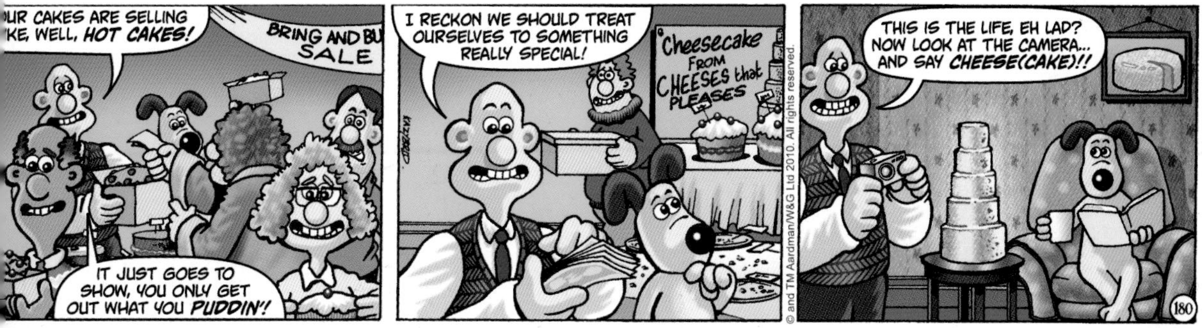

UR CAKES ARE SELLING KE, WELL, ***HOT CAKES!***
BRING AND BU SALE
IT JUST GOES TO SHOW, YOU ONLY GET OUT WHAT YOU ***PUDDIN'!***
I RECKON WE SHOULD TREAT OURSELVES TO SOMETHING REALLY SPECIAL!
Cheesecake FROM CHEESES that PLEASES
THIS IS THE LIFE, EH LAD? NOW LOOK AT THE CAMERA... AND SAY ***CHEESE(CAKE)!!***
180
© and TM Aardman/W&G Ltd 2010. All rights reserved.

The End

Wallace & Gromit - ~~12~~ 6 Days of Christmas

by Aardman & Titan Comic

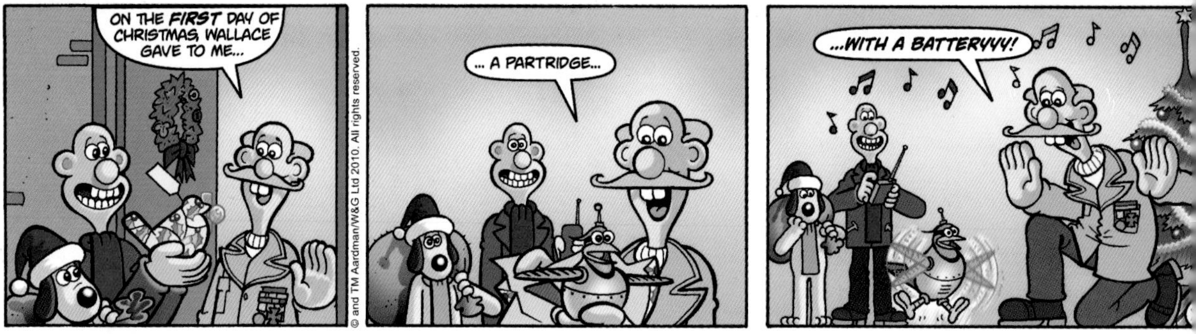
ON THE FIRST DAY OF CHRISTMAS, WALLACE GAVE TO ME...
... A PARTRIDGE...
...WITH A BATTERYYY!

Wallace & Gromit - ~~12~~ 6 Days of Christmas

by Aardman & Titan Comic

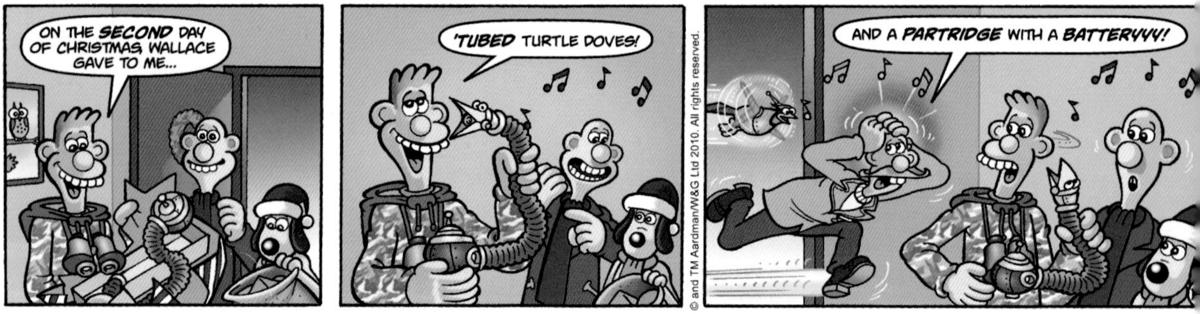
ON THE SECOND DAY OF CHRISTMAS, WALLACE GAVE TO ME...
'TUBED TURTLE DOVES!
AND A PARTRIDGE WITH A BATTERYYY!

Wallace & Gromit - ~~12~~ 6 Days of Christmas

by Aardman & Titan Comic

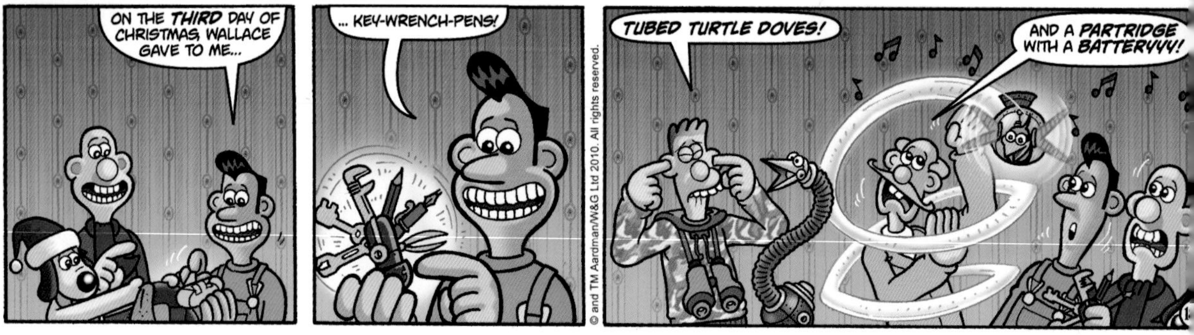
ON THE THIRD DAY OF CHRISTMAS, WALLACE GAVE TO ME...
... KEY-WRENCH-PENS!
TUBED TURTLE DOVES!
AND A PARTRIDGE WITH A BATTERYYY!

Wallace & Gromit - ~~12~~ 6 Days of Christmas — by Aardman & Titan Comics

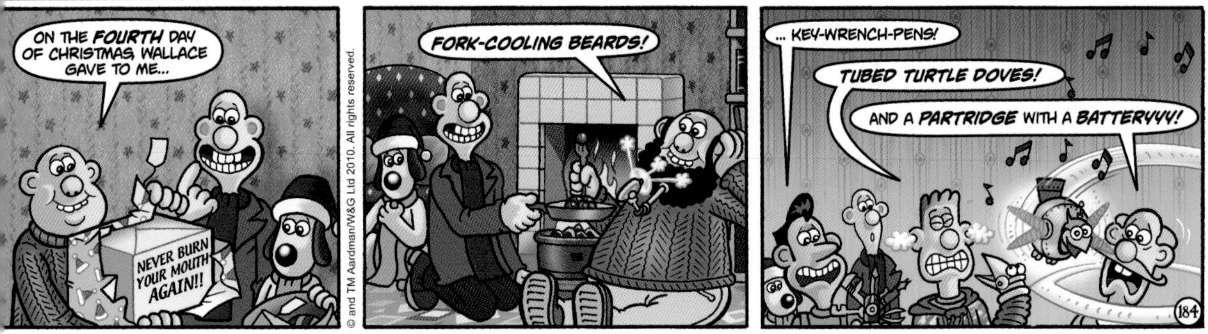
ON THE FOURTH DAY OF CHRISTMAS, WALLACE GAVE TO ME...
NEVER BURN YOUR MOUTH AGAIN!!
FORK-COOLING BEARDS!
... KEY-WRENCH-PENS!
TUBED TURTLE DOVES!
AND A PARTRIDGE WITH A BATTERYYY!
184

Wallace & Gromit - ~~12~~ 6 Days of Christmas — by Aardman & Titan Comics

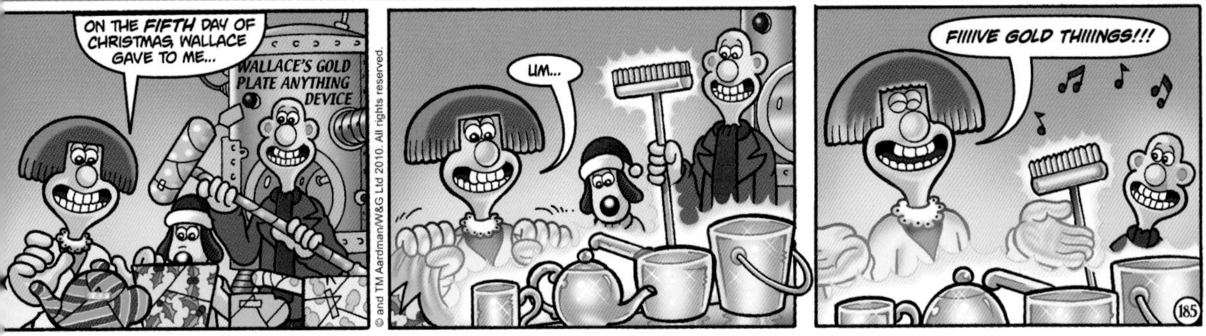
ON THE FIFTH DAY OF CHRISTMAS, WALLACE GAVE TO ME...
WALLACE'S GOLD PLATE ANYTHING DEVICE
UM...
FIIIIVE GOLD THIIINGS!!!
185

Wallace & Gromit - ~~12~~ 6 Days of Christmas — by Aardman & Titan Comics

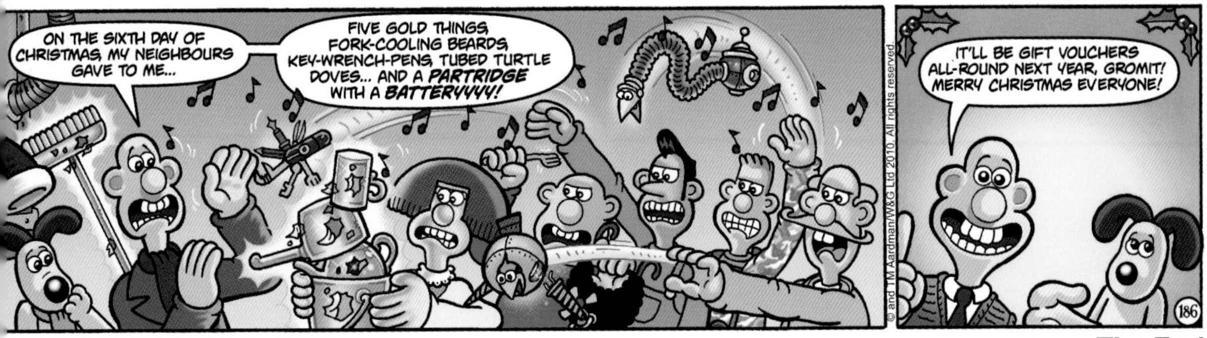
ON THE SIXTH DAY OF CHRISTMAS, MY NEIGHBOURS GAVE TO ME...
FIVE GOLD THINGS, FORK-COOLING BEARDS, KEY-WRENCH-PENS, TUBED TURTLE DOVES... AND A PARTRIDGE WITH A BATTERYYYY!
IT'LL BE GIFT VOUCHERS ALL-ROUND NEXT YEAR, GROMIT! MERRY CHRISTMAS EVERYONE!
186

The End

Wallace & Gromit - Breakfast Gags

by Aardman & Titan Comic

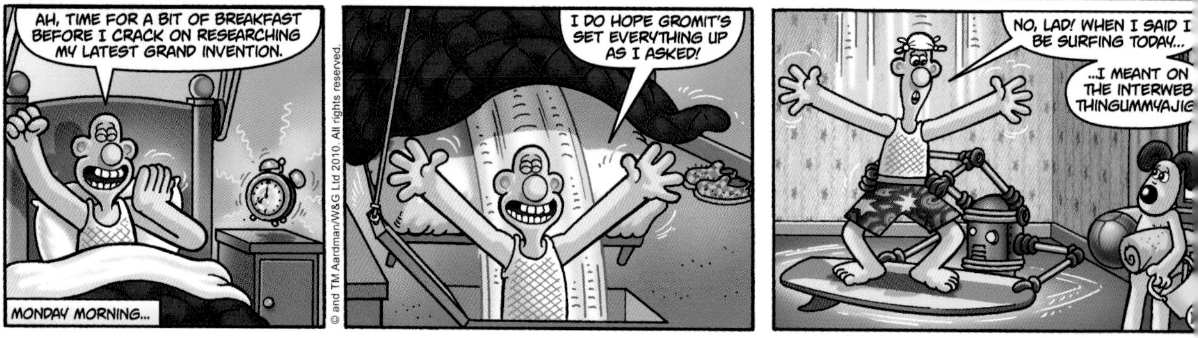

MONDAY MORNING...
AH, TIME FOR A BIT OF BREAKFAST BEFORE I CRACK ON RESEARCHING MY LATEST GRAND INVENTION.
© and TM Aardman/W&G Ltd 2010. All rights reserved.
I DO HOPE GROMIT'S SET EVERYTHING UP AS I ASKED!
NO, LAD! WHEN I SAID I BE SURFING TODAY...
...I MEANT ON THE INTERWEB THINGUMMYAJIG

Wallace & Gromit - Breakfast Gags

by Aardman & Titan Comic

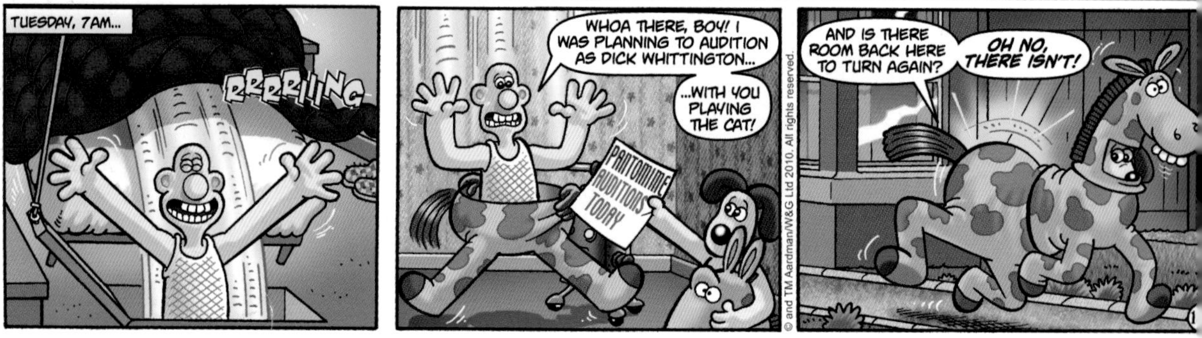

TUESDAY, 7AM...
RRRRIING
WHOA THERE, BOY! I WAS PLANNING TO AUDITION AS DICK WHITTINGTON...
...WITH YOU PLAYING THE CAT!
PANTOMIME AUDITIONS TODAY
© and TM Aardman/W&G Ltd 2010. All rights reserved.
AND IS THERE ROOM BACK HERE TO TURN AGAIN?
OH NO, THERE ISN'T!

Wallace & Gromit - Breakfast Gags

by Aardman & Titan Comic

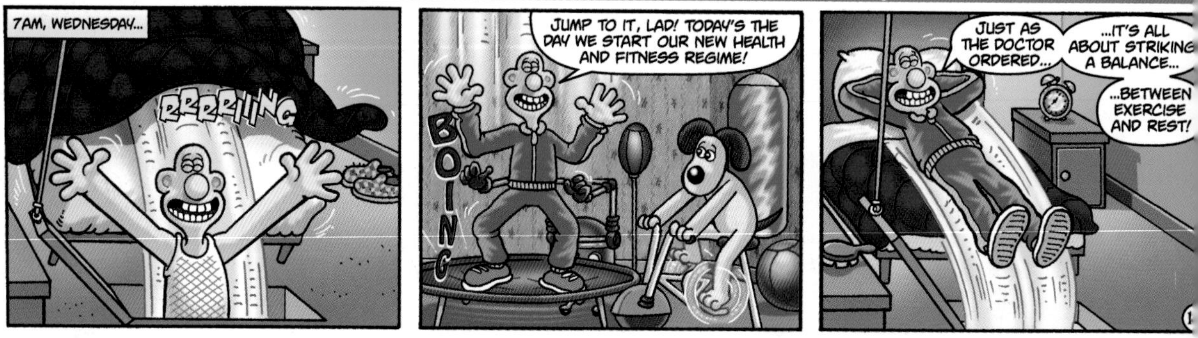

7AM, WEDNESDAY...
RRRRIING
JUMP TO IT, LAD! TODAY'S THE DAY WE START OUR NEW HEALTH AND FITNESS REGIME!
BOING
JUST AS THE DOCTOR ORDERED...
...IT'S ALL ABOUT STRIKING A BALANCE...
...BETWEEN EXERCISE AND REST!

Wallace & Gromit - Breakfast Gags by Aardman & Titan Comics

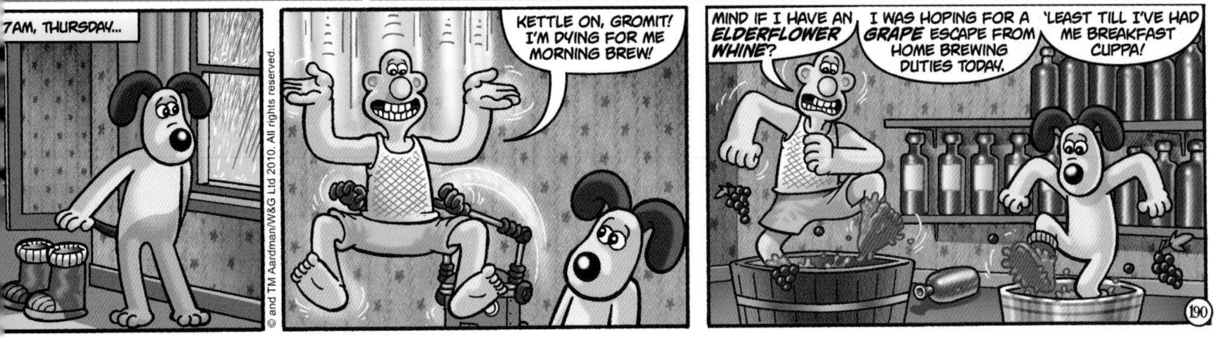
7AM, THURSDAY...
KETTLE ON, GROMIT! I'M DYING FOR ME MORNING BREW!
MIND IF I HAVE AN ELDERFLOWER WHINE?
I WAS HOPING FOR A GRAPE ESCAPE FROM HOME BREWING DUTIES TODAY.
'LEAST TILL I'VE HAD ME BREAKFAST CUPPA!
190

Wallace & Gromit - Breakfast Gags by Aardman & Titan Comics

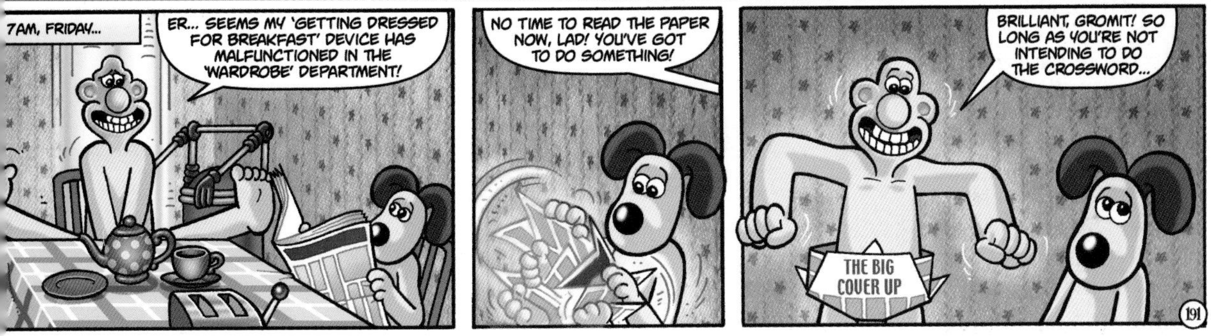
7AM, FRIDAY...
ER... SEEMS MY 'GETTING DRESSED FOR BREAKFAST' DEVICE HAS MALFUNCTIONED IN THE 'WARDROBE' DEPARTMENT!
NO TIME TO READ THE PAPER NOW, LAD! YOU'VE GOT TO DO SOMETHING!
BRILLIANT, GROMIT! SO LONG AS YOU'RE NOT INTENDING TO DO THE CROSSWORD...
THE BIG COVER UP
191

Wallace & Gromit - Breakfast Gags by Aardman & Titan Comics

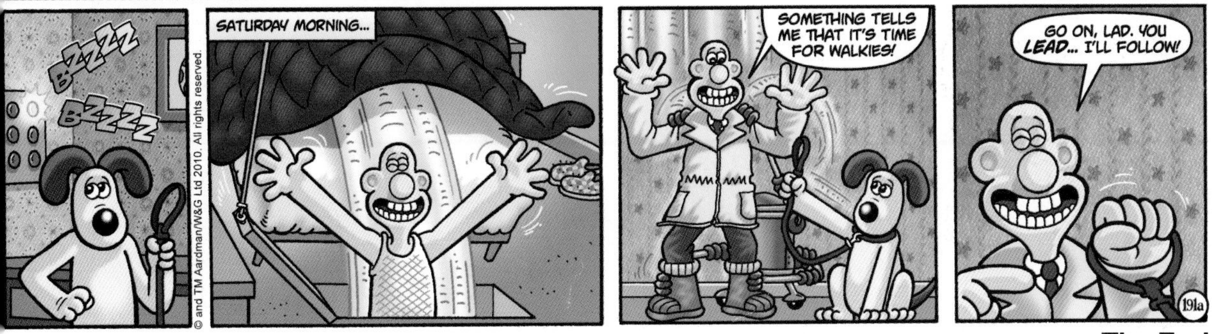
BZZZZ
BZZZZ
SATURDAY MORNING...
SOMETHING TELLS ME THAT IT'S TIME FOR WALKIES!
GO ON, LAD. YOU LEAD... I'LL FOLLOW!
191a

The End

Wallace & Gromit - Ice To See You

by Aardman & Titan Comic

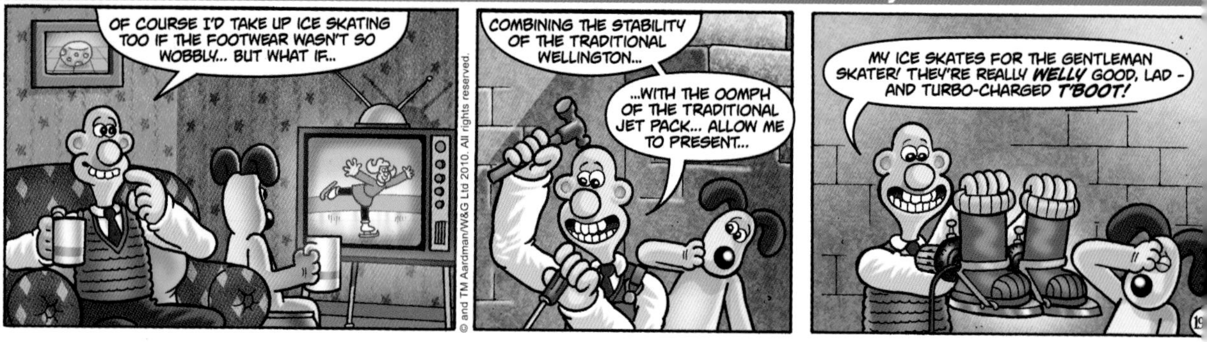

OF COURSE I'D TAKE UP ICE SKATING TOO IF THE FOOTWEAR WASN'T SO WOBBLY... BUT WHAT IF...
© and TM Aardman/W&G Ltd 2010. All rights reserved.
COMBINING THE STABILITY OF THE TRADITIONAL WELLINGTON...
...WITH THE OOMPH OF THE TRADITIONAL JET PACK... ALLOW ME TO PRESENT...
MY ICE SKATES FOR THE GENTLEMAN SKATER! THEY'RE REALLY WELLY GOOD, LAD - AND TURBO-CHARGED T'BOOT!

Wallace & Gromit - Ice To See You

by Aardman & Titan Comic

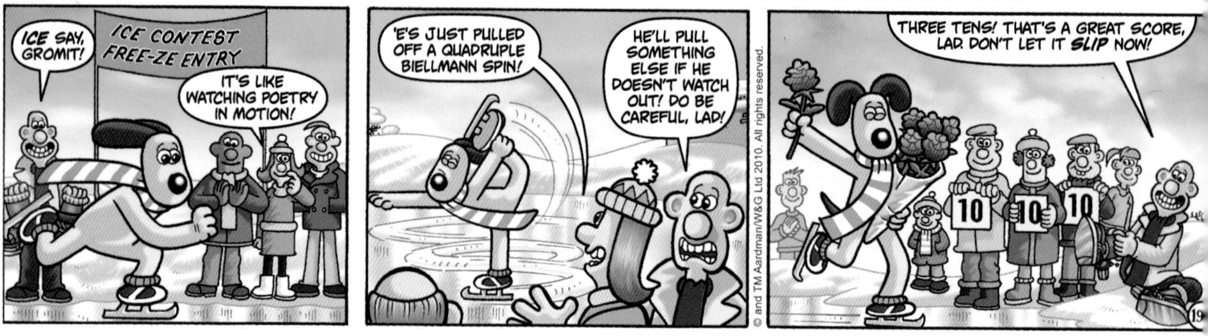

ICE SAY, GROMIT!
ICE CONTEST FREE-ZE ENTRY
IT'S LIKE WATCHING POETRY IN MOTION!
'E'S JUST PULLED OFF A QUADRUPLE BIELLMANN SPIN!
HE'LL PULL SOMETHING ELSE IF HE DOESN'T WATCH OUT! DO BE CAREFUL, LAD!
© and TM Aardman/W&G Ltd 2010. All rights reserved.
THREE TENS! THAT'S A GREAT SCORE, LAD. DON'T LET IT SLIP NOW!
10
10
10

Wallace & Gromit - Ice To See You

by Aardman & Titan Comic

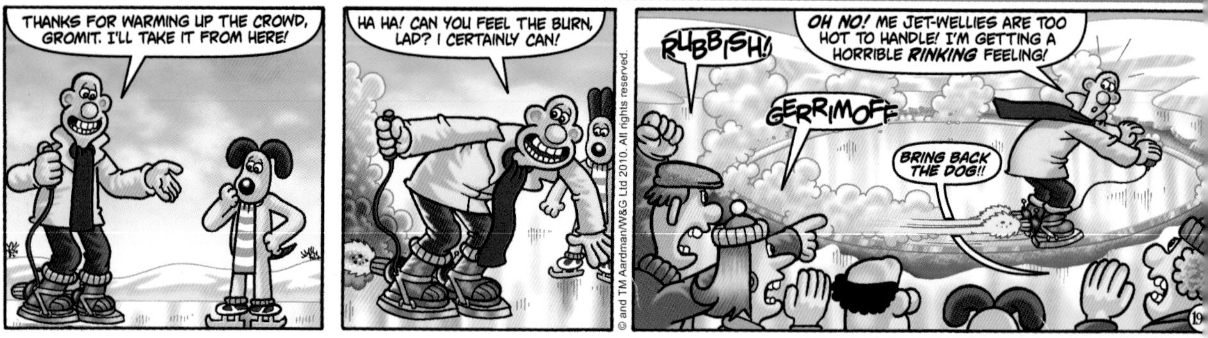

THANKS FOR WARMING UP THE CROWD, GROMIT. I'LL TAKE IT FROM HERE!
HA HA! CAN YOU FEEL THE BURN, LAD? I CERTAINLY CAN!
© and TM Aardman/W&G Ltd 2010. All rights reserved.
RUBBISH!
OH NO! ME JET-WELLIES ARE TOO HOT TO HANDLE! I'M GETTING A HORRIBLE RINKING FEELING!
GERRIMOFF
BRING BACK THE DOG!!

Wallace & Gromit - Ice To See You by Aardman & Titan Comics

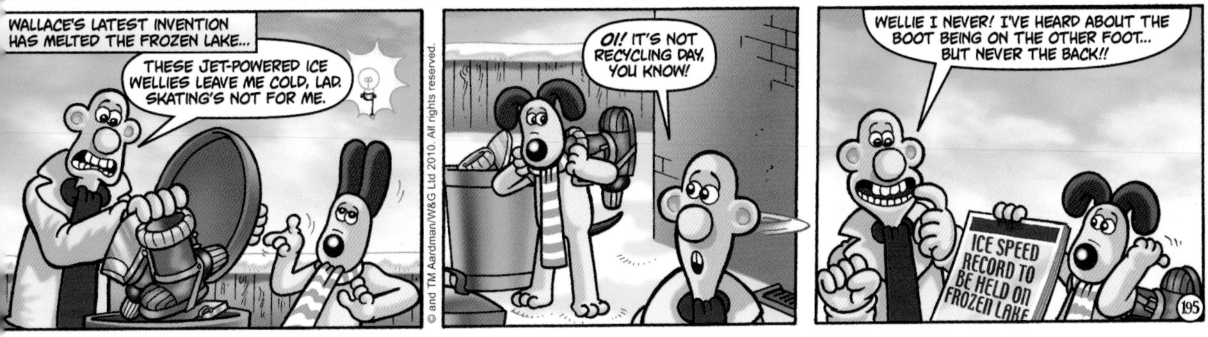

WALLACE'S LATEST INVENTION HAS MELTED THE FROZEN LAKE...
THESE JET-POWERED ICE WELLIES LEAVE ME COLD, LAD. SKATING'S NOT FOR ME.
OI! IT'S NOT RECYCLING DAY, YOU KNOW!
WELLIE I NEVER! I'VE HEARD ABOUT THE BOOT BEING ON THE OTHER FOOT... BUT NEVER THE BACK!!
ICE SPEED RECORD TO BE HELD ON FROZEN LAKE
195

Wallace & Gromit - Ice To See You by Aardman & Titan Comics

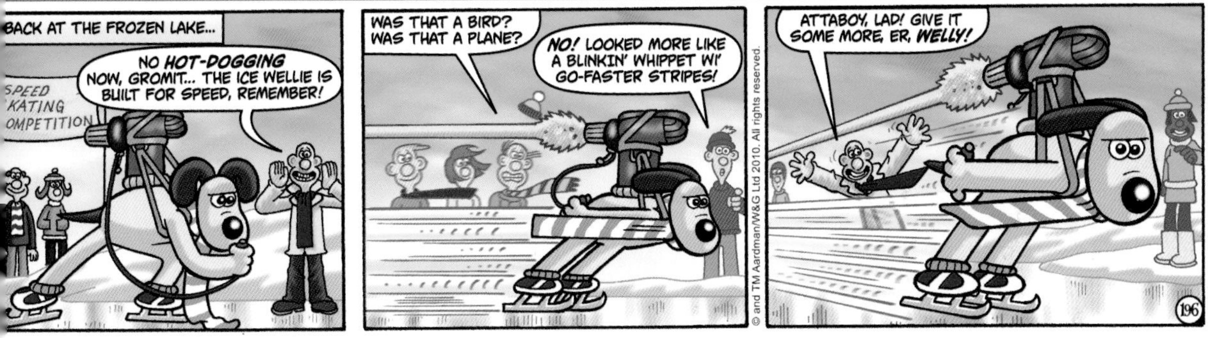

BACK AT THE FROZEN LAKE...
NO HOT-DOGGING NOW, GROMIT... THE ICE WELLIE IS BUILT FOR SPEED, REMEMBER!
SPEED SKATING COMPETITION
WAS THAT A BIRD? WAS THAT A PLANE?
NO! LOOKED MORE LIKE A BLINKIN' WHIPPET WI' GO-FASTER STRIPES!
ATTABOY, LAD! GIVE IT SOME MORE, ER, WELLY!
196

© and TM Aardman/W&G Ltd 2010. All rights reserved.

Wallace & Gromit - Ice To See You by Aardman & Titan Comics

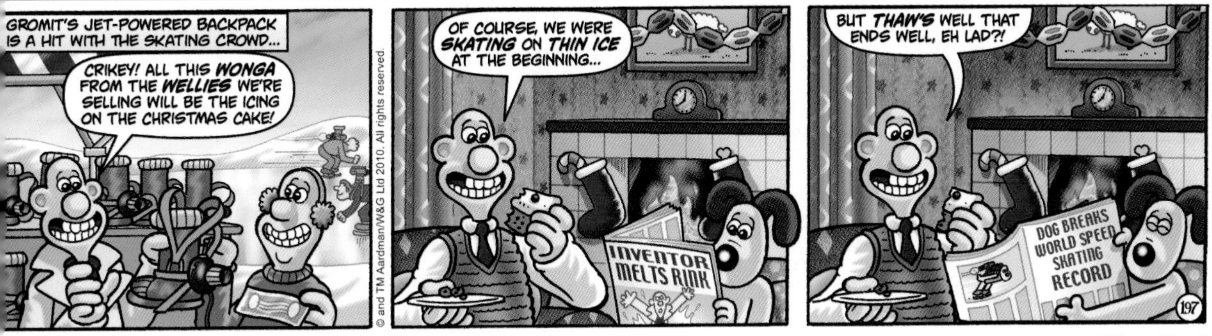

GROMIT'S JET-POWERED BACKPACK IS A HIT WITH THE SKATING CROWD...
CRIKEY! ALL THIS WONGA FROM THE WELLIES WE'RE SELLING WILL BE THE ICING ON THE CHRISTMAS CAKE!
OF COURSE, WE WERE SKATING ON THIN ICE AT THE BEGINNING...
INVENTOR MELTS RINK
BUT THAW'S WELL THAT ENDS WELL, EH LAD?!
DOG BREAKS WORLD SPEED SKATING RECORD
197

© and TM Aardman/W&G Ltd 2010. All rights reserved.

The End

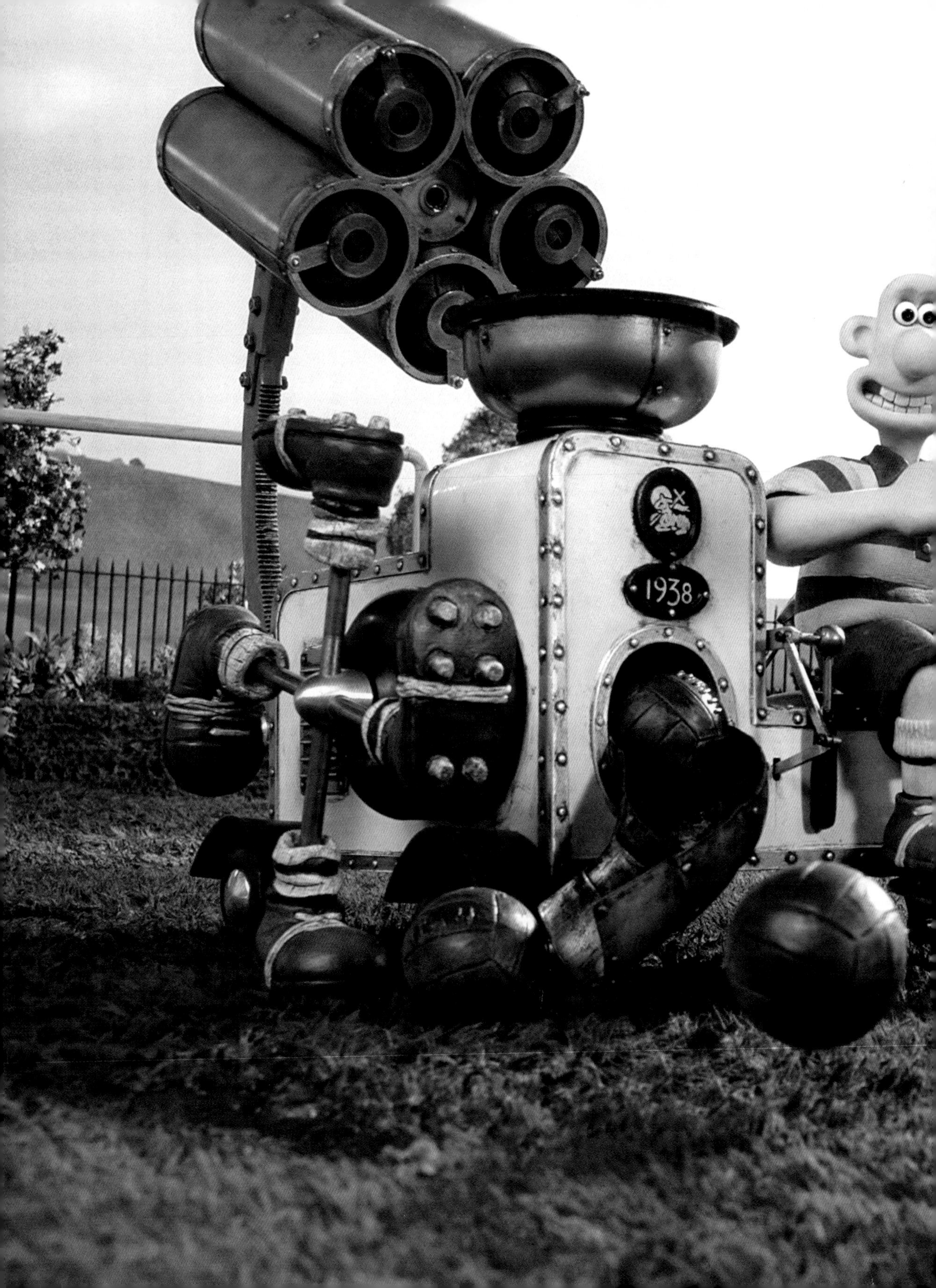
1938

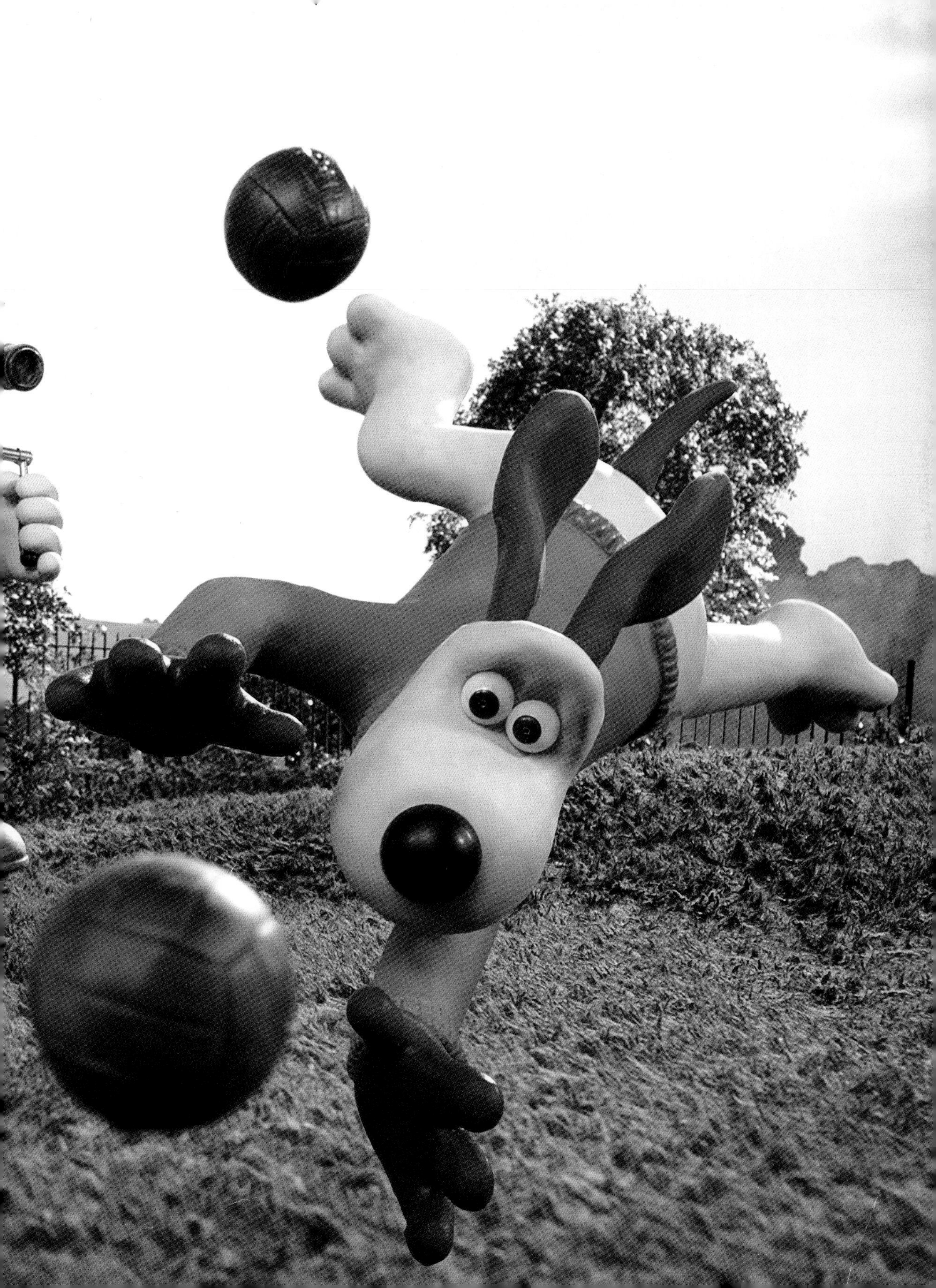

Wallace & Gromit - Scarecrowmatic
by Aardman & Titan Comic

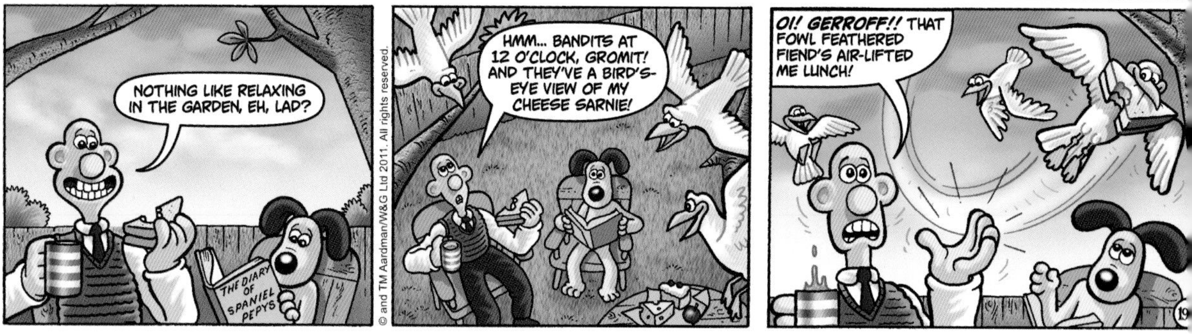
NOTHING LIKE RELAXING IN THE GARDEN, EH, LAD?
THE DIARY OF SPANIEL PEPYS
HMM... BANDITS AT 12 O'CLOCK, GROMIT! AND THEY'VE A BIRD'S-EYE VIEW OF MY CHEESE SARNIE!
OI! GERROFF!! THAT FOWL FEATHERED FIEND'S AIR-LIFTED ME LUNCH!
© and TM Aardman/W&G Ltd 2011. All rights reserved.

Wallace & Gromit - Scarecrowmatic
by Aardman & Titan Comic

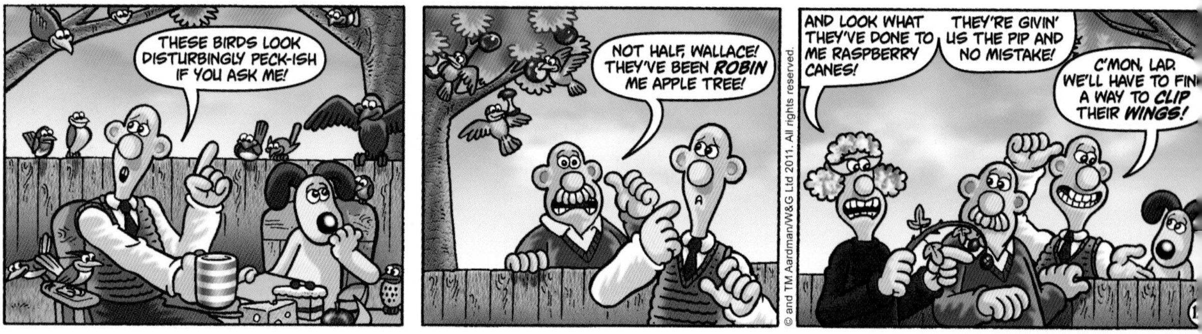
THESE BIRDS LOOK DISTURBINGLY PECK-ISH IF YOU ASK ME!
NOT HALF, WALLACE! THEY'VE BEEN ROBIN ME APPLE TREE!
AND LOOK WHAT THEY'VE DONE TO ME RASPBERRY CANES!
THEY'RE GIVIN' US THE PIP AND NO MISTAKE!
C'MON, LAD. WE'LL HAVE TO FIN A WAY TO CLIP THEIR WINGS!
© and TM Aardman/W&G Ltd 2011. All rights reserved.

Wallace & Gromit - Scarecrowmatic
by Aardman & Titan Comic

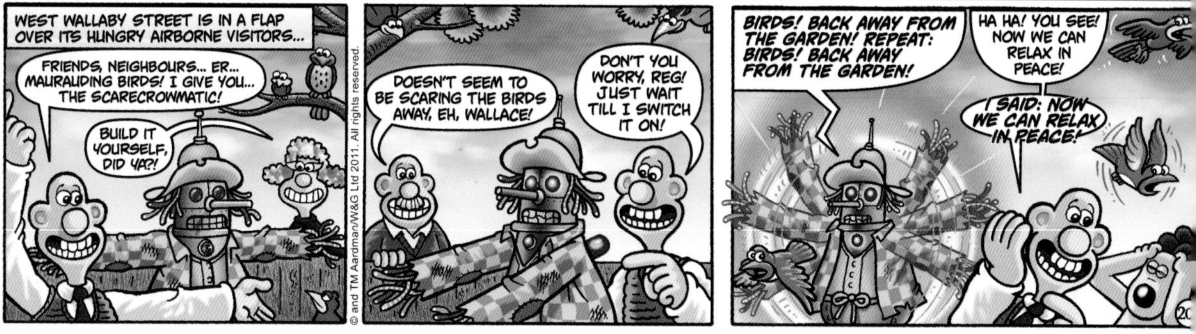
WEST WALLABY STREET IS IN A FLAP OVER ITS HUNGRY AIRBORNE VISITORS...
FRIENDS, NEIGHBOURS... ER... MAURAUDING BIRDS! I GIVE YOU... THE SCARECROWMATIC!
BUILD IT YOURSELF, DID YA?!
DOESN'T SEEM TO BE SCARING THE BIRDS AWAY, EH, WALLACE!
DON'T YOU WORRY, REG! JUST WAIT TILL I SWITCH IT ON!
BIRDS! BACK AWAY FROM THE GARDEN! REPEAT: BIRDS! BACK AWAY FROM THE GARDEN!
HA HA! YOU SEE! NOW WE CAN RELAX IN PEACE!
I SAID: NOW WE CAN RELAX IN PEACE!
© and TM Aardman/W&G Ltd 2011. All rights reserved.

Wallace & Gromit - Scarecrowmatic by Aardman & Titan Comics

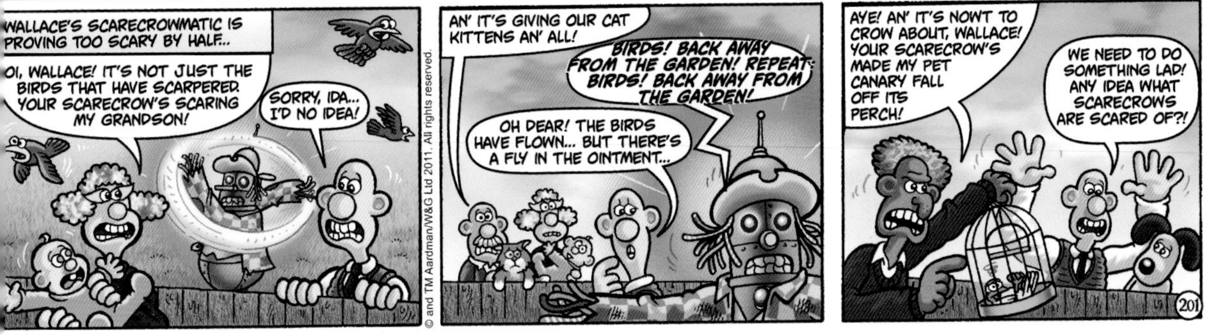

WALLACE'S SCARECROWMATIC IS PROVING TOO SCARY BY HALF...
OI, WALLACE! IT'S NOT JUST THE BIRDS THAT HAVE SCARPERED. YOUR SCARECROW'S SCARING MY GRANDSON!
SORRY, IDA... I'D NO IDEA!
AN' IT'S GIVING OUR CAT KITTENS AN' ALL!
BIRDS! BACK AWAY FROM THE GARDEN! REPEAT: BIRDS! BACK AWAY FROM THE GARDEN!
OH DEAR! THE BIRDS HAVE FLOWN... BUT THERE'S A FLY IN THE OINTMENT...
AYE! AN' IT'S NOWT TO CROW ABOUT, WALLACE! YOUR SCARECROW'S MADE MY PET CANARY FALL OFF ITS PERCH!
WE NEED TO DO SOMETHING LAD! ANY IDEA WHAT SCARECROWS ARE SCARED OF?!
201

Wallace & Gromit - Scarecrowmatic by Aardman & Titan Comics

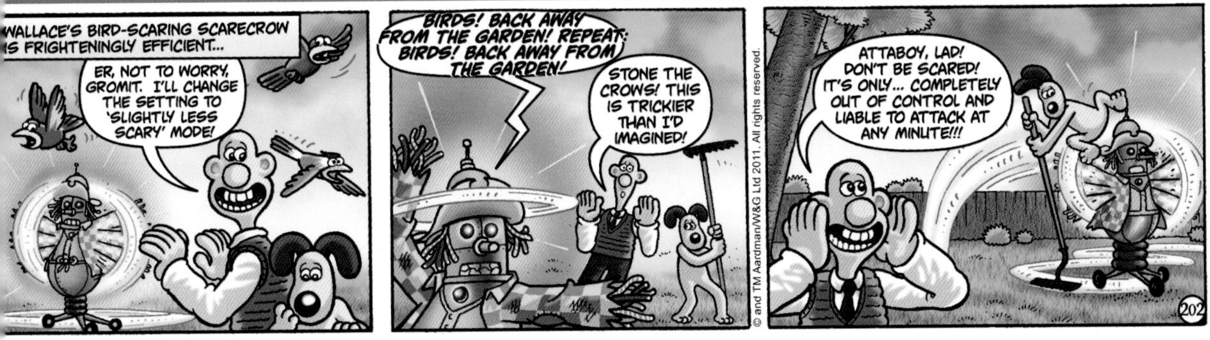

WALLACE'S BIRD-SCARING SCARECROW IS FRIGHTENINGLY EFFICIENT...
ER, NOT TO WORRY, GROMIT. I'LL CHANGE THE SETTING TO 'SLIGHTLY LESS SCARY' MODE!
BIRDS! BACK AWAY FROM THE GARDEN! REPEAT: BIRDS! BACK AWAY FROM THE GARDEN!
STONE THE CROWS! THIS IS TRICKIER THAN I'D IMAGINED!
ATTABOY, LAD! DON'T BE SCARED! IT'S ONLY... COMPLETELY OUT OF CONTROL AND LIABLE TO ATTACK AT ANY MINUTE!!!
202

Wallace & Gromit - Scarecrowmatic by Aardman & Titan Comics

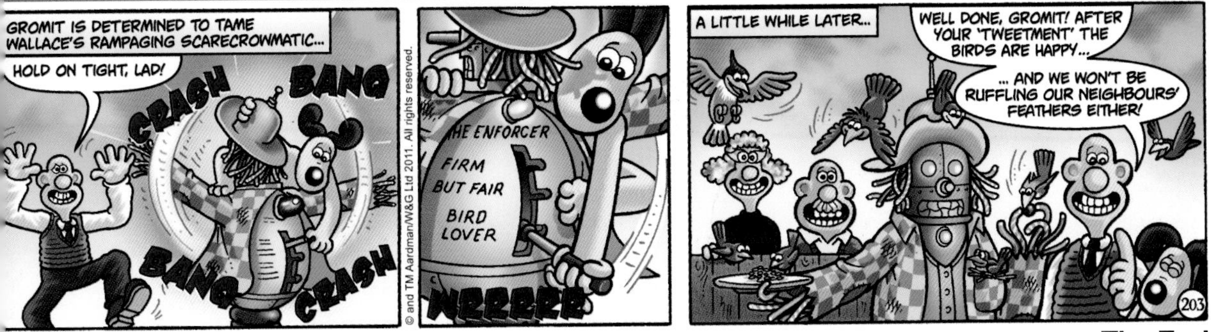

GROMIT IS DETERMINED TO TAME WALLACE'S RAMPAGING SCARECROWMATIC...
HOLD ON TIGHT, LAD!
CRASH
BANG
BANG
CRASH
THE ENFORCER
FIRM
BUT FAIR
BIRD
LOVER
WRRRRR
A LITTLE WHILE LATER...
WELL DONE, GROMIT! AFTER YOUR 'TWEETMENT' THE BIRDS ARE HAPPY...
... AND WE WON'T BE RUFFLING OUR NEIGHBOURS' FEATHERS EITHER!
203

The End

Wallace & Gromit - Hole in One (Hundred)

by Aardman & Titan Comics

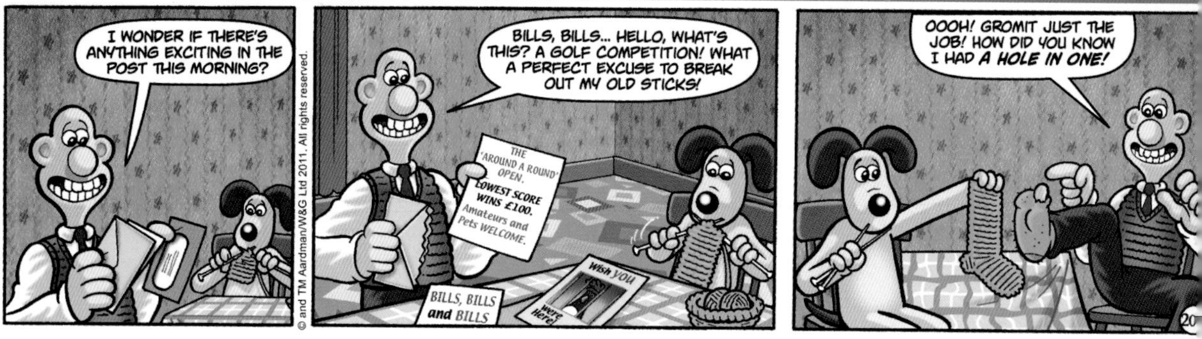
I WONDER IF THERE'S ANYTHING EXCITING IN THE POST THIS MORNING?
BILLS, BILLS... HELLO, WHAT'S THIS? A GOLF COMPETITION! WHAT A PERFECT EXCUSE TO BREAK OUT MY OLD STICKS!
THE 'AROUND A ROUND' OPEN.
LOWEST SCORE WINS £100.
Amateurs and Pets WELCOME.
BILLS, BILLS and BILLS
Wish you were Here!
OOOH! GROMIT JUST THE JOB! HOW DID YOU KNOW I HAD A HOLE IN ONE!
© and TM Aardman/W&G Ltd 2011. All rights reserved.

Wallace & Gromit - Hole in One (Hundred)

by Aardman & Titan Comics

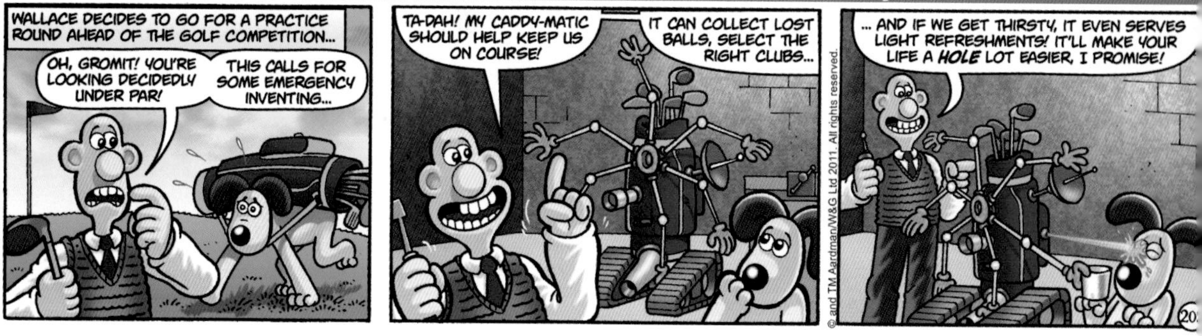
WALLACE DECIDES TO GO FOR A PRACTICE ROUND AHEAD OF THE GOLF COMPETITION...
OH, GROMIT! YOU'RE LOOKING DECIDEDLY UNDER PAR!
THIS CALLS FOR SOME EMERGENCY INVENTING...
TA-DAH! MY CADDY-MATIC SHOULD HELP KEEP US ON COURSE!
IT CAN COLLECT LOST BALLS, SELECT THE RIGHT CLUBS...
... AND IF WE GET THIRSTY, IT EVEN SERVES LIGHT REFRESHMENTS! IT'LL MAKE YOUR LIFE A HOLE LOT EASIER, I PROMISE!
© and TM Aardman/W&G Ltd 2011. All rights reserved.

Wallace & Gromit - Hole in One (Hundred)

by Aardman & Titan Comics

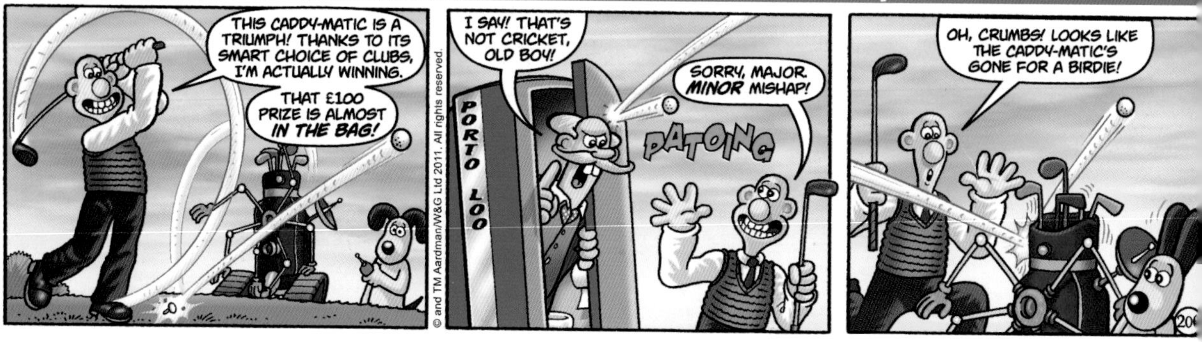
THIS CADDY-MATIC IS A TRIUMPH! THANKS TO ITS SMART CHOICE OF CLUBS, I'M ACTUALLY WINNING.
THAT £100 PRIZE IS ALMOST IN THE BAG!
I SAY! THAT'S NOT CRICKET, OLD BOY!
PORTO LOO
PATOING
SORRY, MAJOR. MINOR MISHAP!
OH, CRUMBS! LOOKS LIKE THE CADDY-MATIC'S GONE FOR A BIRDIE!
© and TM Aardman/W&G Ltd 2011. All rights reserved.

/allace & Gromit - Hole in One (Hundred) by Aardman & Titan Comics

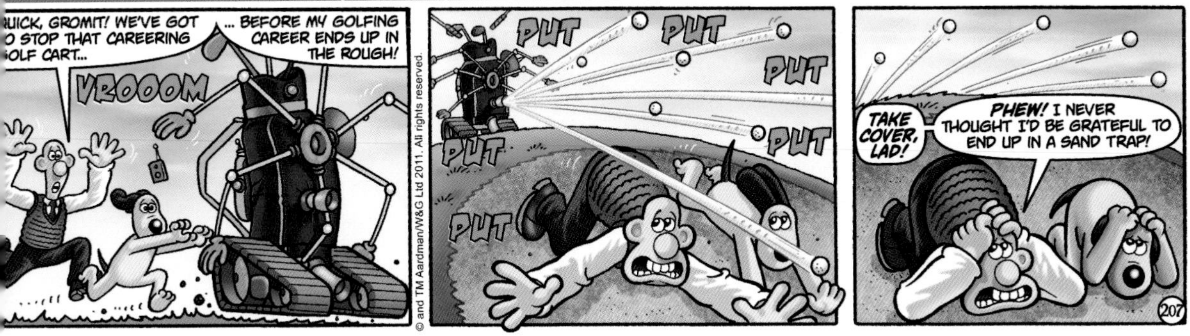

UICK, GROMIT! WE'VE GOT O STOP THAT CAREERING OLF CART...
... BEFORE MY GOLFING CAREER ENDS UP IN THE ROUGH!
VROOOM
PUT
PUT
PUT
PUT
PUT
PUT
TAKE COVER, LAD!
PHEW! I NEVER THOUGHT I'D BE GRATEFUL TO END UP IN A SAND TRAP!
207

/allace & Gromit - Hole in One (Hundred) by Aardman & Titan Comics

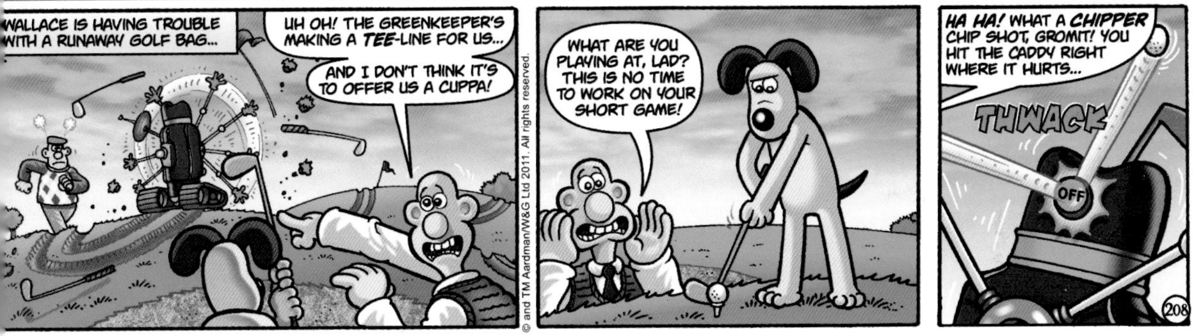

WALLACE IS HAVING TROUBLE WITH A RUNAWAY GOLF BAG...
UH OH! THE GREENKEEPER'S MAKING A TEE-LINE FOR US...
AND I DON'T THINK IT'S TO OFFER US A CUPPA!
WHAT ARE YOU PLAYING AT, LAD? THIS IS NO TIME TO WORK ON YOUR SHORT GAME!
HA HA! WHAT A CHIPPER CHIP SHOT, GROMIT! YOU HIT THE CADDY RIGHT WHERE IT HURTS...
THWACK
OFF
208

/allace & Gromit - Hole in One (Hundred) by Aardman & Titan Comics

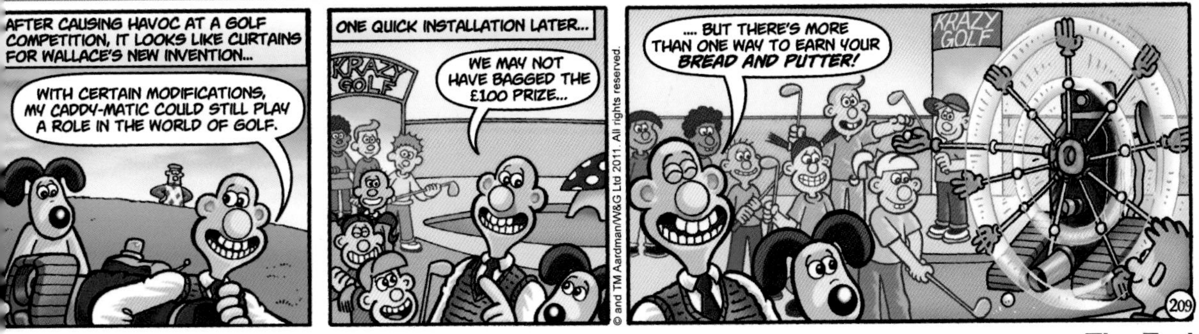

AFTER CAUSING HAVOC AT A GOLF COMPETITION, IT LOOKS LIKE CURTAINS FOR WALLACE'S NEW INVENTION...
WITH CERTAIN MODIFICATIONS, MY CADDY-MATIC COULD STILL PLAY A ROLE IN THE WORLD OF GOLF.
ONE QUICK INSTALLATION LATER...
KRAZY GOLF
WE MAY NOT HAVE BAGGED THE £100 PRIZE...
.... BUT THERE'S MORE THAN ONE WAY TO EARN YOUR BREAD AND PUTTER!
KRAZY GOLF
209

The End

Wallace & Gromit - Abominable Snowman

by Aardman & Titan Comics

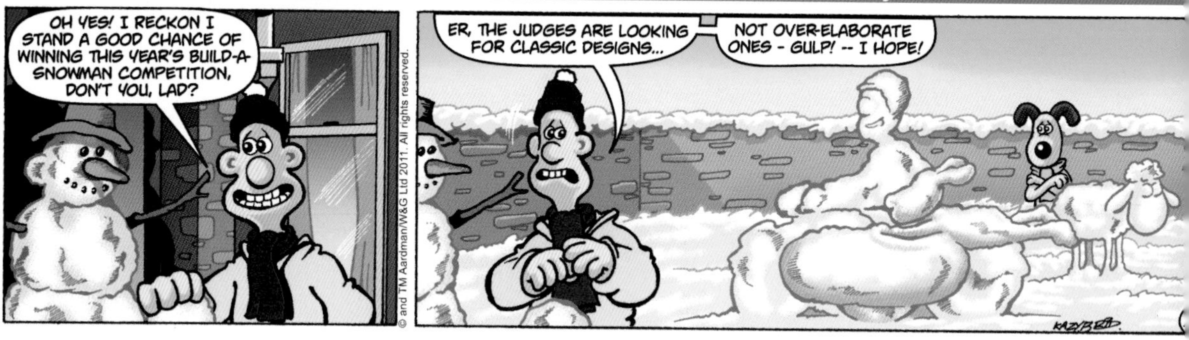

OH YES! I RECKON I STAND A GOOD CHANCE OF WINNING THIS YEAR'S BUILD-A-SNOWMAN COMPETITION, DON'T YOU, LAD?
ER, THE JUDGES ARE LOOKING FOR CLASSIC DESIGNS...
NOT OVER-ELABORATE ONES - GULP! -- I HOPE!

Wallace & Gromit - Abominable Snowman

by Aardman & Titan Comics

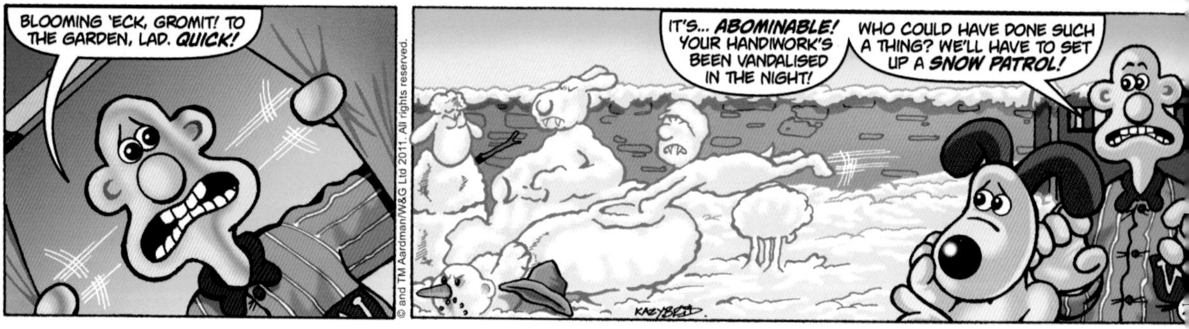

BLOOMING 'ECK, GROMIT! TO THE GARDEN, LAD. *QUICK!*
IT'S... *ABOMINABLE!* YOUR HANDIWORK'S BEEN VANDALISED IN THE NIGHT!
WHO COULD HAVE DONE SUCH A THING? WE'LL HAVE TO SET UP A *SNOW PATROL!*

© and TM Aardman/W&G Ltd 2011. All rights reserved.

Wallace & Gromit - Abominable Snowman

by Aardman & Titan Comics

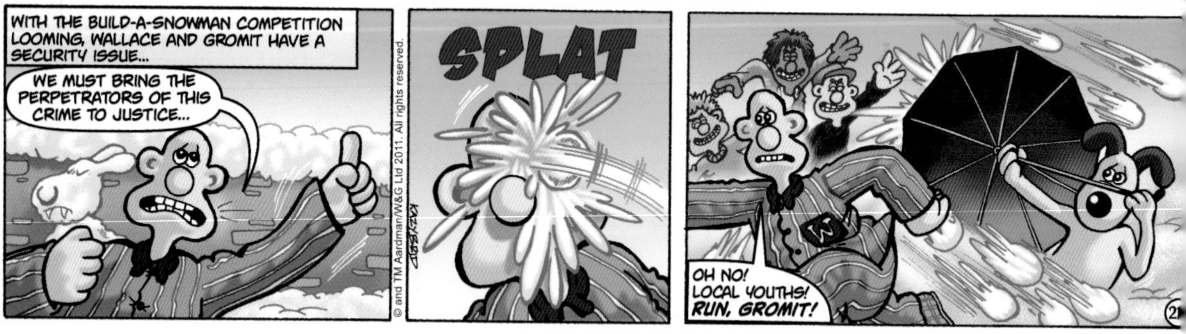

WITH THE BUILD-A-SNOWMAN COMPETITION LOOMING, WALLACE AND GROMIT HAVE A SECURITY ISSUE...
WE MUST BRING THE PERPETRATORS OF THIS CRIME TO JUSTICE...
SPLAT
OH NO! LOCAL YOUTHS! *RUN, GROMIT!*

© and TM Aardman/W&G Ltd 2011. All rights reserved.

allace & Gromit - Abominable Snowman **by Aardman & Titan Comics**

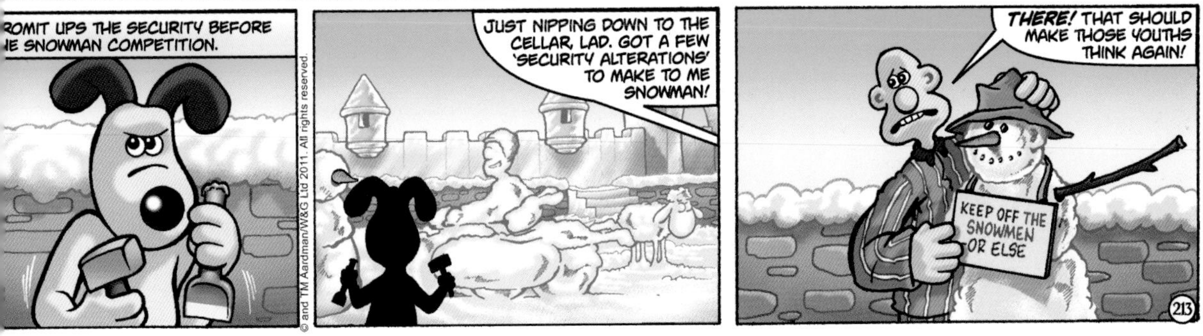

ROMIT UPS THE SECURITY BEFORE
IE SNOWMAN COMPETITION.
© and TM Aardman/W&G Ltd 2011. All rights reserved.
JUST NIPPING DOWN TO THE CELLAR, LAD. GOT A FEW 'SECURITY ALTERATIONS' TO MAKE TO ME SNOWMAN!
THERE! THAT SHOULD MAKE THOSE YOUTHS THINK AGAIN!
KEEP OFF THE SNOWMEN OR ELSE
213

/allace & Gromit - Abominable Snowman **by Aardman & Titan Comics**

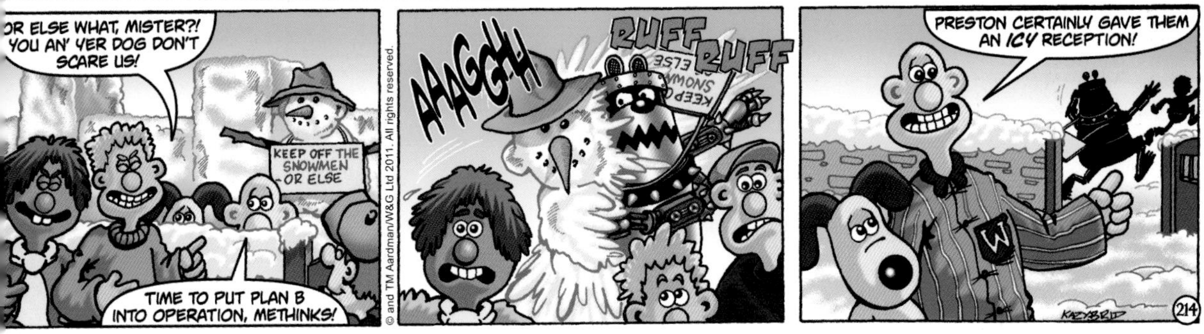

OR ELSE WHAT, MISTER?! YOU AN' YER DOG DON'T SCARE US!
KEEP OFF THE SNOWMEN OR ELSE
TIME TO PUT PLAN B INTO OPERATION, METHINKS!
© and TM Aardman/W&G Ltd 2011. All rights reserved.
AAAGGHH
RUFF RUFF
PRESTON CERTAINLY GAVE THEM AN ICY RECEPTION!
214

/allace & Gromit - Abominable Snowman **by Aardman & Titan Comics**

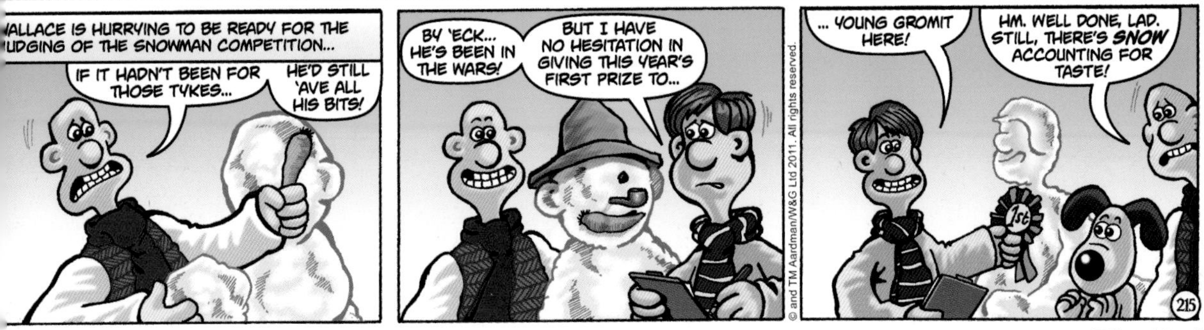

/ALLACE IS HURRYING TO BE READY FOR THE
UDGING OF THE SNOWMAN COMPETITION...
IF IT HADN'T BEEN FOR THOSE TYKES...
HE'D STILL 'AVE ALL HIS BITS!
BY 'ECK... HE'S BEEN IN THE WARS!
BUT I HAVE NO HESITATION IN GIVING THIS YEAR'S FIRST PRIZE TO...
© and TM Aardman/W&G Ltd 2011. All rights reserved.
... YOUNG GROMIT HERE!
HM. WELL DONE, LAD. STILL, THERE'S SNOW ACCOUNTING FOR TASTE!
1st
215

The End

Wallace & Gromit - Perfect Cuppa

by Aardman & Titan Comi

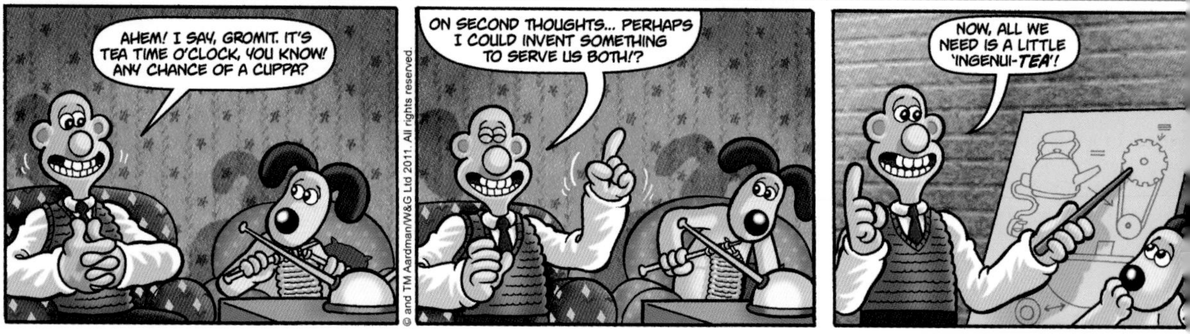
AHEM! I SAY, GROMIT. IT'S TEA TIME O'CLOCK, YOU KNOW! ANY CHANCE OF A CUPPA?
ON SECOND THOUGHTS... PERHAPS I COULD INVENT SOMETHING TO SERVE US BOTH!?
NOW, ALL WE NEED IS A LITTLE 'INGENUI-TEA'!

Wallace & Gromit - Perfect Cuppa

by Aardman & Titan Comi

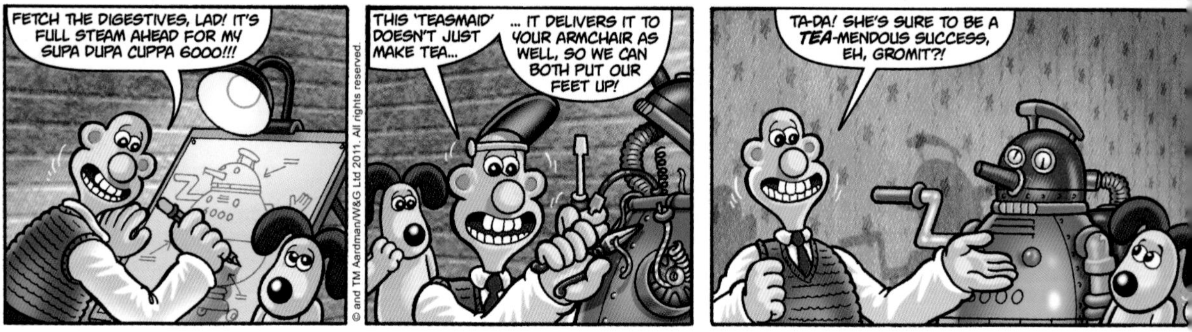
FETCH THE DIGESTIVES, LAD! IT'S FULL STEAM AHEAD FOR MY SUPA DUPA CUPPA 6000!!!
THIS 'TEASMAID' DOESN'T JUST MAKE TEA...
... IT DELIVERS IT TO YOUR ARMCHAIR AS WELL, SO WE CAN BOTH PUT OUR FEET UP!
TA-DA! SHE'S SURE TO BE A TEA-MENDOUS SUCCESS, EH, GROMIT?!

Wallace & Gromit - Perfect Cuppa

by Aardman & Titan Comic

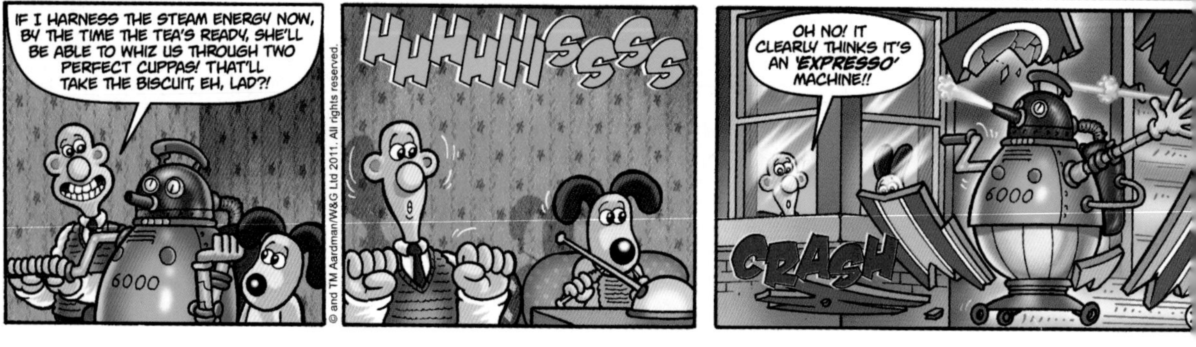
IF I HARNESS THE STEAM ENERGY NOW, BY THE TIME THE TEA'S READY, SHE'LL BE ABLE TO WHIZ US THROUGH TWO PERFECT CUPPAS! THAT'LL TAKE THE BISCUIT, EH, LAD?!
HWHWIIISSSS
OH NO! IT CLEARLY THINKS IT'S AN 'EXPRESSO' MACHINE!!
CRASH

Wallace & Gromit - Perfect Cuppa by Aardman & Titan Comics

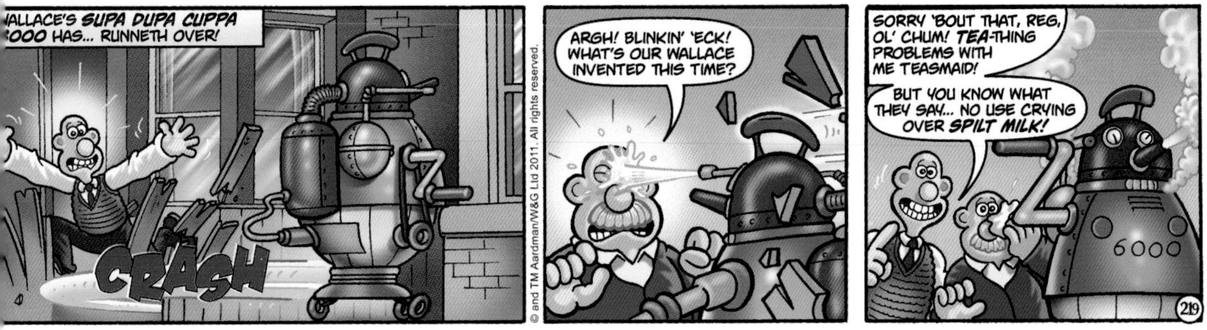

ALLACE'S SUPA DUPA CUPPA OOO HAS... RUNNETH OVER!
CRASH
ARGH! BLINKIN' 'ECK! WHAT'S OUR WALLACE INVENTED THIS TIME?
SORRY 'BOUT THAT, REG, OL' CHUM! TEA-THING PROBLEMS WITH ME TEASMAID!
BUT YOU KNOW WHAT THEY SAY... NO USE CRYING OVER SPILT MILK!
6000
219

Wallace & Gromit - Perfect Cuppa by Aardman & Titan Comics

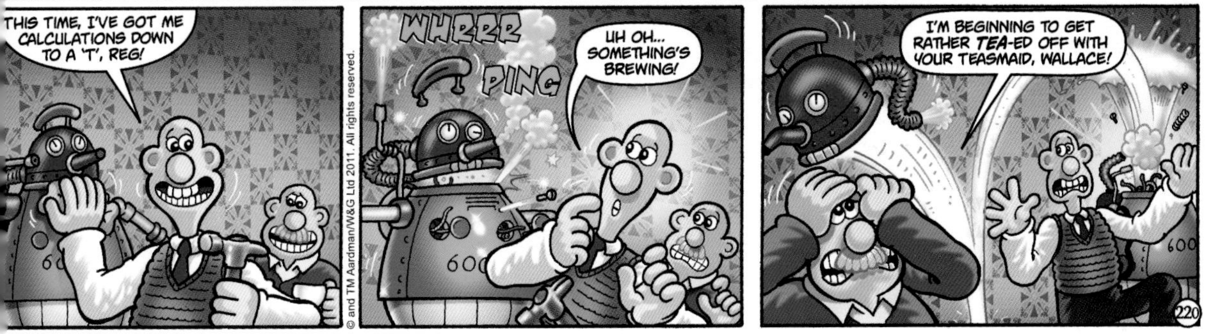

THIS TIME, I'VE GOT ME CALCULATIONS DOWN TO A 'T', REG!
WHRRR
PING
UH OH... SOMETHING'S BREWING!
I'M BEGINNING TO GET RATHER TEA-ED OFF WITH YOUR TEASMAID, WALLACE!
220

© and TM Aardman/W&G Ltd 2011. All rights reserved.

Wallace & Gromit - Perfect Cuppa by Aardman & Titan Comics

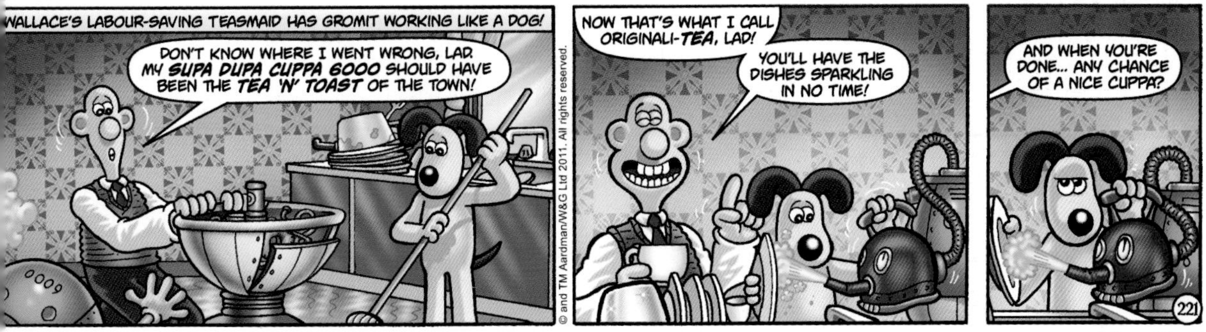

WALLACE'S LABOUR-SAVING TEASMAID HAS GROMIT WORKING LIKE A DOG!
DON'T KNOW WHERE I WENT WRONG, LAD. MY SUPA DUPA CUPPA 6000 SHOULD HAVE BEEN THE TEA 'N' TOAST OF THE TOWN!
NOW THAT'S WHAT I CALL ORIGINALI-TEA, LAD!
YOU'LL HAVE THE DISHES SPARKLING IN NO TIME!
AND WHEN YOU'RE DONE... ANY CHANCE OF A NICE CUPPA?
221

© and TM Aardman/W&G Ltd 2011. All rights reserved.

The End

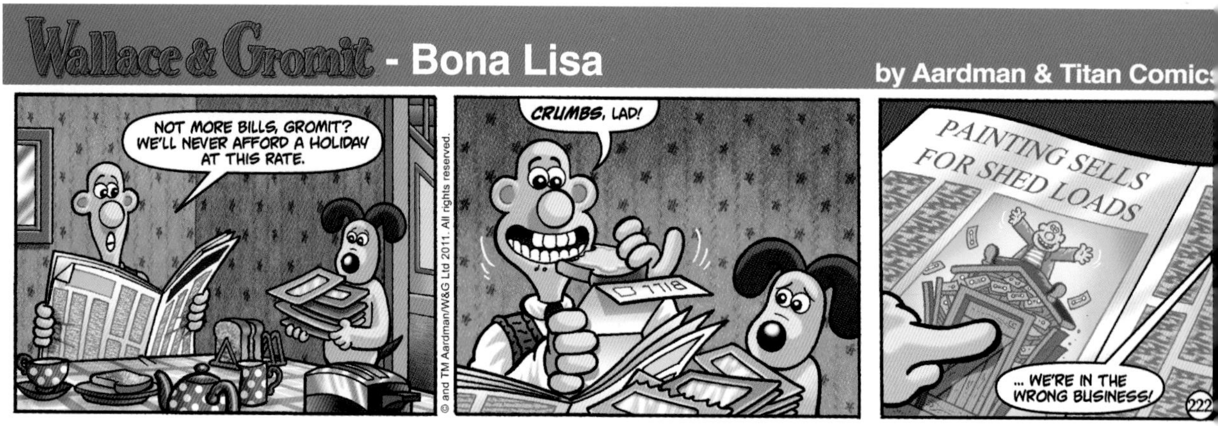
Wallace & Gromit - Bona Lisa
by Aardman & Titan Comics
NOT MORE BILLS, GROMIT? WE'LL NEVER AFFORD A HOLIDAY AT THIS RATE.
CRUMBS, LAD!
PAINTING SELLS FOR SHED LOADS
... WE'RE IN THE WRONG BUSINESS!
© and TM Aardman/W&G Ltd 2011. All rights reserved.
222

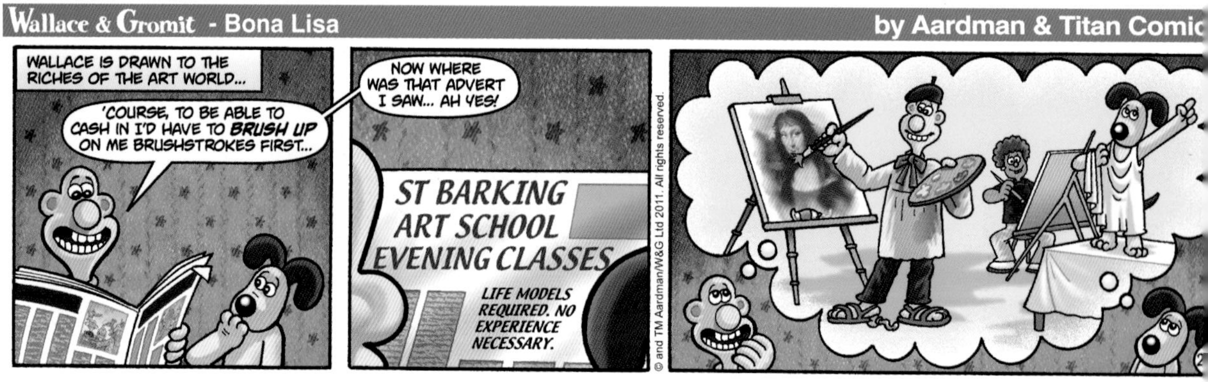
Wallace & Gromit - Bona Lisa
by Aardman & Titan Comics
WALLACE IS DRAWN TO THE RICHES OF THE ART WORLD...
'COURSE, TO BE ABLE TO CASH IN I'D HAVE TO BRUSH UP ON ME BRUSHSTROKES FIRST...
NOW WHERE WAS THAT ADVERT I SAW... AH YES!
ST BARKING ART SCHOOL EVENING CLASSES
LIFE MODELS REQUIRED. NO EXPERIENCE NECESSARY.
© and TM Aardman/W&G Ltd 2011. All rights reserved.

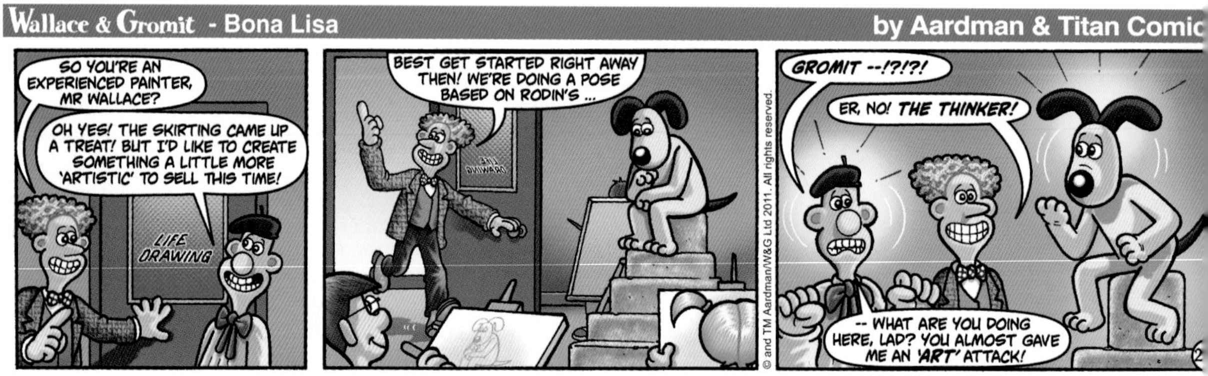
Wallace & Gromit - Bona Lisa
by Aardman & Titan Comics
SO YOU'RE AN EXPERIENCED PAINTER, MR WALLACE?
OH YES! THE SKIRTING CAME UP A TREAT! BUT I'D LIKE TO CREATE SOMETHING A LITTLE MORE 'ARTISTIC' TO SELL THIS TIME!
LIFE DRAWING
BEST GET STARTED RIGHT AWAY THEN! WE'RE DOING A POSE BASED ON RODIN'S ...
GROMIT --!?!?!
ER, NO! THE THINKER!
-- WHAT ARE YOU DOING HERE, LAD? YOU ALMOST GAVE ME AN 'ART' ATTACK!
© and TM Aardman/W&G Ltd 2011. All rights reserved.

Vallace & Gromit - Bona Lisa by Aardman & Titan Comics

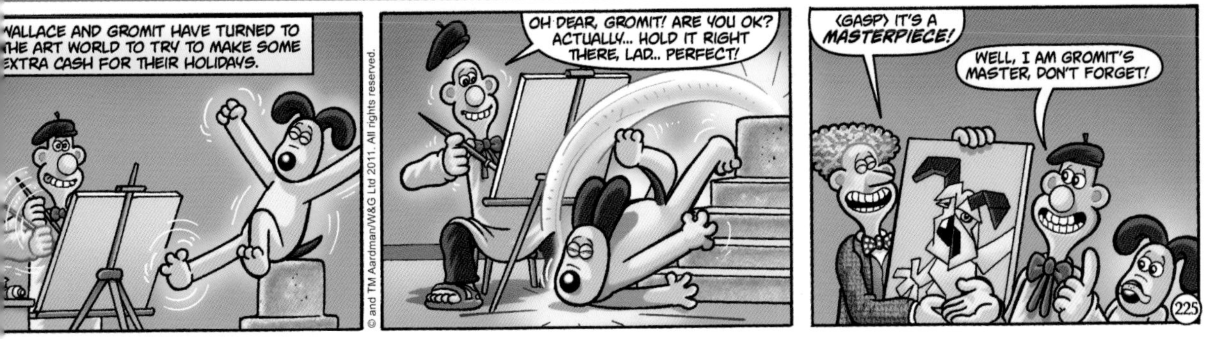

/ALLACE AND GROMIT HAVE TURNED TO
HE ART WORLD TO TRY TO MAKE SOME
EXTRA CASH FOR THEIR HOLIDAYS.
OH DEAR, GROMIT! ARE YOU OK? ACTUALLY... HOLD IT RIGHT THERE, LAD... PERFECT!
(GASP) IT'S A MASTERPIECE!
WELL, I AM GROMIT'S MASTER, DON'T FORGET!
225

Vallace & Gromit - Bona Lisa by Aardman & Titan Comics

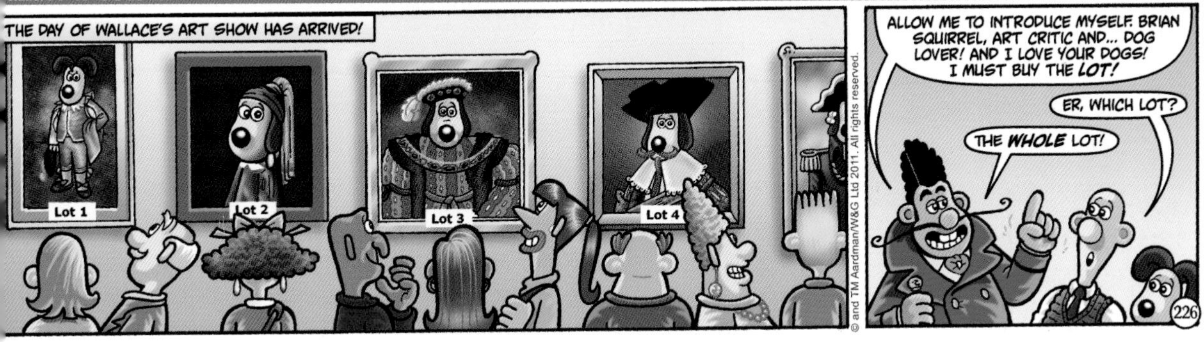

THE DAY OF WALLACE'S ART SHOW HAS ARRIVED!
Lot 1
Lot 2
Lot 3
Lot 4
ALLOW ME TO INTRODUCE MYSELF. BRIAN SQUIRREL, ART CRITIC AND... DOG LOVER! AND I LOVE YOUR DOGS! I MUST BUY THE LOT!
ER, WHICH LOT?
THE WHOLE LOT!
226

Vallace & Gromit - Bona Lisa by Aardman & Titan Comics

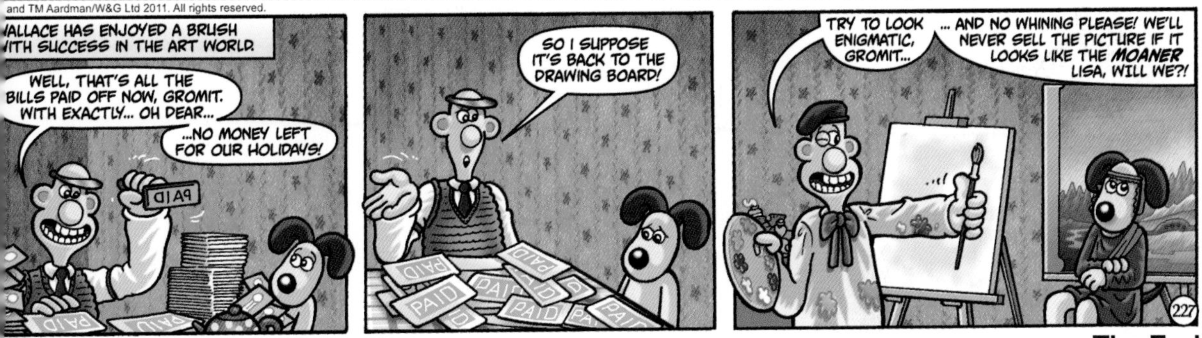

/ALLACE HAS ENJOYED A BRUSH
/ITH SUCCESS IN THE ART WORLD.
WELL, THAT'S ALL THE BILLS PAID OFF NOW, GROMIT. WITH EXACTLY... OH DEAR...
...NO MONEY LEFT FOR OUR HOLIDAYS!
PAID
SO I SUPPOSE IT'S BACK TO THE DRAWING BOARD!
TRY TO LOOK ENIGMATIC, GROMIT...
... AND NO WHINING PLEASE! WE'LL NEVER SELL THE PICTURE IF IT LOOKS LIKE THE MOANER LISA, WILL WE?!
227

The End

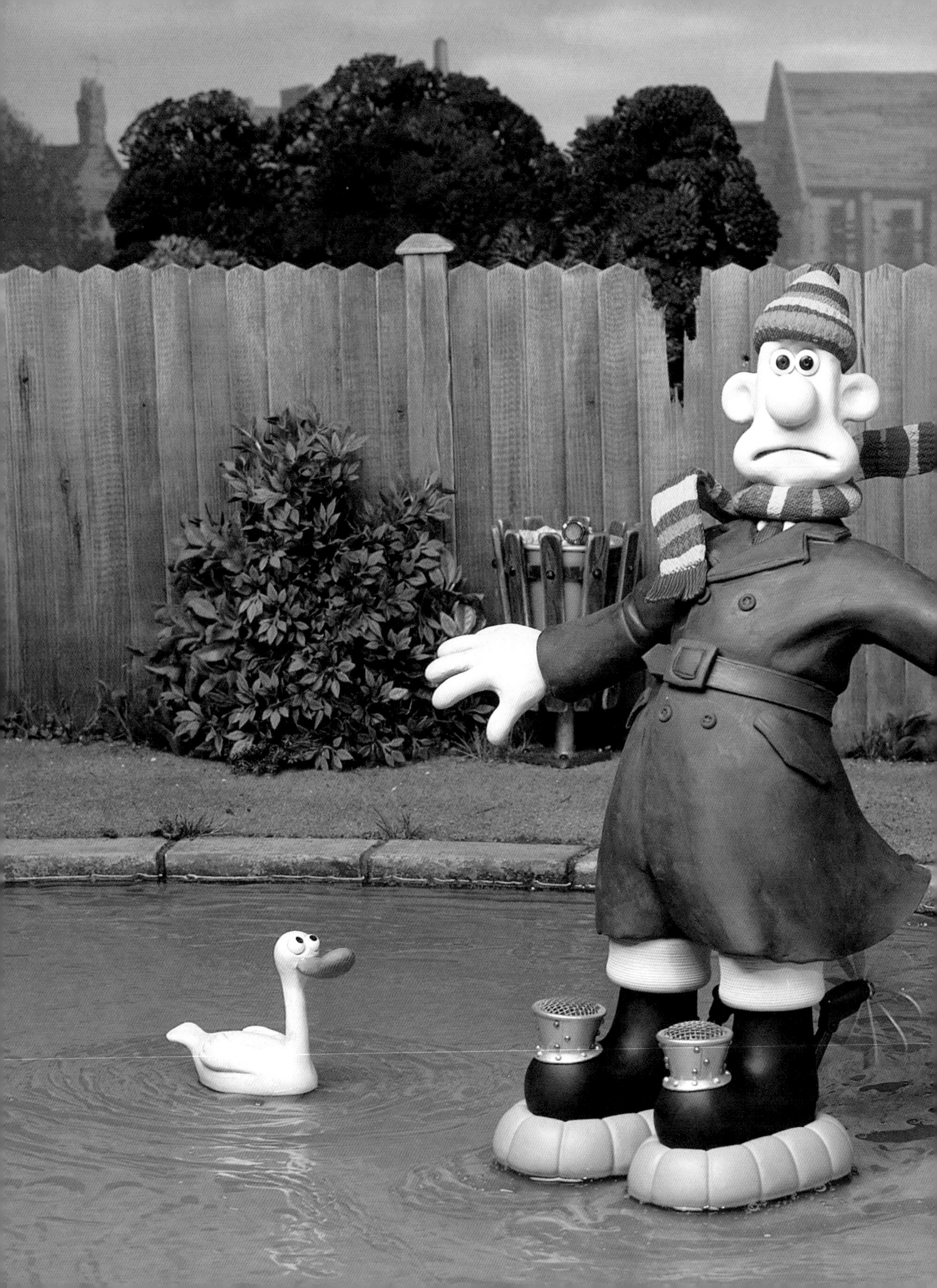

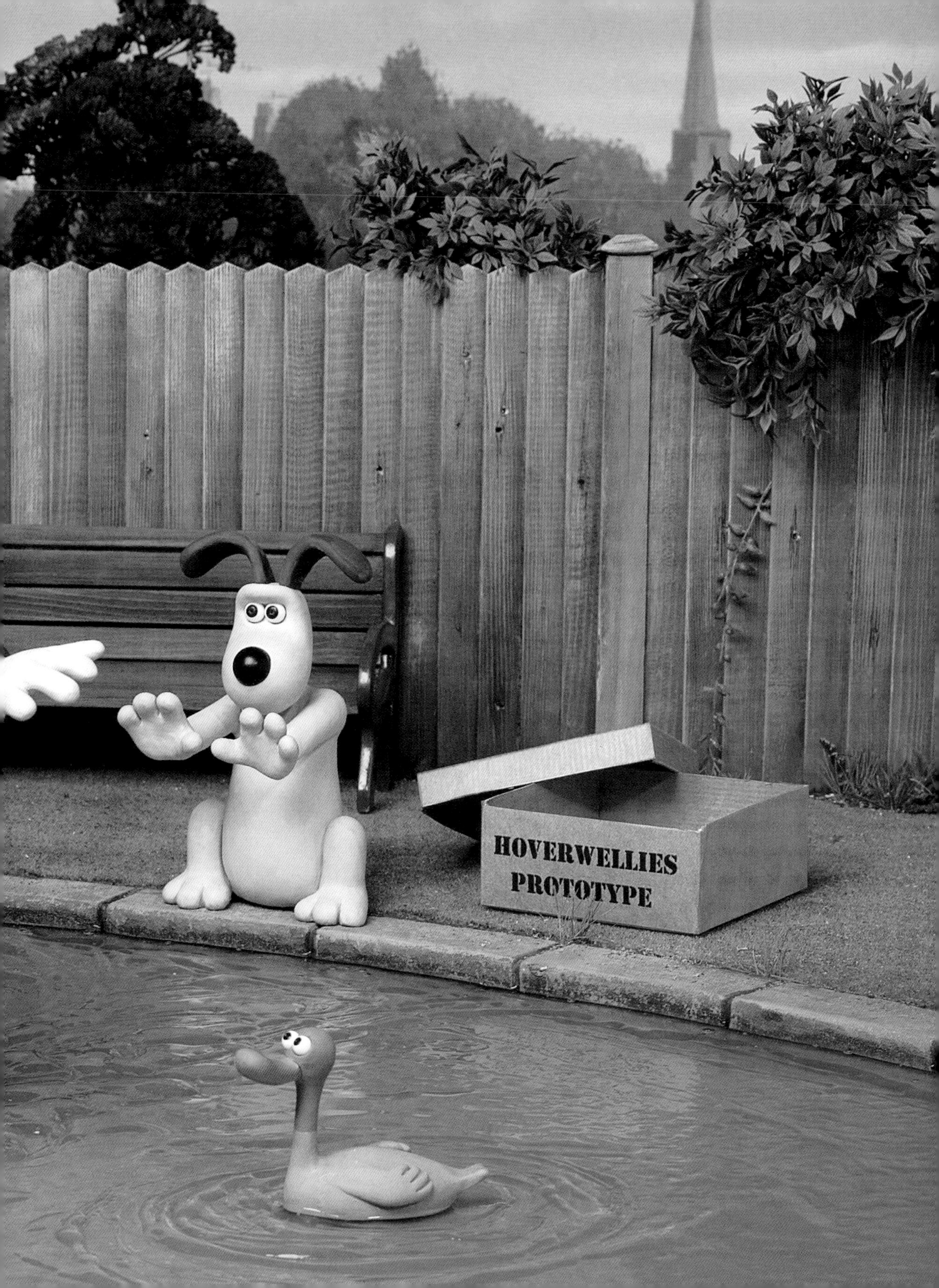
HOVERWELLIES
PROTOTYPE

Wallace & Gromit - Bit of a Jam

by Aardman & Titan Comics

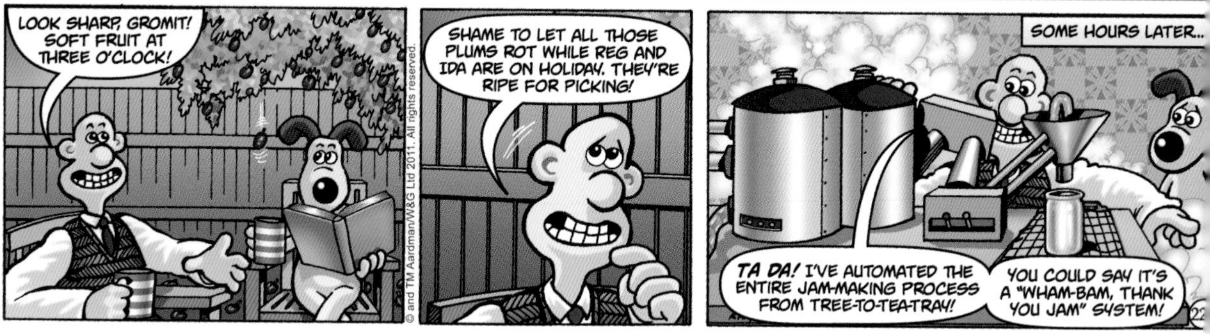
LOOK SHARP, GROMIT! SOFT FRUIT AT THREE O'CLOCK!
SHAME TO LET ALL THOSE PLUMS ROT WHILE REG AND IDA ARE ON HOLIDAY. THEY'RE RIPE FOR PICKING!
© and TM Aardman/W&G Ltd 2011. All rights reserved.
SOME HOURS LATER...
TA DA! I'VE AUTOMATED THE ENTIRE JAM-MAKING PROCESS FROM TREE-TO-TEA-TRAY!
YOU COULD SAY IT'S A "WHAM-BAM, THANK YOU JAM" SYSTEM!

Wallace & Gromit - Bit of a Jam

by Aardman & Titan Comics

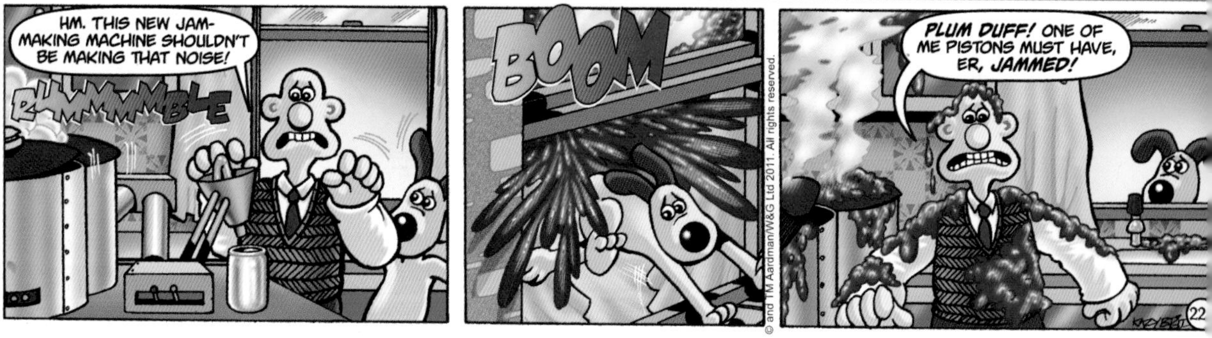
HM. THIS NEW JAM-MAKING MACHINE SHOULDN'T BE MAKING THAT NOISE!
RUMMMMBLE
BOOM
© and TM Aardman/W&G Ltd 2011. All rights reserved.
PLUM DUFF! ONE OF ME PISTONS MUST HAVE, ER, JAMMED!

Wallace & Gromit - Bit of a Jam

by Aardman & Titan Comics

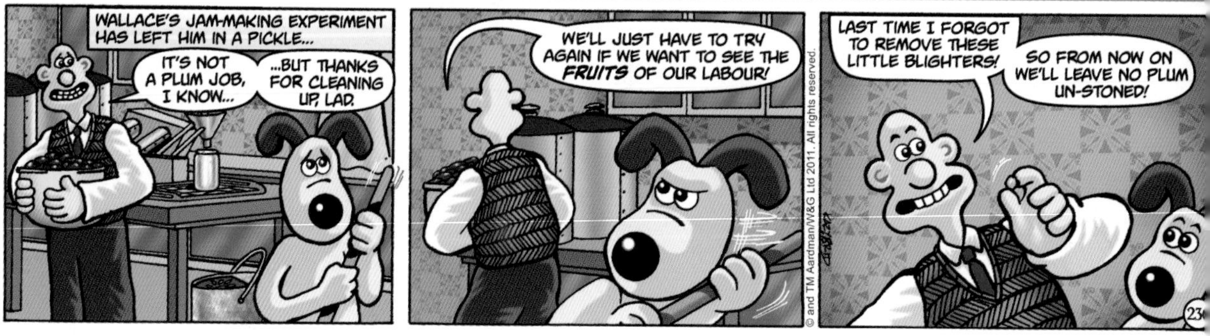
WALLACE'S JAM-MAKING EXPERIMENT HAS LEFT HIM IN A PICKLE...
IT'S NOT A PLUM JOB, I KNOW...
...BUT THANKS FOR CLEANING UP, LAD.
WE'LL JUST HAVE TO TRY AGAIN IF WE WANT TO SEE THE FRUITS OF OUR LABOUR!
© and TM Aardman/W&G Ltd 2011. All rights reserved.
LAST TIME I FORGOT TO REMOVE THESE LITTLE BLIGHTERS!
SO FROM NOW ON WE'LL LEAVE NO PLUM UN-STONED!

Wallace & Gromit - Bit of a Jam

by Aardman & Titan Comics

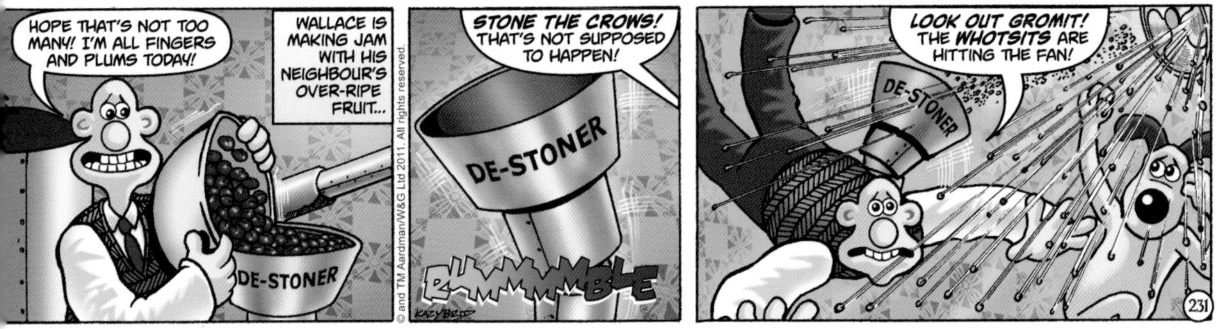

HOPE THAT'S NOT TOO MANY! I'M ALL FINGERS AND PLUMS TODAY!
WALLACE IS MAKING JAM WITH HIS NEIGHBOUR'S OVER-RIPE FRUIT...
DE-STONER
© and TM Aardman/W&G Ltd 2011. All rights reserved.
STONE THE CROWS! THAT'S NOT SUPPOSED TO HAPPEN!
DE-STONER
RUMMMMBLE
LOOK OUT GROMIT! THE WHOTSITS ARE HITTING THE FAN!
DE-STONER
231

Wallace & Gromit - Bit of a Jam

by Aardman & Titan Comics

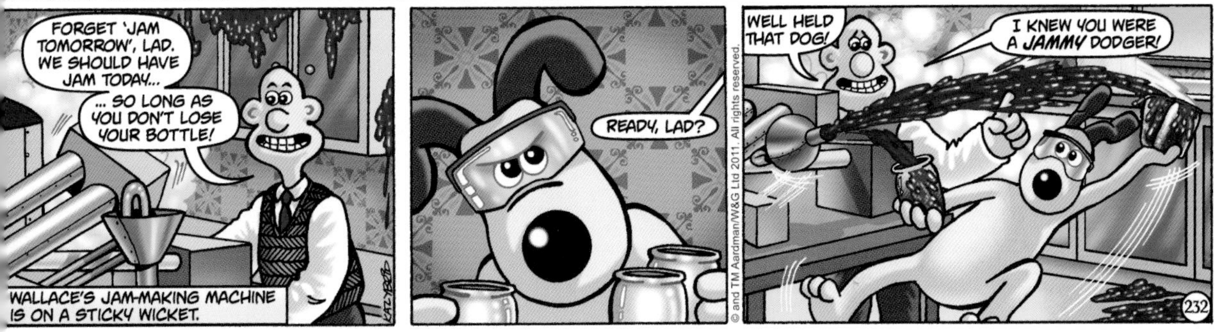

FORGET 'JAM TOMORROW', LAD. WE SHOULD HAVE JAM TODAY...
... SO LONG AS YOU DON'T LOSE YOUR BOTTLE!
WALLACE'S JAM-MAKING MACHINE IS ON A STICKY WICKET.
READY, LAD?
© and TM Aardman/W&G Ltd 2011. All rights reserved.
WELL HELD THAT DOG!
I KNEW YOU WERE A JAMMY DODGER!
232

Wallace & Gromit - Bit of a Jam

by Aardman & Titan Comics

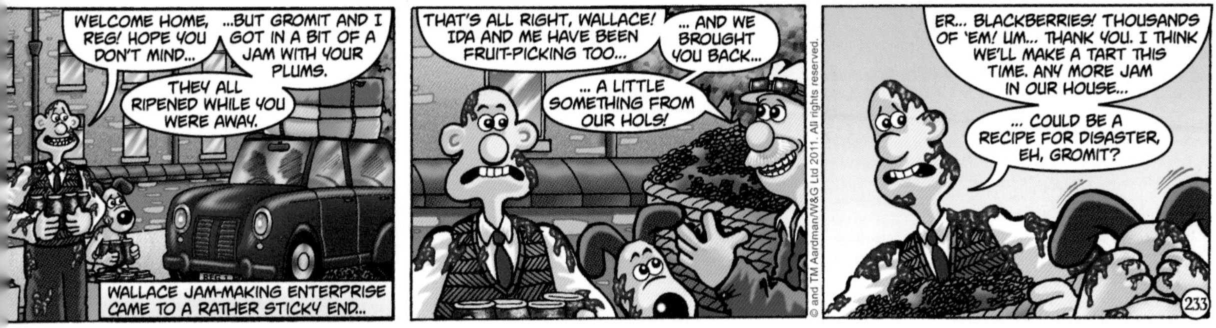

WELCOME HOME, REG! HOPE YOU DON'T MIND...
...BUT GROMIT AND I GOT IN A BIT OF A JAM WITH YOUR PLUMS.
THEY ALL RIPENED WHILE YOU WERE AWAY.
WALLACE JAM-MAKING ENTERPRISE CAME TO A RATHER STICKY END...
THAT'S ALL RIGHT, WALLACE! IDA AND ME HAVE BEEN FRUIT-PICKING TOO...
... AND WE BROUGHT YOU BACK...
... A LITTLE SOMETHING FROM OUR HOLS!
© and TM Aardman/W&G Ltd 2011. All rights reserved.
ER... BLACKBERRIES! THOUSANDS OF 'EM! UM... THANK YOU. I THINK WE'LL MAKE A TART THIS TIME. ANY MORE JAM IN OUR HOUSE...
... COULD BE A RECIPE FOR DISASTER, EH, GROMIT?
233

The End

Wallace & Gromit - Love is in the Air
by Aardman & Titan Comics

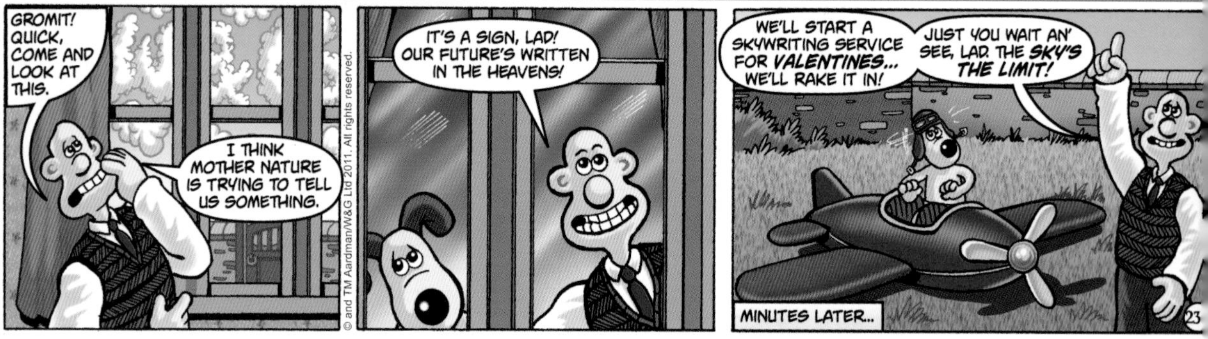
GROMIT! QUICK, COME AND LOOK AT THIS.
I THINK MOTHER NATURE IS TRYING TO TELL US SOMETHING.
IT'S A SIGN, LAD! OUR FUTURE'S WRITTEN IN THE HEAVENS!
WE'LL START A SKYWRITING SERVICE FOR VALENTINES... WE'LL RAKE IT IN!
JUST YOU WAIT AN' SEE, LAD. THE SKY'S THE LIMIT!
MINUTES LATER...

Wallace & Gromit - Love is in the Air
by Aardman & Titan Comics

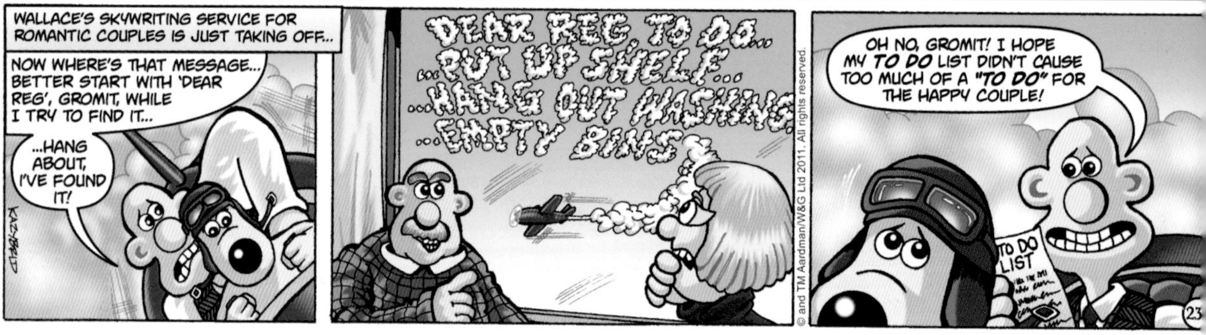
WALLACE'S SKYWRITING SERVICE FOR ROMANTIC COUPLES IS JUST TAKING OFF...
NOW WHERE'S THAT MESSAGE... BETTER START WITH 'DEAR REG', GROMIT, WHILE I TRY TO FIND IT...
...HANG ABOUT, I'VE FOUND IT!
DEAR REG TO DO...
...PUT UP SHELF...
...HANG OUT WASHING
...EMPTY BINS
OH NO, GROMIT! I HOPE MY TO DO LIST DIDN'T CAUSE TOO MUCH OF A "TO DO" FOR THE HAPPY COUPLE!
TO DO LIST

Wallace & Gromit - Love is in the Air
by Aardman & Titan Comics

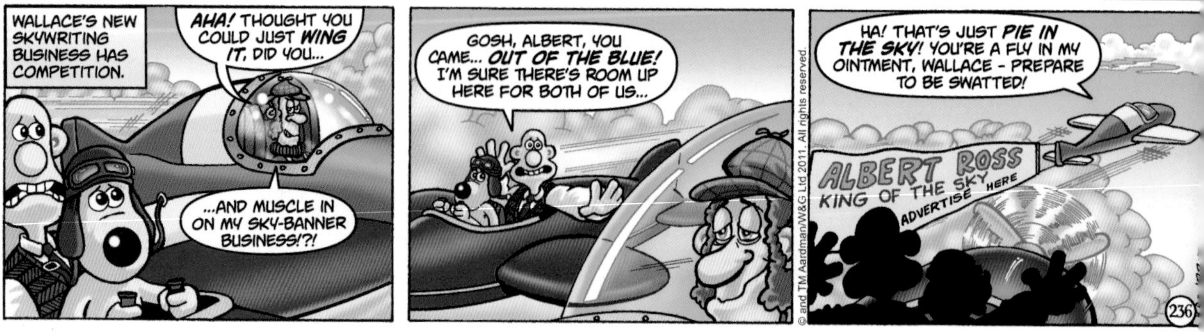
WALLACE'S NEW SKYWRITING BUSINESS HAS COMPETITION.
AHA! THOUGHT YOU COULD JUST WING IT, DID YOU...
...AND MUSCLE IN ON MY SKY-BANNER BUSINESS!?!
GOSH, ALBERT, YOU CAME... OUT OF THE BLUE! I'M SURE THERE'S ROOM UP HERE FOR BOTH OF US...
HA! THAT'S JUST PIE IN THE SKY! YOU'RE A FLY IN MY OINTMENT, WALLACE - PREPARE TO BE SWATTED!
ALBERT ROSS
KING OF THE SKY
ADVERTISE HERE
236

Wallace & Gromit - Love is in the Air by Aardman & Titan Comics

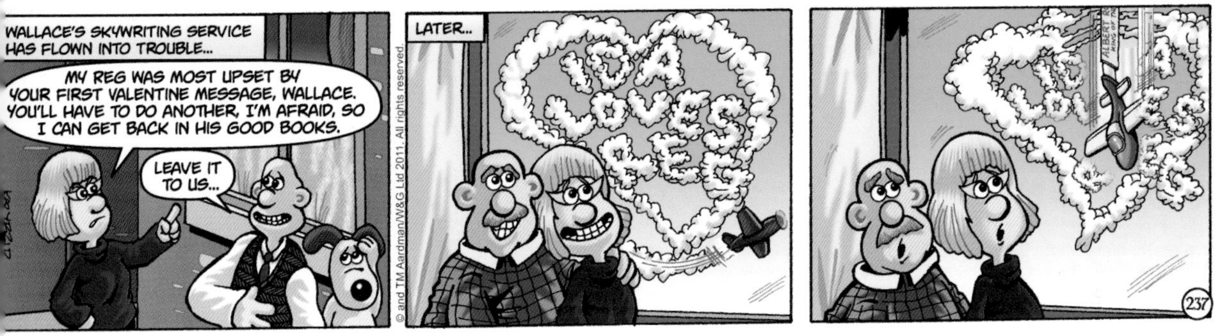
WALLACE'S SKYWRITING SERVICE HAS FLOWN INTO TROUBLE...
MY REG WAS MOST UPSET BY YOUR FIRST VALENTINE MESSAGE, WALLACE. YOU'LL HAVE TO DO ANOTHER, I'M AFRAID, SO I CAN GET BACK IN HIS GOOD BOOKS.
LEAVE IT TO US...
LATER...
IDA LOVES REG
© and TM Aardman/W&G Ltd 2011. All rights reserved.
237

Wallace & Gromit - Love is in the Air by Aardman & Titan Comics

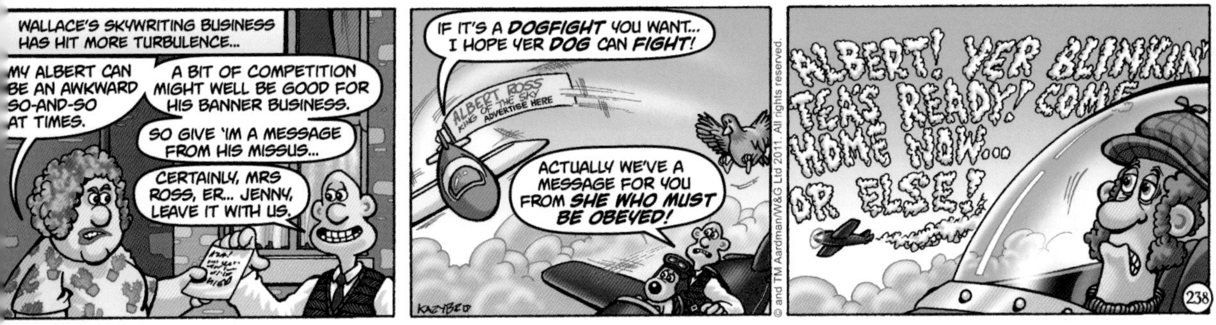
WALLACE'S SKYWRITING BUSINESS HAS HIT MORE TURBULENCE...
MY ALBERT CAN BE AN AWKWARD SO-AND-SO AT TIMES.
A BIT OF COMPETITION MIGHT WELL BE GOOD FOR HIS BANNER BUSINESS.
SO GIVE 'IM A MESSAGE FROM HIS MISSUS...
CERTAINLY, MRS ROSS, ER... JENNY, LEAVE IT WITH US.
IF IT'S A DOGFIGHT YOU WANT... I HOPE YER DOG CAN FIGHT!
ALBERT ROSS KING OF THE SKY ADVERTISE HERE
ACTUALLY WE'VE A MESSAGE FOR YOU FROM SHE WHO MUST BE OBEYED!
© and TM Aardman/W&G Ltd 2011. All rights reserved.
ALBERT! YER BLINKIN' TEA'S READY! COME HOME NOW... OR ELSE!
238

Wallace & Gromit - Love is in the Air by Aardman & Titan Comics

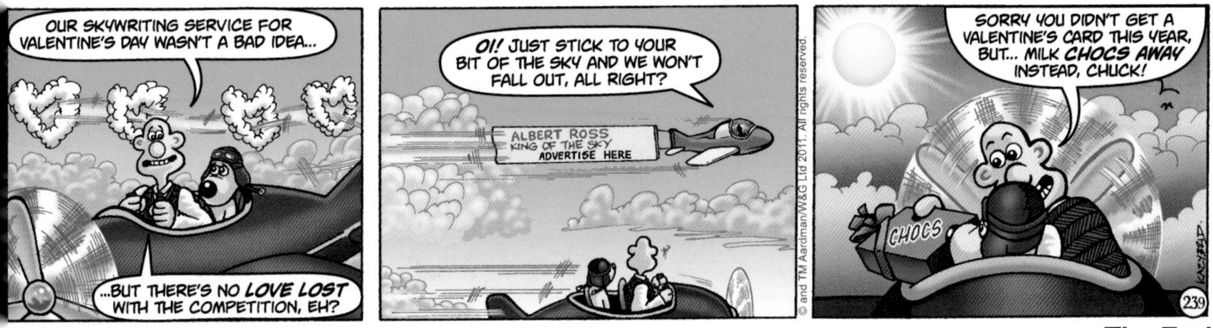
OUR SKYWRITING SERVICE FOR VALENTINE'S DAY WASN'T A BAD IDEA...
...BUT THERE'S NO LOVE LOST WITH THE COMPETITION, EH?
OI! JUST STICK TO YOUR BIT OF THE SKY AND WE WON'T FALL OUT, ALL RIGHT?
ALBERT ROSS KING OF THE SKY ADVERTISE HERE
© and TM Aardman/W&G Ltd 2011. All rights reserved.
SORRY YOU DIDN'T GET A VALENTINE'S CARD THIS YEAR, BUT... MILK CHOCS AWAY INSTEAD, CHUCK!
CHOCS
239

The End

Wallace & Gromit - For the Birds
by Aardman & Titan Comic

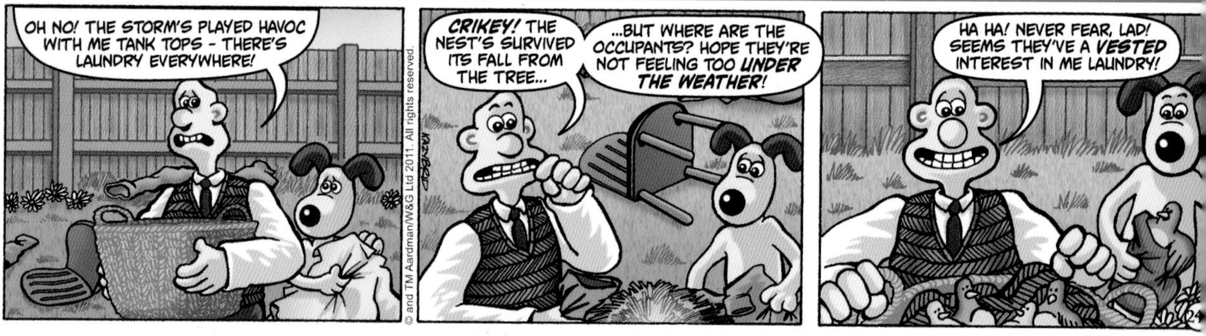

OH NO! THE STORM'S PLAYED HAVOC WITH ME TANK TOPS - THERE'S LAUNDRY EVERYWHERE!
CRIKEY! THE NEST'S SURVIVED ITS FALL FROM THE TREE...
...BUT WHERE ARE THE OCCUPANTS? HOPE THEY'RE NOT FEELING TOO UNDER THE WEATHER!
HA HA! NEVER FEAR, LAD! SEEMS THEY'VE A VESTED INTEREST IN ME LAUNDRY!
© and TM Aardman/W&G Ltd 2011. All rights reserved.

Wallace & Gromit - For the Birds
by Aardman & Titan Comic

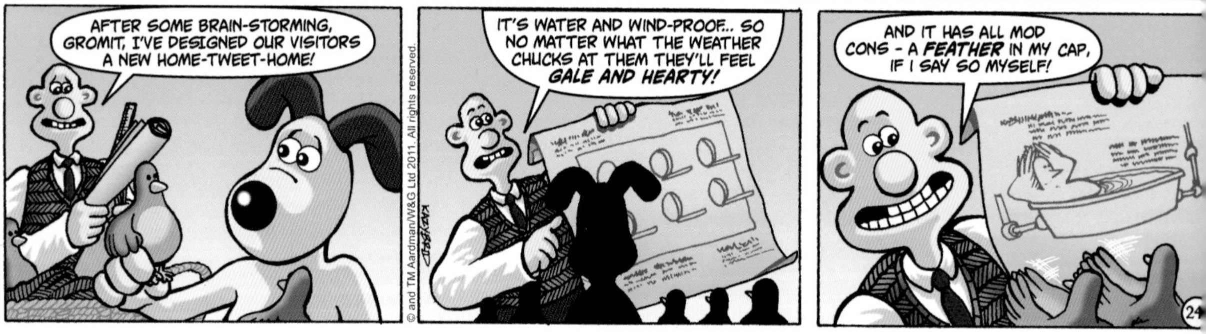

AFTER SOME BRAIN-STORMING, GROMIT, I'VE DESIGNED OUR VISITORS A NEW HOME-TWEET-HOME!
IT'S WATER AND WIND-PROOF.. SO NO MATTER WHAT THE WEATHER CHUCKS AT THEM THEY'LL FEEL GALE AND HEARTY!
AND IT HAS ALL MOD CONS - A FEATHER IN MY CAP, IF I SAY SO MYSELF!
© and TM Aardman/W&G Ltd 2011. All rights reserved.

Wallace & Gromit - For the Birds
by Aardman & Titan Comic

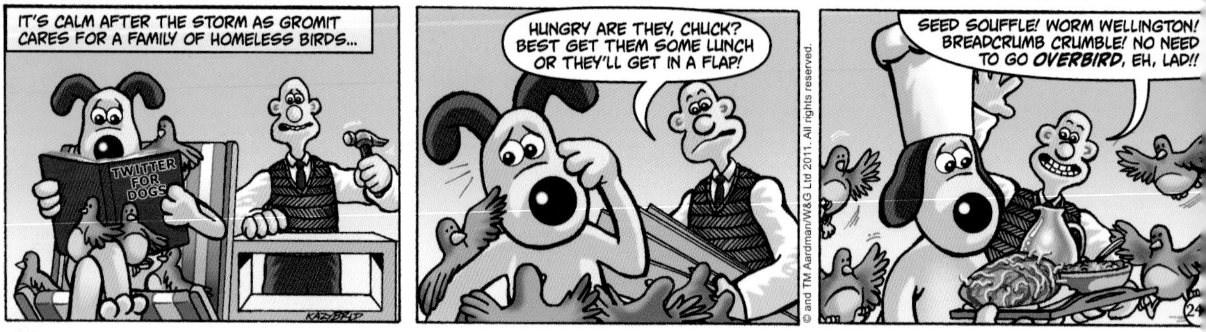

IT'S CALM AFTER THE STORM AS GROMIT CARES FOR A FAMILY OF HOMELESS BIRDS...
TWITTER FOR DOGS
HUNGRY ARE THEY, CHUCK? BEST GET THEM SOME LUNCH OR THEY'LL GET IN A FLAP!
SEED SOUFFLE! WORM WELLINGTON! BREADCRUMB CRUMBLE! NO NEED TO GO OVERBIRD, EH, LAD!!
© and TM Aardman/W&G Ltd 2011. All rights reserved.

Wallace & Gromit - For the Birds by Aardman & Titan Comics

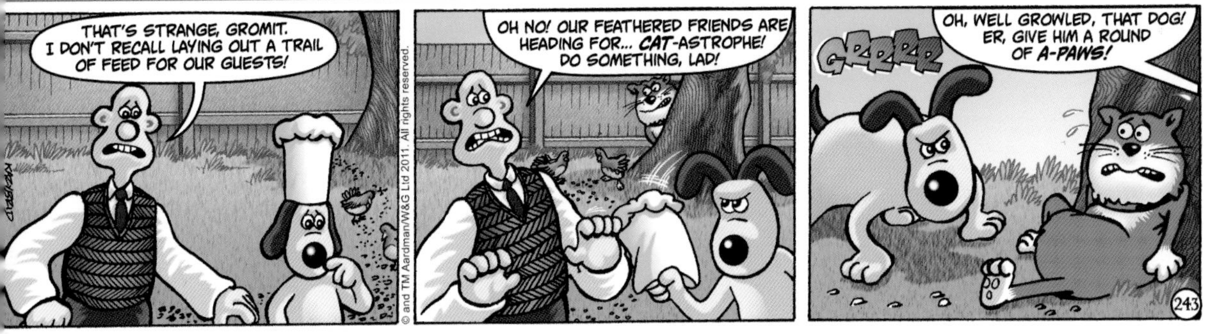

THAT'S STRANGE, GROMIT. I DON'T RECALL LAYING OUT A TRAIL OF FEED FOR OUR GUESTS!
OH NO! OUR FEATHERED FRIENDS ARE HEADING FOR... CAT-ASTROPHE! DO SOMETHING, LAD!
© and TM Aardman/W&G Ltd 2011. All rights reserved.
GRRRR
OH, WELL GROWLED, THAT DOG! ER, GIVE HIM A ROUND OF A-PAWS!
243

Wallace & Gromit - For the Birds by Aardman & Titan Comics

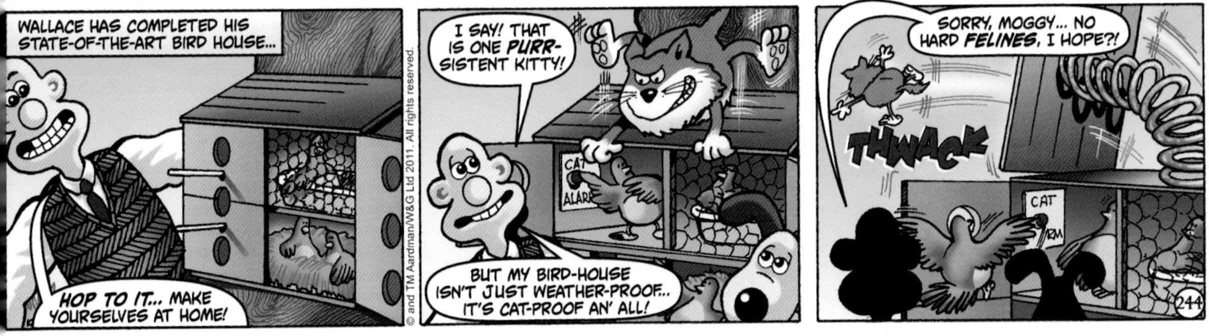

WALLACE HAS COMPLETED HIS STATE-OF-THE-ART BIRD HOUSE...
HOP TO IT... MAKE YOURSELVES AT HOME!
© and TM Aardman/W&G Ltd 2011. All rights reserved.
I SAY! THAT IS ONE PURR-SISTENT KITTY!
BUT MY BIRD-HOUSE ISN'T JUST WEATHER-PROOF.. IT'S CAT-PROOF AN' ALL!
SORRY, MOGGY... NO HARD FELINES, I HOPE?!
THWACK
CAT
244

Wallace & Gromit - For the Birds by Aardman & Titan Comics

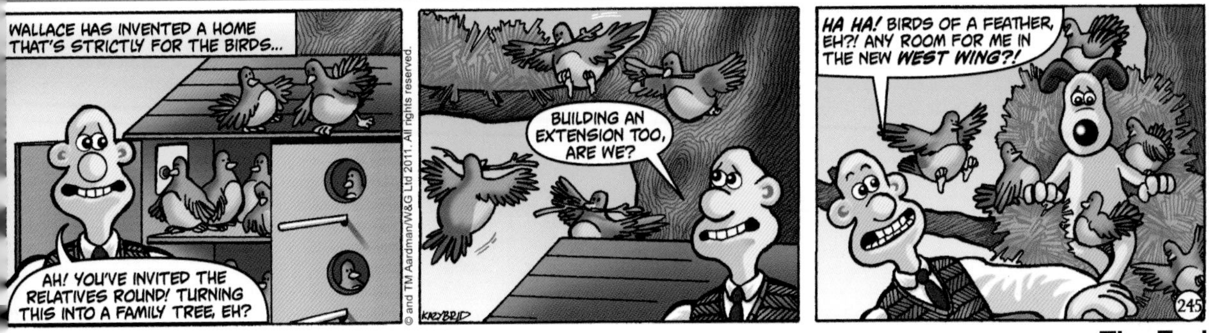

WALLACE HAS INVENTED A HOME THAT'S STRICTLY FOR THE BIRDS...
AH! YOU'VE INVITED THE RELATIVES ROUND! TURNING THIS INTO A FAMILY TREE, EH?
© and TM Aardman/W&G Ltd 2011. All rights reserved.
BUILDING AN EXTENSION TOO, ARE WE?
HA HA! BIRDS OF A FEATHER, EH?! ANY ROOM FOR ME IN THE NEW WEST WING?!
245

The End

Wallace & Gromit - Sweet Dreams are Made of Cheese by Aardman & Titan Comics

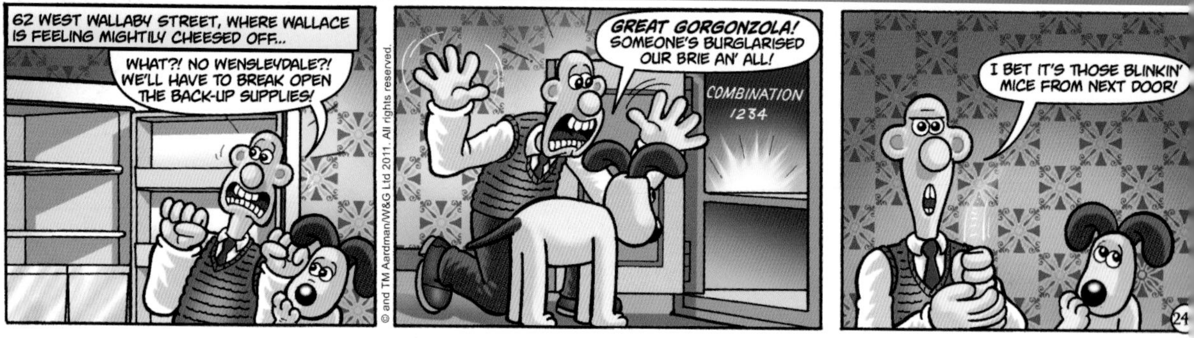
62 WEST WALLABY STREET, WHERE WALLACE IS FEELING MIGHTILY CHEESED OFF...
WHAT?! NO WENSLEYDALE?! WE'LL HAVE TO BREAK OPEN THE BACK-UP SUPPLIES!
GREAT GORGONZOLA! SOMEONE'S BURGLARISED OUR BRIE AN' ALL!
COMBINATION 1234
I BET IT'S THOSE BLINKIN' MICE FROM NEXT DOOR!

Wallace & Gromit - Sweet Dreams are Made of Cheese by Aardman & Titan Comics

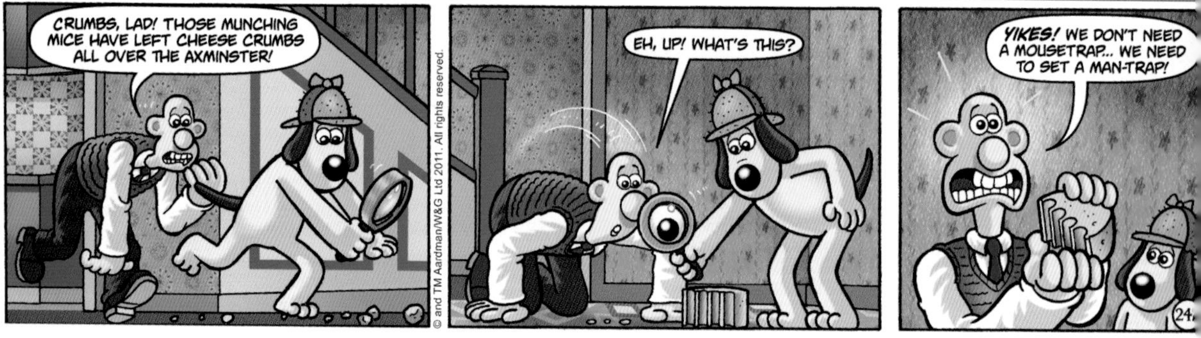
CRUMBS, LAD! THOSE MUNCHING MICE HAVE LEFT CHEESE CRUMBS ALL OVER THE AXMINSTER!
EH, UP! WHAT'S THIS?
YIKES! WE DON'T NEED A MOUSETRAP... WE NEED TO SET A MAN-TRAP!

Wallace & Gromit - Sweet Dreams are Made of Cheese by Aardman & Titan Comics

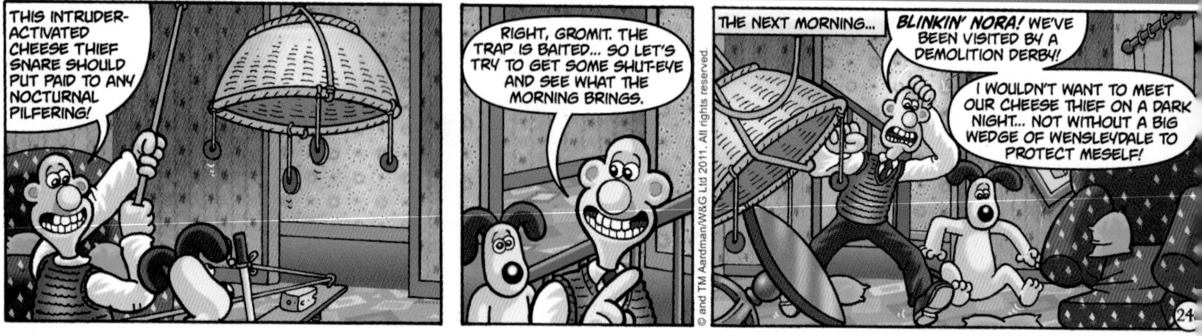
THIS INTRUDER-ACTIVATED CHEESE THIEF SNARE SHOULD PUT PAID TO ANY NOCTURNAL PILFERING!
RIGHT, GROMIT. THE TRAP IS BAITED... SO LET'S TRY TO GET SOME SHUT-EYE AND SEE WHAT THE MORNING BRINGS.
THE NEXT MORNING...
BLINKIN' NORA! WE'VE BEEN VISITED BY A DEMOLITION DERBY!
I WOULDN'T WANT TO MEET OUR CHEESE THIEF ON A DARK NIGHT... NOT WITHOUT A BIG WEDGE OF WENSLEYDALE TO PROTECT MESELF!

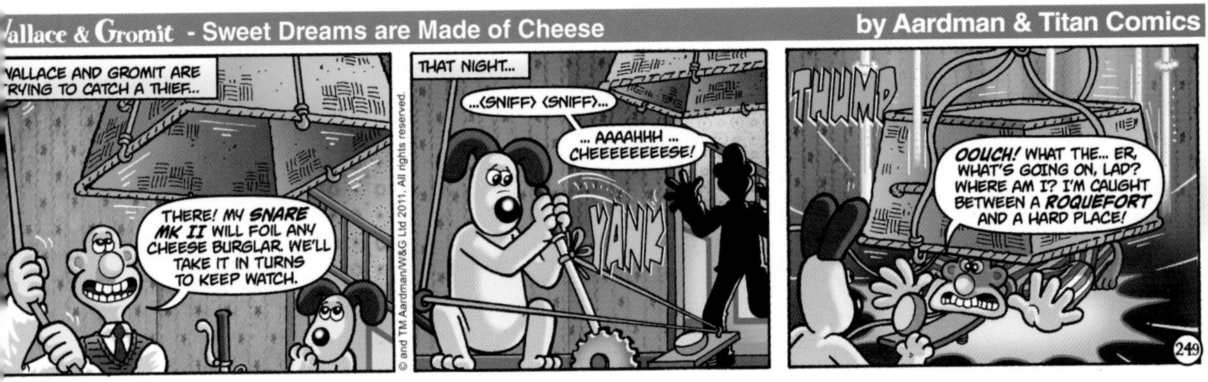
Wallace & Gromit - Sweet Dreams are Made of Cheese
by Aardman & Titan Comics
WALLACE AND GROMIT ARE TRYING TO CATCH A THIEF...
THERE! MY SNARE MK II WILL FOIL ANY CHEESE BURGLAR. WE'LL TAKE IT IN TURNS TO KEEP WATCH.
THAT NIGHT...
...(SNIFF) (SNIFF)...
... AAAAHHH ... CHEEEEEEEEESE!
YANK
© and TM Aardman/W&G Ltd 2011. All rights reserved.
THUMP
OOUCH! WHAT THE... ER, WHAT'S GOING ON, LAD? WHERE AM I? I'M CAUGHT BETWEEN A ROQUEFORT AND A HARD PLACE!
249

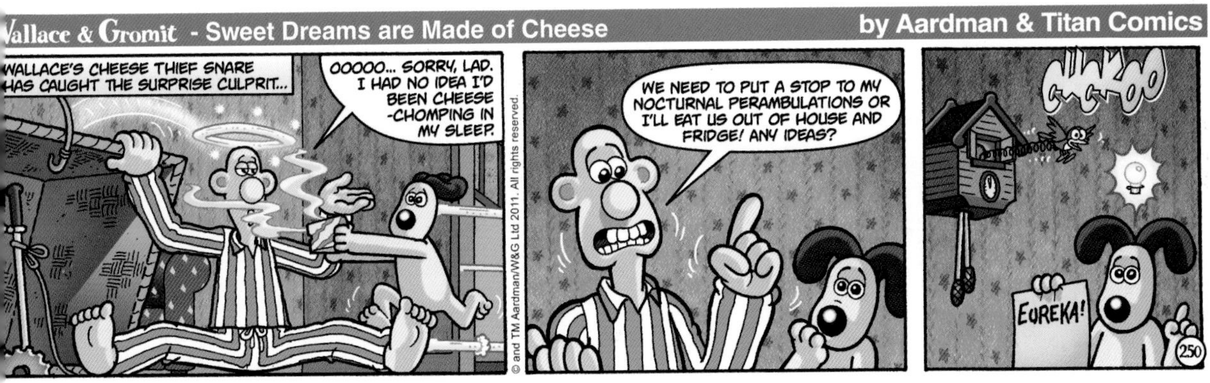
Wallace & Gromit - Sweet Dreams are Made of Cheese
by Aardman & Titan Comics
WALLACE'S CHEESE THIEF SNARE HAS CAUGHT THE SURPRISE CULPRIT...
OOOOO... SORRY, LAD. I HAD NO IDEA I'D BEEN CHEESE -CHOMPING IN MY SLEEP.
© and TM Aardman/W&G Ltd 2011. All rights reserved.
WE NEED TO PUT A STOP TO MY NOCTURNAL PERAMBULATIONS OR I'LL EAT US OUT OF HOUSE AND FRIDGE! ANY IDEAS?
CUCKOO
EUREKA!
250

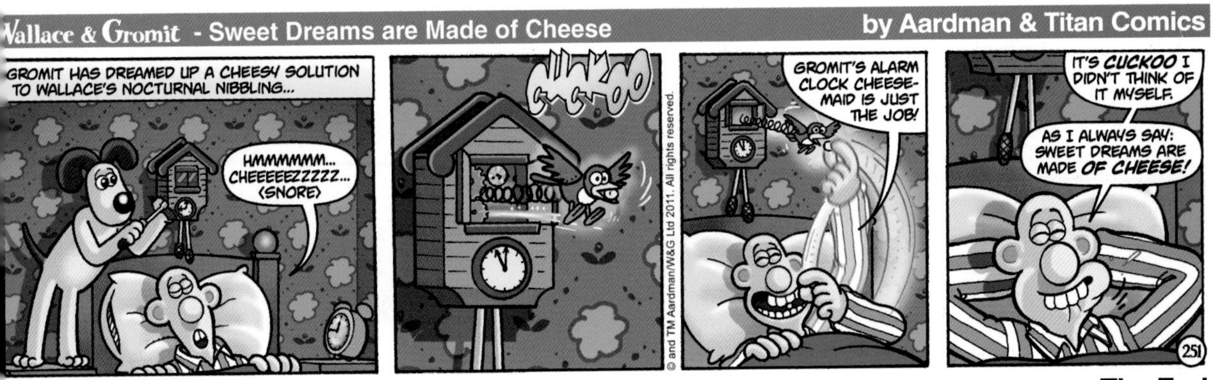
Wallace & Gromit - Sweet Dreams are Made of Cheese
by Aardman & Titan Comics
GROMIT HAS DREAMED UP A CHEESY SOLUTION TO WALLACE'S NOCTURNAL NIBBLING...
HMMMMMM... CHEEEEEZZZZZ... (SNORE)
CUCKOO
© and TM Aardman/W&G Ltd 2011. All rights reserved.
GROMIT'S ALARM CLOCK CHEESE-MAID IS JUST THE JOB!
IT'S CUCKOO I DIDN'T THINK OF IT MYSELF.
AS I ALWAYS SAY: SWEET DREAMS ARE MADE OF CHEESE!
251

The End

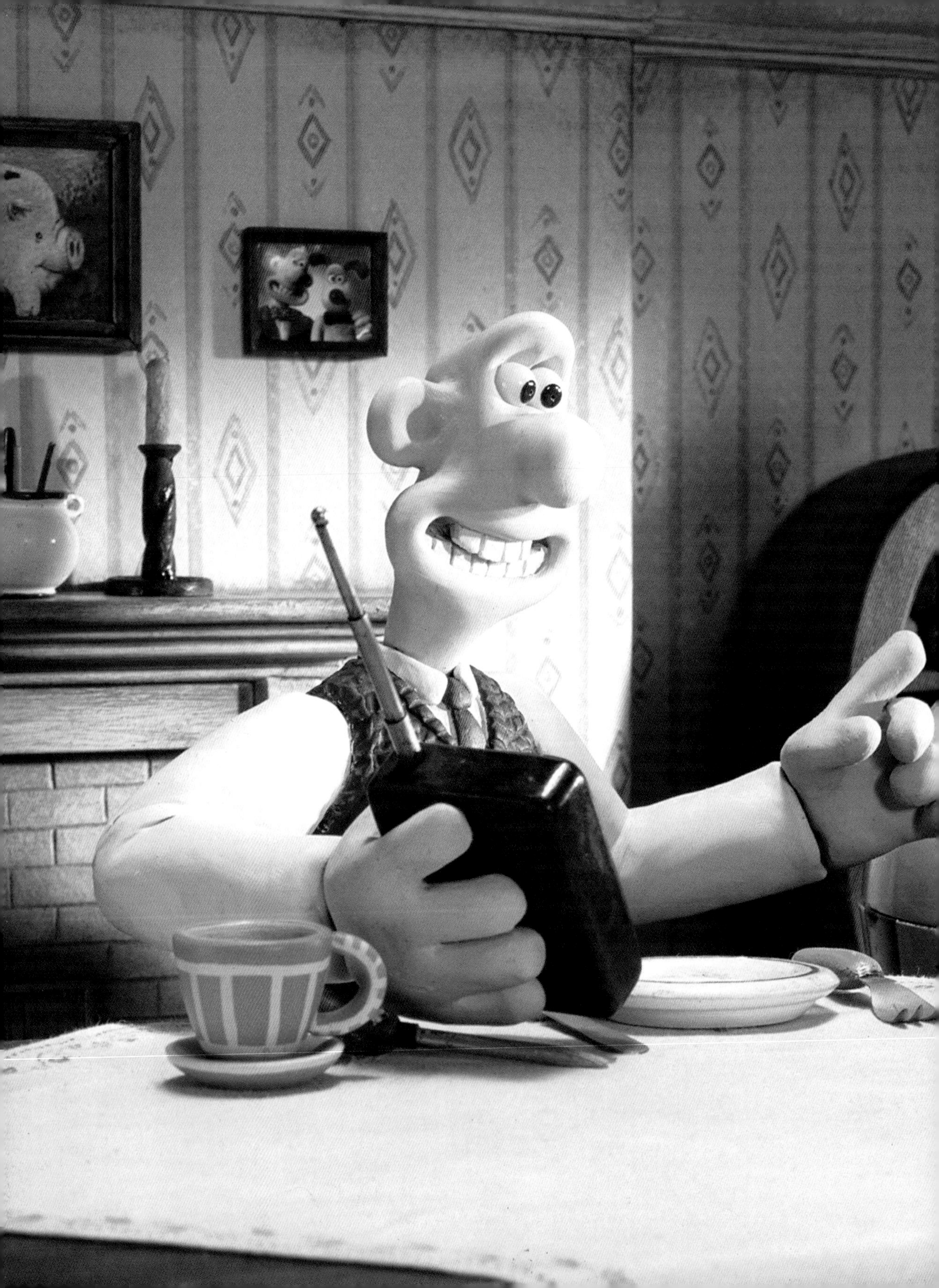

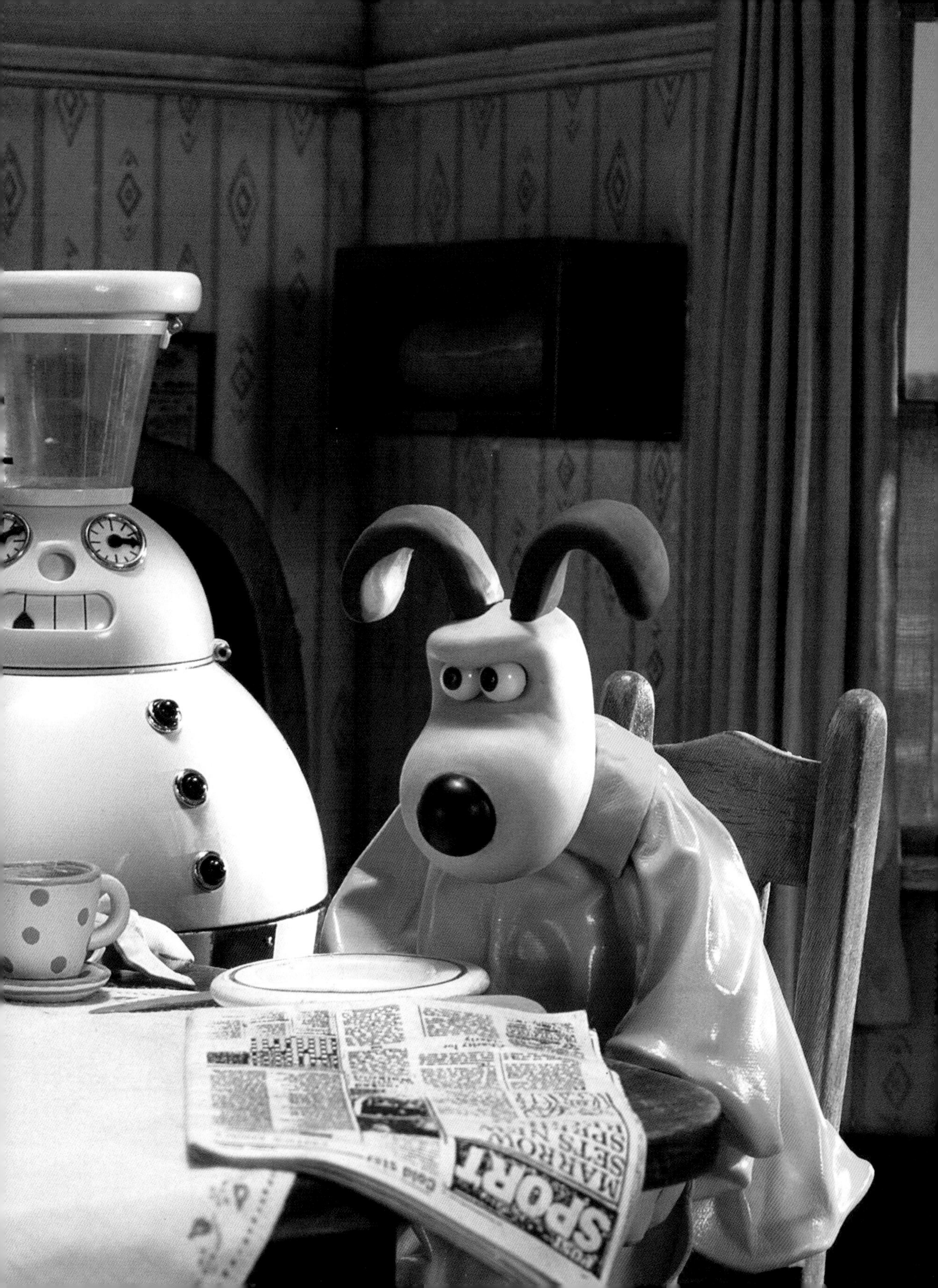
SPORT

Wallace & Gromit - Another Grand Day Out by Aardman & Titan Comic

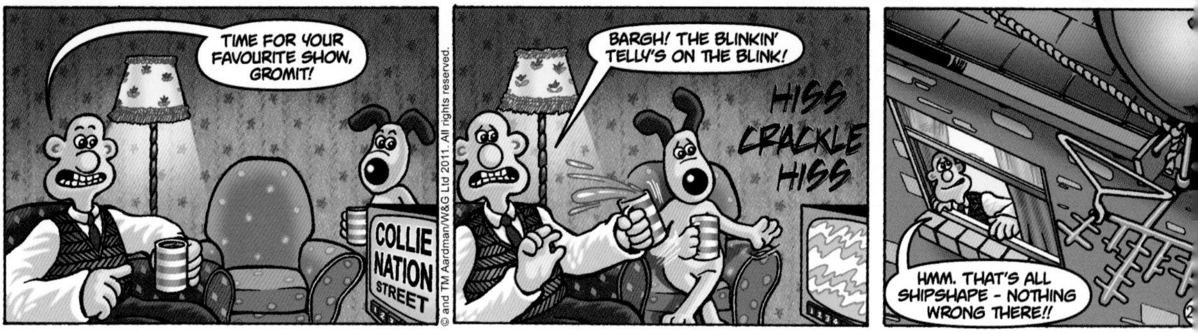
TIME FOR YOUR FAVOURITE SHOW, GROMIT!
COLLIE NATION STREET
© and TM Aardman/W&G Ltd 2011. All rights reserved.
BARGH! THE BLINKIN' TELLY'S ON THE BLINK!
HISS CRACKLE HISS
HMM. THAT'S ALL SHIPSHAPE - NOTHING WRONG THERE!!

Wallace & Gromit - Another Grand Day Out by Aardman & Titan Comic

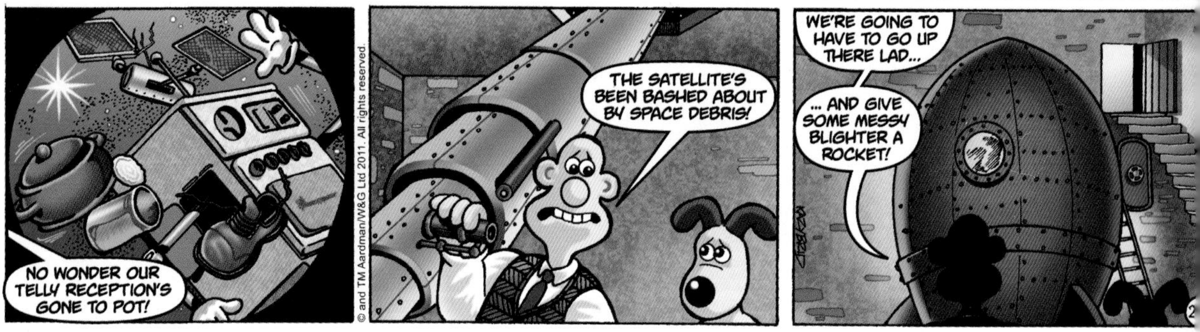
NO WONDER OUR TELLY RECEPTION'S GONE TO POT!
© and TM Aardman/W&G Ltd 2011. All rights reserved.
THE SATELLITE'S BEEN BASHED ABOUT BY SPACE DEBRIS!
WE'RE GOING TO HAVE TO GO UP THERE LAD...
... AND GIVE SOME MESSY BLIGHTER A ROCKET!

Wallace & Gromit - Another Grand Day Out by Aardman & Titan Comic

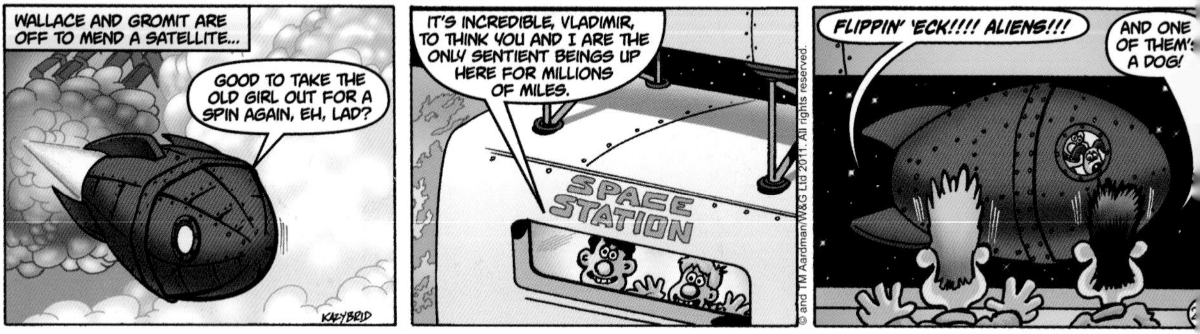
WALLACE AND GROMIT ARE OFF TO MEND A SATELLITE...
GOOD TO TAKE THE OLD GIRL OUT FOR A SPIN AGAIN, EH, LAD?
IT'S INCREDIBLE, VLADIMIR, TO THINK YOU AND I ARE THE ONLY SENTIENT BEINGS UP HERE FOR MILLIONS OF MILES.
SPACE STATION
© and TM Aardman/W&G Ltd 2011. All rights reserved.
FLIPPIN' 'ECK!!!! ALIENS!!!
AND ONE OF THEM'S A DOG!

Vallace & Gromit - Another Grand Day Out by Aardman & Titan Comics

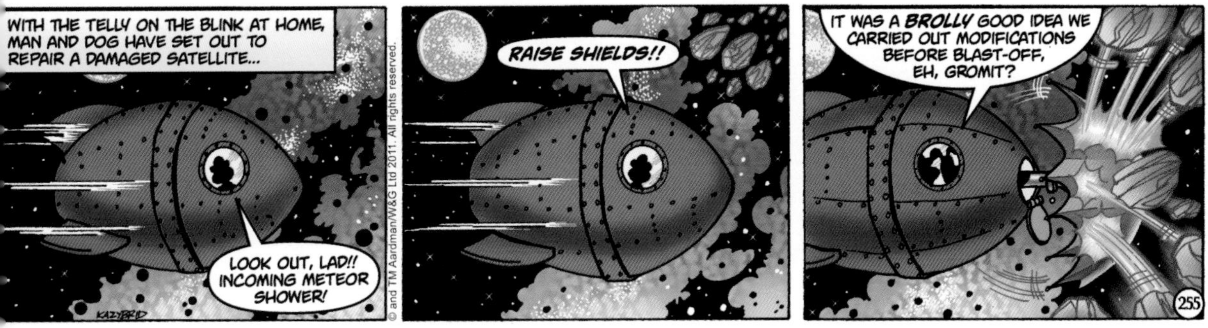

WITH THE TELLY ON THE BLINK AT HOME, MAN AND DOG HAVE SET OUT TO REPAIR A DAMAGED SATELLITE...
LOOK OUT, LAD!! INCOMING METEOR SHOWER!
KAZYBRID
© and TM Aardman/W&G Ltd 2011. All rights reserved.
RAISE SHIELDS!!
IT WAS A BROLLY GOOD IDEA WE CARRIED OUT MODIFICATIONS BEFORE BLAST-OFF, EH, GROMIT?
255

Vallace & Gromit - Another Grand Day Out by Aardman & Titan Comics

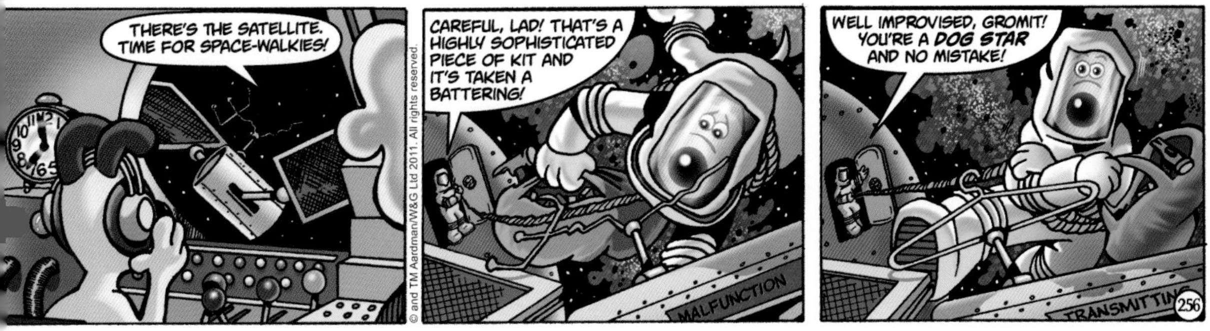

THERE'S THE SATELLITE. TIME FOR SPACE-WALKIES!
© and TM Aardman/W&G Ltd 2011. All rights reserved.
CAREFUL, LAD! THAT'S A HIGHLY SOPHISTICATED PIECE OF KIT AND IT'S TAKEN A BATTERING!
MALFUNCTION
WELL IMPROVISED, GROMIT! YOU'RE A DOG STAR AND NO MISTAKE!
TRANSMITTING
256

Vallace & Gromit - Another Grand Day Out by Aardman & Titan Comics

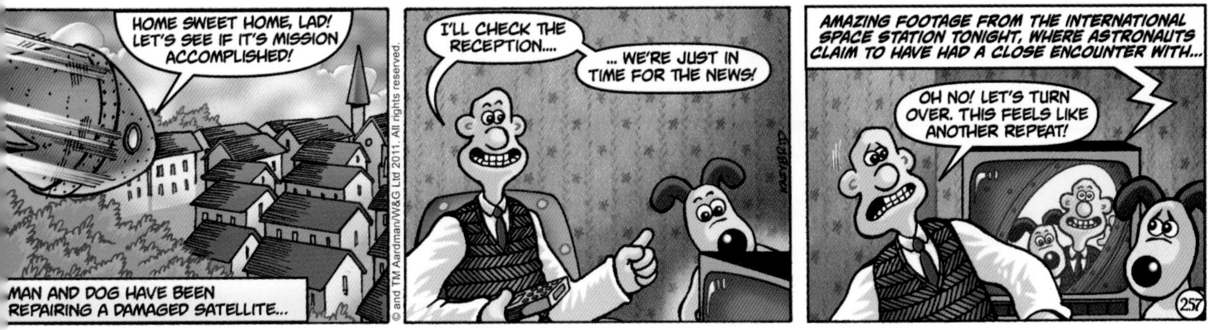

HOME SWEET HOME, LAD! LET'S SEE IF IT'S MISSION ACCOMPLISHED!
MAN AND DOG HAVE BEEN REPAIRING A DAMAGED SATELLITE...
© and TM Aardman/W&G Ltd 2011. All rights reserved.
I'LL CHECK THE RECEPTION....
... WE'RE JUST IN TIME FOR THE NEWS!
AMAZING FOOTAGE FROM THE INTERNATIONAL SPACE STATION TONIGHT, WHERE ASTRONAUTS CLAIM TO HAVE HAD A CLOSE ENCOUNTER WITH...
OH NO! LET'S TURN OVER. THIS FEELS LIKE ANOTHER REPEAT!
257

The End

Wallace & Gromit - Leaf it to Wallace

by Aardman & Titan Comic

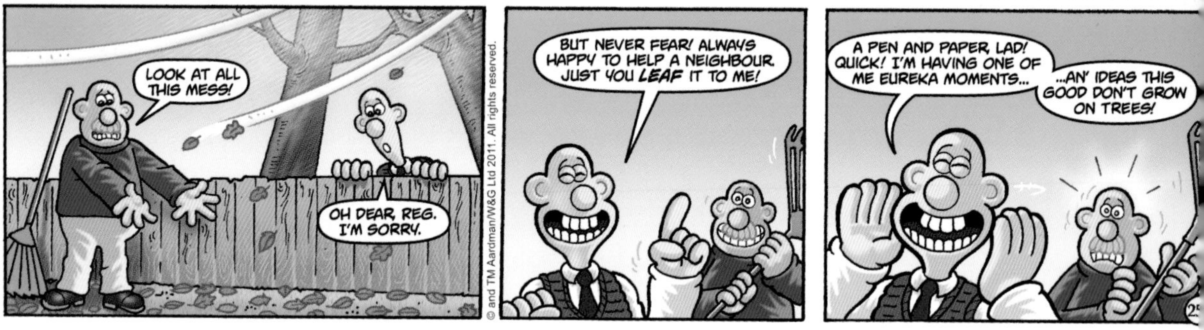
LOOK AT ALL THIS MESS!
OH DEAR, REG. I'M SORRY.
© and TM Aardman/W&G Ltd 2011. All rights reserved.
BUT NEVER FEAR! ALWAYS HAPPY TO HELP A NEIGHBOUR. JUST YOU LEAF IT TO ME!
A PEN AND PAPER, LAD! QUICK! I'M HAVING ONE OF ME EUREKA MOMENTS...
...AN' IDEAS THIS GOOD DON'T GROW ON TREES!

Wallace & Gromit - Leaf it to Wallace

by Aardman & Titan Comic

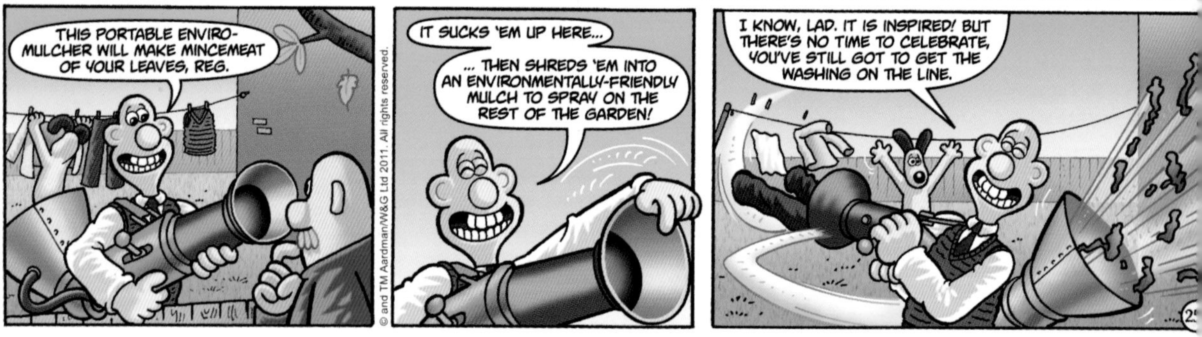
THIS PORTABLE ENVIRO-MULCHER WILL MAKE MINCEMEAT OF YOUR LEAVES, REG.
© and TM Aardman/W&G Ltd 2011. All rights reserved.
IT SUCKS 'EM UP HERE...
... THEN SHREDS 'EM INTO AN ENVIRONMENTALLY-FRIENDLY MULCH TO SPRAY ON THE REST OF THE GARDEN!
I KNOW, LAD. IT IS INSPIRED! BUT THERE'S NO TIME TO CELEBRATE, YOU'VE STILL GOT TO GET THE WASHING ON THE LINE.

Wallace & Gromit - Leaf it to Wallace

by Aardman & Titan Comic

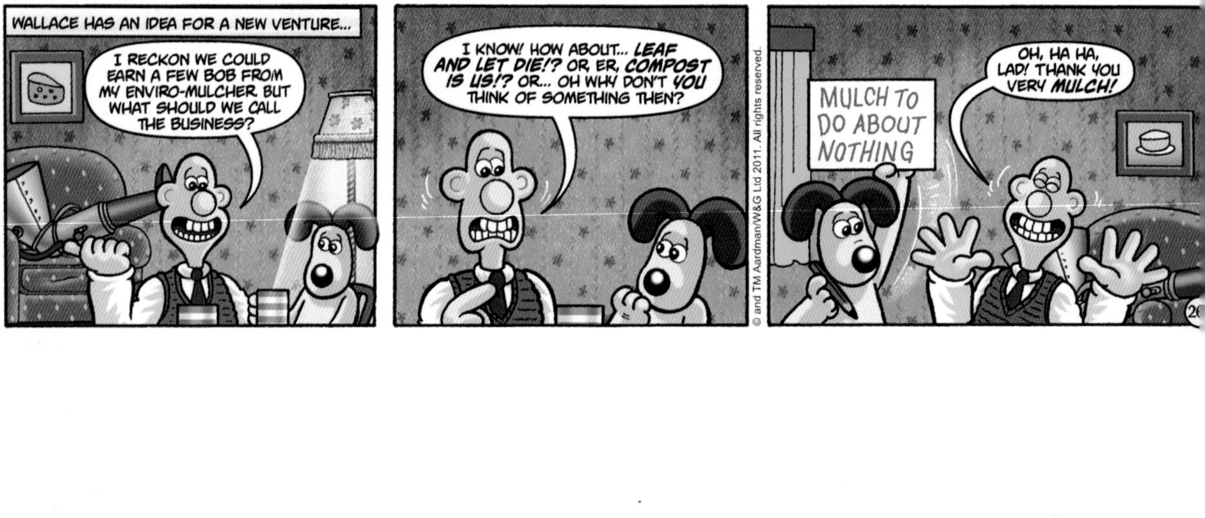
WALLACE HAS AN IDEA FOR A NEW VENTURE...
I RECKON WE COULD EARN A FEW BOB FROM MY ENVIRO-MULCHER. BUT WHAT SHOULD WE CALL THE BUSINESS?
I KNOW! HOW ABOUT... LEAF AND LET DIE!? OR, ER, COMPOST IS US!? OR... OH WHY DON'T YOU THINK OF SOMETHING THEN?
© and TM Aardman/W&G Ltd 2011. All rights reserved.
MULCH TO DO ABOUT NOTHING
OH, HA HA, LAD! THANK YOU VERY MULCH!

Wallace & Gromit - Leaf it to Wallace by Aardman & Titan Comics

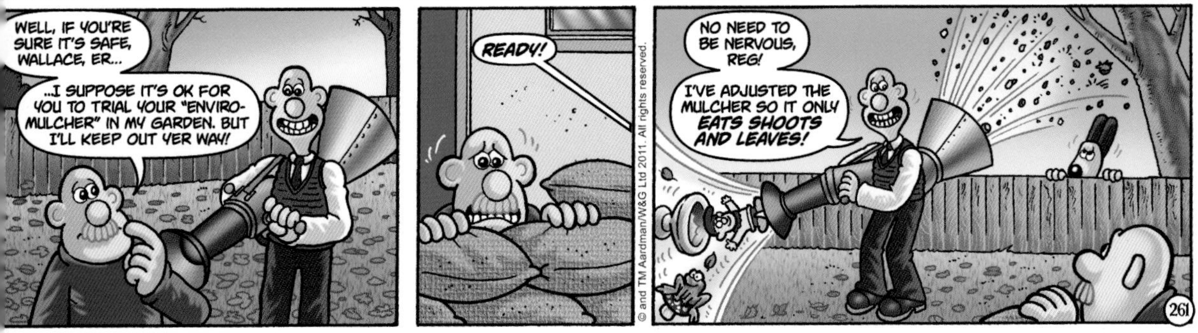
WELL, IF YOU'RE SURE IT'S SAFE, WALLACE, ER...
...I SUPPOSE IT'S OK FOR YOU TO TRIAL YOUR "ENVIRO-MULCHER" IN MY GARDEN. BUT I'LL KEEP OUT YER WAY!
READY!
NO NEED TO BE NERVOUS, REG!
I'VE ADJUSTED THE MULCHER SO IT ONLY **EATS SHOOTS AND LEAVES!**
261

Wallace & Gromit - Leaf it to Wallace by Aardman & Titan Comics

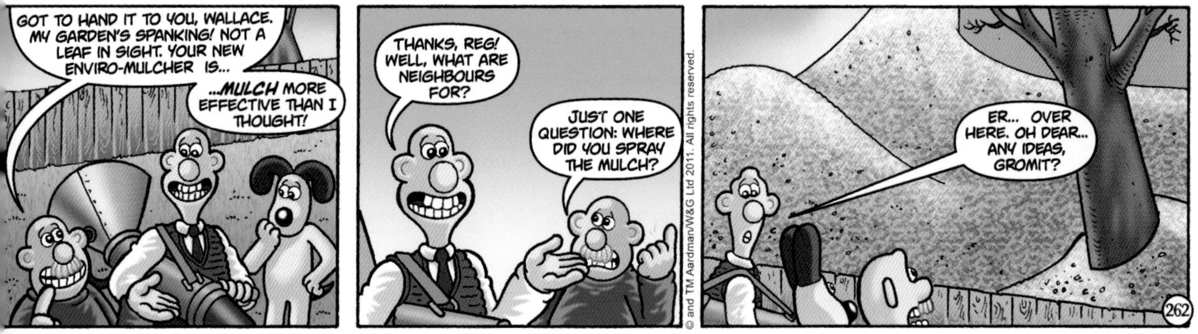
GOT TO HAND IT TO YOU, WALLACE. MY GARDEN'S SPANKING! NOT A LEAF IN SIGHT. YOUR NEW ENVIRO-MULCHER IS...
...**MULCH** MORE EFFECTIVE THAN I THOUGHT!
THANKS, REG! WELL, WHAT ARE NEIGHBOURS FOR?
JUST ONE QUESTION: WHERE DID YOU SPRAY THE MULCH?
ER... OVER HERE. OH DEAR... ANY IDEAS, GROMIT?
262

Wallace & Gromit - Leaf it to Wallace by Aardman & Titan Comics

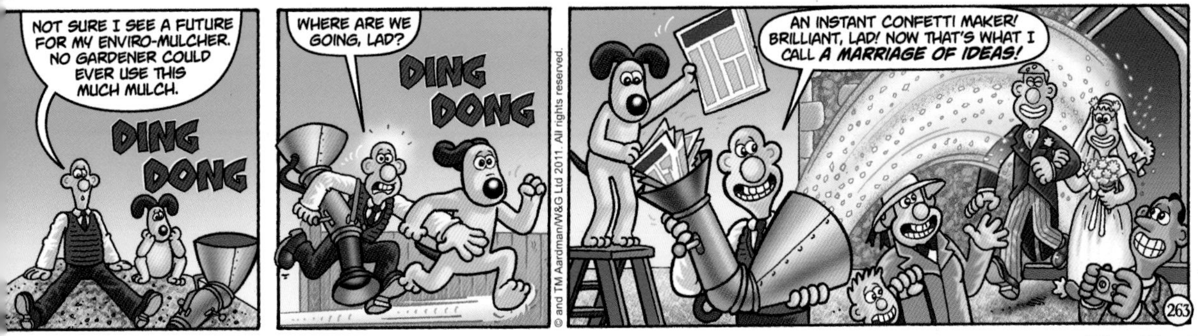
NOT SURE I SEE A FUTURE FOR MY ENVIRO-MULCHER. NO GARDENER COULD EVER USE THIS MUCH MULCH.
DING DONG
WHERE ARE WE GOING, LAD?
DING DONG
AN INSTANT CONFETTI MAKER! BRILLIANT, LAD! NOW THAT'S WHAT I CALL ***A MARRIAGE OF IDEAS!***
263

The End

Wallace & Gromit - Paper Hound

by Aardman & Titan Comic

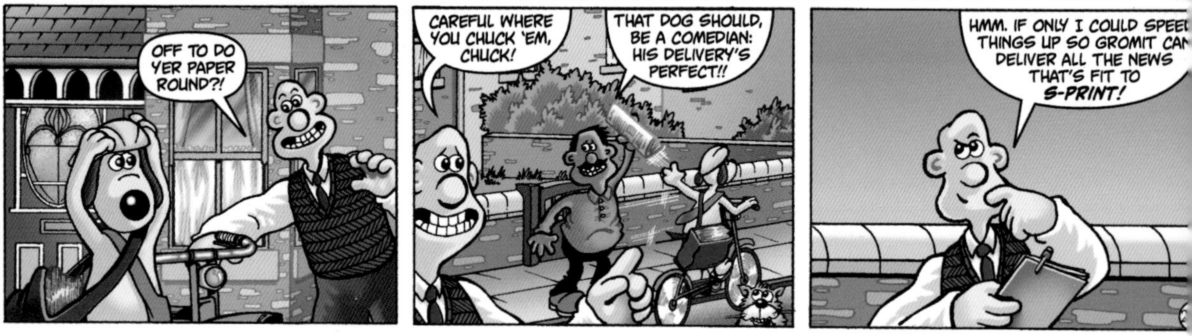

OFF TO DO YER PAPER ROUND?!
CAREFUL WHERE YOU CHUCK 'EM, CHUCK!
THAT DOG SHOULD, BE A COMEDIAN: HIS DELIVERY'S PERFECT!!
HMM. IF ONLY I COULD SPEE THINGS UP SO GROMIT CA DELIVER ALL THE NEWS THAT'S FIT TO S-PRINT!

Wallace & Gromit - Paper Hound

by Aardman & Titan Comic

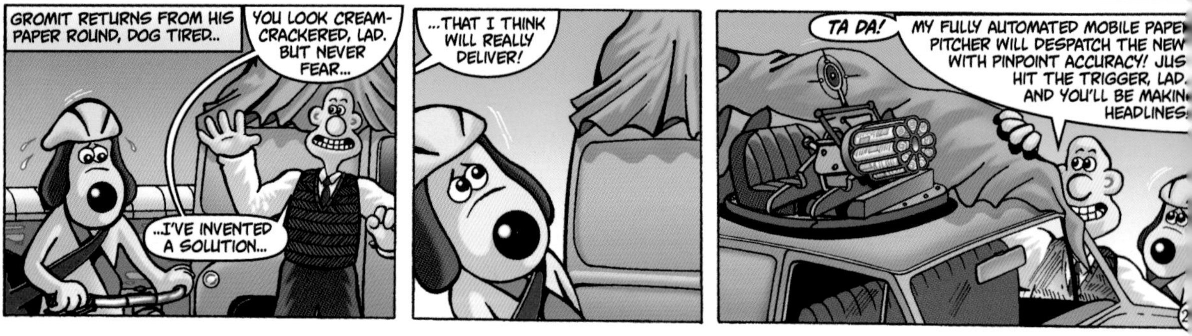

GROMIT RETURNS FROM HIS PAPER ROUND, DOG TIRED...
YOU LOOK CREAM-CRACKERED, LAD. BUT NEVER FEAR...
...I'VE INVENTED A SOLUTION...
...THAT I THINK WILL REALLY DELIVER!
TA DA!
MY FULLY AUTOMATED MOBILE PAPE PITCHER WILL DESPATCH THE NEW WITH PINPOINT ACCURACY! JUS HIT THE TRIGGER, LAD. AND YOU'LL BE MAKIN HEADLINES!

Wallace & Gromit - Paper Hound

by Aardman & Titan Comic

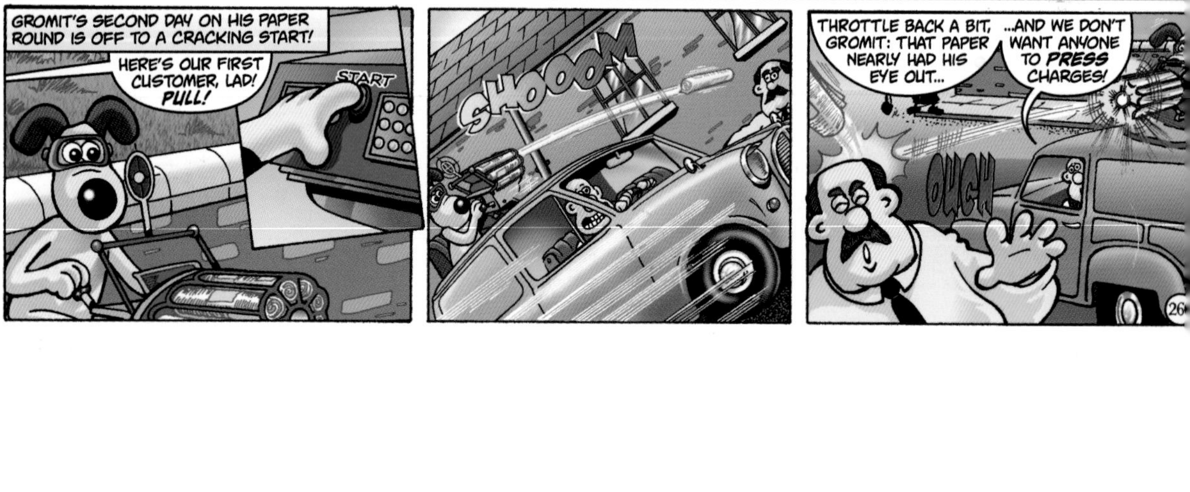

GROMIT'S SECOND DAY ON HIS PAPER ROUND IS OFF TO A CRACKING START!
HERE'S OUR FIRST CUSTOMER, LAD! PULL!
START
SHOOOM
THROTTLE BACK A BIT, GROMIT: THAT PAPER NEARLY HAD HIS EYE OUT...
...AND WE DON'T WANT ANYONE TO PRESS CHARGES!
OUCH

Wallace & Gromit - Paper Hound by Aardman & Titan Comics

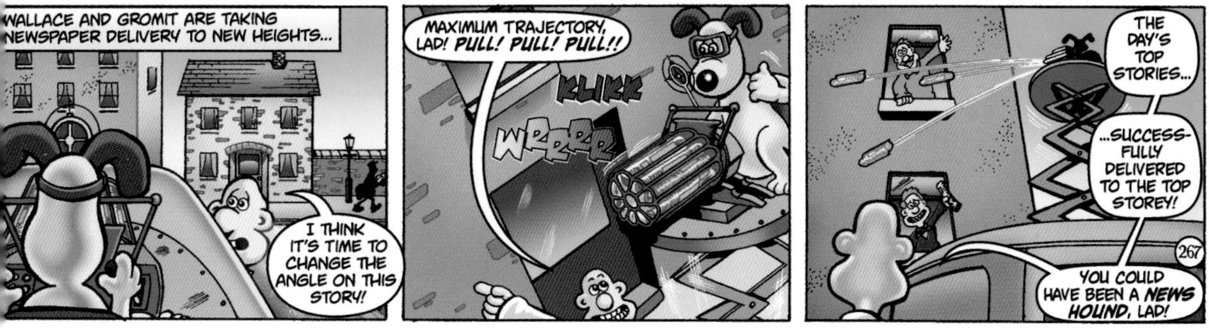
WALLACE AND GROMIT ARE TAKING NEWSPAPER DELIVERY TO NEW HEIGHTS...
I THINK IT'S TIME TO CHANGE THE ANGLE ON THIS STORY!
MAXIMUM TRAJECTORY, LAD! PULL! PULL! PULL!!
KLIKK
THE DAY'S TOP STORIES...
...SUCCESSFULLY DELIVERED TO THE TOP STOREY!
YOU COULD HAVE BEEN A NEWS HOUND, LAD!
267

Wallace & Gromit - Paper Hound by Aardman & Titan Comics

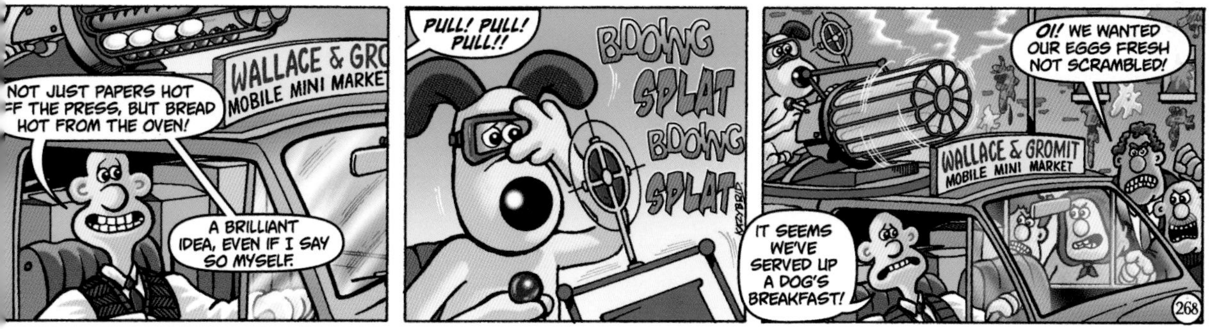
WALLACE & GRO
MOBILE MINI MARKET
NOT JUST PAPERS HOT F THE PRESS, BUT BREAD HOT FROM THE OVEN!
A BRILLIANT IDEA, EVEN IF I SAY SO MYSELF.
PULL! PULL! PULL!!
BDOING
SPLAT
BDOING
SPLAT
OI! WE WANTED OUR EGGS FRESH NOT SCRAMBLED!
WALLACE & GROMIT
MOBILE MINI MARKET
IT SEEMS WE'VE SERVED UP A DOG'S BREAKFAST!
268

Wallace & Gromit - Paper Hound by Aardman & Titan Comics

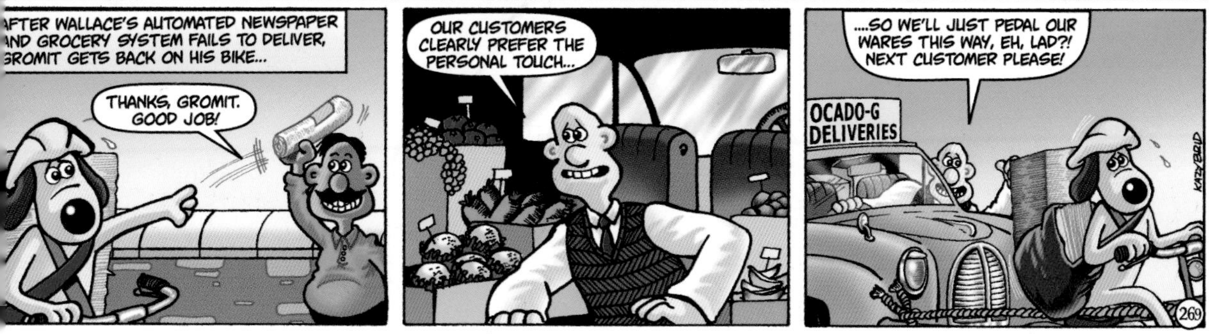
AFTER WALLACE'S AUTOMATED NEWSPAPER AND GROCERY SYSTEM FAILS TO DELIVER, GROMIT GETS BACK ON HIS BIKE...
THANKS, GROMIT. GOOD JOB!
OUR CUSTOMERS CLEARLY PREFER THE PERSONAL TOUCH...
...SO WE'LL JUST PEDAL OUR WARES THIS WAY, EH, LAD?! NEXT CUSTOMER PLEASE!
OCADO-G DELIVERIES
269

The End

Wallace & Gromit - The Pup-pet Show

by Aardman & Titan Comic

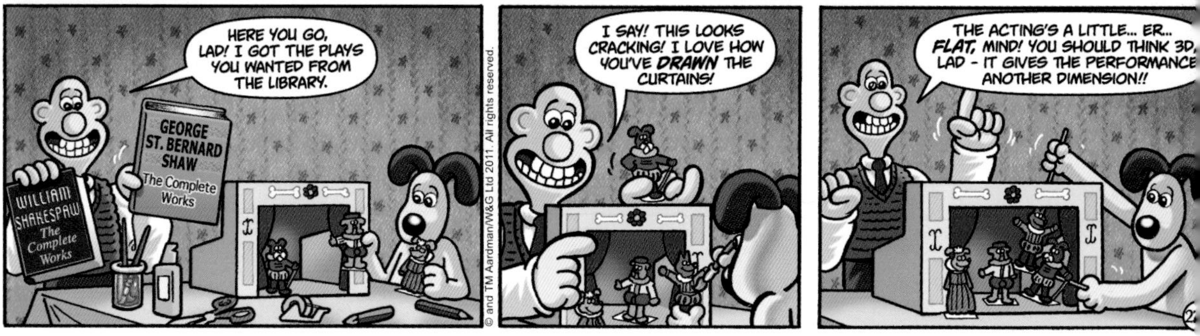

HERE YOU GO, LAD! I GOT THE PLAYS YOU WANTED FROM THE LIBRARY.
GEORGE ST. BERNARD SHAW The Complete Works
WILLIAM SHAKESPAW The Complete Works
I SAY! THIS LOOKS CRACKING! I LOVE HOW YOU'VE **DRAWN** THE CURTAINS!
THE ACTING'S A LITTLE... ER... **FLAT,** MIND! YOU SHOULD THINK 3D, LAD - IT GIVES THE PERFORMANCE ANOTHER DIMENSION!!

Wallace & Gromit - The Pup-pet Show

by Aardman & Titan Comic

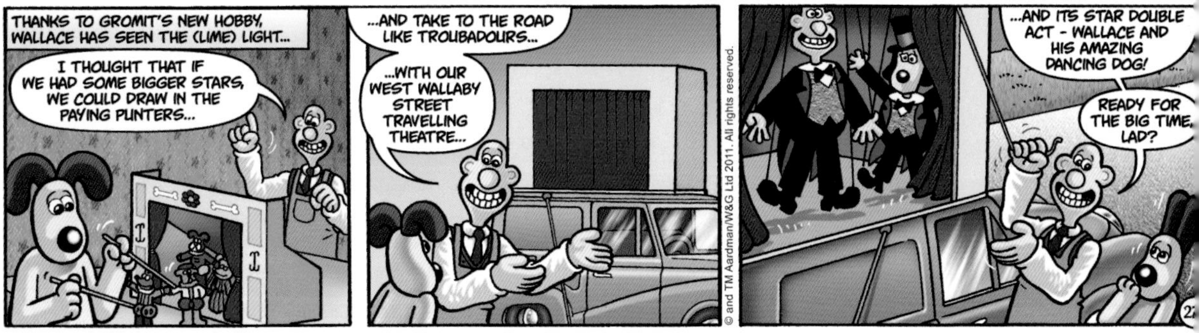

THANKS TO GROMIT'S NEW HOBBY, WALLACE HAS SEEN THE (LIME) LIGHT...
I THOUGHT THAT IF WE HAD SOME BIGGER STARS, WE COULD DRAW IN THE PAYING PUNTERS...
...AND TAKE TO THE ROAD LIKE TROUBADOURS...
...WITH OUR WEST WALLABY STREET TRAVELLING THEATRE...
...AND ITS STAR DOUBLE ACT - WALLACE AND HIS AMAZING DANCING DOG!
READY FOR THE BIG TIME, LAD?

Wallace & Gromit - The Pup-pet Show

by Aardman & Titan Comic

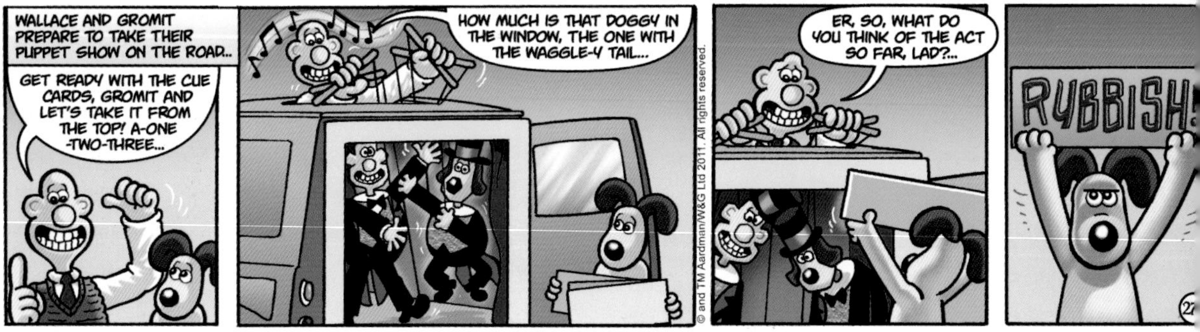

WALLACE AND GROMIT PREPARE TO TAKE THEIR PUPPET SHOW ON THE ROAD...
GET READY WITH THE CUE CARDS, GROMIT AND LET'S TAKE IT FROM THE TOP! A-ONE -TWO-THREE...
HOW MUCH IS THAT DOGGY IN THE WINDOW, THE ONE WITH THE WAGGLE-Y TAIL...
ER, SO, WHAT DO YOU THINK OF THE ACT SO FAR, LAD?...
RUBBISH!

Wallace & Gromit - The Pup-pet Show by Aardman & Titan Comics

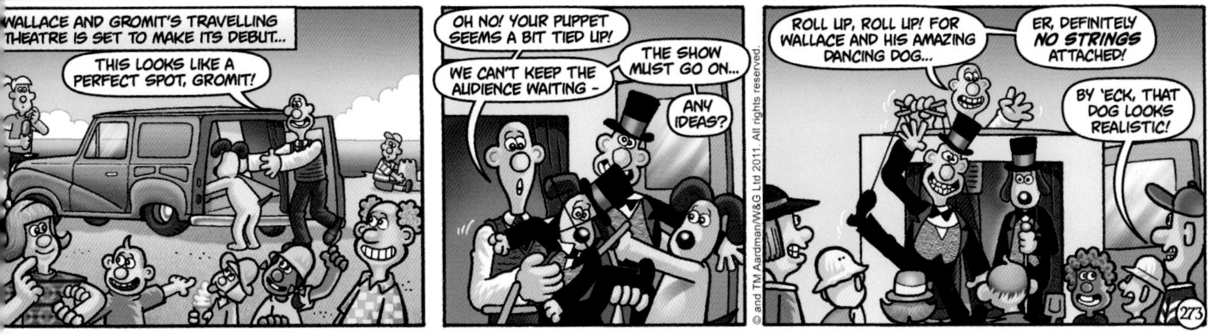
WALLACE AND GROMIT'S TRAVELLING THEATRE IS SET TO MAKE ITS DEBUT...
THIS LOOKS LIKE A PERFECT SPOT, GROMIT!
OH NO! YOUR PUPPET SEEMS A BIT TIED UP!
WE CAN'T KEEP THE AUDIENCE WAITING -
THE SHOW MUST GO ON...
ANY IDEAS?
© and TM Aardman/W&G Ltd 2011. All rights reserved.
ROLL UP, ROLL UP! FOR WALLACE AND HIS AMAZING DANCING DOG...
ER, DEFINITELY NO STRINGS ATTACHED!
BY 'ECK, THAT DOG LOOKS REALISTIC!
273

Wallace & Gromit - The Pup-pet Show by Aardman & Titan Comics

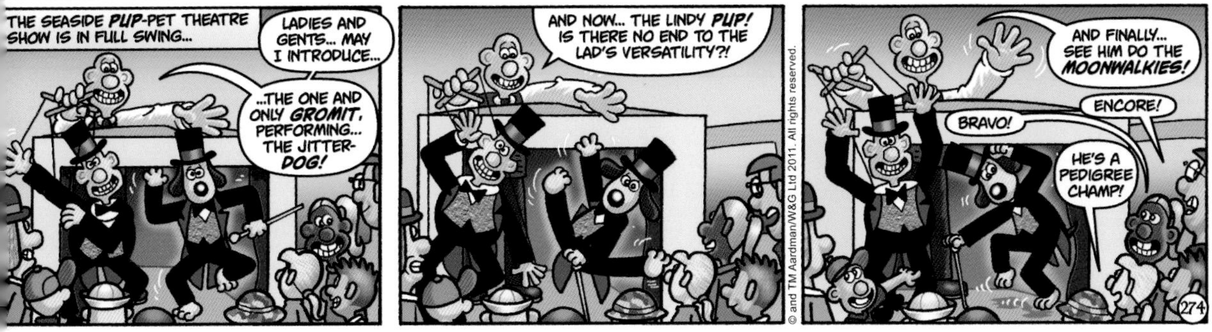
THE SEASIDE PUP-PET THEATRE SHOW IS IN FULL SWING...
LADIES AND GENTS... MAY I INTRODUCE...
...THE ONE AND ONLY GROMIT, PERFORMING... THE JITTER-DOG!
AND NOW... THE LINDY PUP! IS THERE NO END TO THE LAD'S VERSATILITY?!
© and TM Aardman/W&G Ltd 2011. All rights reserved.
AND FINALLY... SEE HIM DO THE MOONWALKIES!
ENCORE!
BRAVO!
HE'S A PEDIGREE CHAMP!
274

Wallace & Gromit - The Pup-pet Show by Aardman & Titan Comics

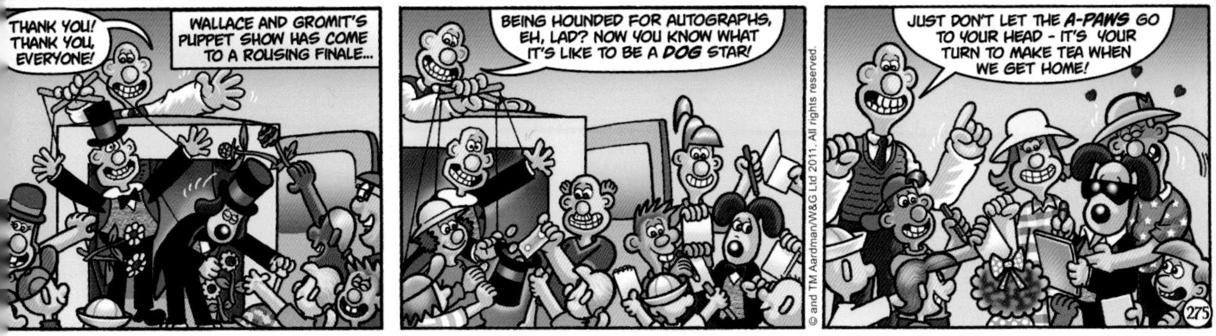
THANK YOU! THANK YOU, EVERYONE!
WALLACE AND GROMIT'S PUPPET SHOW HAS COME TO A ROUSING FINALE...
BEING HOUNDED FOR AUTOGRAPHS, EH, LAD? NOW YOU KNOW WHAT IT'S LIKE TO BE A DOG STAR!
© and TM Aardman/W&G Ltd 2011. All rights reserved.
JUST DON'T LET THE A-PAWS GO TO YOUR HEAD - IT'S YOUR TURN TO MAKE TEA WHEN WE GET HOME!
275

The End

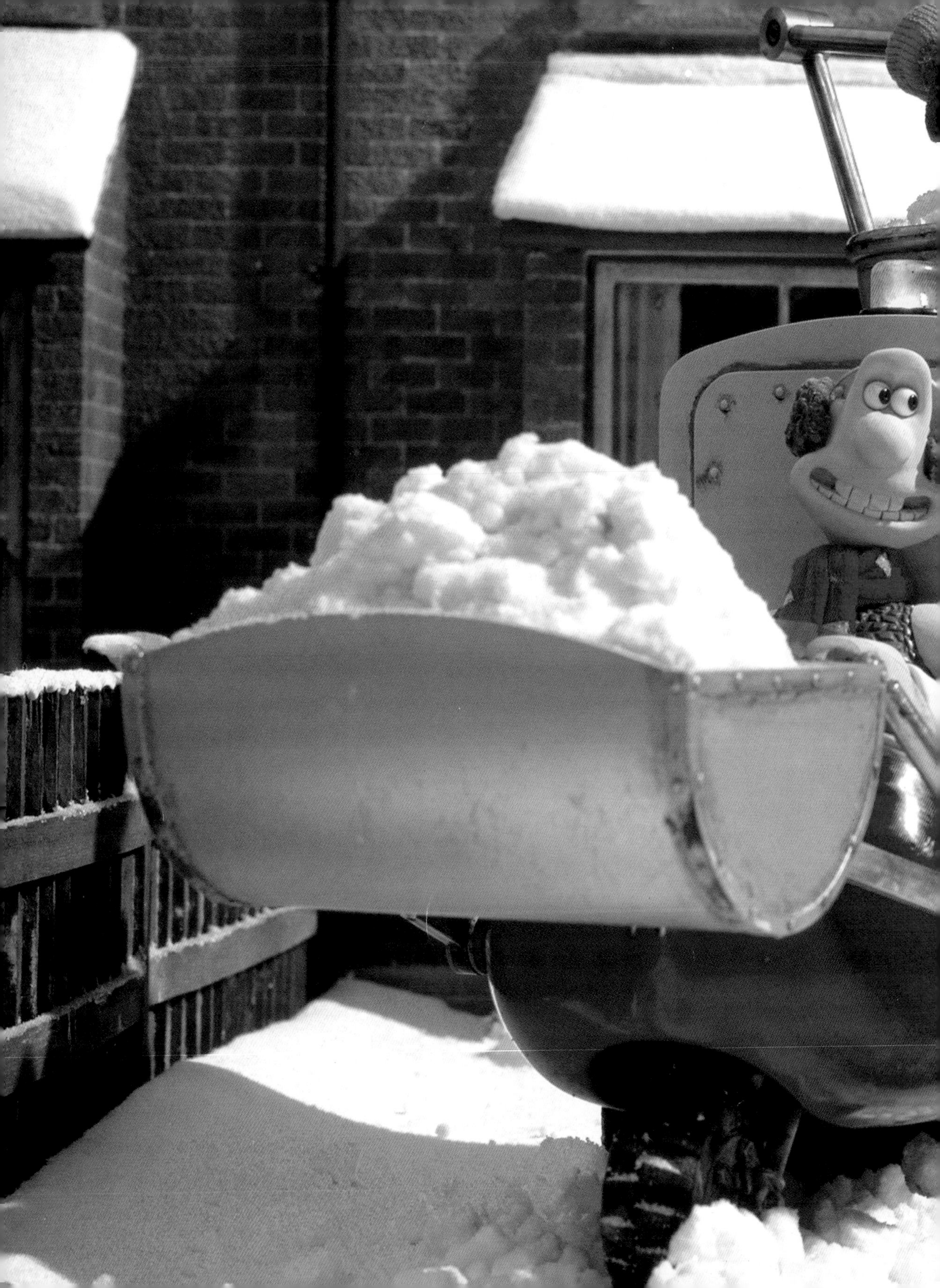

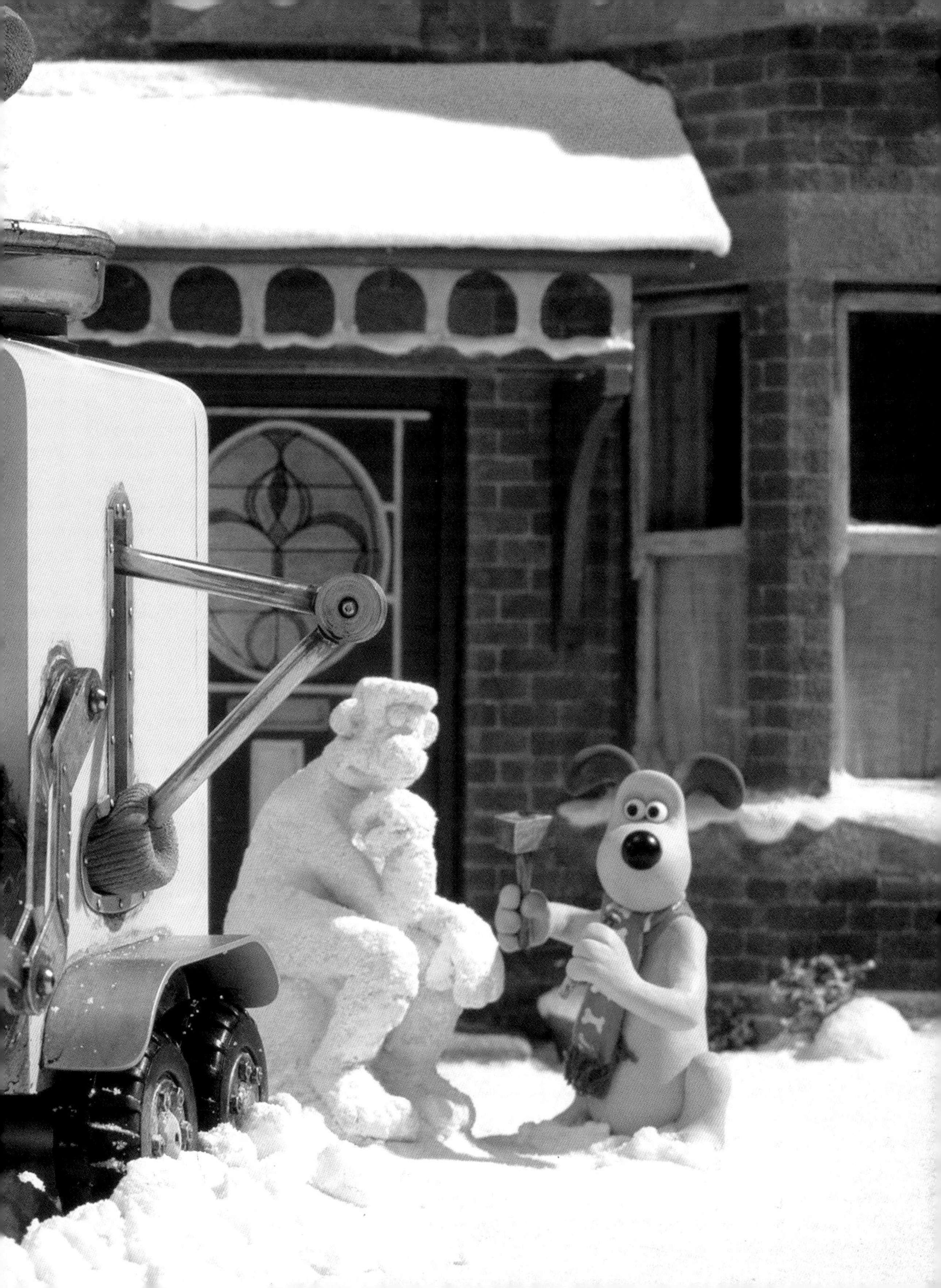

Wallace & Gromit - The Hard Work Hardware Shop by Aardman & Titan Comics

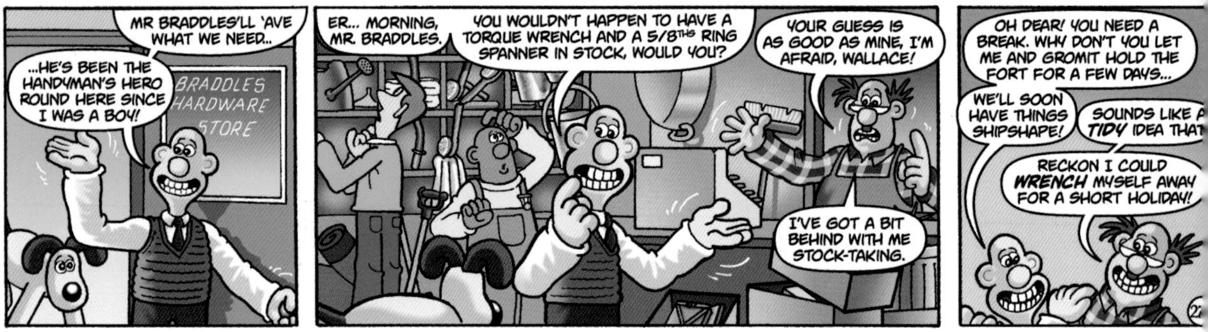
MR BRADDLES'LL 'AVE WHAT WE NEED...
...HE'S BEEN THE HANDYMAN'S HERO ROUND HERE SINCE I WAS A BOY!
BRADDLES HARDWARE STORE
ER... MORNING, MR. BRADDLES.
YOU WOULDN'T HAPPEN TO HAVE A TORQUE WRENCH AND A 5/8THS RING SPANNER IN STOCK, WOULD YOU?
YOUR GUESS IS AS GOOD AS MINE, I'M AFRAID, WALLACE!
I'VE GOT A BIT BEHIND WITH ME STOCK-TAKING.
OH DEAR! YOU NEED A BREAK. WHY DON'T YOU LET ME AND GROMIT HOLD THE FORT FOR A FEW DAYS...
WE'LL SOON HAVE THINGS SHIPSHAPE!
SOUNDS LIKE A *TIDY* IDEA THAT
RECKON I COULD *WRENCH* MYSELF AWAY FOR A SHORT HOLIDAY!

Wallace & Gromit - The Hard Work Hardware Shop by Aardman & Titan Comics

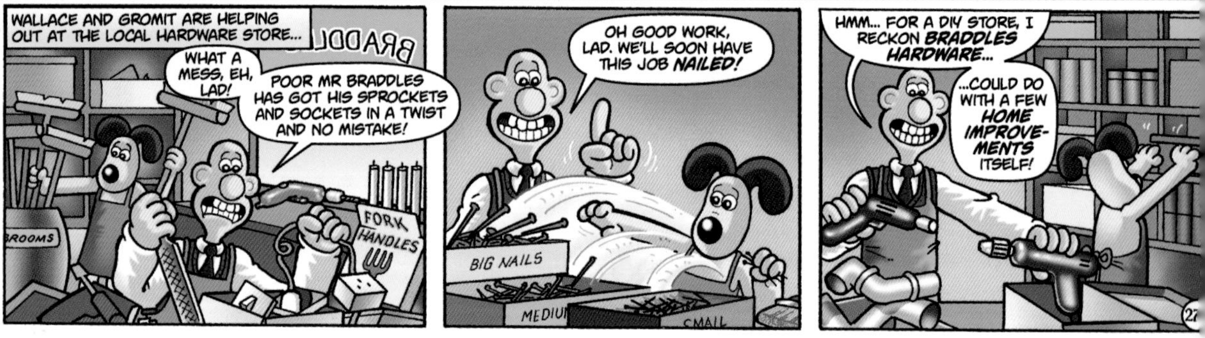
WALLACE AND GROMIT ARE HELPING OUT AT THE LOCAL HARDWARE STORE...
WHAT A MESS, EH, LAD!
POOR MR BRADDLES HAS GOT HIS SPROCKETS AND SOCKETS IN A TWIST AND NO MISTAKE!
BROOMS
FORK HANDLES
OH GOOD WORK, LAD. WE'LL SOON HAVE THIS JOB *NAILED!*
BIG NAILS
MEDIUM
SMALL
HMM... FOR A DIY STORE, I RECKON *BRADDLES HARDWARE*...
...COULD DO WITH A FEW *HOME IMPROVEMENTS* ITSELF!

Wallace & Gromit - The Hard Work Hardware Shop by Aardman & Titan Comics

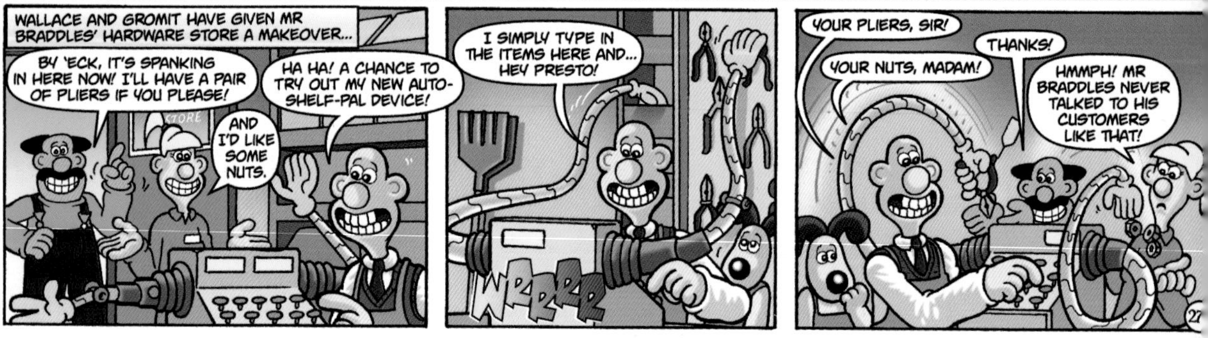
WALLACE AND GROMIT HAVE GIVEN MR BRADDLES' HARDWARE STORE A MAKEOVER...
BY 'ECK, IT'S SPANKING IN HERE NOW! I'LL HAVE A PAIR OF PLIERS IF YOU PLEASE!
AND I'D LIKE SOME NUTS.
HA HA! A CHANCE TO TRY OUT MY NEW AUTO-SHELF-PAL DEVICE!
I SIMPLY TYPE IN THE ITEMS HERE AND... HEY PRESTO!
WRRRR
YOUR PLIERS, SIR!
YOUR NUTS, MADAM!
THANKS!
HMMPH! MR BRADDLES NEVER TALKED TO HIS CUSTOMERS LIKE THAT!

Vallace & Gromit - The Hard Work Hardware Shop by Aardman & Titan Comics

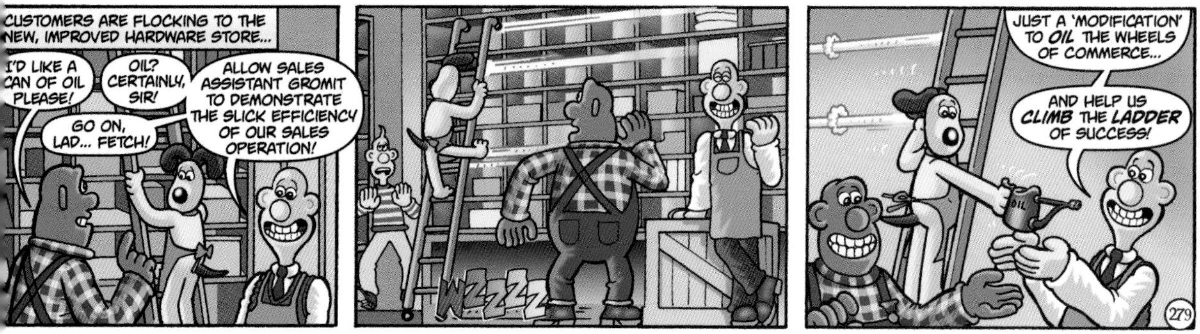

CUSTOMERS ARE FLOCKING TO THE NEW, IMPROVED HARDWARE STORE...
I'D LIKE A CAN OF OIL PLEASE!
OIL? CERTAINLY, SIR!
ALLOW SALES ASSISTANT GROMIT TO DEMONSTRATE THE SLICK EFFICIENCY OF OUR SALES OPERATION!
GO ON, LAD... FETCH!
WZZZZ
JUST A 'MODIFICATION' TO OIL THE WHEELS OF COMMERCE...
AND HELP US CLIMB THE LADDER OF SUCCESS!
OIL
279

Vallace & Gromit - The Hard Work Hardware Shop by Aardman & Titan Comics

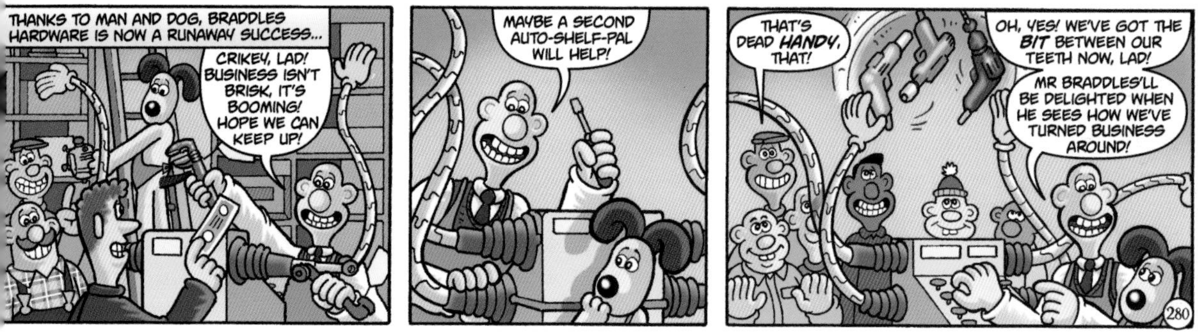

THANKS TO MAN AND DOG, BRADDLES HARDWARE IS NOW A RUNAWAY SUCCESS...
CRIKEY, LAD! BUSINESS ISN'T BRISK, IT'S BOOMING! HOPE WE CAN KEEP UP!
MAYBE A SECOND AUTO-SHELF-PAL WILL HELP!
THAT'S DEAD HANDY, THAT!
OH, YES! WE'VE GOT THE BIT BETWEEN OUR TEETH NOW, LAD!
MR BRADDLES'LL BE DELIGHTED WHEN HE SEES HOW WE'VE TURNED BUSINESS AROUND!
280

Vallace & Gromit - The Hard Work Hardware Shop by Aardman & Titan Comics

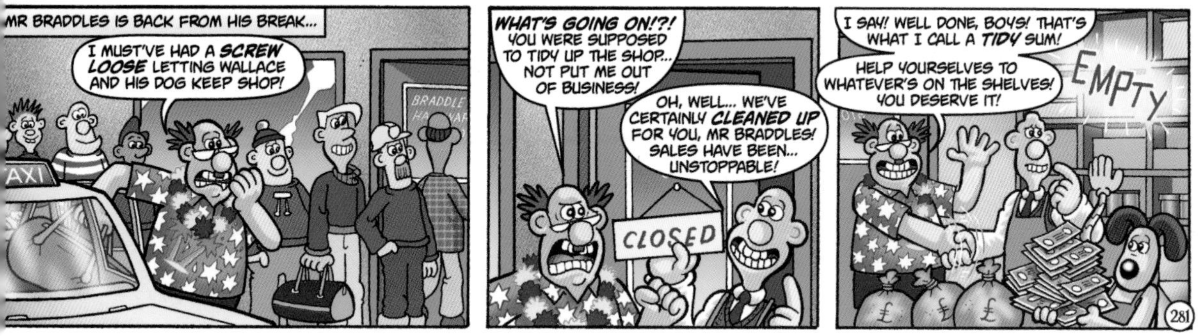

MR BRADDLES IS BACK FROM HIS BREAK...
I MUST'VE HAD A SCREW LOOSE LETTING WALLACE AND HIS DOG KEEP SHOP!
AXI
WHAT'S GOING ON!?! YOU WERE SUPPOSED TO TIDY UP THE SHOP... NOT PUT ME OUT OF BUSINESS!
OH, WELL... WE'VE CERTAINLY CLEANED UP FOR YOU, MR BRADDLES! SALES HAVE BEEN... UNSTOPPABLE!
CLOSED
I SAY! WELL DONE, BOYS! THAT'S WHAT I CALL A TIDY SUM!
HELP YOURSELVES TO WHATEVER'S ON THE SHELVES! YOU DESERVE IT!
EMPTY
281

The End

Wallace & Gromit - Hook, Line and Stinker

by Aardman & Titan Comic

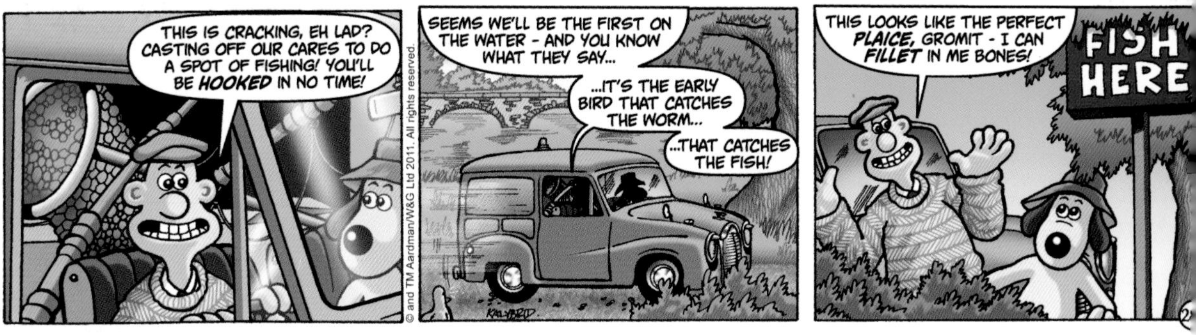
THIS IS CRACKING, EH LAD? CASTING OFF OUR CARES TO DO A SPOT OF FISHING! YOU'LL BE *HOOKED* IN NO TIME!
© and TM Aardman/W&G Ltd 2011. All rights reserved.
SEEMS WE'LL BE THE FIRST ON THE WATER - AND YOU KNOW WHAT THEY SAY...
...IT'S THE EARLY BIRD THAT CATCHES THE WORM...
...THAT CATCHES THE FISH!
THIS LOOKS LIKE THE PERFECT *PLAICE*, GROMIT - I CAN *FILLET* IN ME BONES!
FISH HERE

Wallace & Gromit - Hook, Line and Stinker

by Aardman & Titan Comic

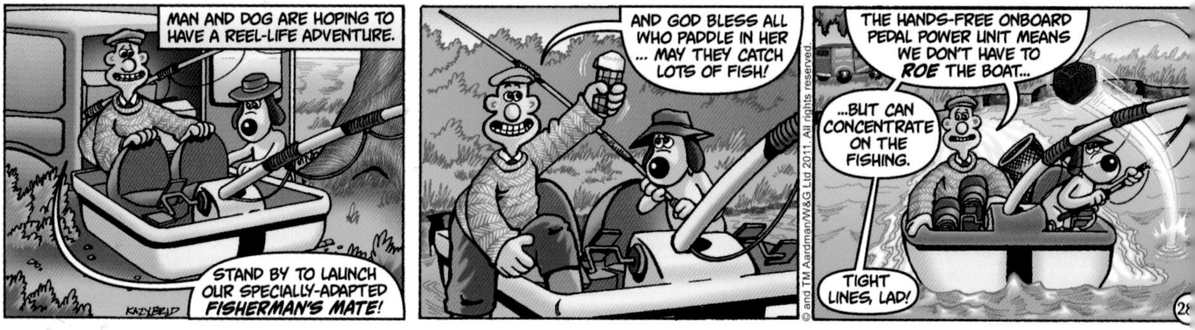
MAN AND DOG ARE HOPING TO HAVE A REEL-LIFE ADVENTURE.
STAND BY TO LAUNCH OUR SPECIALLY-ADAPTED *FISHERMAN'S MATE*!
AND GOD BLESS ALL WHO PADDLE IN HER ... MAY THEY CATCH LOTS OF FISH!
© and TM Aardman/W&G Ltd 2011. All rights reserved.
THE HANDS-FREE ONBOARD PEDAL POWER UNIT MEANS WE DON'T HAVE TO *ROE* THE BOAT...
...BUT CAN CONCENTRATE ON THE FISHING.
TIGHT LINES, LAD!

Wallace & Gromit - Hook, Line and Stinker

by Aardman & Titan Comic

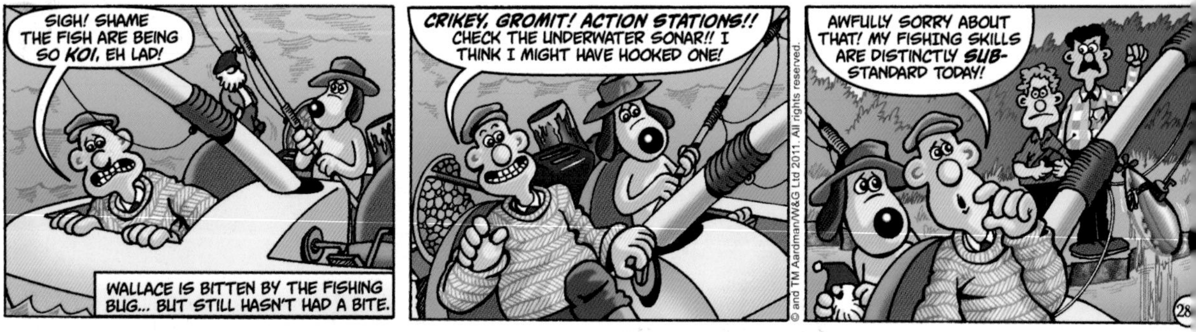
SIGH! SHAME THE FISH ARE BEING SO *KOI*, EH LAD!
WALLACE IS BITTEN BY THE FISHING BUG... BUT STILL HASN'T HAD A BITE.
CRIKEY, GROMIT! ACTION STATIONS!! CHECK THE UNDERWATER SONAR!! I THINK I MIGHT HAVE HOOKED ONE!
© and TM Aardman/W&G Ltd 2011. All rights reserved.
AWFULLY SORRY ABOUT THAT! MY FISHING SKILLS ARE DISTINCTLY *SUB*-STANDARD TODAY!

Wallace & Gromit - Hook, Line and Stinker by Aardman & Titan Comics

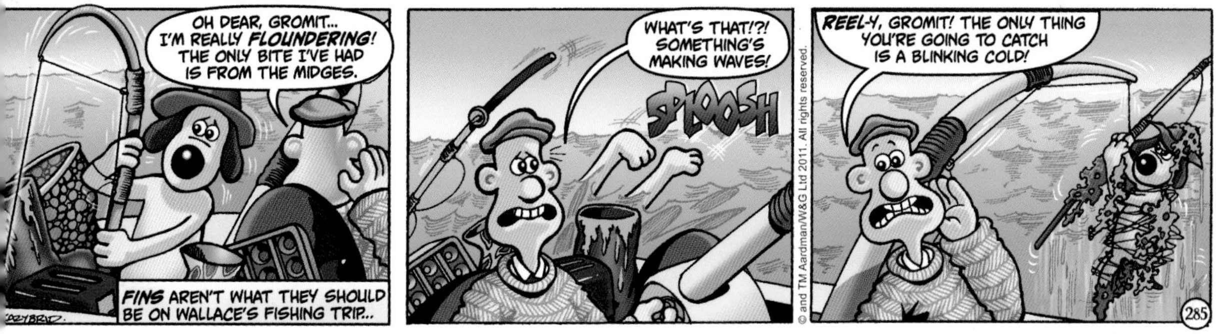

OH DEAR, GROMIT... I'M REALLY FLOUNDERING! THE ONLY BITE I'VE HAD IS FROM THE MIDGES.
FINS AREN'T WHAT THEY SHOULD BE ON WALLACE'S FISHING TRIP...
WHAT'S THAT!?! SOMETHING'S MAKING WAVES!
SPLOOSH
© and TM Aardman/W&G Ltd 2011. All rights reserved.
REEL-Y, GROMIT! THE ONLY THING YOU'RE GOING TO CATCH IS A BLINKING COLD!
285

Wallace & Gromit - Hook, Line and Stinker by Aardman & Titan Comics

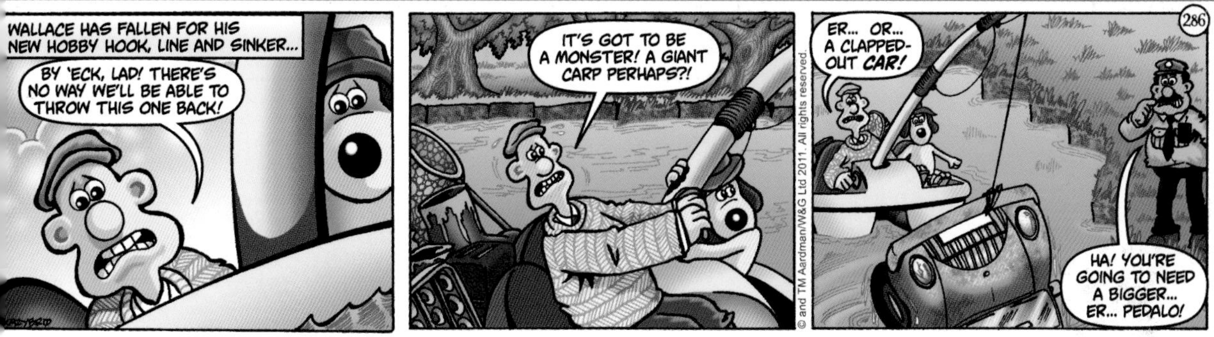

WALLACE HAS FALLEN FOR HIS NEW HOBBY HOOK, LINE AND SINKER...
BY 'ECK, LAD! THERE'S NO WAY WE'LL BE ABLE TO THROW THIS ONE BACK!
IT'S GOT TO BE A MONSTER! A GIANT CARP PERHAPS?!
© and TM Aardman/W&G Ltd 2011. All rights reserved.
286
ER... OR... A CLAPPED-OUT CAR!
HA! YOU'RE GOING TO NEED A BIGGER... ER... PEDALO!

Wallace & Gromit - Hook, Line and Stinker by Aardman & Titan Comics

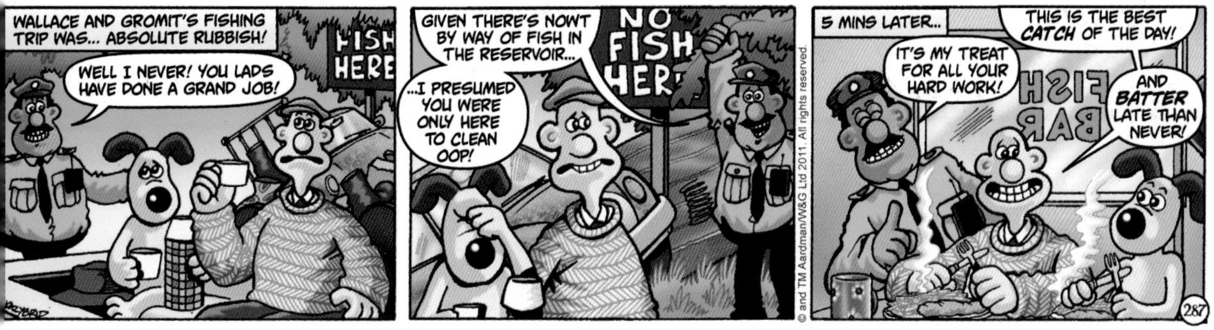

WALLACE AND GROMIT'S FISHING TRIP WAS... ABSOLUTE RUBBISH!
WELL I NEVER! YOU LADS HAVE DONE A GRAND JOB!
FISH HERE
GIVEN THERE'S NOWT BY WAY OF FISH IN THE RESERVOIR...
...I PRESUMED YOU WERE ONLY HERE TO CLEAN OOP!
NO FISH HER
© and TM Aardman/W&G Ltd 2011. All rights reserved.
5 MINS LATER..
THIS IS THE BEST CATCH OF THE DAY!
IT'S MY TREAT FOR ALL YOUR HARD WORK!
AND BATTER LATE THAN NEVER!
287

The End

Wallace & Gromit - The Faver-Heigh Egg

by Aardman & Titan Comics

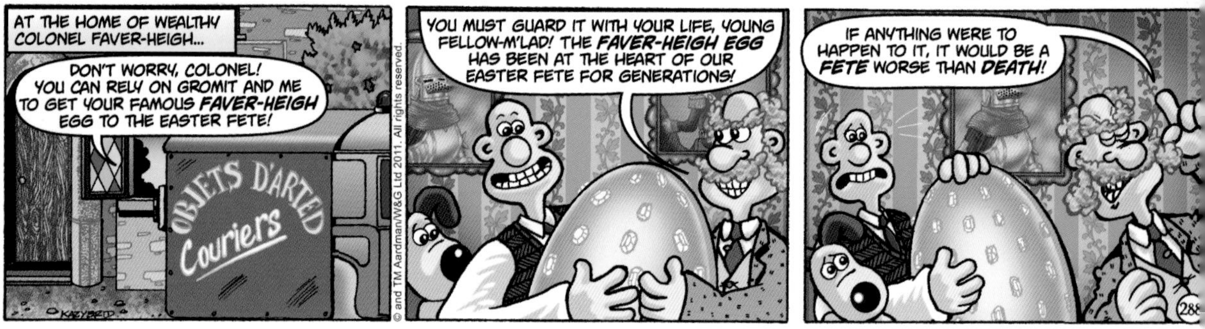
AT THE HOME OF WEALTHY COLONEL FAVER-HEIGH...
DON'T WORRY, COLONEL! YOU CAN RELY ON GROMIT AND ME TO GET YOUR FAMOUS ***FAVER-HEIGH*** EGG TO THE EASTER FETE!
OBJETS D'ARTED Couriers
KAZYBRID
© and TM Aardman/W&G Ltd 2011. All rights reserved.
YOU MUST GUARD IT WITH YOUR LIFE, YOUNG FELLOW-M'LAD! THE ***FAVER-HEIGH EGG*** HAS BEEN AT THE HEART OF OUR EASTER FETE FOR GENERATIONS!
IF ANYTHING WERE TO HAPPEN TO IT, IT WOULD BE A ***FETE*** WORSE THAN ***DEATH***!
288

Wallace & Gromit - The Faver-Heigh Egg

by Aardman & Titan Comics

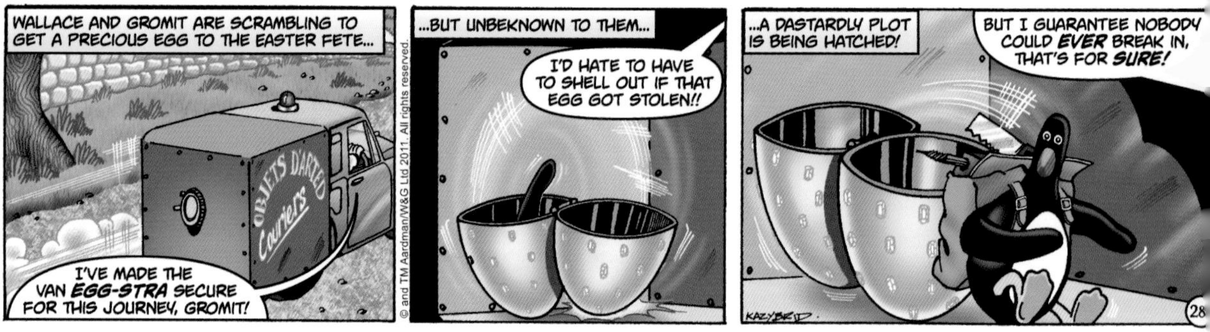
WALLACE AND GROMIT ARE SCRAMBLING TO GET A PRECIOUS EGG TO THE EASTER FETE...
OBJETS D'ARTED Couriers
I'VE MADE THE VAN ***EGG-STRA*** SECURE FOR THIS JOURNEY, GROMIT!
© and TM Aardman/W&G Ltd 2011. All rights reserved.
...BUT UNBEKNOWN TO THEM...
I'D HATE TO HAVE TO SHELL OUT IF THAT EGG GOT STOLEN!!
...A DASTARDLY PLOT IS BEING HATCHED!
BUT I GUARANTEE NOBODY COULD ***EVER*** BREAK IN, THAT'S FOR ***SURE!***
KAZYBRID

Wallace & Gromit - The Faver-Heigh Egg

by Aardman & Titan Comics

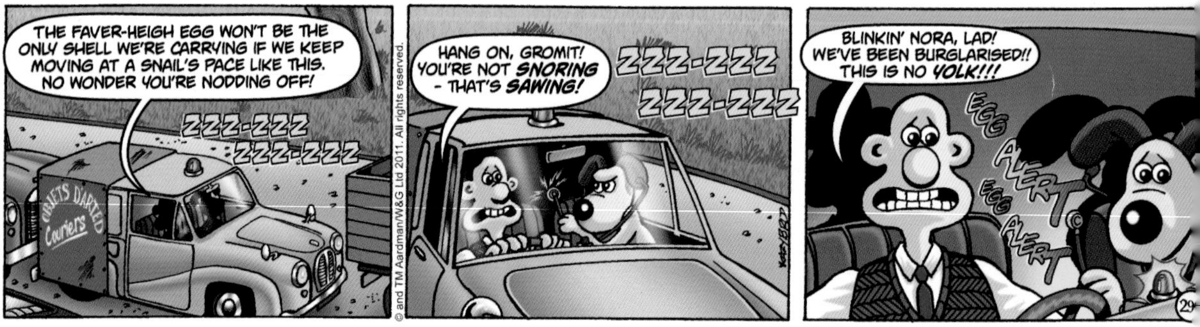
THE FAVER-HEIGH EGG WON'T BE THE ONLY SHELL WE'RE CARRYING IF WE KEEP MOVING AT A SNAIL'S PACE LIKE THIS. NO WONDER YOU'RE NODDING OFF!
ZZZ-ZZZ
ZZZ-ZZZ
OBJETS D'ARTED Couriers
© and TM Aardman/W&G Ltd 2011. All rights reserved.
HANG ON, GROMIT! YOU'RE NOT ***SNORING*** - THAT'S ***SAWING!***
ZZZ-ZZZ
ZZZ-ZZZ
KAZYBRID
BLINKIN' NORA, LAD! WE'VE BEEN BURGLARISED!! THIS IS NO ***YOLK!!!***
EGG ALERT
EGG ALERT

Wallace & Gromit - The Faver-Heigh Egg by Aardman & Titan Comics

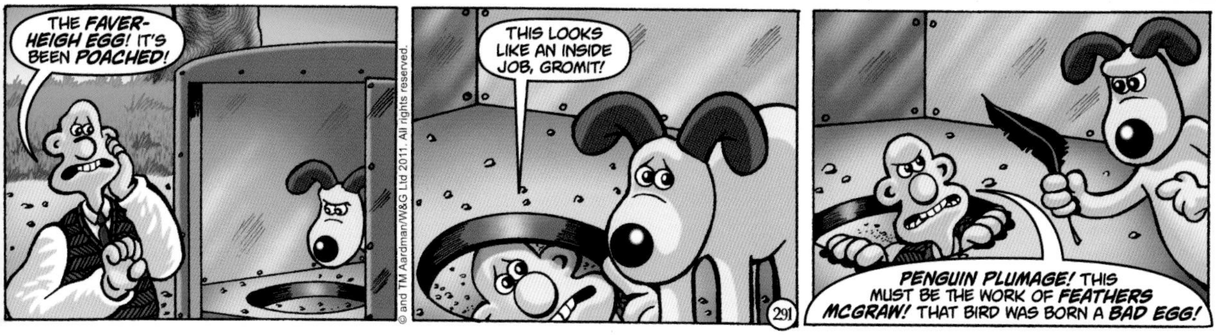
THE FAVER-HEIGH EGG! IT'S BEEN POACHED!
THIS LOOKS LIKE AN INSIDE JOB, GROMIT!
© and TM Aardman/W&G Ltd 2011. All rights reserved.
291
PENGUIN PLUMAGE! THIS MUST BE THE WORK OF FEATHERS MCGRAW! THAT BIRD WAS BORN A BAD EGG!

Wallace & Gromit - The Faver-Heigh Egg by Aardman & Titan Comics

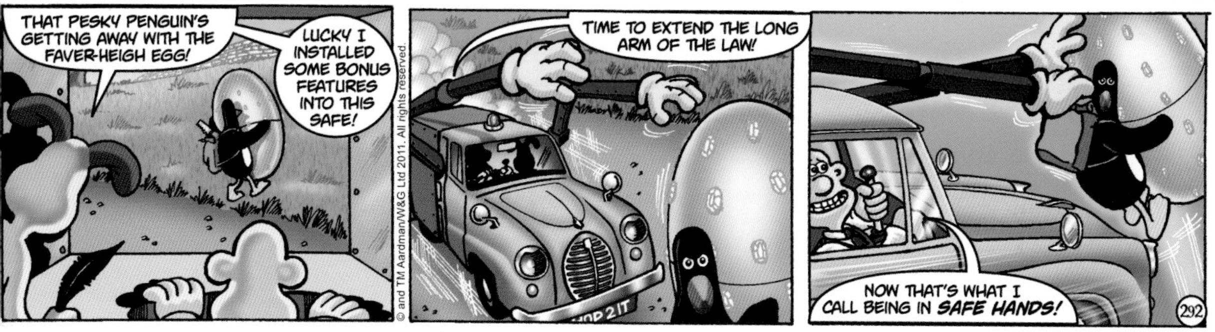
THAT PESKY PENGUIN'S GETTING AWAY WITH THE FAVER-HEIGH EGG!
LUCKY I INSTALLED SOME BONUS FEATURES INTO THIS SAFE!
© and TM Aardman/W&G Ltd 2011. All rights reserved.
TIME TO EXTEND THE LONG ARM OF THE LAW!
NOW THAT'S WHAT I CALL BEING IN SAFE HANDS!
292

Wallace & Gromit - The Faver-Heigh Egg by Aardman & Titan Comics

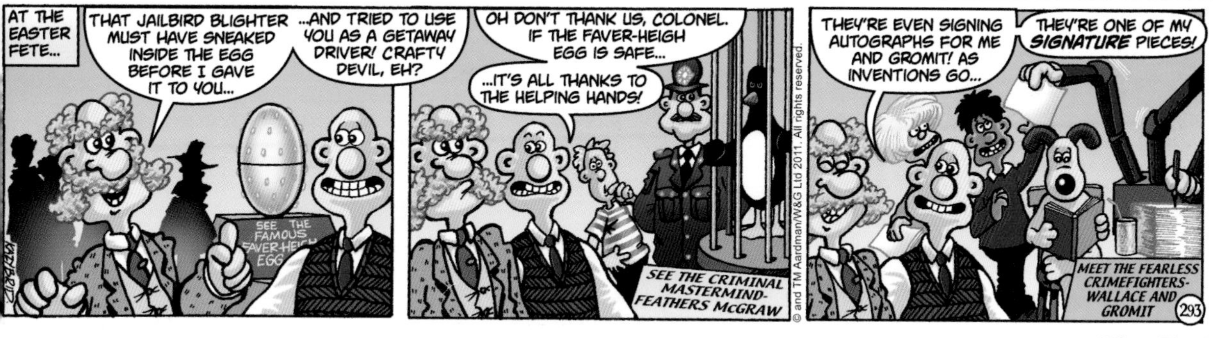
AT THE EASTER FETE...
THAT JAILBIRD BLIGHTER MUST HAVE SNEAKED INSIDE THE EGG BEFORE I GAVE IT TO YOU...
...AND TRIED TO USE YOU AS A GETAWAY DRIVER! CRAFTY DEVIL, EH?
SEE THE FAMOUS FAVER-HEIGH EGG
OH DON'T THANK US, COLONEL. IF THE FAVER-HEIGH EGG IS SAFE...
...IT'S ALL THANKS TO THE HELPING HANDS!
SEE THE CRIMINAL MASTERMIND-FEATHERS McGRAW
© and TM Aardman/W&G Ltd 2011. All rights reserved.
THEY'RE EVEN SIGNING AUTOGRAPHS FOR ME AND GROMIT! AS INVENTIONS GO...
THEY'RE ONE OF MY SIGNATURE PIECES!
MEET THE FEARLESS CRIMEFIGHTERS-WALLACE AND GROMIT
293

The End

Wallace & Gromit - A Right Royal Knees Up
by Aardman & Titan Comics

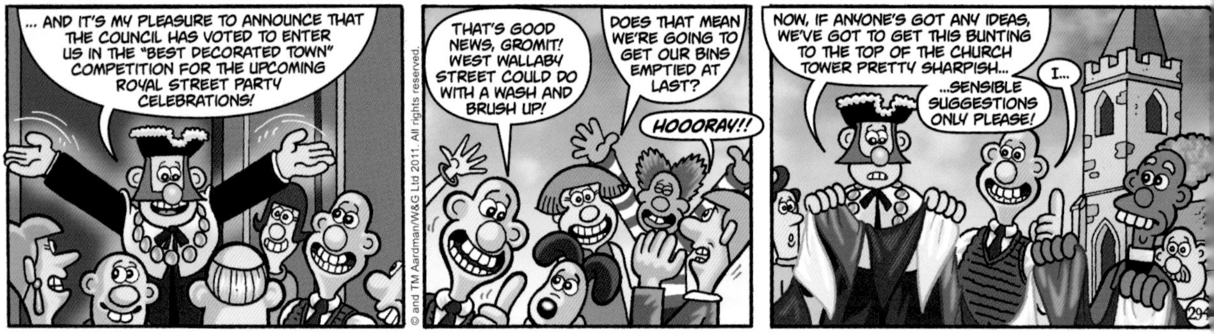
... AND IT'S MY PLEASURE TO ANNOUNCE THAT THE COUNCIL HAS VOTED TO ENTER US IN THE "BEST DECORATED TOWN" COMPETITION FOR THE UPCOMING ROYAL STREET PARTY CELEBRATIONS!
THAT'S GOOD NEWS, GROMIT! WEST WALLABY STREET COULD DO WITH A WASH AND BRUSH UP!
DOES THAT MEAN WE'RE GOING TO GET OUR BINS EMPTIED AT LAST?
HOOORAY!!
NOW, IF ANYONE'S GOT ANY IDEAS, WE'VE GOT TO GET THIS BUNTING TO THE TOP OF THE CHURCH TOWER PRETTY SHARPISH...
...SENSIBLE SUGGESTIONS ONLY PLEASE!
I...
© and TM Aardman/W&G Ltd 2011. All rights reserved.
294

Wallace & Gromit - A Right Royal Knees Up
by Aardman & Titan Comics

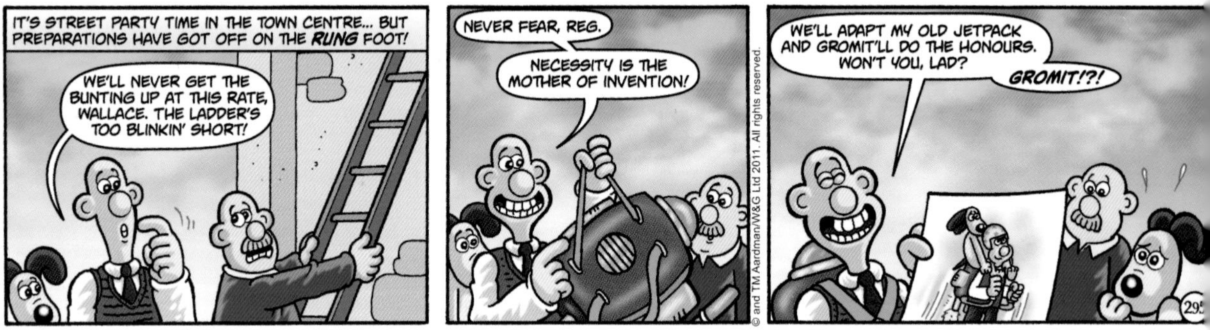
IT'S STREET PARTY TIME IN THE TOWN CENTRE... BUT PREPARATIONS HAVE GOT OFF ON THE RUNG FOOT!
WE'LL NEVER GET THE BUNTING UP AT THIS RATE, WALLACE. THE LADDER'S TOO BLINKIN' SHORT!
NEVER FEAR, REG.
NECESSITY IS THE MOTHER OF INVENTION!
WE'LL ADAPT MY OLD JETPACK AND GROMIT'LL DO THE HONOURS. WON'T YOU, LAD?
GROMIT!?!
© and TM Aardman/W&G Ltd 2011. All rights reserved.
295

Wallace & Gromit - A Right Royal Knees Up
by Aardman & Titan Comics

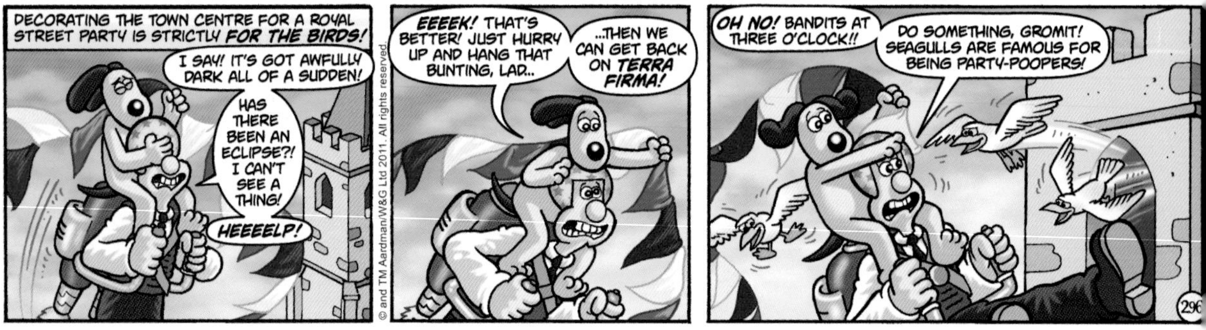
DECORATING THE TOWN CENTRE FOR A ROYAL STREET PARTY IS STRICTLY FOR THE BIRDS!
I SAY! IT'S GOT AWFULLY DARK ALL OF A SUDDEN!
HAS THERE BEEN AN ECLIPSE?! I CAN'T SEE A THING!
HEEEELP!
EEEEK! THAT'S BETTER! JUST HURRY UP AND HANG THAT BUNTING, LAD...
...THEN WE CAN GET BACK ON TERRA FIRMA!
OH NO! BANDITS AT THREE O'CLOCK!!
DO SOMETHING, GROMIT! SEAGULLS ARE FAMOUS FOR BEING PARTY-POOPERS!
© and TM Aardman/W&G Ltd 2011. All rights reserved.
296

Wallace & Gromit - A Right Royal Knees Up by Aardman & Titan Comics

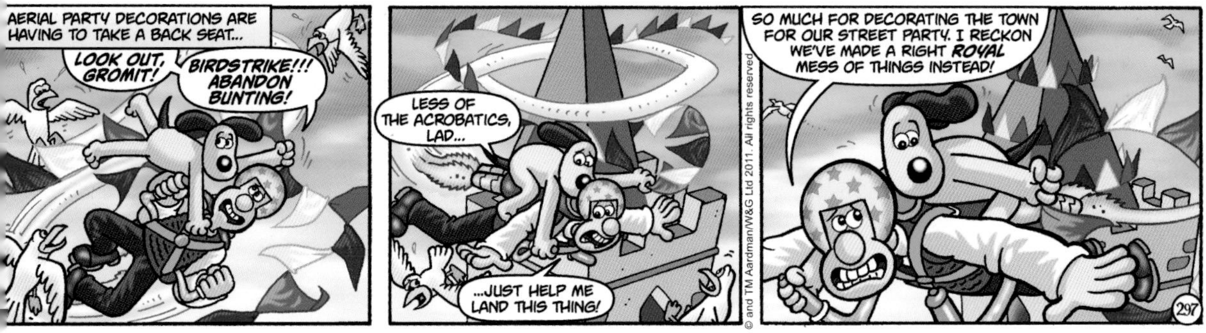
AERIAL PARTY DECORATIONS ARE HAVING TO TAKE A BACK SEAT...
LOOK OUT, GROMIT!
BIRDSTRIKE!!! ABANDON BUNTING!
LESS OF THE ACROBATICS, LAD...
...JUST HELP ME LAND THIS THING!
SO MUCH FOR DECORATING THE TOWN FOR OUR STREET PARTY. I RECKON WE'VE MADE A RIGHT ROYAL MESS OF THINGS INSTEAD!
297

Wallace & Gromit - A Right Royal Knees Up by Aardman & Titan Comics

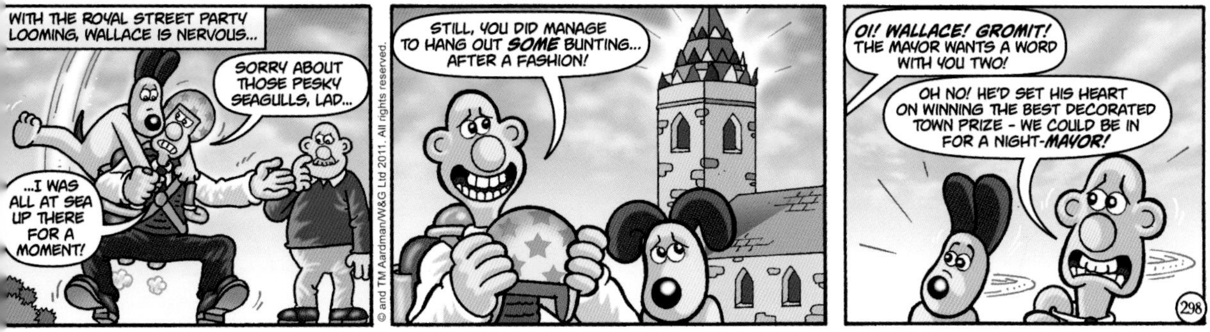
WITH THE ROYAL STREET PARTY LOOMING, WALLACE IS NERVOUS...
SORRY ABOUT THOSE PESKY SEAGULLS, LAD...
...I WAS ALL AT SEA UP THERE FOR A MOMENT!
STILL, YOU DID MANAGE TO HANG OUT SOME BUNTING... AFTER A FASHION!
OI! WALLACE! GROMIT! THE MAYOR WANTS A WORD WITH YOU TWO!
OH NO! HE'D SET HIS HEART ON WINNING THE BEST DECORATED TOWN PRIZE - WE COULD BE IN FOR A NIGHT-MAYOR!
298

Wallace & Gromit - A Right Royal Knees Up by Aardman & Titan Comics

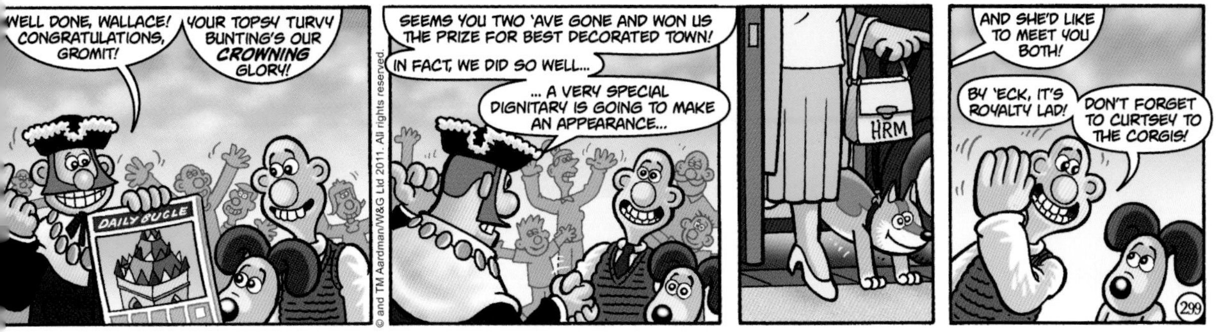
WELL DONE, WALLACE! CONGRATULATIONS, GROMIT!
YOUR TOPSY TURVY BUNTING'S OUR CROWNING GLORY!
DAILY BUGLE
SEEMS YOU TWO 'AVE GONE AND WON US THE PRIZE FOR BEST DECORATED TOWN!
IN FACT, WE DID SO WELL...
... A VERY SPECIAL DIGNITARY IS GOING TO MAKE AN APPEARANCE...
HRM
AND SHE'D LIKE TO MEET YOU BOTH!
BY 'ECK, IT'S ROYALTY LAD!
DON'T FORGET TO CURTSEY TO THE CORGIS!
299

The End

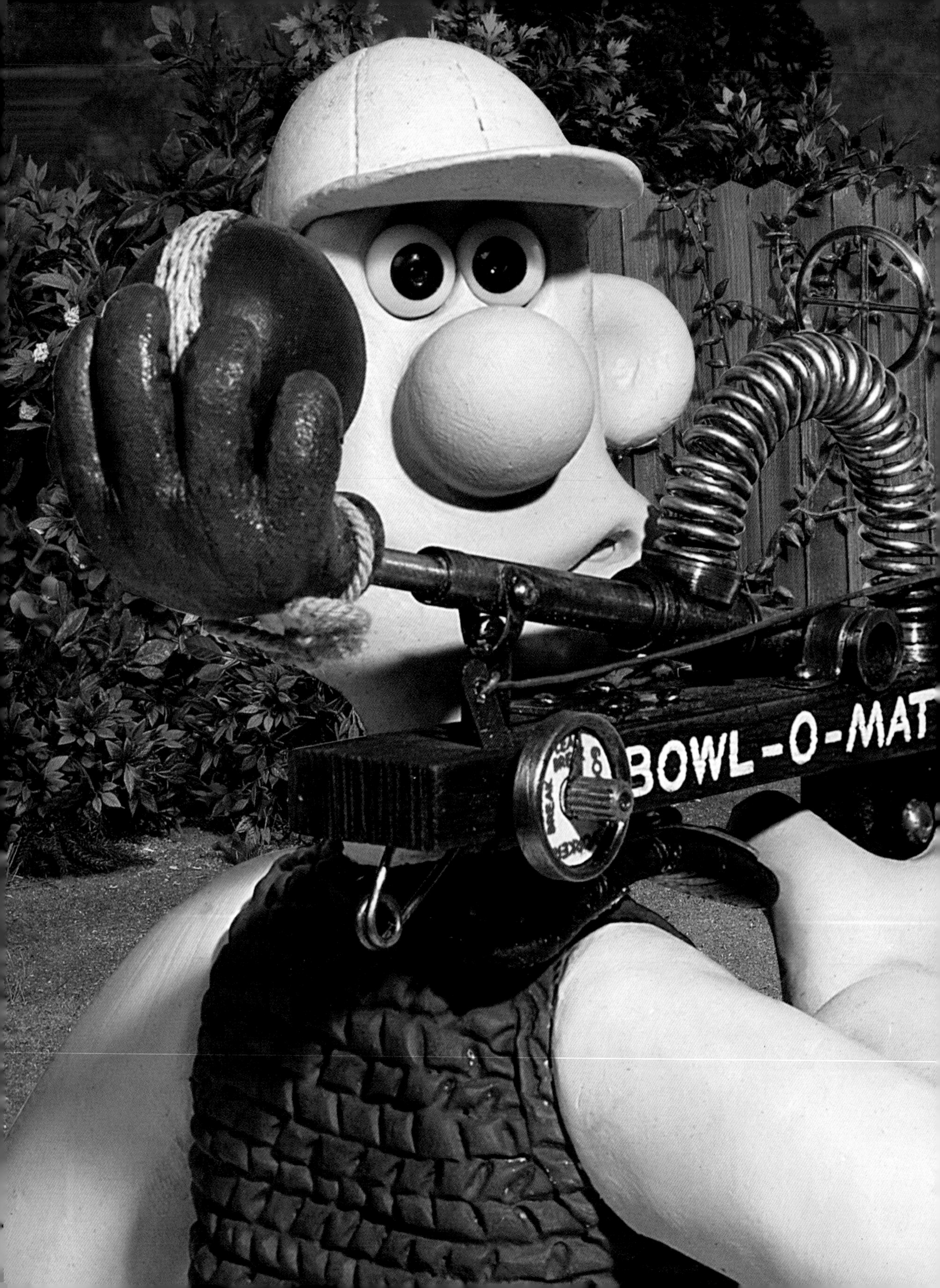
BOWL-O-MAT

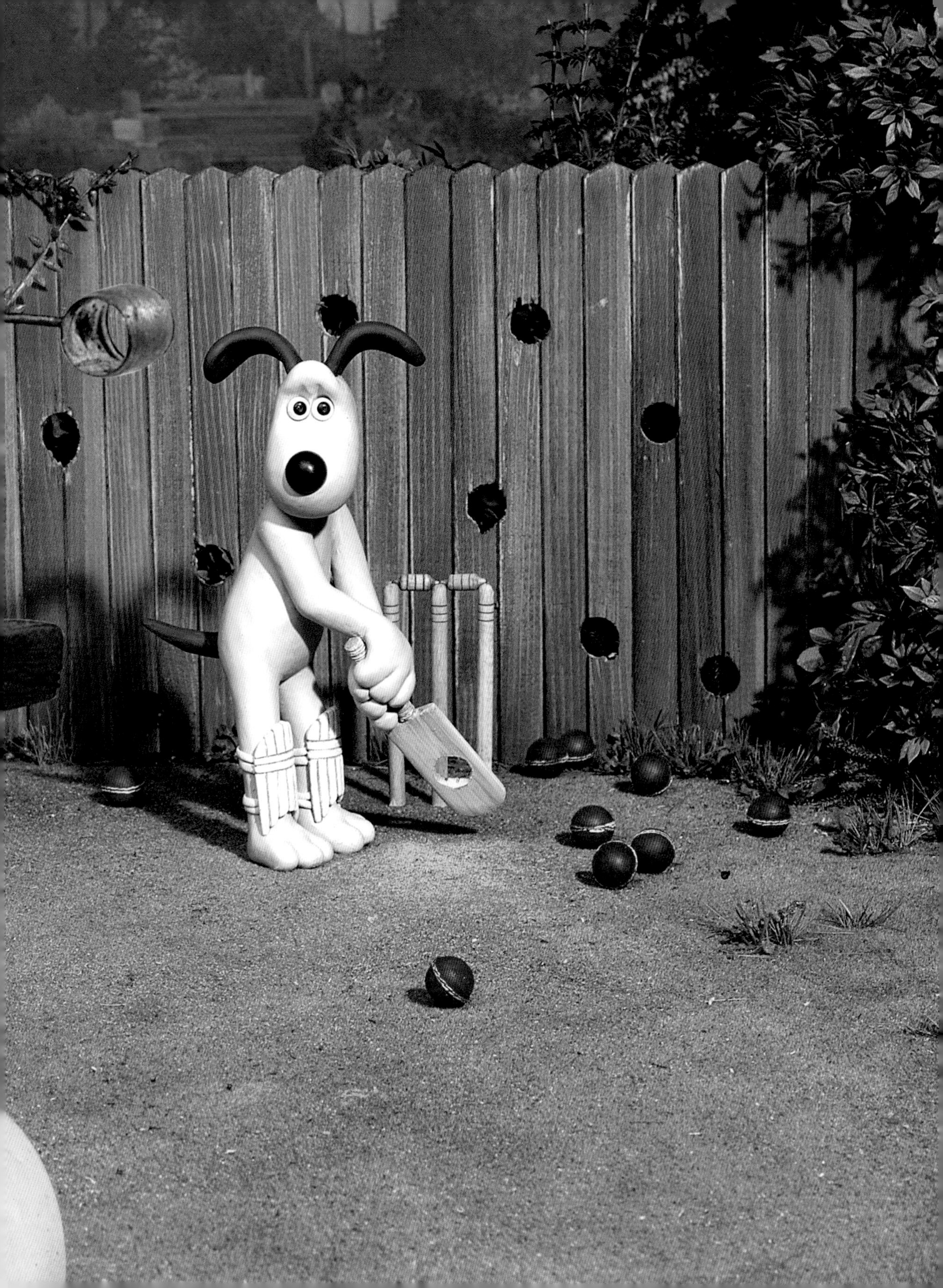

Wallace & Gromit - Caped Crusaders

by Aardman & Titan Comics

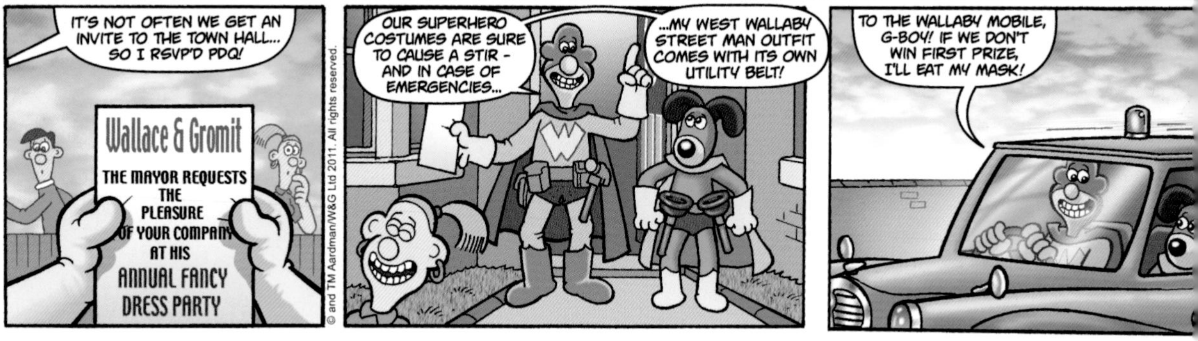

IT'S NOT OFTEN WE GET AN INVITE TO THE TOWN HALL... SO I RSVP'D PDQ!
Wallace & Gromit
THE MAYOR REQUESTS THE PLEASURE OF YOUR COMPANY AT HIS ANNUAL FANCY DRESS PARTY
© and TM Aardman/W&G Ltd 2011. All rights reserved.
OUR SUPERHERO COSTUMES ARE SURE TO CAUSE A STIR - AND IN CASE OF EMERGENCIES...
...MY WEST WALLABY STREET MAN OUTFIT COMES WITH ITS OWN UTILITY BELT!
TO THE WALLABY MOBILE, G-BOY! IF WE DON'T WIN FIRST PRIZE, I'LL EAT MY MASK!

Wallace & Gromit - Caped Crusaders

by Aardman & Titan Comics

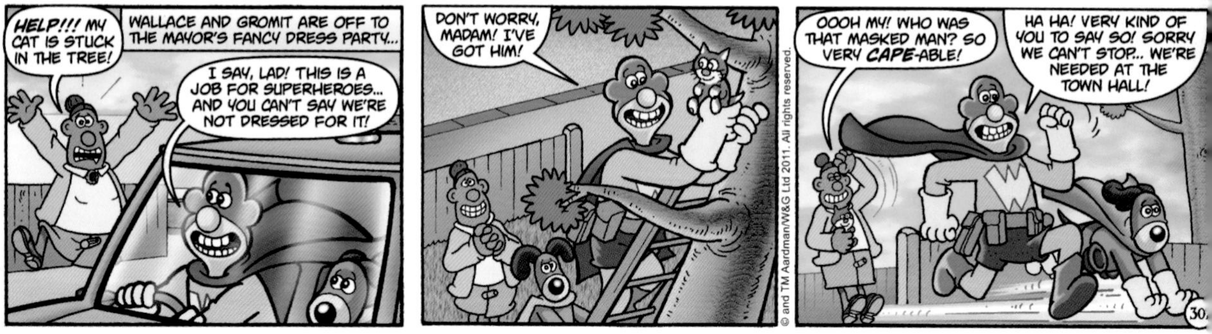

HELP!!! MY CAT IS STUCK IN THE TREE!
WALLACE AND GROMIT ARE OFF TO THE MAYOR'S FANCY DRESS PARTY...
I SAY, LAD! THIS IS A JOB FOR SUPERHEROES... AND YOU CAN'T SAY WE'RE NOT DRESSED FOR IT!
DON'T WORRY, MADAM! I'VE GOT HIM!
© and TM Aardman/W&G Ltd 2011. All rights reserved.
OOOH MY! WHO WAS THAT MASKED MAN? SO VERY CAPE-ABLE!
HA HA! VERY KIND OF YOU TO SAY SO! SORRY WE CAN'T STOP... WE'RE NEEDED AT THE TOWN HALL!

Wallace & Gromit - Caped Crusaders

by Aardman & Titan Comics

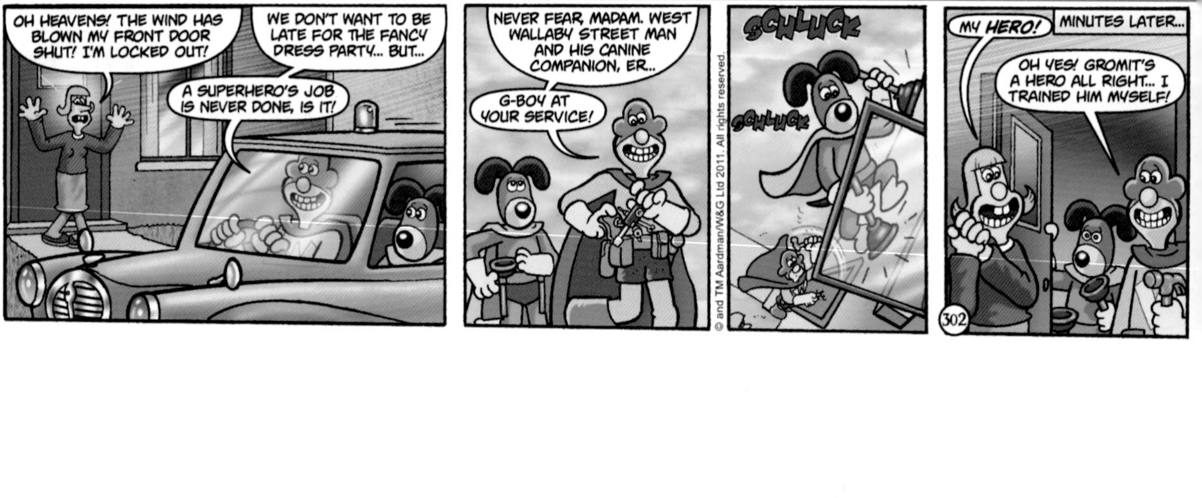

OH HEAVENS! THE WIND HAS BLOWN MY FRONT DOOR SHUT! I'M LOCKED OUT!
WE DON'T WANT TO BE LATE FOR THE FANCY DRESS PARTY... BUT...
A SUPERHERO'S JOB IS NEVER DONE, IS IT!
NEVER FEAR, MADAM. WEST WALLABY STREET MAN AND HIS CANINE COMPANION, ER...
G-BOY AT YOUR SERVICE!
© and TM Aardman/W&G Ltd 2011. All rights reserved.
SCHLUCK
SCHLUCK
MY HERO!
MINUTES LATER...
OH YES! GROMIT'S A HERO ALL RIGHT... I TRAINED HIM MYSELF!
302

Wallace & Gromit - Caped Crusaders by Aardman & Titan Comics

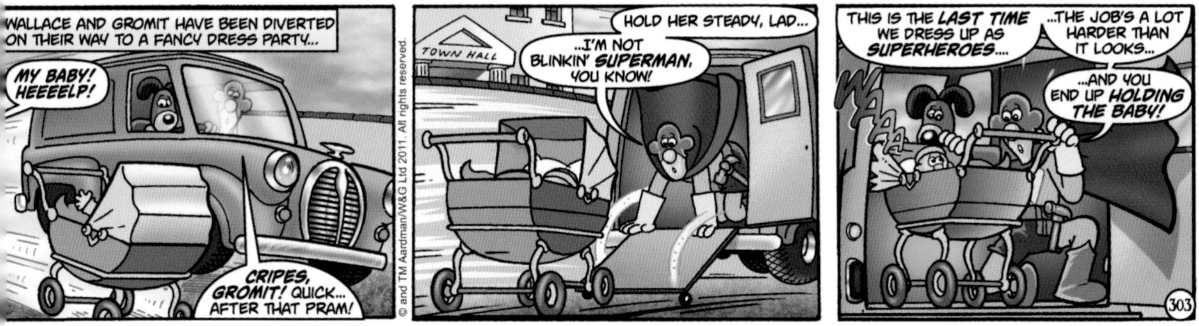
WALLACE AND GROMIT HAVE BEEN DIVERTED ON THEIR WAY TO A FANCY DRESS PARTY...
MY BABY! HEEEELP!
CRIPES, GROMIT! QUICK... AFTER THAT PRAM!
© and TM Aardman/W&G Ltd 2011. All rights reserved.
TOWN HALL
HOLD HER STEADY, LAD...
...I'M NOT BLINKIN' SUPERMAN, YOU KNOW!
THIS IS THE LAST TIME WE DRESS UP AS SUPERHEROES....
...THE JOB'S A LOT HARDER THAN IT LOOKS...
...AND YOU END UP HOLDING THE BABY!
WAAA
303

Wallace & Gromit - Caped Crusaders by Aardman & Titan Comics

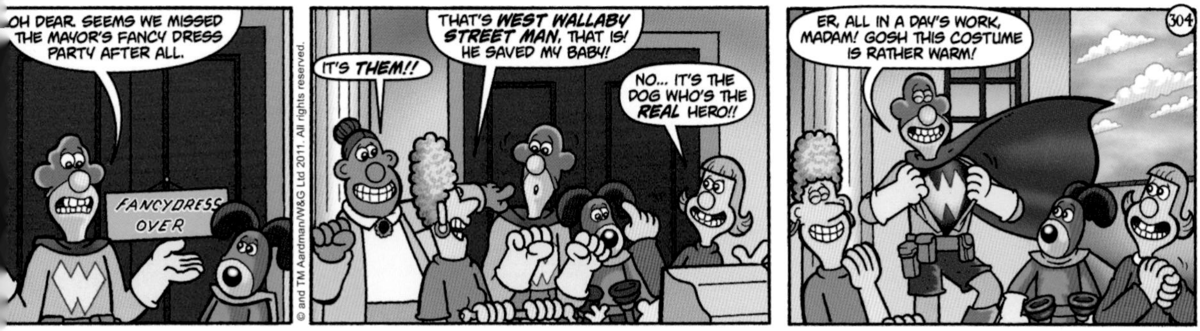
OH DEAR. SEEMS WE MISSED THE MAYOR'S FANCY DRESS PARTY AFTER ALL.
FANCYDRESS OVER
© and TM Aardman/W&G Ltd 2011. All rights reserved.
IT'S THEM!!
THAT'S WEST WALLABY STREET MAN, THAT IS! HE SAVED MY BABY!
NO... IT'S THE DOG WHO'S THE REAL HERO!!
ER, ALL IN A DAY'S WORK, MADAM! GOSH THIS COSTUME IS RATHER WARM!
304

Wallace & Gromit - Caped Crusaders by Aardman & Titan Comics

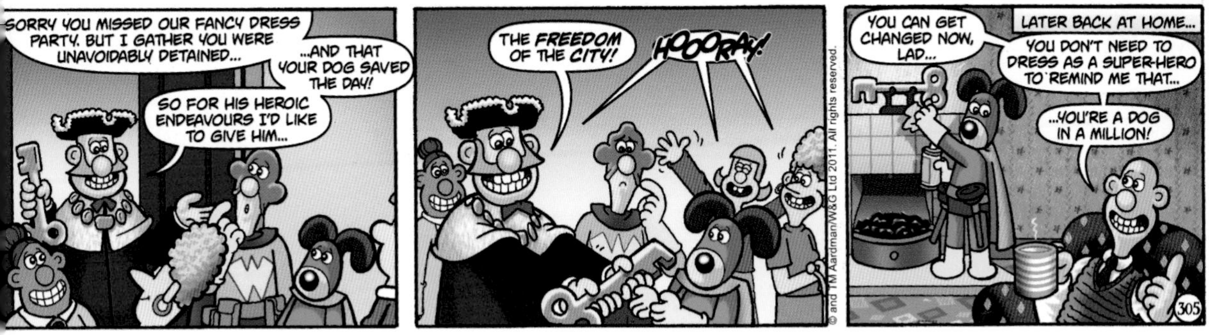
SORRY YOU MISSED OUR FANCY DRESS PARTY. BUT I GATHER YOU WERE UNAVOIDABLY DETAINED...
...AND THAT YOUR DOG SAVED THE DAY!
SO FOR HIS HEROIC ENDEAVOURS I'D LIKE TO GIVE HIM...
THE FREEDOM OF THE CITY!
HOOORAY!
© and TM Aardman/W&G Ltd 2011. All rights reserved.
YOU CAN GET CHANGED NOW, LAD...
LATER BACK AT HOME...
YOU DON'T NEED TO DRESS AS A SUPER-HERO TO REMIND ME THAT...
...YOU'RE A DOG IN A MILLION!
305

The End

Wallace & Gromit - Movers and Shakers

by Aardman & Titan Comics

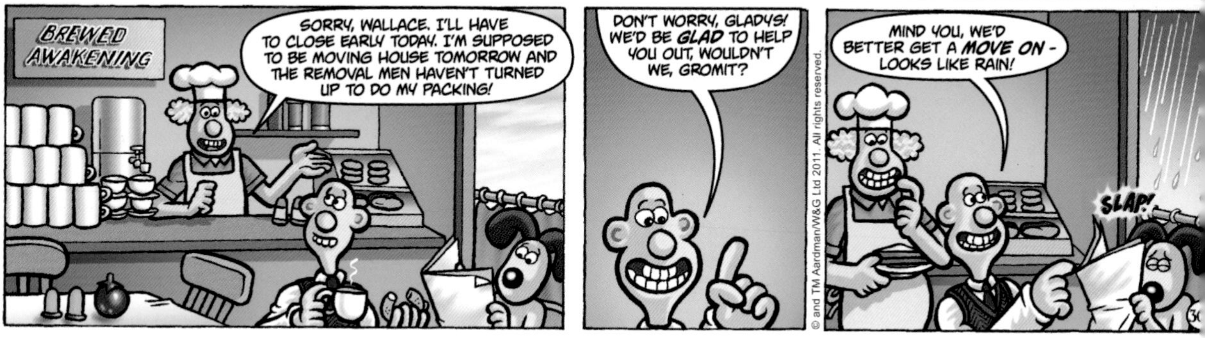

BREWED AWAKENING
SORRY, WALLACE. I'LL HAVE TO CLOSE EARLY TODAY. I'M SUPPOSED TO BE MOVING HOUSE TOMORROW AND THE REMOVAL MEN HAVEN'T TURNED UP TO DO MY PACKING!
DON'T WORRY, GLADYS! WE'D BE GLAD TO HELP YOU OUT, WOULDN'T WE, GROMIT?
© and TM Aardman/W&G Ltd 2011. All rights reserved.
MIND YOU, WE'D BETTER GET A MOVE ON - LOOKS LIKE RAIN!
SLAP!

Wallace & Gromit - Movers and Shakers

by Aardman & Titan Comics

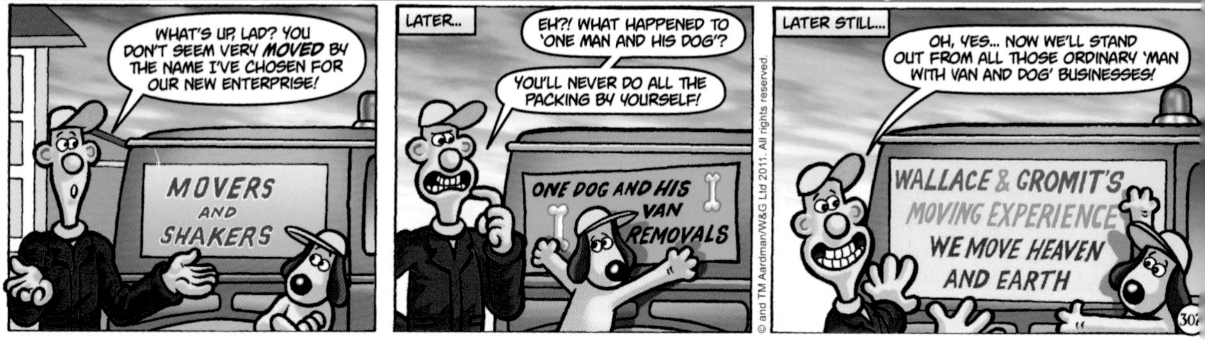

WHAT'S UP, LAD? YOU DON'T SEEM VERY MOVED BY THE NAME I'VE CHOSEN FOR OUR NEW ENTERPRISE!
MOVERS AND SHAKERS
LATER...
EH?! WHAT HAPPENED TO 'ONE MAN AND HIS DOG'?
YOU'LL NEVER DO ALL THE PACKING BY YOURSELF!
ONE DOG AND HIS VAN REMOVALS
© and TM Aardman/W&G Ltd 2011. All rights reserved.
LATER STILL...
OH, YES... NOW WE'LL STAND OUT FROM ALL THOSE ORDINARY 'MAN WITH VAN AND DOG' BUSINESSES!
WALLACE & GROMIT'S MOVING EXPERIENCE WE MOVE HEAVEN AND EARTH

Wallace & Gromit - Movers and Shakers

by Aardman & Titan Comics

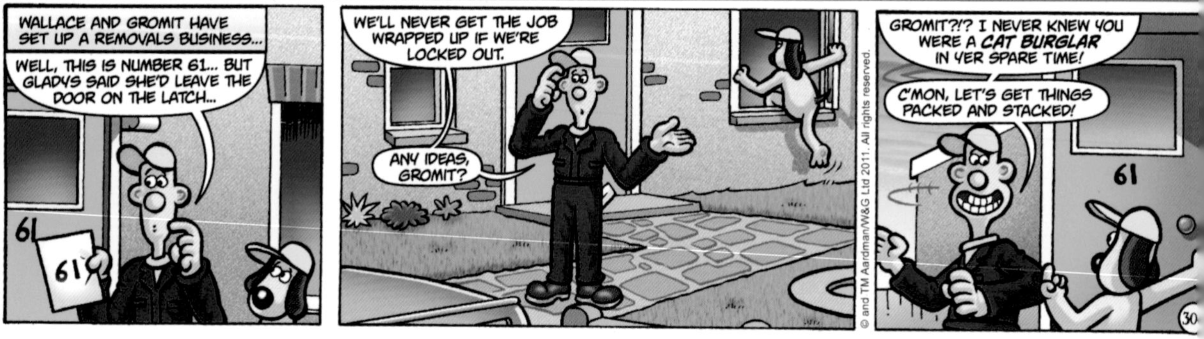

WALLACE AND GROMIT HAVE SET UP A REMOVALS BUSINESS...
WELL, THIS IS NUMBER 61... BUT GLADYS SAID SHE'D LEAVE THE DOOR ON THE LATCH...
61
61
WE'LL NEVER GET THE JOB WRAPPED UP IF WE'RE LOCKED OUT.
ANY IDEAS, GROMIT?
© and TM Aardman/W&G Ltd 2011. All rights reserved.
GROMIT?!? I NEVER KNEW YOU WERE A CAT BURGLAR IN YER SPARE TIME!
C'MON, LET'S GET THINGS PACKED AND STACKED!
61

Wallace & Gromit - Movers and Shakers by Aardman & Titan Comics

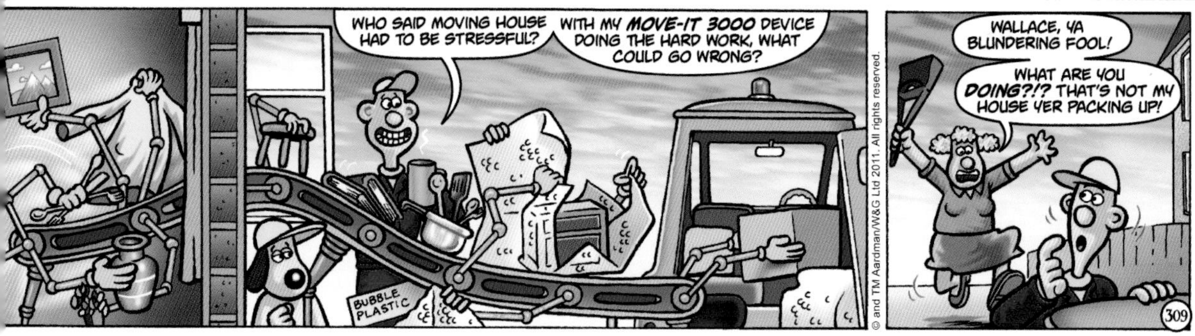

WHO SAID MOVING HOUSE HAD TO BE STRESSFUL?
WITH MY MOVE-IT 3000 DEVICE DOING THE HARD WORK, WHAT COULD GO WRONG?
BUBBLE PLASTIC
© and TM Aardman/W&G Ltd 2011. All rights reserved.
WALLACE, YA BLUNDERING FOOL!
WHAT ARE YOU DOING?!? THAT'S NOT MY HOUSE YER PACKING UP!
309

Wallace & Gromit - Movers and Shakers by Aardman & Titan Comics

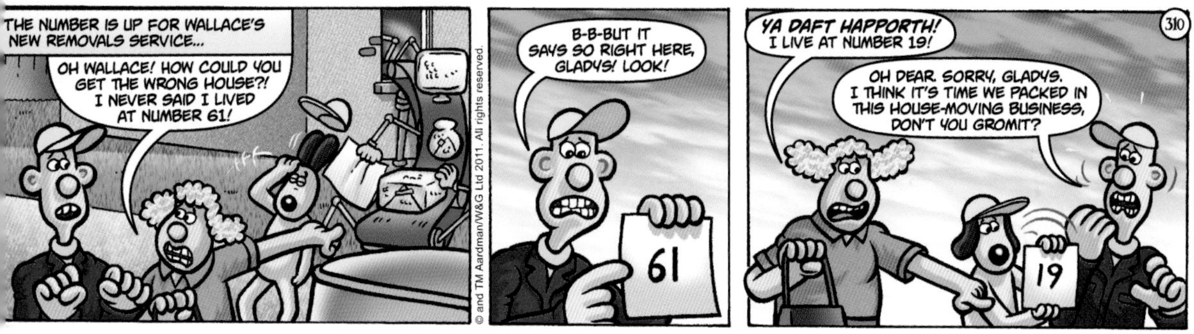

THE NUMBER IS UP FOR WALLACE'S NEW REMOVALS SERVICE...
OH WALLACE! HOW COULD YOU GET THE WRONG HOUSE?! I NEVER SAID I LIVED AT NUMBER 61!
© and TM Aardman/W&G Ltd 2011. All rights reserved.
B-B-BUT IT SAYS SO RIGHT HERE, GLADYS! LOOK!
61
YA DAFT HAPPORTH! I LIVE AT NUMBER 19!
OH DEAR. SORRY, GLADYS. I THINK IT'S TIME WE PACKED IN THIS HOUSE-MOVING BUSINESS, DON'T YOU GROMIT?
19
310

Wallace & Gromit - Movers and Shakers by Aardman & Titan Comics

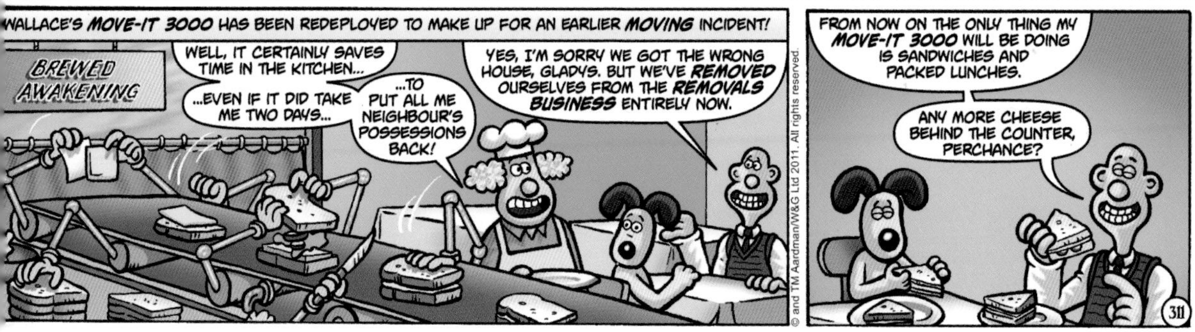

WALLACE'S MOVE-IT 3000 HAS BEEN REDEPLOYED TO MAKE UP FOR AN EARLIER MOVING INCIDENT!
BREWED AWAKENING
WELL, IT CERTAINLY SAVES TIME IN THE KITCHEN...
...EVEN IF IT DID TAKE ME TWO DAYS...
...TO PUT ALL ME NEIGHBOUR'S POSSESSIONS BACK!
YES, I'M SORRY WE GOT THE WRONG HOUSE, GLADYS. BUT WE'VE REMOVED OURSELVES FROM THE REMOVALS BUSINESS ENTIRELY NOW.
© and TM Aardman/W&G Ltd 2011. All rights reserved.
FROM NOW ON THE ONLY THING MY MOVE-IT 3000 WILL BE DOING IS SANDWICHES AND PACKED LUNCHES.
ANY MORE CHEESE BEHIND THE COUNTER, PERCHANCE?
311

The End

Tomb of the unknown artist.

We thought we'd take this moment to credit the unsung heroes of the Wallace & Gromit newspaper comic strip. Those brave men and women who every day climb up onto their stools and chairs, pick up a pencil or mouse, paintbrush or keyboard, and do battle with that dreaded enemy – the blank sheet of paper – all in the name of Wallace & Gromit!

Each of the six-day comic strips featured in this collection started out life as an idea thrown around in creative brainstorming sessions held here in Titan Towers by the Titan Think Tank (TTT, or TTTT if you're counting the 'The'). Successful ideas were then written up into story pitches which, once approved by Aardman, were assigned to writers who wrote them up into full scripts. After those scripts were green-lit by Aardman, various artists were commissioned to pencil, ink, colour and, finally, letter the comic strips before The Sun published them.

These are some of the many people who have all helped and contributed in the creation of the Wallace & Gromit newspaper comic strip over the last three years.

Writers: (This collection) Richy Chandler, Robert Etherington,
Ned Hartley, Rik Hoskin, David Leach, J.P. Rutter & Rona Simpson.
Also: Gordon Volke, Mike Garley and Luke Paton.
Artists: (This collection) Jimmy Hansen & Mychailo Kazybrid.
Also: Sylvia Bennion, Jay Clarke, Viv Heath & Brian Williamson.
Inker: Bambos
Colourist: John Burns
Also: Digikore
Editors: Steve White, Rona Simpson & David Leach
Letterers: Rona Simpson & David Leach
Special thanks to: Mark McKenzie-Ray and Hannah Tibbets.
Book cover: David Leach, **writer**. Jay Clarke, **artist**. John Burns, **colourist**.

And a big thanks to Aardman and Nick Park

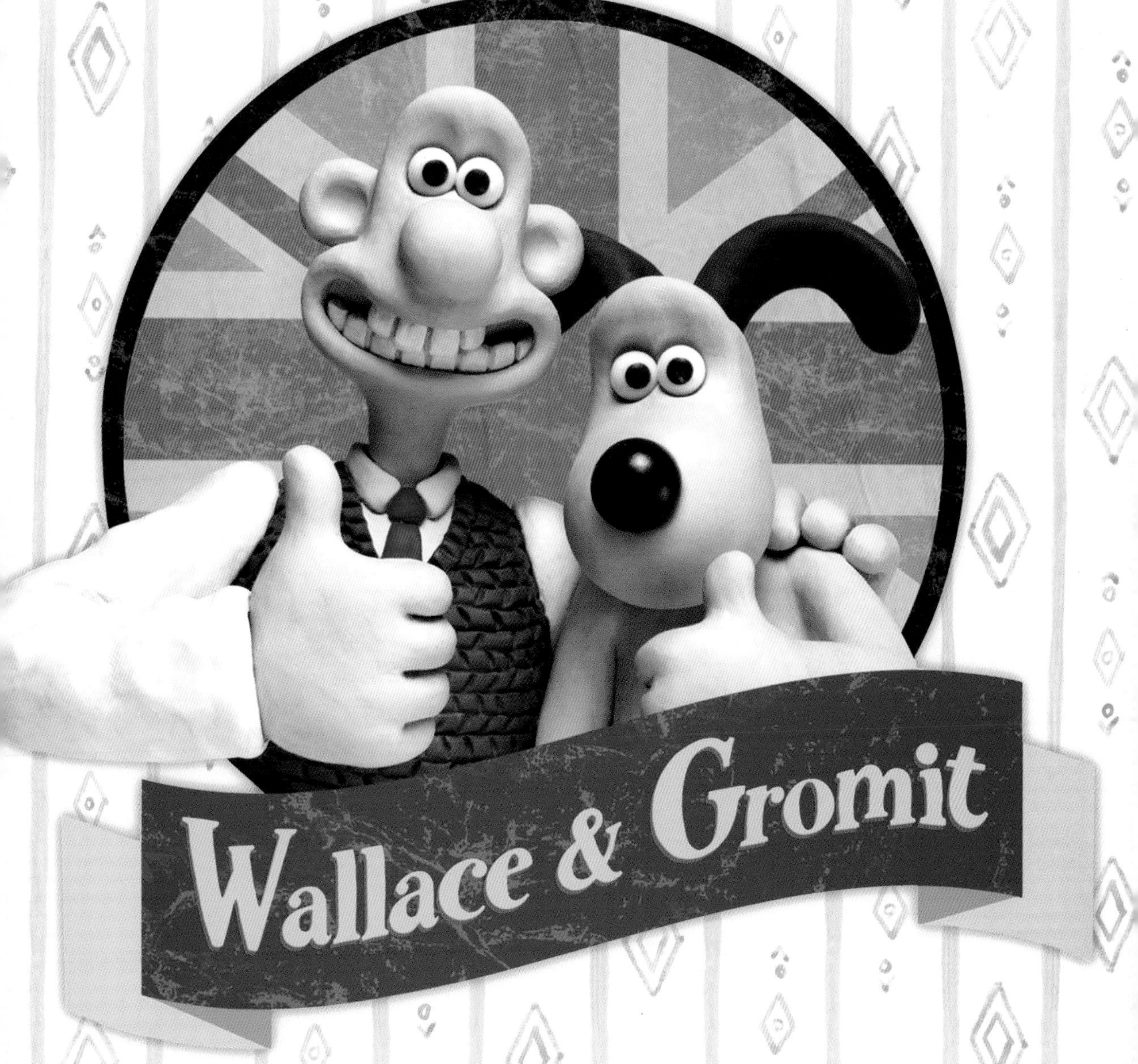
Wallace & Gromit

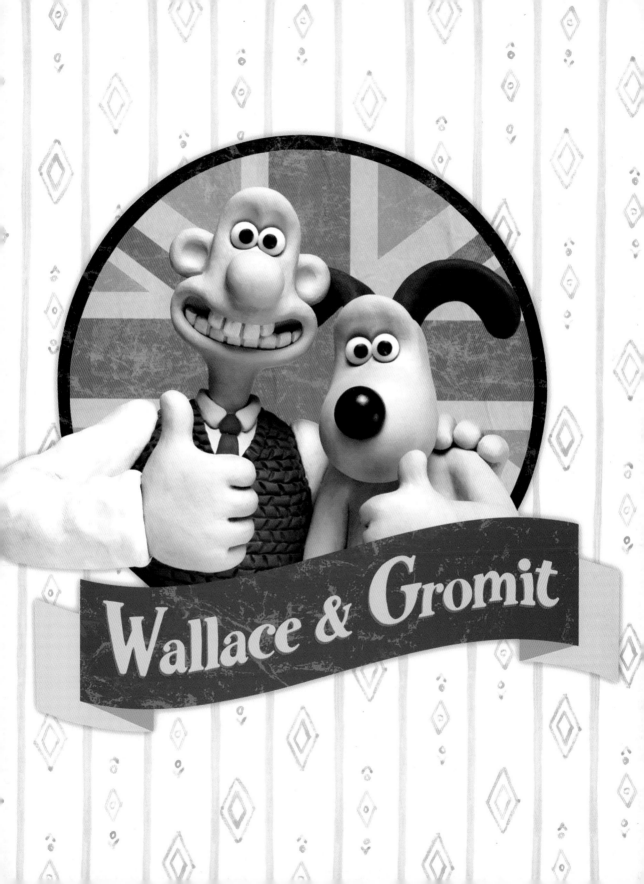